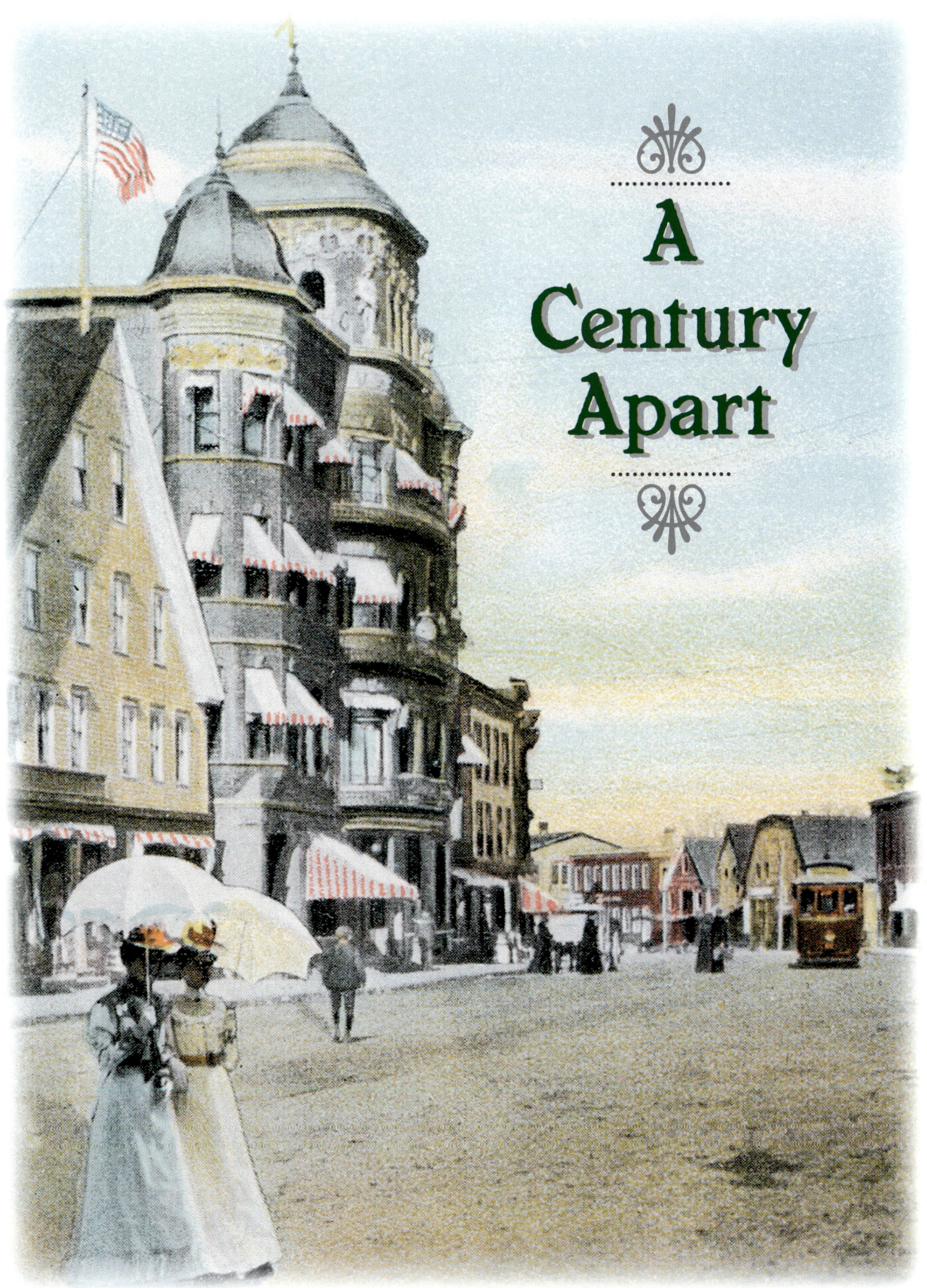
A Century Apart

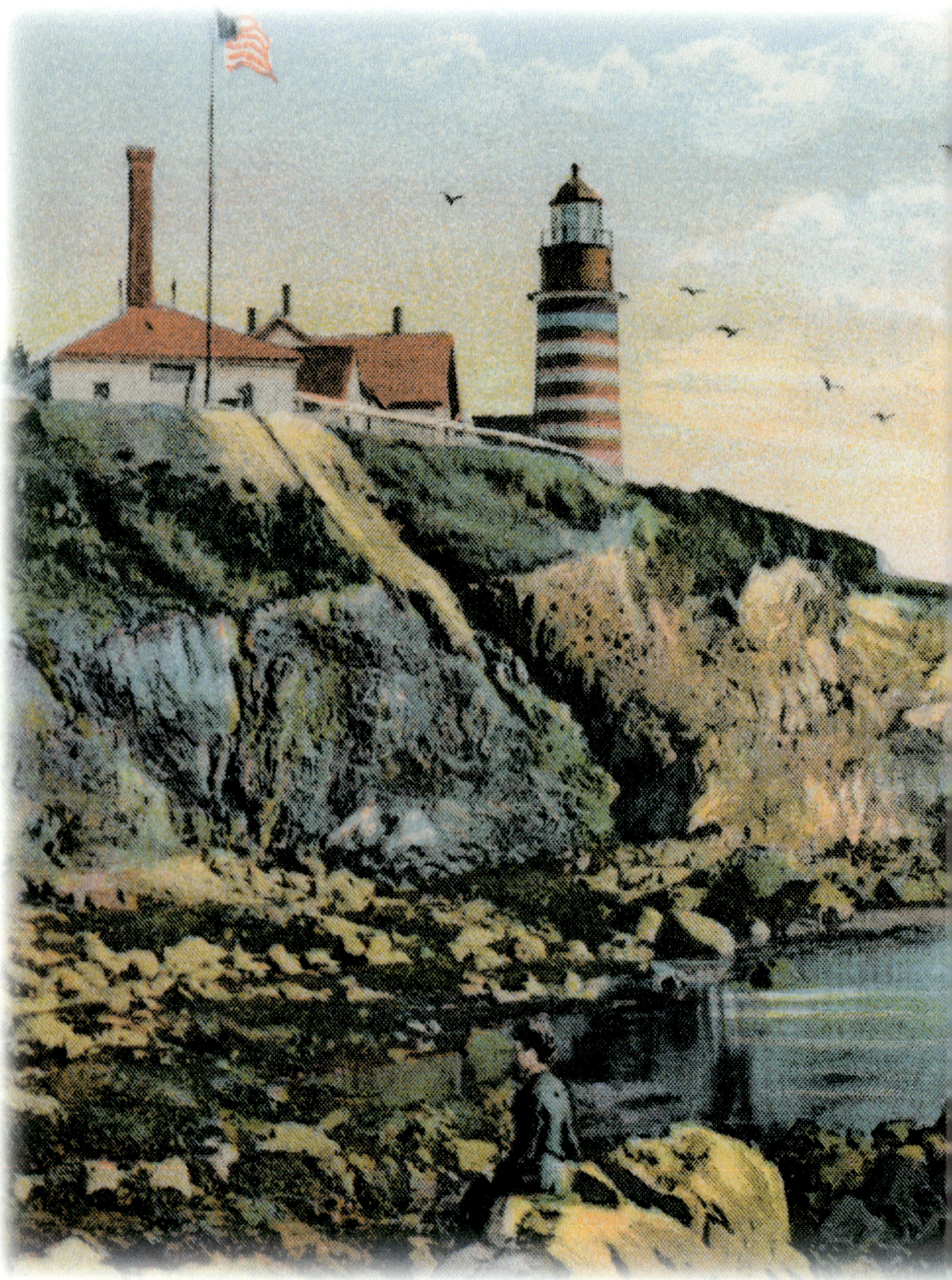

A Century Apart

MAINE THEN & NOW

Cindy McIntyre

DOWN EAST BOOKS

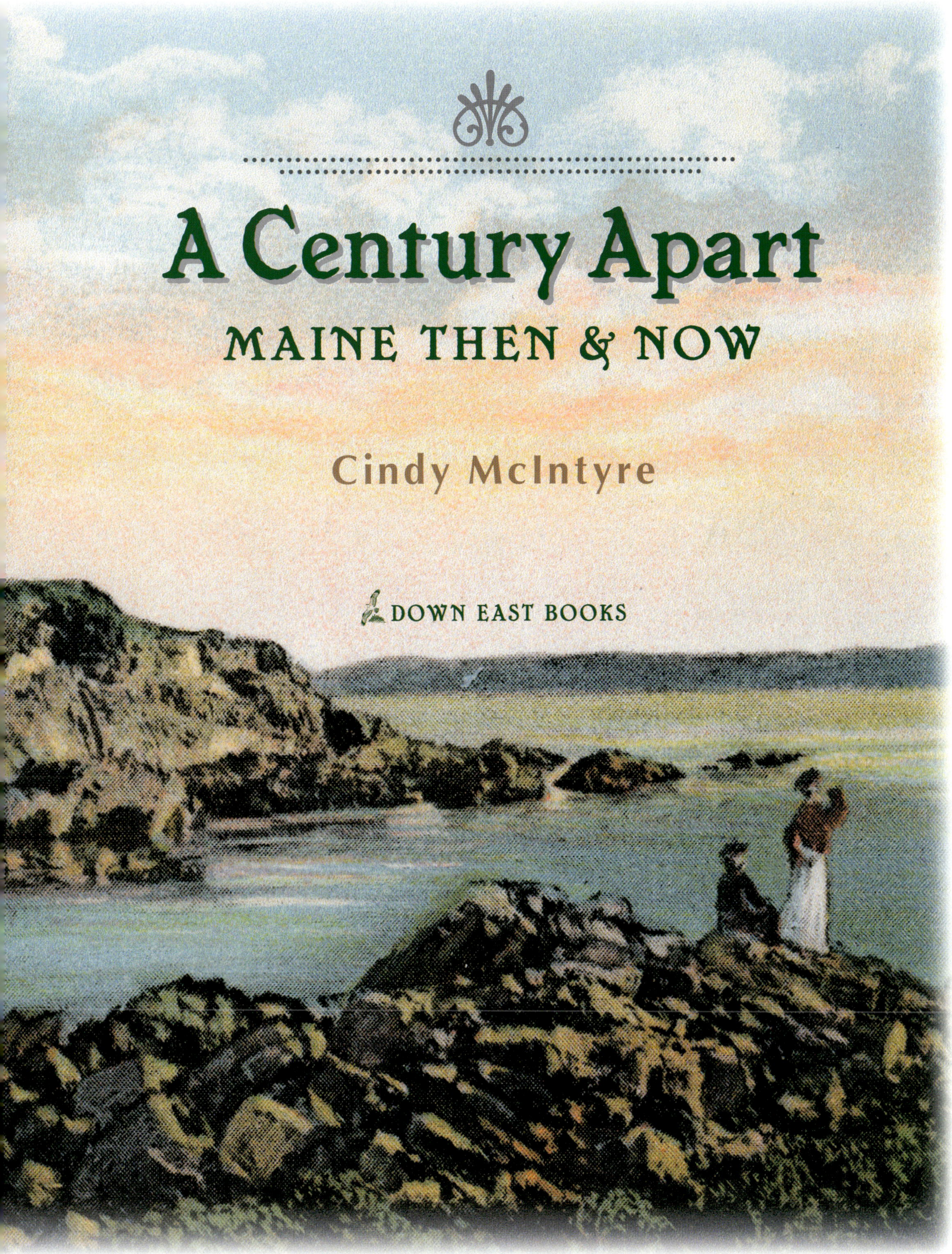

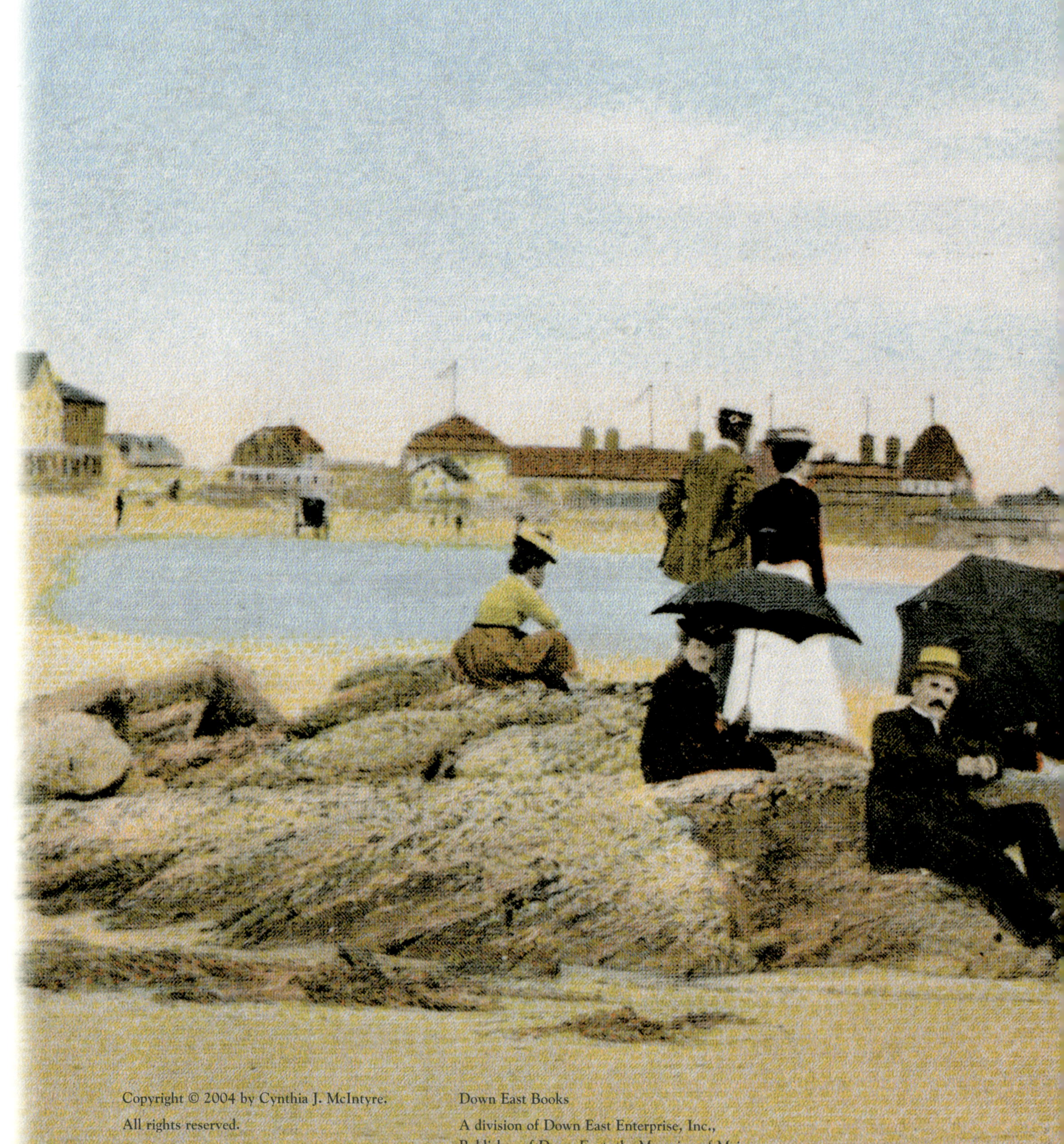

ISBN: 0-89272-613-X
LCCN: 2003113885
Cover and interior by Lurelle Cheverie
Printed in China / FCI
5 4 3 2 1

Down East Books
A division of Down East Enterprise, Inc.,
Publisher of *Down East*, the Magazine of Maine
Book orders: 1-800-685-7962
www.downeastbooks.com

To

"Miss" Joy McGraw,

my seventh-grade teacher

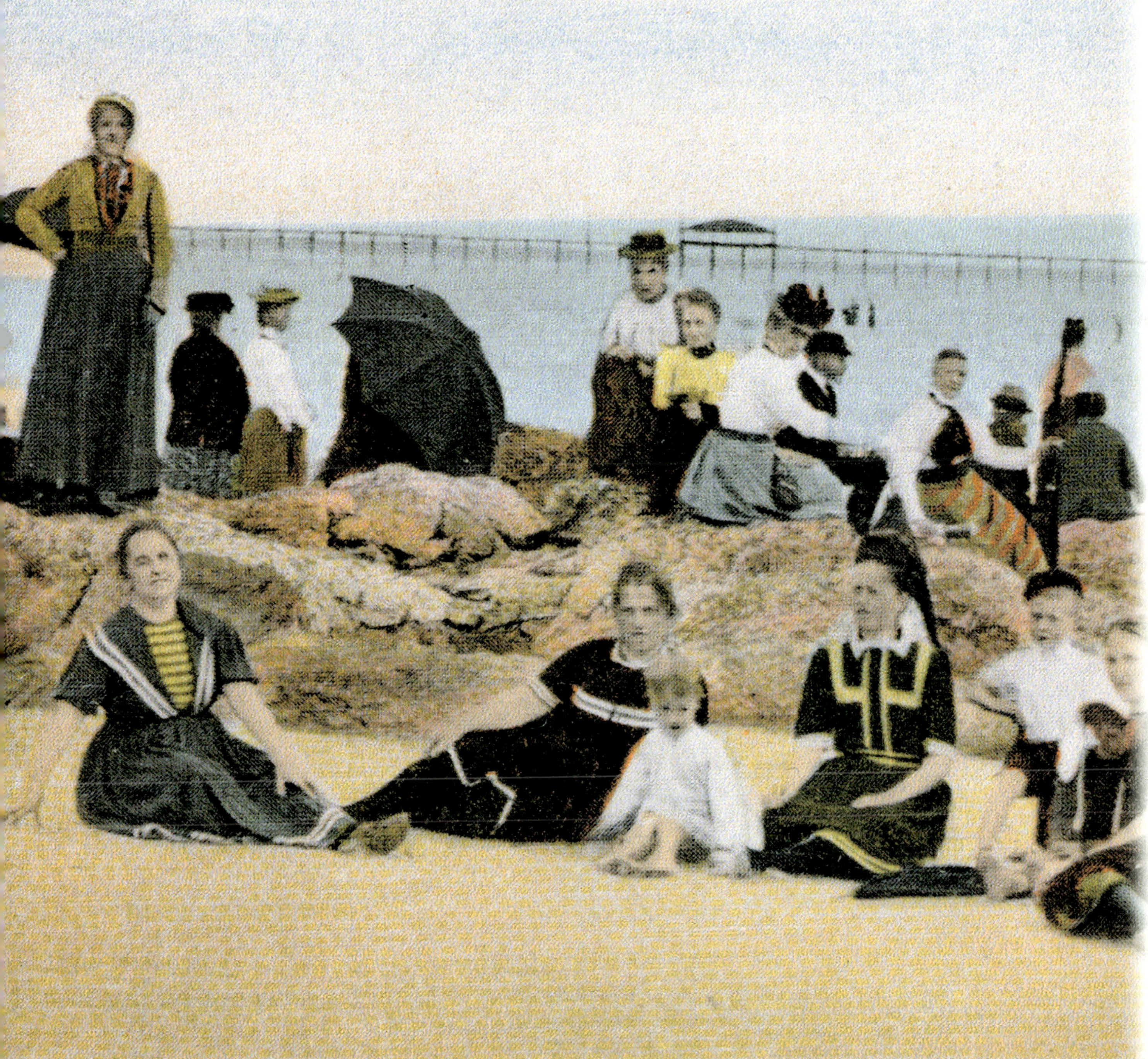

Contents

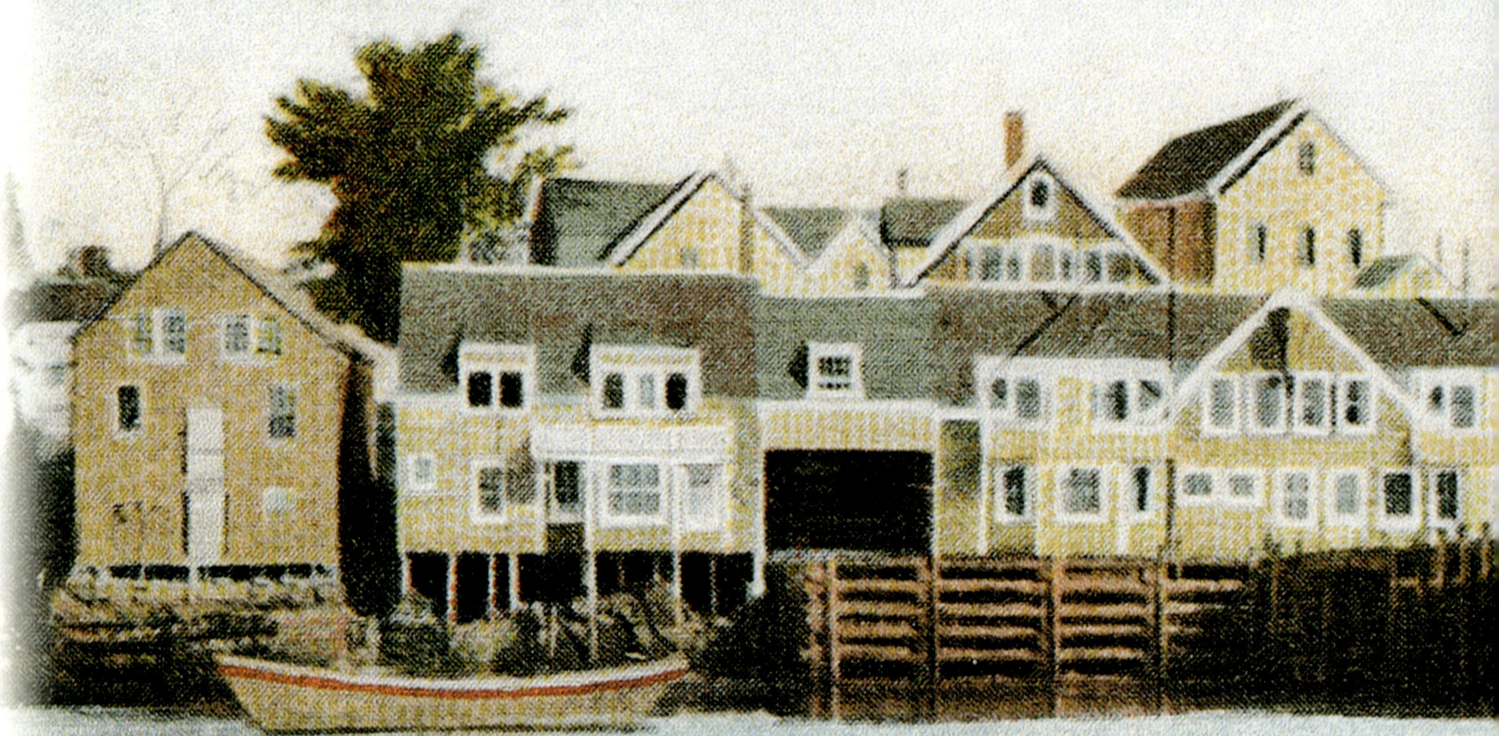

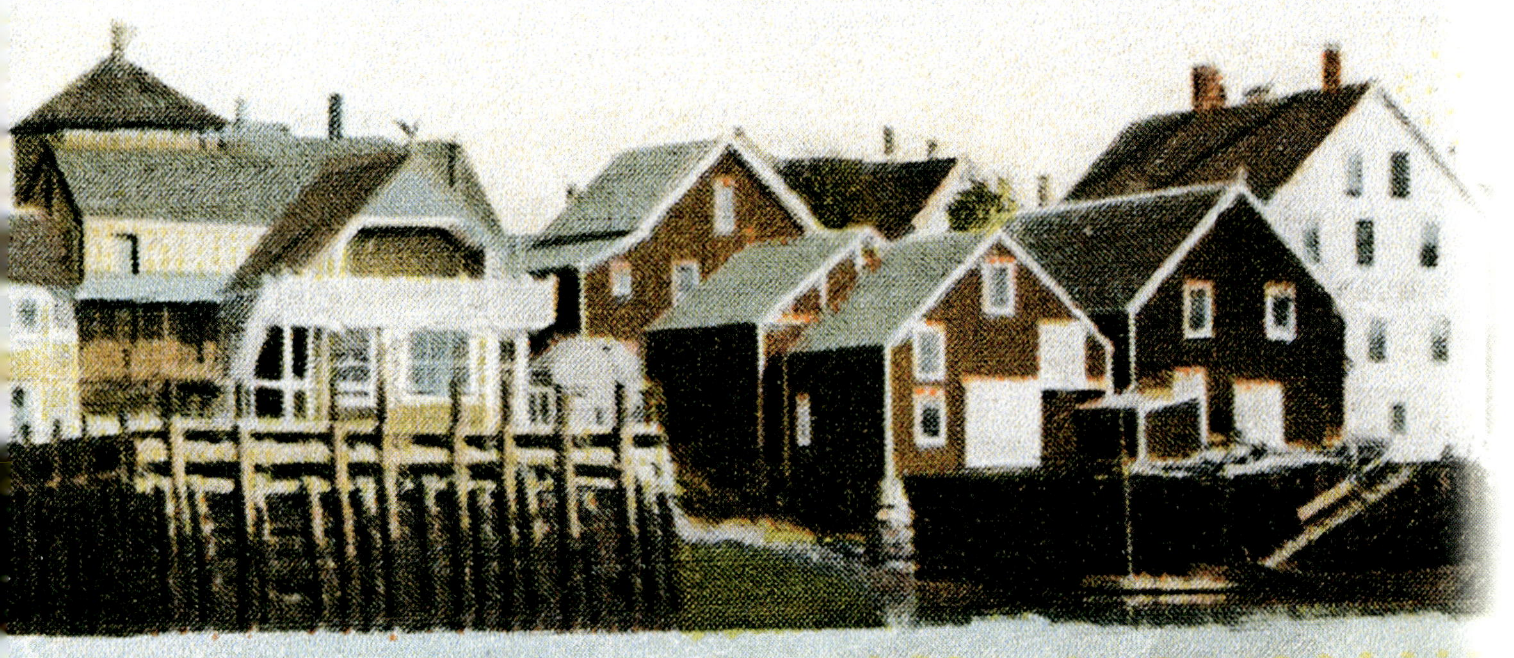

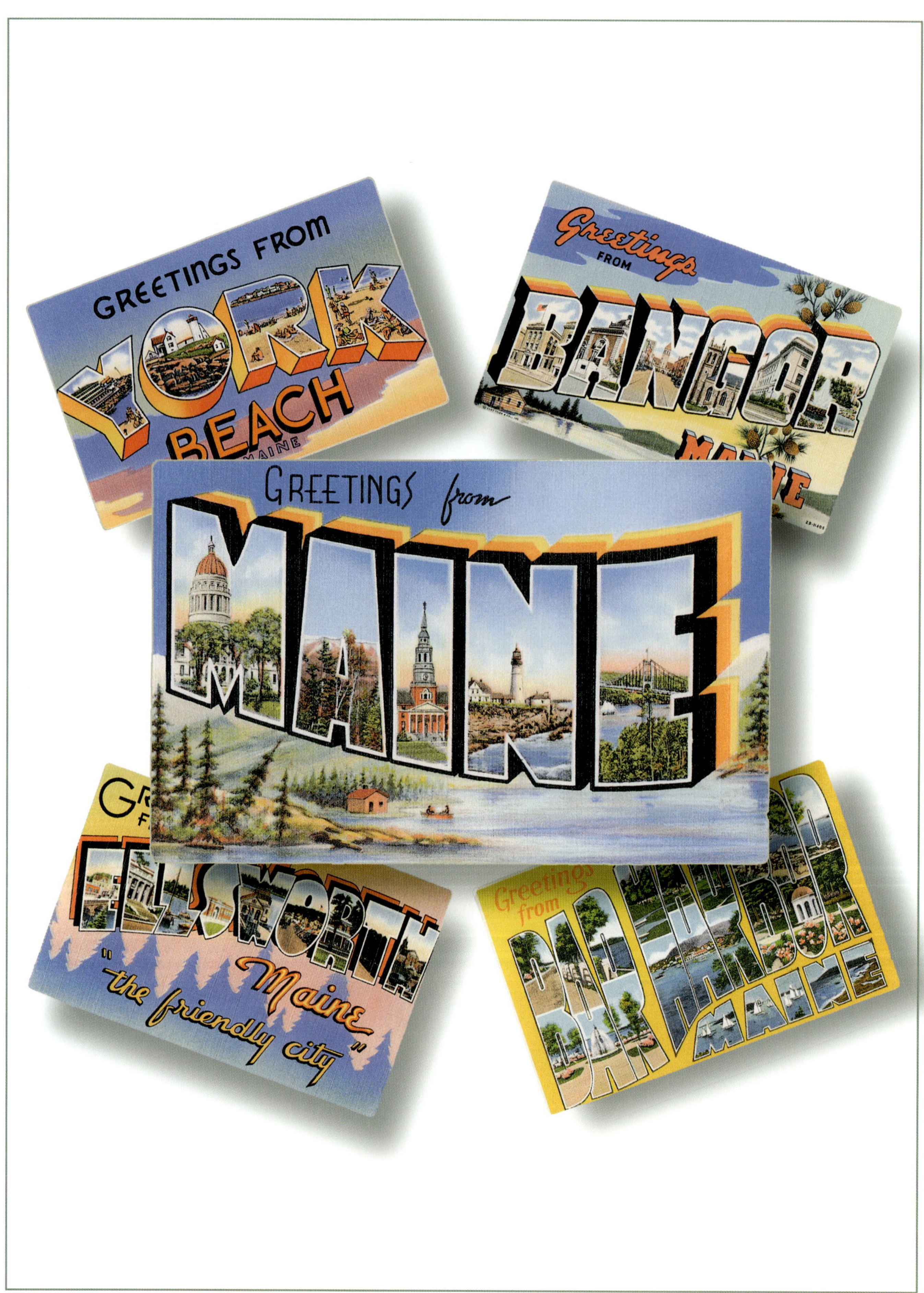
GREETINGS FROM
YORK
BEACH
Greetings
FROM
BANGOR
GREETINGS from
MAINE
"the friendly city"
Maine
Greetings
from
BAR HARBOR
MAINE

Introduction

The paired vintage and modern photographs in this book are not always a century apart in the literal sense (although most *are* nearly a hundred years apart), but in the figurative sense of visually comparing two very different centuries. This is a sampler of Maine, then and now. Represented are thirty towns, fifteen cities, four villages, two lighthouses, Maine's one national park, and one fort. As the years pass, people who can identify the details of the old postcards are themselves becoming bygones. Here is a small attempt to preserve what is known.

POSTCARDS IN THE GOLDEN AGE

In the first decade of the twentieth century, literally billions of postcards were printed, mailed, and collected. It seems that every town, no matter how small, had at least one postcard boasting of its attributes. The establishment of Rural Free Delivery by the U.S. Postal Service before the turn of the century may have aided the popularity of postcards. Prior to that, free home delivery was available only in towns with populations of at least ten thousand, and only a quarter of the country's population lived in such urban centers at that time.

Until 1952, it cost only one penny to mail a postcard (with the exception of two brief periods when it cost two cents). Before March 1907, people were not allowed to write messages on the backs of postcards—only the address, which was usually rendered in the typical sweeping penmanship of the day. These undivided-back cards often contained a tiny area on the front for jotting just a few words. Even when divided-back cards were introduced in 1907, messages were often cursory and mundane: "Arrived safely." "Feeling better." "Weather's too cold/hot." Never-the-less, postcards allowed the recipient a little armchair traveling, and cards were often collected with the sole purpose of placing them in one of the ubiquitous souvenir albums of the day.

A satiric magazine article published in 1906 called this new fad "postal carditis . . . an incipient mania for cherishing the useless." One facet of this mania was the postcard shower, in which the recipient could receive dozens of postcards for her collection. In 1909, the Baltimore post office handled more than a million postcards during the Christmas season. A St. Louis post office processed two and a half tons of postcards in one day during the height of the mania. And in 1913, 900 million postcards were mailed in the United States.

Today's collector of vintage cards often specializes by subject. Some collect every view ever made of a par-

A card from before 1912, when the Moosehead Inn burned. Currier's Flying Service now occupies this site in Greenville.

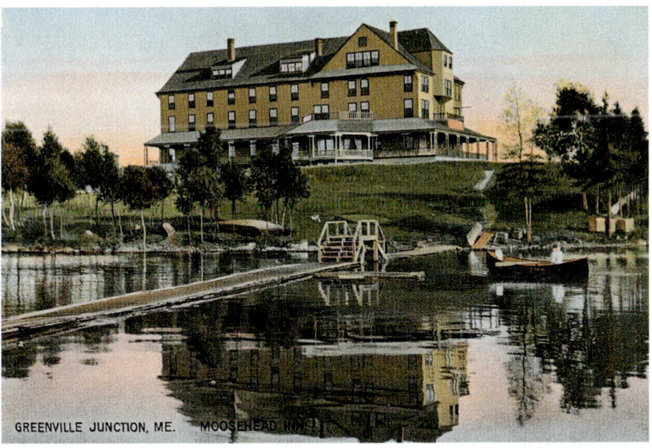

Union River, Ellsworth, at the turn of the twentieth century. The mills and factories are gone now.

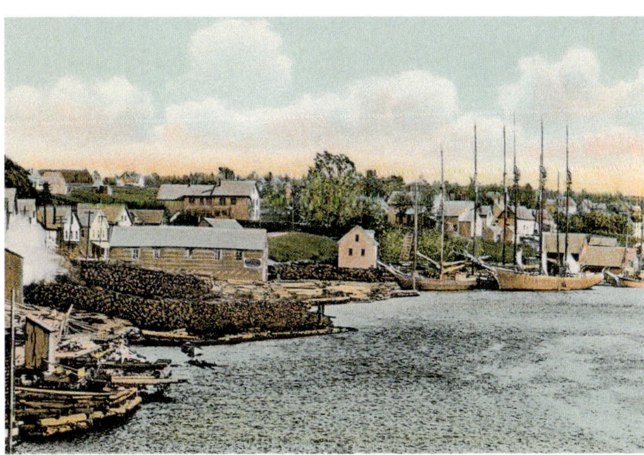

ticular town. Some collect postcards of television shows or dogs or Native Americans. Some only want real photo cards (printed on photographic paper, not lithographed). Others want to collect every numbered card made by a particular publisher. (One sees these collectors at ephemera shows with their shopping lists of numbers yet to be found.) I personally need a few linen "Greetings from . . ." state cards to round out my collection.

I began collecting Maine postcards six years ago. As a fine-art photographer who hand-paints my black-and-white photographs, I felt a kinship with the old tinted cards. I found a few for a quarter apiece, and I was hooked. Aesthetics of color and charm attracted me, leading me on a drive to see how the town turned out a century later. Often I buy a town view before I ever visit the place.

In Maine we are blessed that our *Mayberry RFD* economy has kept the bane of urban renewal at bay—at least, when compared to other regions. Nonetheless, some towns succumbed, and sad is the street that lost its old buildings with intricate brick decor and tin ceilings, with the carved and molded handiwork of a lost aesthetic. It was the destruction of these buildings by those who valued only function, not soul, that led to the historic preservation movement across the country. Today, many towns are re-creating the bygone architecture. (A Denver, Colorado, suburb even tore down a shopping mall to replace it with an old-fashioned Main Street!) In Maine, towns such as Ellsworth, Rockland, and Winthrop have in recent years installed vintage-style lampposts on their Main Streets in appreciation of their retro charm.

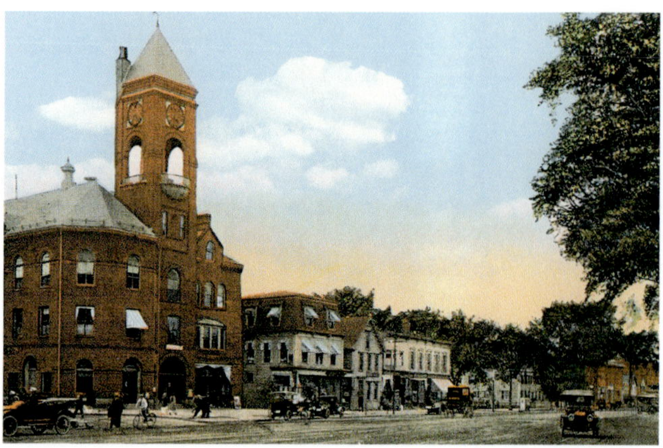

Maine Street, Brunswick, in the 1920s. This appears to be an early Tichnor Brothers card, one of the "white border" cards produced after World War I.

Hallet's Drug Store clock on Front Street in Bath today.

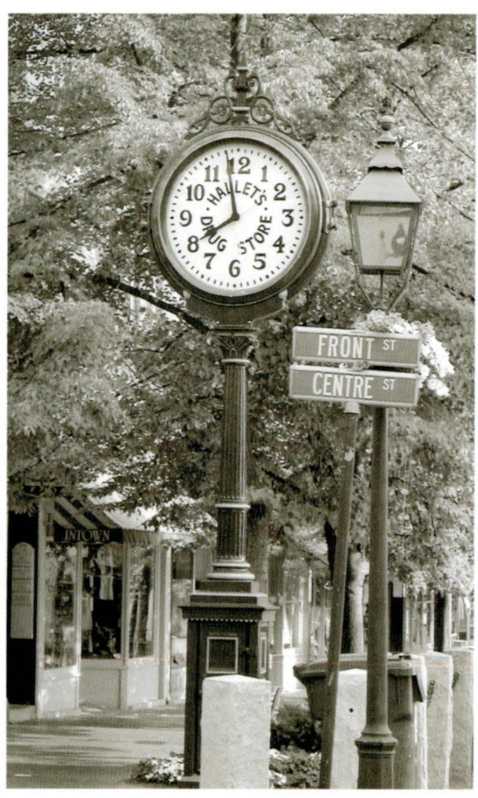

PHOTOGRAPHIC TECHNOLOGY THEN AND NOW

I've found little written information about the photographers who created the postcard images a century ago. None were given credit lines, and the companies that produced the cards are long gone. Local photographers probably supplied the publishers with most of the negatives. Some images were even sold to several publishers, in much the same way that freelancers today license images for multiple uses. (That may explain the day/night versions of the Bangor view shown on page 14.) It is not unusual to find several color variations of the same image, or even a black-and-white "real photo" version.

Eastern Illustrating, of Belfast, Maine, produced many of these "real photo" postcards beginning in the early twentieth century. But most people, when they refer to early-day postcards, mean the lithographed or

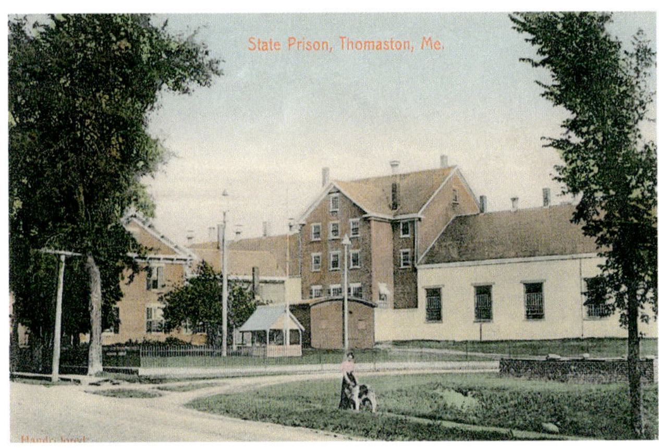

This card of the old state prison in Thomaston is one of the few printed in Austria. Published by Huston's Book Store, Rockland.

hand-tinted cards done in color. Most Maine postcards in the first decade of the twentieth century were printed by the Hugh C. Leighton and George W. Morris companies in Portland. Those color cards were almost always printed in Germany, where the world's finest lithographers produced quality unmatched in their day. According to author R. Brewster Harding, the Leighton company had published nearly thirty thousand different images by 1911, totaling ten million cards imported from German printers. The Detroit Publishing Company, which produced around 350 views of southern Maine subjects, had a stable of salaried photographers who traveled the country, including the venerable William Henry Jackson.

However, many towns were too small for those companies to bother with, so often an enterprising businessman would act as his own publisher, often featuring his own establishment. Occasionally one can even find a Maine card printed by Raphael Tuck and Sons of London. My personal favorites are the cards by Albertype, a Brooklyn, N.Y., company that printed their cards on an absorbent photographic paper and hand-tinted them with watercolors. The clarity and artistry of the colors on these cards are unsurpassed, but even a small drop of water could cause the paint to run. The Albertype Company hired hundreds of people ("starving artists" was the term used by one writer) to do the coloring on millions of cards published between 1915 and 1940.

The cameras of yesteryear were mostly view cameras, meaning the lens was separated from the film plane by an extendable bellows. Because the lens was situated on rails, it could be swung and tilted to provide a range of foreground to background sharpness. Such an arrangement also allowed for parallax correction.

Parallax is when the parallel lines of a building converge at the top due to both lens and film plane being tipped upward. This is considered unacceptable in professional architectural photography. With today's 35mm and digital cameras, parallax is unavoidable since the lens cannot swing and tilt in relation to the film plane. However, minor corrections can be made in the darkroom by tilting the darkroom easel during exposure, and with certain digital editing tools, the perspective control function accomplishes a similar correction.

In the days before color film was invented, coloring instructions were provided when the photographs or negatives were shipped to Germany for lithographic printing. Lithography involved the making of

The Russian Orthodox Church in Richmond as it looks today.

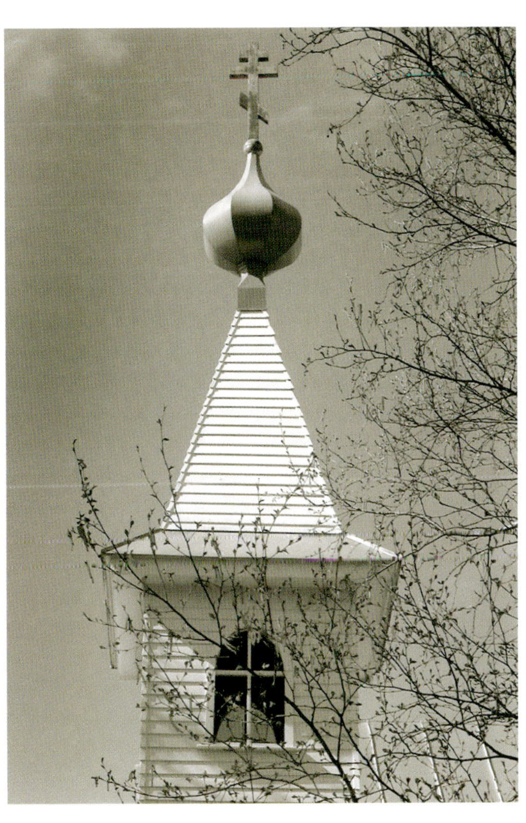

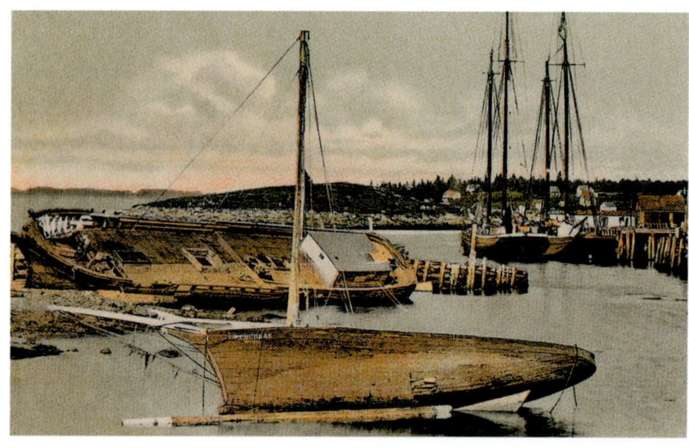

Schooner graveyard at Port Clyde in the early 1900s.

In the old postcards, sometimes objects such as automobiles and airplanes were stripped in by the printer, while in other scenes, the trolley cars are real enough, but the utility and streetcar wires do not show because they were too fine for the printing process to record. Or maybe they were "erased," explaining why some trolleys shown on certain old postcards seem to run on trackless dirt roads.

I used digital editing tools to clean off specks, stains, and tears and to remove the titles stamped on the postcards themselves. My preference was to present them as art prints, restored to their original clarity. Their contemporary counterparts were photographed from the same vantage point wherever possible, using vintage Canon cameras and black-and-white film or an Olympus digital camera, which I switched to using in 2003. Sometimes, due to obstructions or aesthetics, I chose another angle to convey the idea of change.

When World War I commenced, German printers stopped doing any work for American companies, but years earlier, passage of the Payne-Aldrich Tariff in 1909 had already slowed the importation of German-printed cards. Importers stockpiled what they could get in anticipation of the tariff, and oversupply encouraged price-cutting. The National Postcard Asso-ciation was formed shortly afterward to bring some stability back into the industry. In the 1910s, folded greeting cards became popular, and fifteen American publishers had stopped producing

stone or metal plates, each of which would print a different color of ink. Sometimes the colors were not accurate, but the goal was to have them look as pleasing as possible. Delightful clouds were often painted in by the lithographer, adding interest to what may have been a bare sky.

Today's black-and-white films do not "see" blue very well, and I often used a red filter to be sure clouds would be visible in the modern-day photos in this book. During the digital printing I also often used burning tools to darken the skies and edges, a vignetting technique commonly used by portrait and fine-art photographers, including Ansel Adams. I wasn't above adding a few cloud streaks myself, but the accuracy of the contemporary scenes is otherwise unchanged, even though I was *so* often tempted to take out the power lines!

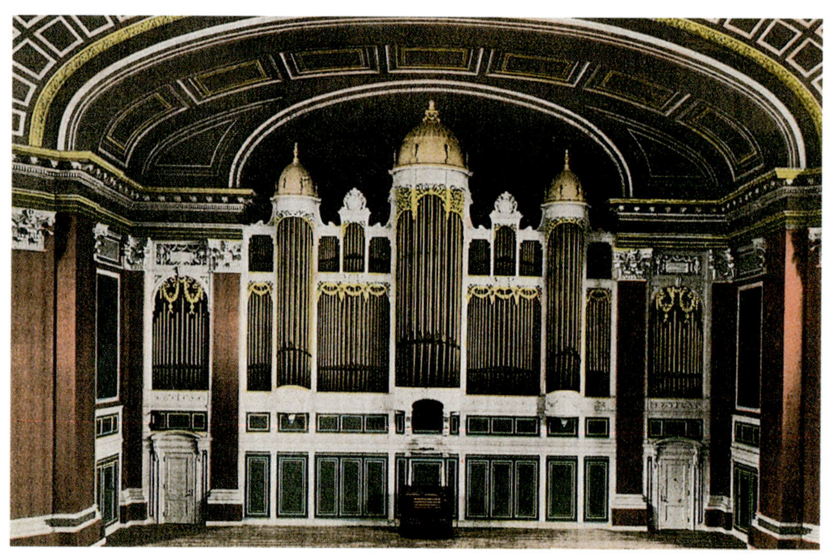

The Herman Kotzschmar Memorial Organ at Portland City Hall, 1920. Published by the Eastern News Company, Portland.

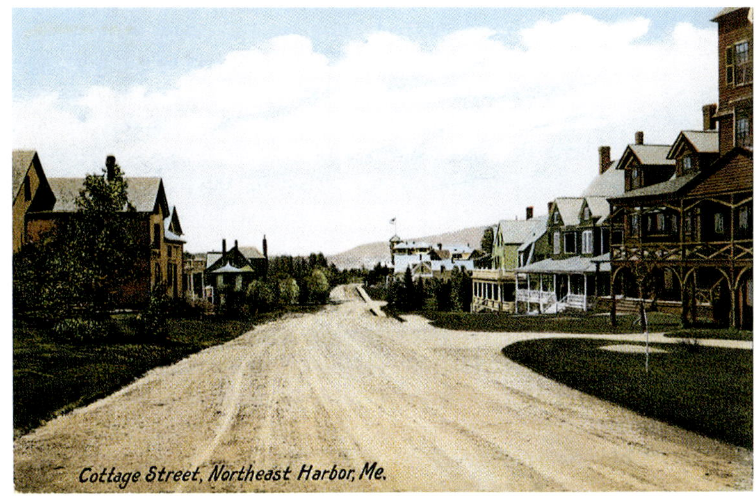

Cottage Street, Northeast Harbor, in 1907. Published by Hugh C. Leighton Co., Portland.

postcards by 1913. By the time war broke out in 1914, interest in postcard collecting had waned and the golden age of postcards was over.

However, postcards were far from extinct, even though American-printed cards were much inferior in quality. These cards were printed with white borders to save ink. The "linens," so called because of the heavily textured surface, were hardly an improvement. First produced around 1930, they utilized garish, comic-strip coloration and "drawn" details, and remained in vogue until about 1945. Tichnor Bros. and Curt Teich were primary publishers of the linens. They were followed in the 1950s by the "chromes," full-color views like the ones we see today. Occasionally they had little souvenirs attached. I remember buying a chrome with a little bag of Great Salt Lake salt attached while on a 1969 vacation to Utah. After I became a professional photographer, I, too, sold dozens of images for postcards of Washington state and Maine, as well as one image of the Expo '86 World's Fair buildings in Vancouver, British Columbia.

David Hastings, of Tenants Harbor, owned the Eastern Illustrating Company during some of its chrome years, and did most of the photography from the mid-1970s to the mid-1980s. He said his day rate for shooting postcards was about a tenth of what he'd made as a commercial photographer in New York. He hired photographers on occasion, and also bought photographs from freelancers. "I couldn't face a photographer with a straight face and tell him what we paid," he said. (I can attest that rates haven't changed much in thirty years, either.) He sold the business to Down East Enterprise, who then donated most of the historic negatives and glass plates to the Maine Photographic Workshops in Rockport, which makes them available to the public. Maine Scene, Inc., of Union, bought the rest of the Down East postcard business in 1978 and operates a thriving enterprise to this day. Today's high-quality scenic postcards—like everything else—are usually printed overseas because it is cheaper.

RESEARCHING THE TOWN HISTORIES

Maine comprises 435 towns, 22 cities, 32 plantations, 16 counties, and three Indian nations. It became the twenty-third state in the union in 1820, when the

Sanders Store in Greenville, in the late 1940s.

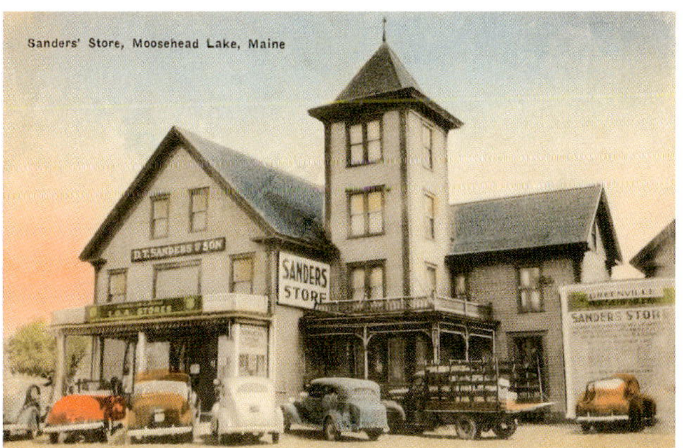

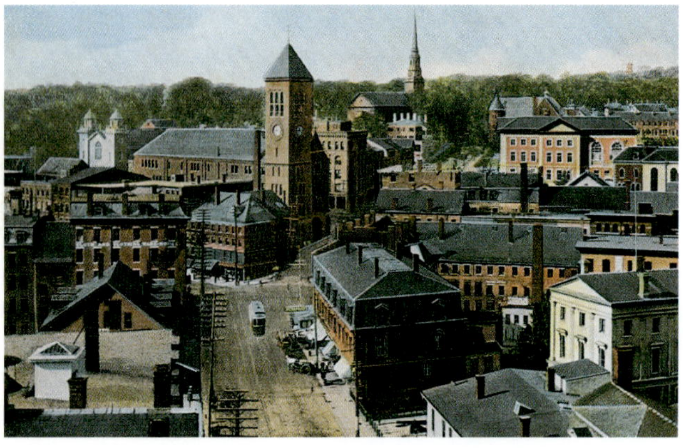

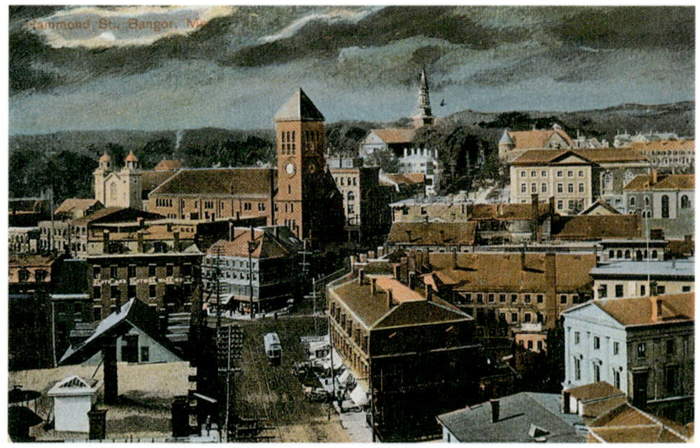

(Left) Hammond Street in Bangor, 1907. Published by the Metropolitan News Co., Boston. The same photograph *(right)* was used by the Robbins Brothers of Boston, but colored to look like nighttime.

Missouri Compromise allowed it to be admitted as a free state, with Missouri joining a year later as a slave state. State population in 1900 was 694,466. In 2000 it was nearly double, at 1,274,923.

In the brief histories on the following pages, the ranking of when each entity became an official Maine town takes into account the fact that some later became cities, or changed names, or merged with another and lost its individual identity. Thus, even though there are 435 towns now, Dover-Foxcroft is ranked as the 485th town because of this reason. Sometimes several towns were incorporated on the same day, so the rank may not agree from one source to the next. Town incorporation dates also vary from one published source to another. A town could use the date the petition was approved, the date the first town meeting was held or the first mayor elected, or some other event.

Superlatives sometimes raise contention, so we have to study the subtleties. For instance, Lubec is the country's easternmost *town*, Eastport is its easternmost *city*, but Lubec has the easternmost *rock*, which sees sunlight a millisecond sooner.

Rites of passage are as important to communities as they are to families. People tend to keep mental landmarks in their heads, such as when a favorite store closed or a certain bridge was opened. I've included the dates of significant fires, since they often dramatically altered a commercial district. In these thumbnail histories, my emphasis was on the twentieth century, since, of course, most of the historic cards date from then. Most Native American history falls outside the scope of this book; its omission is not a judgment of its importance, but merely reflects the limitations of this project.

The articles that accompany each set of then-and-now photographs are the distillation of thousands of words in books and news clippings. My role has been as a gleaner of facts and tidbits, lacing together the

The Gerald Hotel in Fairfield, 1905. Signs on the left front read "Stables" and "J C Byrns." To the right on the ground floor was Lawry Brothers Furniture. Mercury, god of speed, tops the dome.

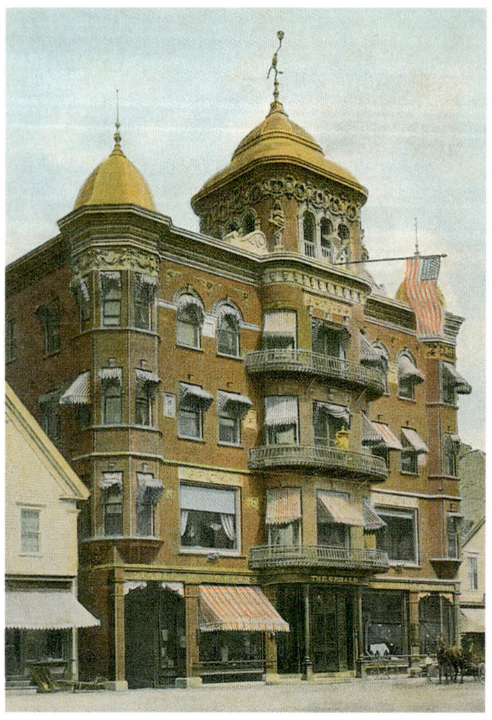

research of hundreds of historians and journalists who did the grueling work of wading through archaic tomes of stilted language and faded penmanship. Many kind souls checked my efforts—often at the last minute. Nonetheless, any errors are mine alone.

THE OLDEN DAYS

Historian W. H. Bunting in *A Day's Work* writes, "[P]eople have always acted pretty much as people always have, and still do, for better and for worse." One thing I learned, while researching Maine town histories, is that folks then fought over every little change, same as we do now. A new bridge, a town name, whether to support the indigent or run them out of town—all were a focus for argument. Then, as today, it could take years, sometimes with townspeople voting and re-voting, before anything actually happened. People have always needed a little time to adjust to change.

History has demonstrated the sheer resilience of Maine families and communities. When a mill or poultry-processing plant closed, many towns were proactive in enticing new businesses to move in. Some were more successful, or luckier than others. The mid-1800s were especially prosperous times for Maine, but when the cod, herring, and virgin pine forests were gone, livelihoods disappeared, too. When plaster was replaced by gypsum drywall, the lime industry folded. When it became cheaper to make cloth in Southern states, mills closed. When technology changed, ice cutters and harness makers put away their tools. The things that defined a town disappeared. New definitions arose: tourist town, summer colony, credit card center.

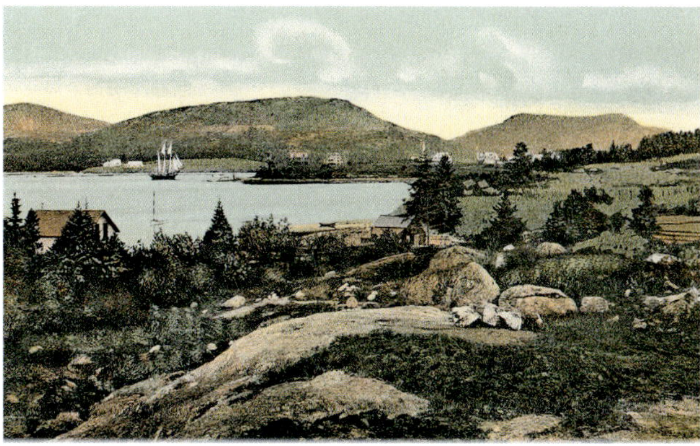

Somes Sound, on Mt. Desert Island, circa 1905, published by G. W. Morris, Portland. This was an undivided-back card, meaning only the address was allowed on the back.

ADVICE TO HISTORIANS

Today, we have a tendency to dismiss our current enterprises as pedestrian, even crass. Video rentals,

Fish Houses at Monhegan, 1907. Another G. W. Morris card. The Morris cards have a certain look—in the greener color of the skies and the fluffier clouds, compared to the Leighton Company cards.

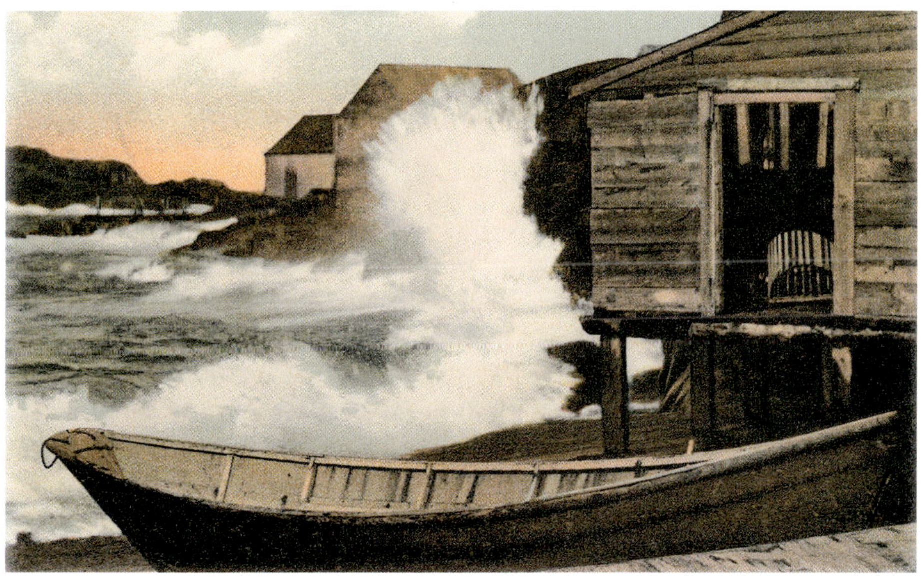

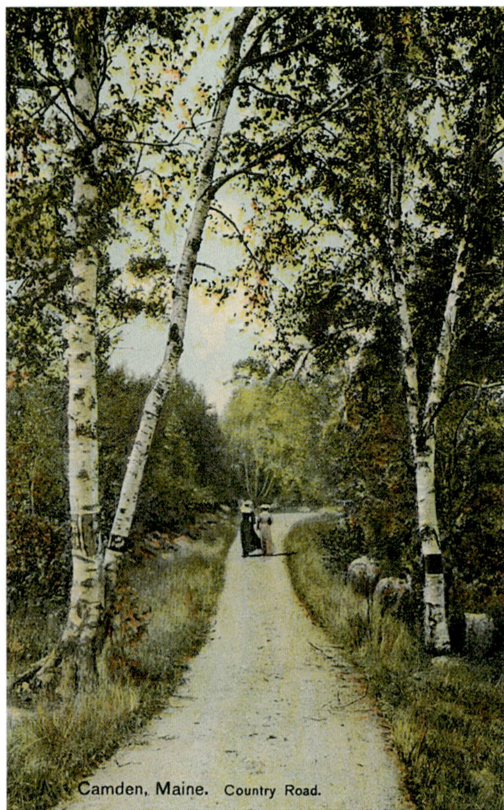

The message written on the back of this card from the early twentieth century reads: "Hello Johnnie— It is 98 degrees in the shade to-day. . . . We have lots of excitement here—dances—driving—berrying etc. I think I have gained six lbs. already so don't get scared when you see me back home. Olive "

tattoo parlors, strip malls, and so on—they all seem so . . . unromantic compared to the general stores, telegraph offices, and cobblers of old. I, too, plead guilty. It is difficult to imagine a historian in 2104 *ooh*ing and *aah*ing over a 1990s beauty salon that was replaced in 2079 by the Transporter to Mars. How many newspaper clippings have I failed to add to my research folder, just because it was "today's news"?

It seems that a century needs to pass before people get excited about a past era. In the dozens of town histories I perused, I found much written about the first footfall of the first settler, but comparatively little about what happened in the 1960s. Even town historians writing at the time of their local bicentennial celebrations revere the most ancient of histories and genealogies and often take only a cursory glance at the history that they themselves have lived. Some wonderful exceptions have been *The History of Belfast in the 20th Century* by Jay Davis and Tim Hughes, and Jasper J. Stahl's *History of Old Broad Bay and Waldoboro*. Perhaps the recent political controversies are still too fresh, and people who may be offended are still alive.

It occurs to me that today's documents should be as carefully archived and coveted as those now-scarce items historians pry out of attics and yard sales. We cringe to think of all the glass negatives that met their demise on a town dump, yet we toss out our own negatives with careless abandon. The Maine Historic Preservation Commission compiles lists of early photographers whose thin histories are now revered, and much study is devoted to their works long after they are gone. Why not begin now to archive the work of today's photographers, writers, journalists, and artists so it is preserved accurately and effortlessly for the historians a century hence?

Maybe one way of funding such historical work is to create a library of contemporary photographs in collaboration with those making them today. Many photographers derive income from licensing the use of their images. Perhaps older images could be co-

This sculpture on today's waterfront in Auburn's Festival Park commemorates the shoe industry of days gone by.

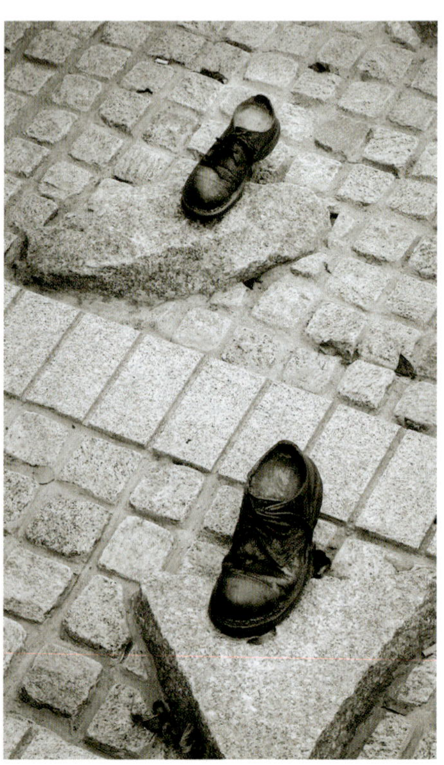

licensed by the historical associations so the photographer has an incentive to share today's work. Or they could be earmarked to be held in trust until a designated time when the images are "retired." Eventually the copyrights will expire and works will be in the public domain—and, if properly arranged, safely in the archives of a historical society.

Then again, maybe the thrill of the hunt is part of what drives historic preservation, and today's boring collections will be tomorrow's exciting "finds." (Assuming they'll be around to find.)

Town historians can also make sets of "then and now" images by pairing vintage pictures from their archives with modern photographs showing how the landmarks look today.

I was distressed to find a few historical societies that were somewhat reluctant to share their resources. When an organization of volunteers charges twenty dollars an hour to help a researcher clarify a few facts, then the business of history becomes elitist. Perhaps there is another way to fund the work of these societies without shutting out legitimate inquiries. We're not talking about a family's personal genealogy research, but about a book that seeks to represent a town, and presumably a historical society would want to see its town represented accurately. Fortunately, though, the great majority of the people I contacted were passionate about their work and eager to be helpful.

Some tips for those embarking on the weighty job of publishing a town history: First, name names. Don't say, "The textile mill, the town's largest employer, closed in 1955" without mentioning somewhere in the previous pages the actual name of the mill. Second, photographs with only vague captions are a missed opportunity; go the extra mile and describe them with as much detail as you can. Third, dates are critical. If you have 'em, print 'em. Fourth, *correct* dates are critical. If they're wrong, people like me will only repeat the error. Fifth, don't assume everybody reading knows the backstory. They don't, and they certainly won't fifty years later. Sixth, keep a logical chronology in your presentation, not a scattershot layout of photos and information. Do these things, and compilers like me will adore you!

I welcome your questions and information about the history of your town. Write to **cindy@cindymcintyre.com**. To see more of my hand-colored photographs, visit **www.cindymcintyre.com**.

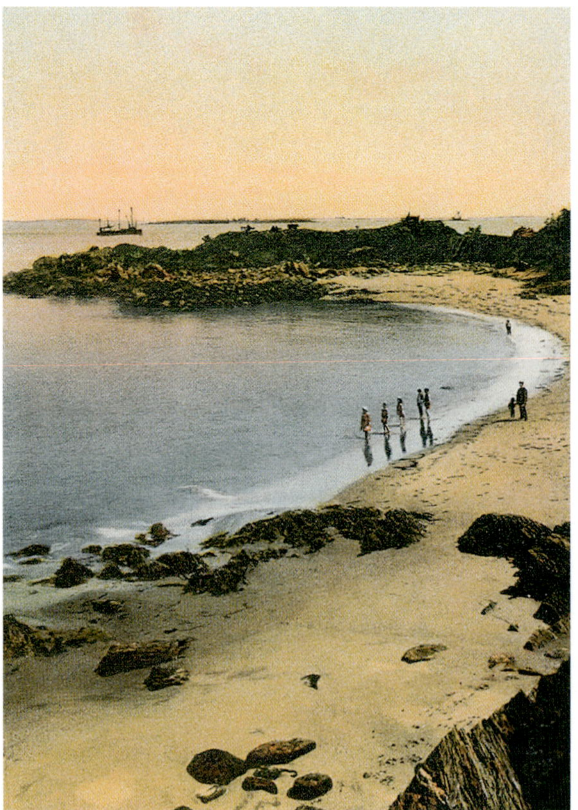

The beach at Cape Casino in Cape Elizabeth, looking toward Ram Island, early 1900s.

The Oddfellows Building in Madison today.

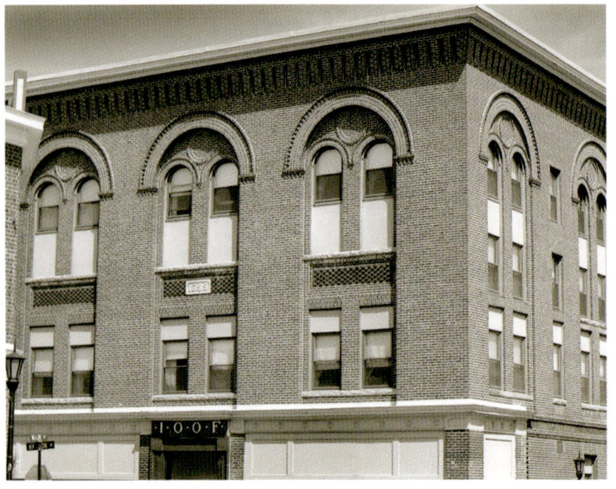

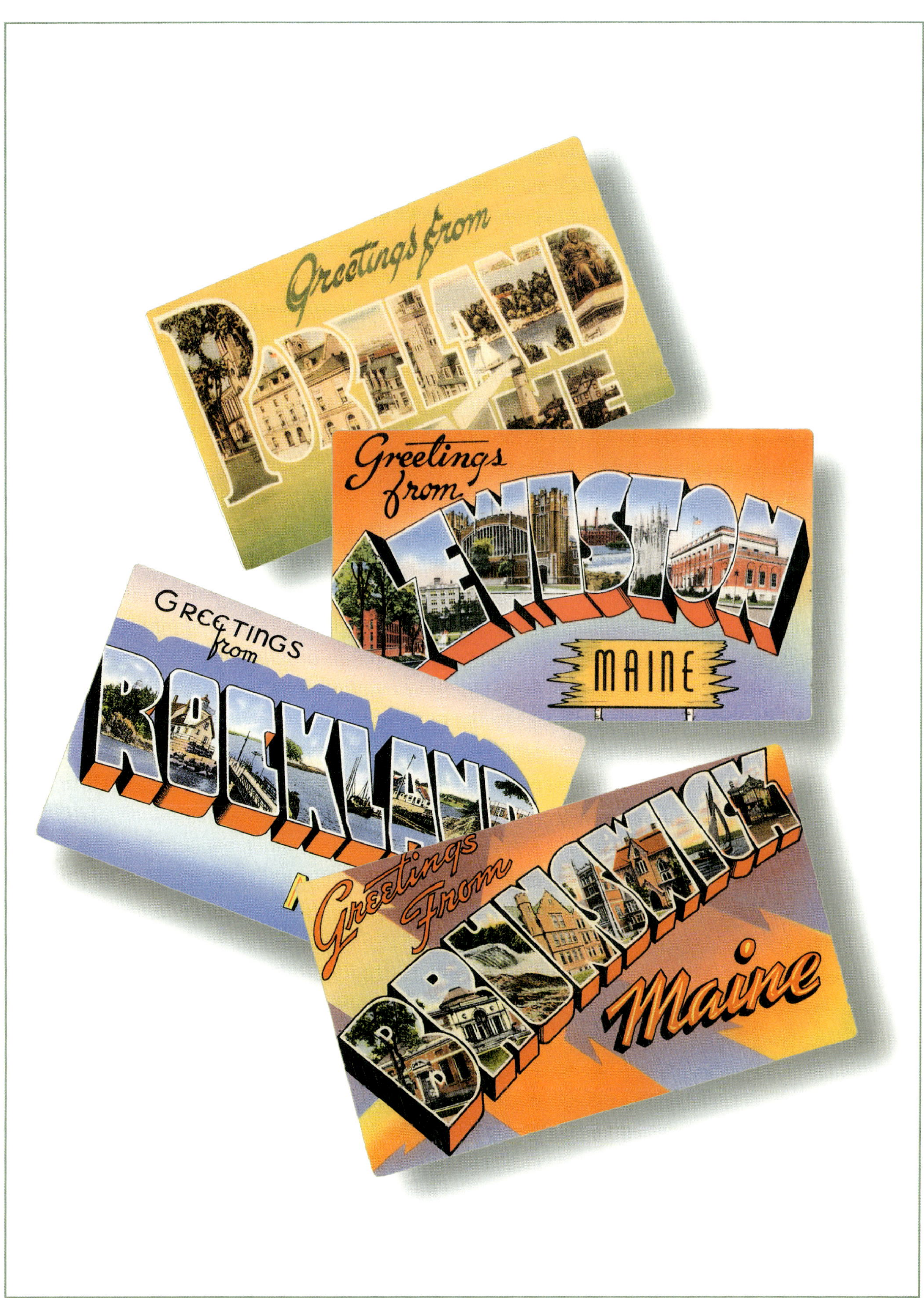
Greetings from
PORTLAND
Greetings from
LEWISTON
MAINE
GREETINGS from
ROCKLAND
Greetings From
BRUNSWICK
Maine

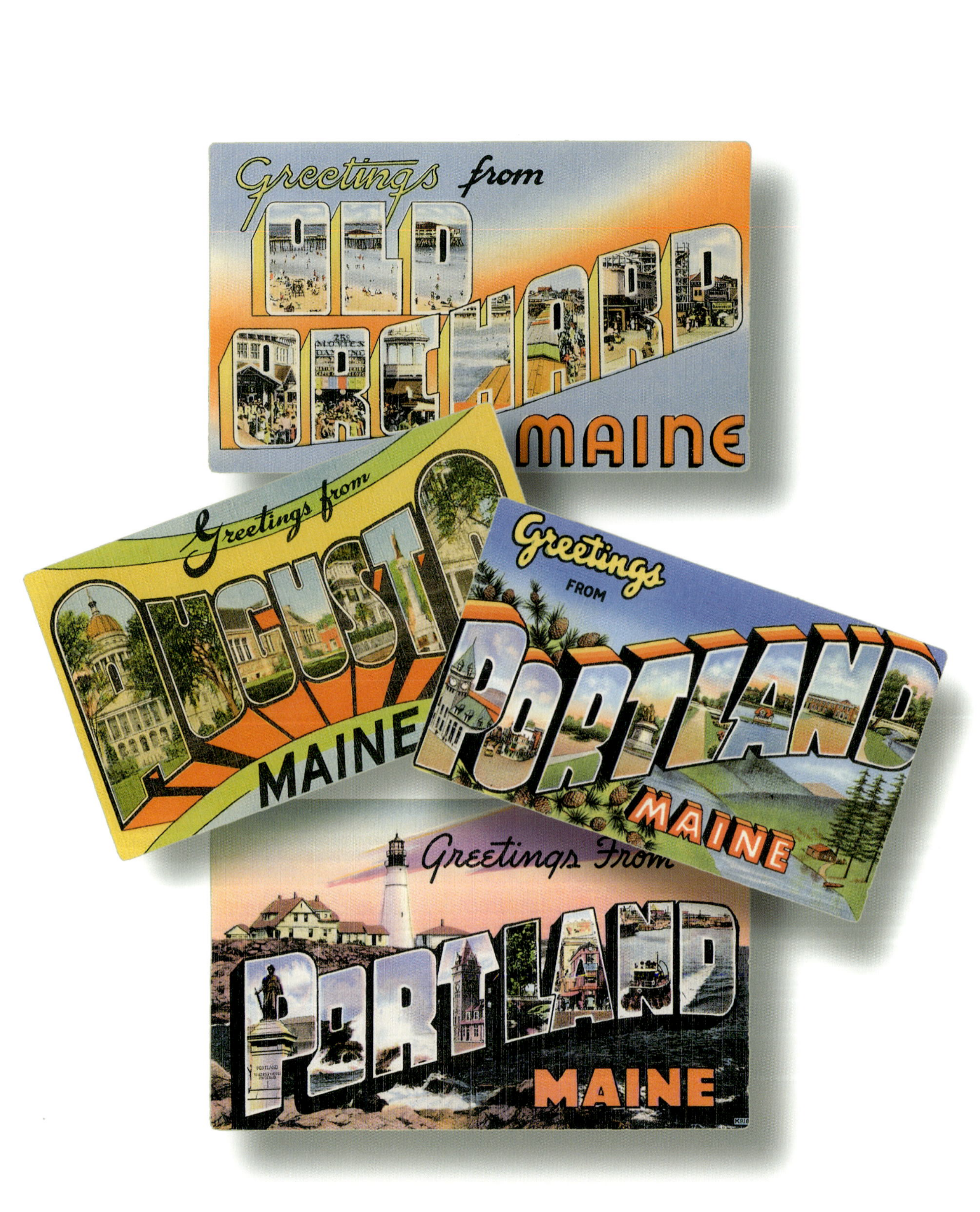
Greetings from
OLD ORCHARD
MAINE
Greetings from
AUGUSTA
MAINE
Greetings FROM
PORTLAND
MAINE
Greetings From
PORTLAND
MAINE

Acadia National Park

Oddly enough, the gasoline-powered sawmill and the automobile were responsible for Acadia National Park. Wealthy summer residents were alarmed at the rate of "progress" on Mount Desert Island at the turn of the twentieth century, and feared their idyllic retreat in the forests, mountains, and seashores would be forever lost. But when they formed an organization to preserve the scenic lands, they weren't just thinking of themselves. Almost all of the land now enjoyed by the public was donated by the privileged, who could have afforded to keep it off limits.

The coalition, formed in 1901 by Harvard president Charles W. Eliot and George B. Dorr, Boston textile magnate, accumulated more than 5,000 acres, which they presented to the federal government. The "bold and ebullient" Dorr ceaselessly petitioned Washington to accept the land trust's holdings, and on July 8, 1916, the Sieur de Monts National Monument was born. The coalition kept adding to its holdings, and on February 16, 1919, it became Lafayette National Park, named after the Marquis de Lafayette who supported the colonists during the American Revolution. In 1929 the park was renamed Acadia.

Dorr spent forty-three years and eventually went broke buying land for the park, which today encompasses over 35,000 acres—30,000 of them on Mount Desert Island. Beginning in 1913, the carriage roads were financed, designed, and constructed by John D. Rockefeller Jr., and Frederick Law Olmsted contributed his expertise in the 1930s. The picturesque roads were engineered for gentle slopes and wide passages to accommodate horse-drawn carriages, and are supported by sixteen major bridges over or under the auto roads on Mount Desert Island.

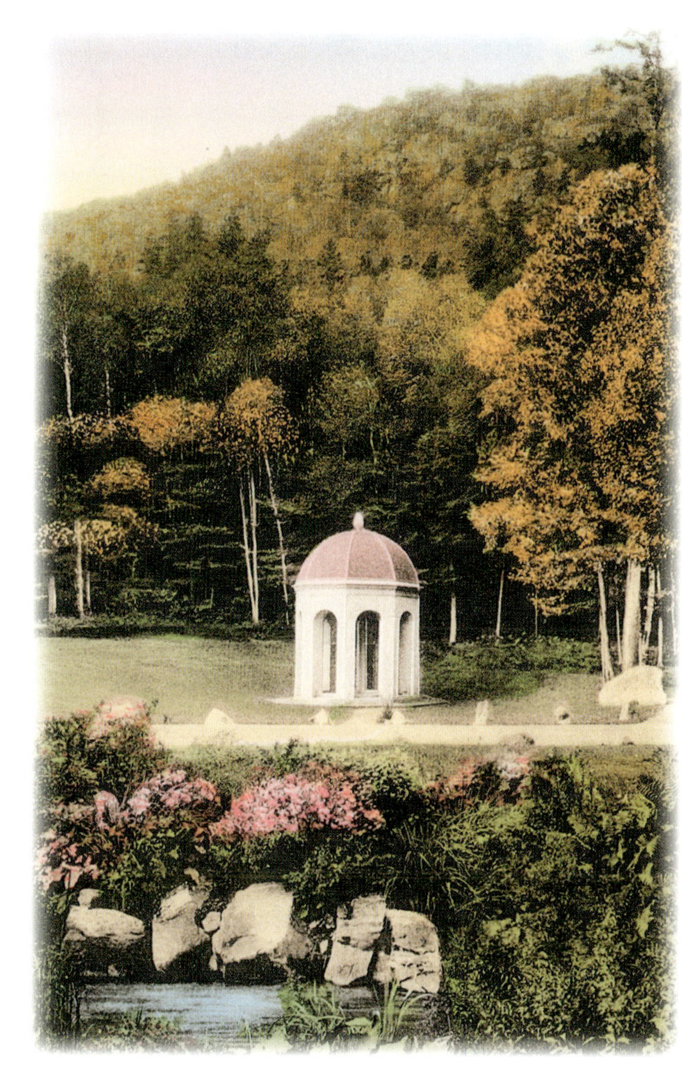

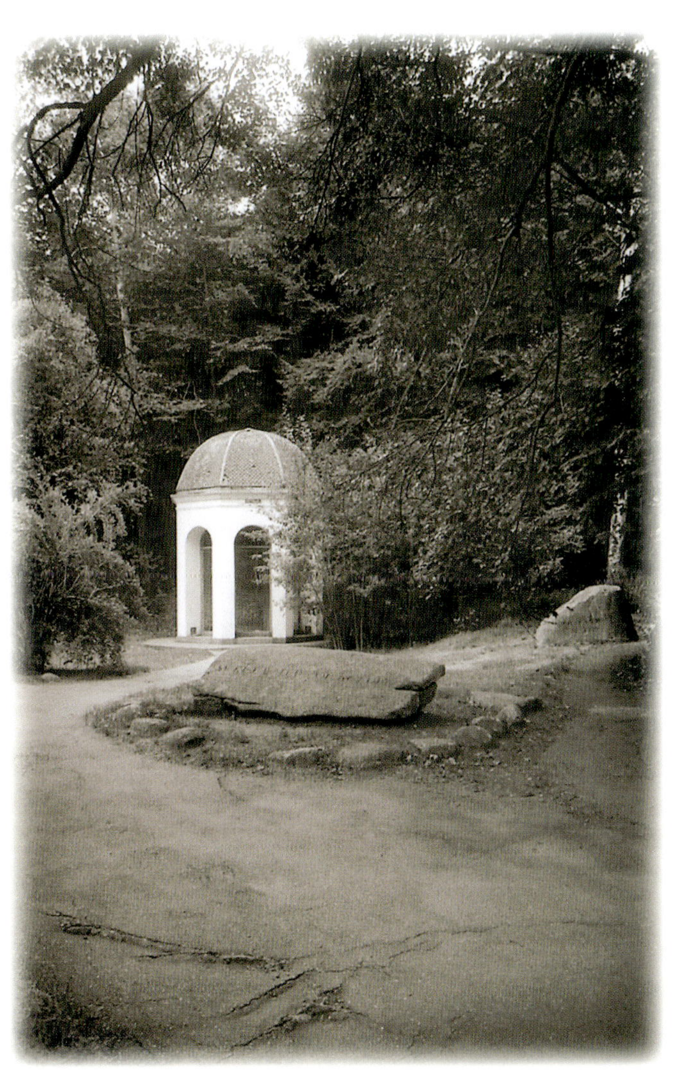

George Dorr purchased the Sieur de Monts Spring (pictured in the postcard at left) from a group of men who had found that commercially bottling the water wasn't very profitable. He built the octagonal, tile-roofed cover house in a Florentine design. The spring opening was covered with glass so people could see "the water gushing out in a generous rush." He named the spring after a nobleman and friend of King Henri IV, who was with Samuel de Champlain when he named the island *l'Isle de Mont Desert*, because of its bare (deserted) mountaintops.

Dorr wrote, "Springs, from boyhood on, have always held a singular interest for me, an interest heightened by years of travel abroad where, from the earliest historic period on, they have been objects of mystery and worship. And this spring was wonderfully placed, with the mountains rising steeply up beside it, contrasting with the Great and Little Meadow lands on either side." The hand-colored postcard shows the spring with the Flying Squadron Mountain in the background.

A great fire in 1947 burned 17,000 acres of Mount Desert Island, including many of the wealthy residents' cottages in and around Bar Harbor. The springhouse, however, was spared. Ten thousand acres of parkland were consumed, transforming a spruce and fir forest into what is today a more scenic and varied landscape. Hardwoods such as maple, aspen, and birch were the first to recolonize the burned ground, and these sun-loving trees provide the shade needed by the young evergreens, which may eventually replace the hardwoods once again.

The Bubble Pond Bridge, built in 1928.

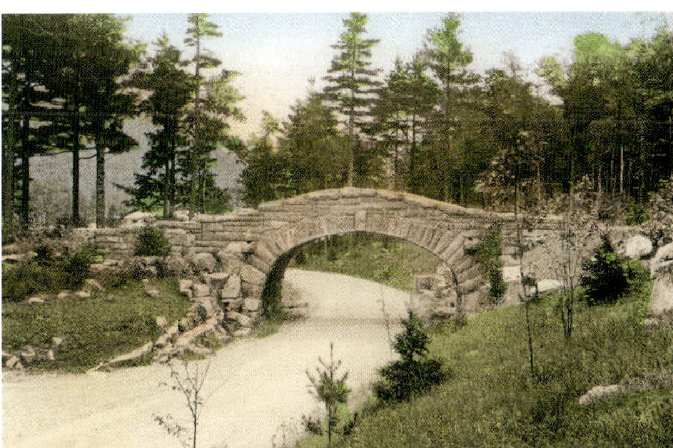

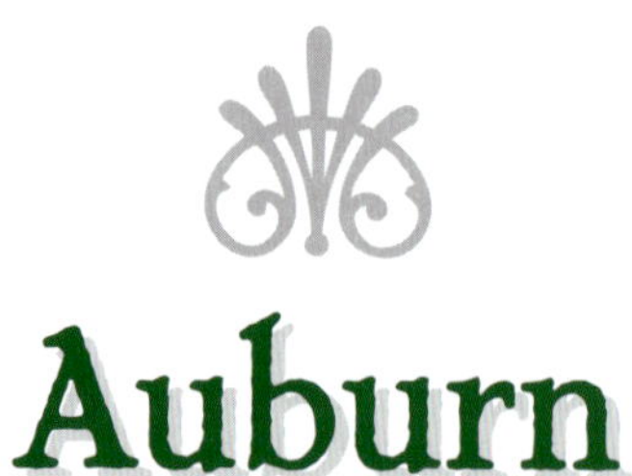

Auburn

INCORPORATED AS MAINE'S
356TH TOWN ON FEBRUARY 24, 1842

INCORPORATED AS MAINE'S
13TH CITY ON FEBRUARY 22, 1869

POPULATION IN 1900: 12,951

POPULATION IN 2000: 23,203

"Sweet Auburn! loveliest village of the plain . . ."

That line of poetry, from Oliver Goldsmith's "The Deserted Village," inspired the name of the bustling new town. Written in 1770, the poem—about a fictional English hamlet laid waste—oddly foreshadowed the darker days Auburn would face in the future. Formerly part of Minot, which itself was part of Poland, Auburn became the seat of Androscoggin County in 1854.

Lying across the Androscoggin River from its industrial sister city, Lewiston, Auburn had traditionally been seen as the "better" of the two. Where Lewiston's huge brick mills drew thousands of immigrants who lived in company-built tenements, the mill owners often chose to live in Auburn, despite its own plethora of factories. Over the years, the cities found themselves competing for tax breaks and other benefits, and an attempt in 1978 to bring about official cooperation almost failed. Recently, however, the cities have engaged in joint management and planning, acknowledging their long-shared economic and social ties.

Those factories in sweet Auburn were nearly all related to the shoe industry. The state's first shoe factory, Minot Shoe Company, was built in what later became West Auburn in 1836. In 1922 Auburn was the fifth-largest shoe producer in the U.S., employing eight thousand people in twelve factories.

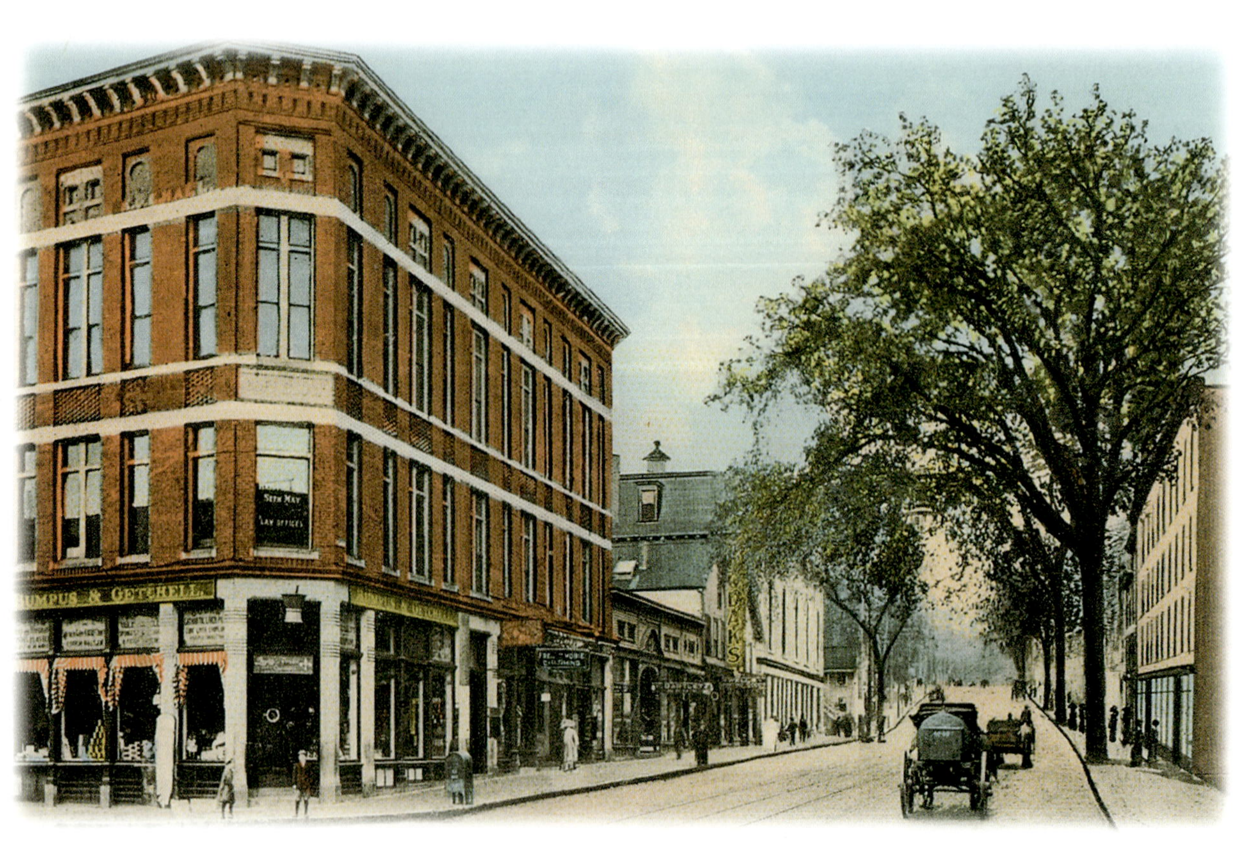

And desolation saddens all thy green . . .
Far, far away, thy children leave the land . . .

By the mid-1950s, Auburn was faced with a bleak future as its major economic base declined. Several companies operated through the sixties, but most of the factories have long since been demolished. Through a determined citizens' effort, new industries were lured to the city, neighborhoods were improved, and community problems were resolved. For these remarkable efforts, Auburn won an All-America City Award in 1968 from the National Municipal League and *Look* magazine.

The postcard shows the 1873 Goff Block at the corner of Court and Main. Downtown Auburn was once known as Goff's Corner because of the store operated by James Goff in 1823. Today the building is the Midnight Blues Club and Muddy Waters Café.

Down the street is the mansard-roofed Auburn Hall, built in 1865 after fire destroyed the Auburn City Building the previous year. City offices moved out in 1897, but city government meetings were held there until 1916. The police station was under the stairway of the ground-floor entrance, and the jail was in the basement. Ground-floor shops included Flanders Clothing and Packards Pharmacy. Through-out the twentieth century, Auburn Hall drew the community together for festivals, band concerts, fund-raising dances, minstrel shows, and the like. During the 1940s the stage and balconies were removed and the hall partitioned, and from 1946 to 1961, it was occupied by the State Department of Health and Welfare. Saved from the wrecking ball, it was remodeled in 2003–04 to once again house municipal offices.

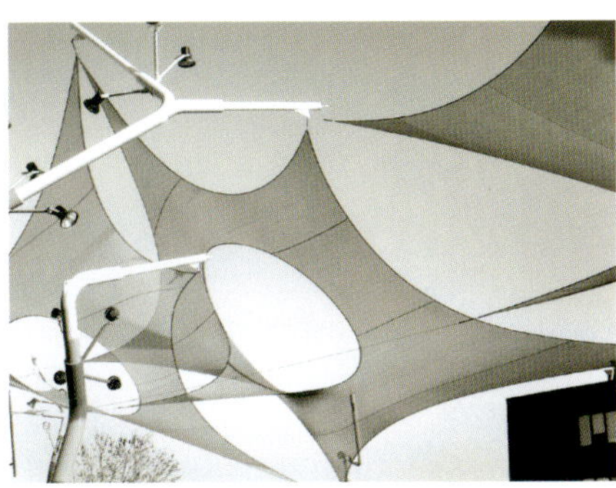

Colorful canopies and sculptures decorate Festival Plaza Park, on the Androscoggin River waterfront

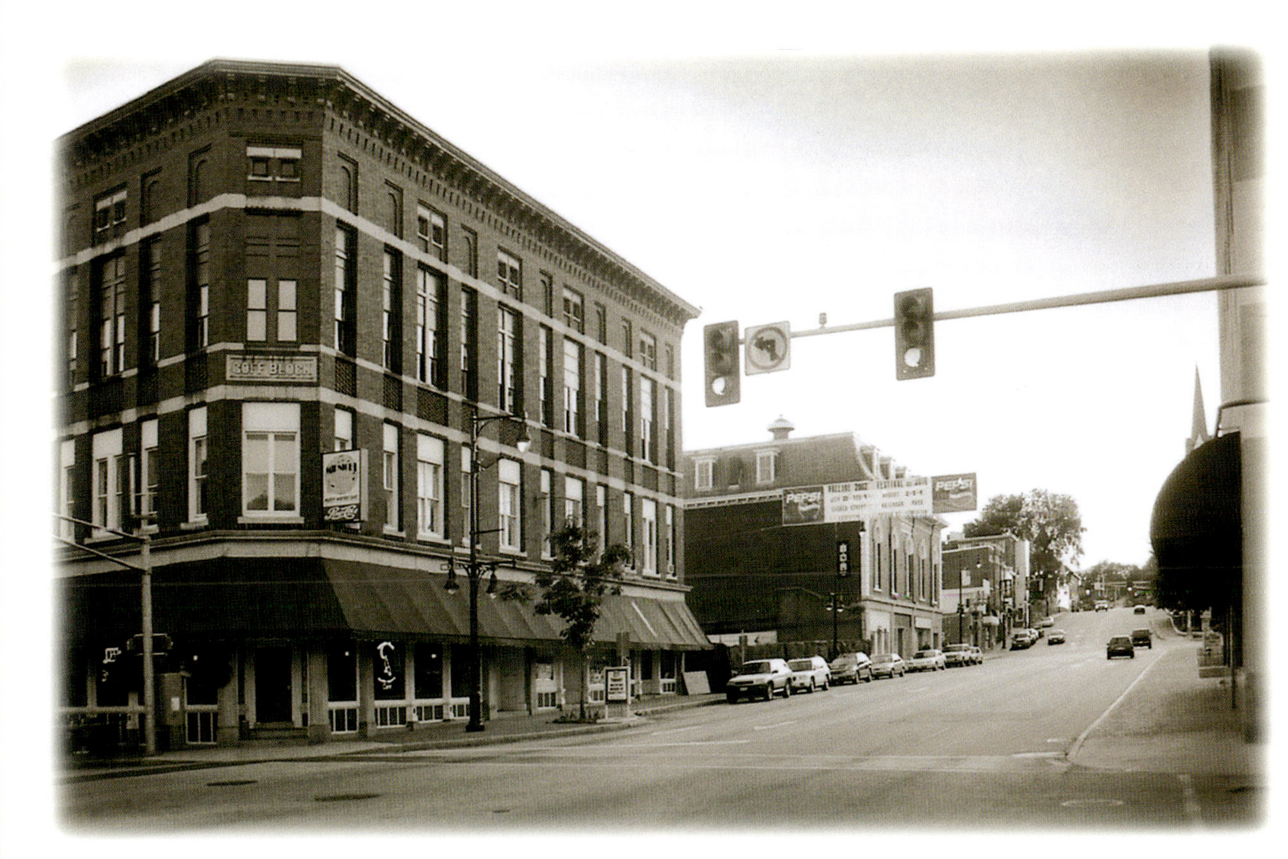

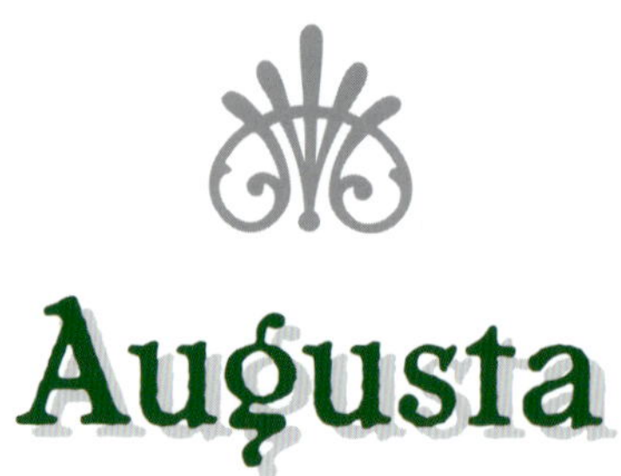

Augusta

INCORPORATED AS MAINE'S
109TH TOWN ON FEBRUARY 20, 1797

INCORPORATED AS MAINE'S
4TH CITY ON JULY 23, 1849

SHIRETOWN OF KENNEBEC COUNTY
AND STATE CAPITAL SINCE 1827

POPULATION IN 1900: 11,683

POPULATION IN 2000: 18,560

The first permanent settlement of Augusta began when Fort Western was erected in 1754. Originally part of Hallowell, the town was set off in 1797 and named for Lord Harrington, a distinguished English patriot. Although the lore suggests Harrington changed its name by June of that year because its detractors nicknamed it "herringtown," perhaps it bothered the town fathers to honor a Brit so soon after the Revolutionary War. At any rate, a more "august" name was found in the personage of Pamela Augusta Dearborn, daughter of Revolutionary War hero, Henry Dearborn. He marched with Benedict Arnold through Maine to Quebec in 1775, passing through the settlement.

Augusta was also seen as second rate by those who made continued attempts to move the state capital to Portland, which could then be done by a simple legislative vote. Governor Enoch Lincoln in 1827 decreed by legislative bill that Augusta was the seat of the state government, even though legislators had been meeting in Portland. It was deemed that Augusta was the center of the most populous "wheel" of the state, and thus provided fairer access to legislators who twice a year had to travel there by horseback or stagecoach. The effort to snatch Augusta's economic advantages and prestige as the seat of state government failed for the final time in 1911, when an amendment to the state constitution confirmed the city as Maine's capital.

The city straddles the Kennebec River, which has provided power to Edwards Manufacturing Company's textile mills, among others. The paper, textile, and shoe factories attracted a large population of French-speaking workers from Canada. By 1908 nearly a fifth of Augusta's population was French. Augusta was home to several large publishing houses that fueled its economic engine in the late 1800s, and contributed to the doubling of the post office's size in 1910, and again in 1940. Indeed, the city was known as the mail-order publishing capital of the world, boasting the first million-circulation magazine, *Comfort*, published by Gannett Publishing. By 1910, *The American Woman* and *Needlecraft*, published by Vickery & Hill, enjoyed national distribution. *Comfort* ceased publication in 1934, and the era ended in 1942, with only the Gannett publishing empire re-

Water Street and the Post Office in the 1930s, with the Woolworth Co. store on left.

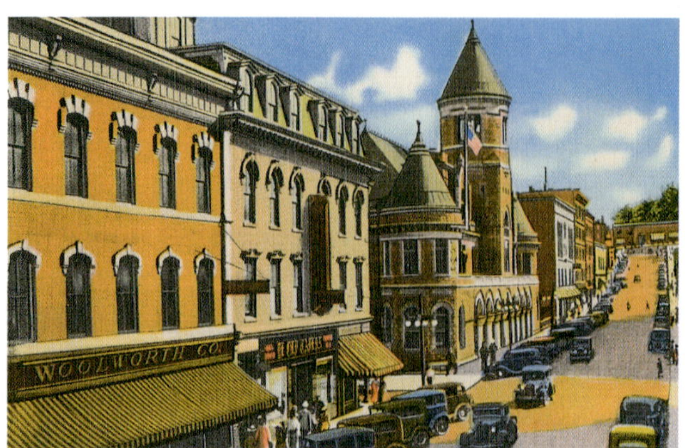

The Post Office in the 1940s.

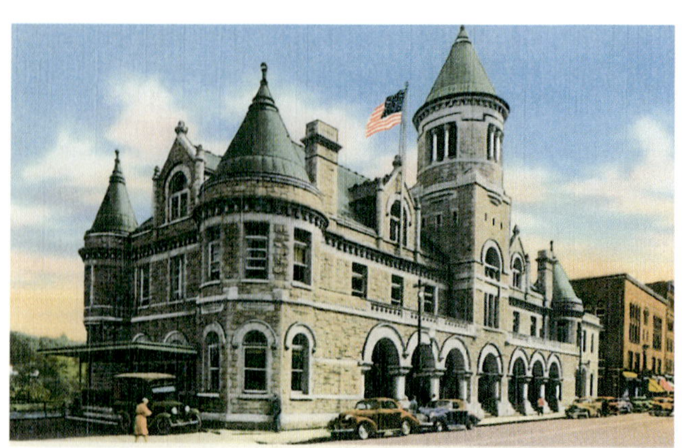

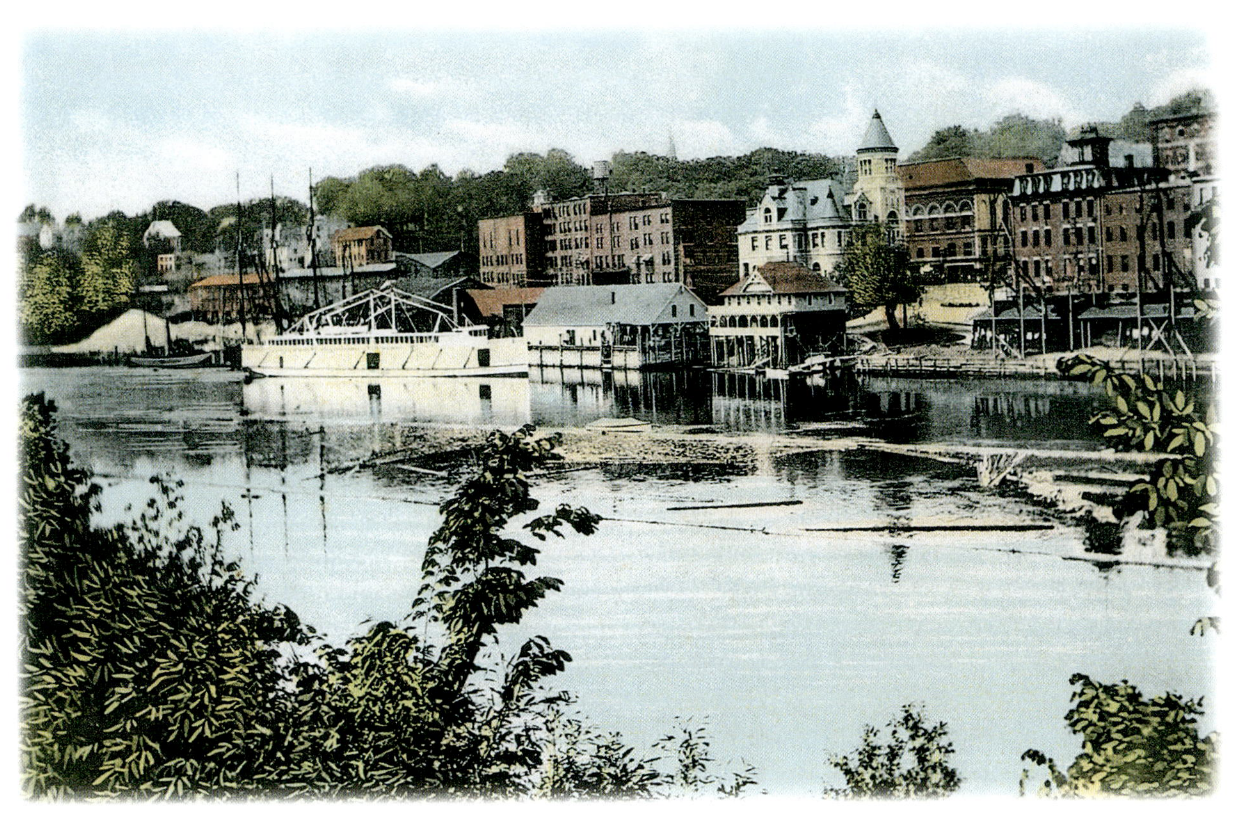

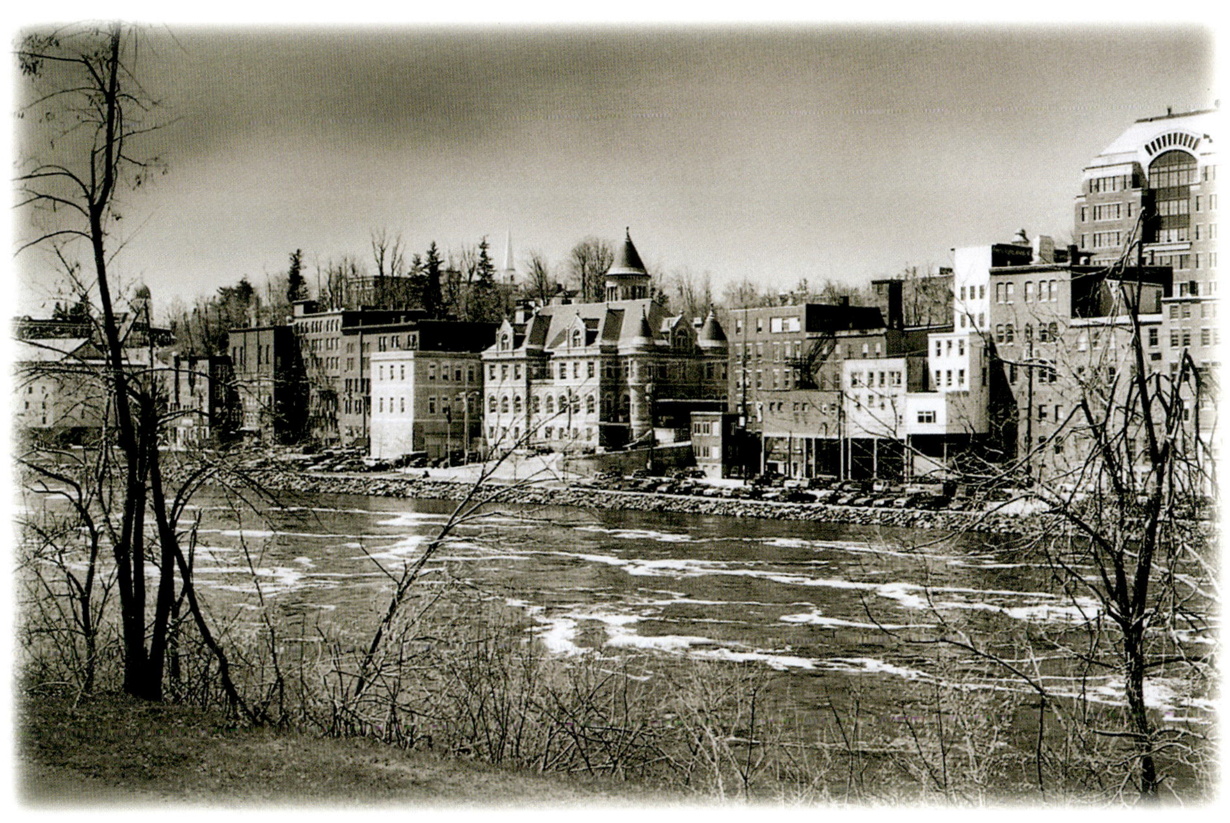

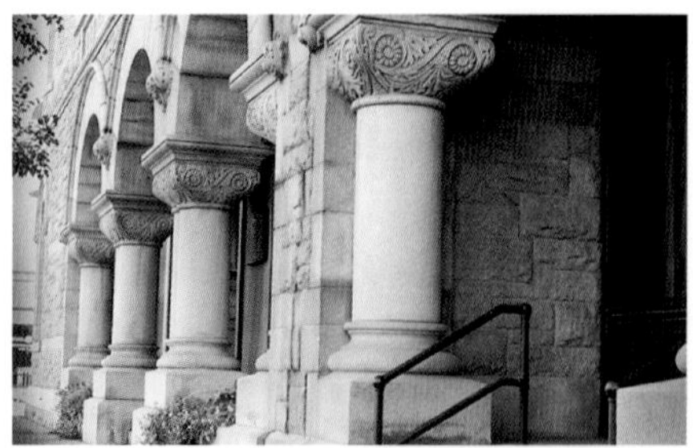

Details of the Post Office building today.

maining to this day, albeit headquartered in Portland. (This company bears no relation to the publicly held Gannett Co.)

Most of the commercial district was rebuilt after a fire in 1865 destroyed eighty buildings, and another fire damaged the east side in 1904. Most of the buildings retain their ornate facades, though some have had a '60s scouring. Nevertheless, twelve buildings on Water Street are on the National Register of Historic Places. The 1987 Key Plaza is a striking postmodern high-rise (framed by the lamps on the left side of today's picture on page 27). Seven buildings formerly occupied the site, including a hotel that was demolished in 1966 for a parking lot.

The postcard view of Water Street looks toward the castle-like Old Post Office, built in 1890 in Romanesque-Revival style with Hallowell granite. While it still houses a postal branch, the main post office and federal offices have moved to Western Avenue. From the Old Post Office toward the foreground were the E. C. Allen Publishing Company (pioneer of mail-order periodicals), the gorgeous Vickery Building (built in 1893 of Hallowell granite), and the old Brooks Hardware building.

In the center of the block, but not appreciably visible in the photo, is a stunning Art Deco two-story built for the S. S. Kresge Co. in 1932, replacing a row of three Italianate buildings that were home to Dirigo Business College. It is now Stacy's office supply store. Farther up the street toward the viewer is a granite row built where the 1865 fire began. The Italianate buildings ending with the Barker Block now house a variety store and travel agency. Signs on that side of the street in the postcard include Swift & Turner, Union Mutual Life, and Crawford Cooking Ranges.

On the right side of Water Street, the Mid-State College holds the foreground position today. Formerly the Cony House hotel, it was built in 1866 with a mansard roof and cupola, which was removed after 1913, later replaced, and then removed again. By 1902 it was owned by Augusta Real Estate Association. Adjacent, going down the street, were the Augusta Supply Company and the Quality Shoe Company. The building on the corner eventually housed Fleet Bank (now vacant).

Western Avenue became an exit for the Maine Turnpike in 1955, and soon found its grand residential area swamped by commercial development. It was inevitable that downtown commerce would flee, starting with the Augusta Supply Company that same year. By the mid-1960s, Augusta's schools were aged and overcrowded, the high school had lost its accreditation, the Kennebec was polluted, and the Bates Mill was about to close.

In an effort to reverse this decline, the newly formed Augusta Board of Trade helped establish the Hallowell Shoe Factory, which employed four hundred people for two decades, as well as other manufacturers in the Augusta Business Park. The city's first shopping mall, Augusta Plaza, was completed on the site of the Haynes Estate in 1961, and in 1973 the Augusta Civic Center was built in the north end. In 1970 the University of Maine at Augusta moved onto its new 165-acre campus. The Edwards Dam, which supplied power to Edwards Manufacturing's textile mill and its predecessors for over 160 years, was removed in 1999 to restore fisheries to the eighteen-mile stretch of the Kennebec River between Augusta and Waterville.

NOTABLE NATIVE:

Guy Gannett, the publishing baron, was born in Augusta in 1881.

REMARKABLE RESIDENT:

James Gillespie Blaine helped found the Republican Party in Maine and was state chairman from 1859 to 1881. He ran unsuccessfully for president against Grover Cleveland in 1884.

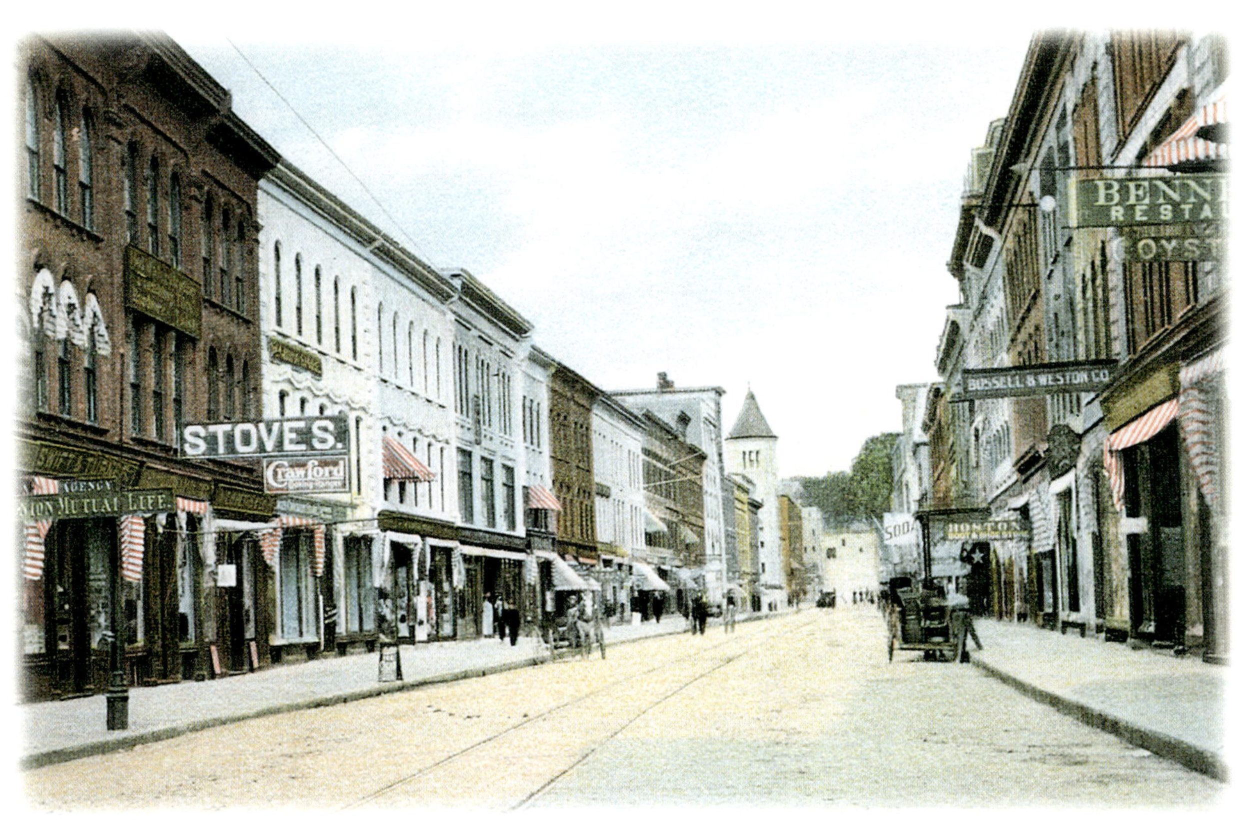
STOVES.
Crawford
BOSSELL & WESTON CO.

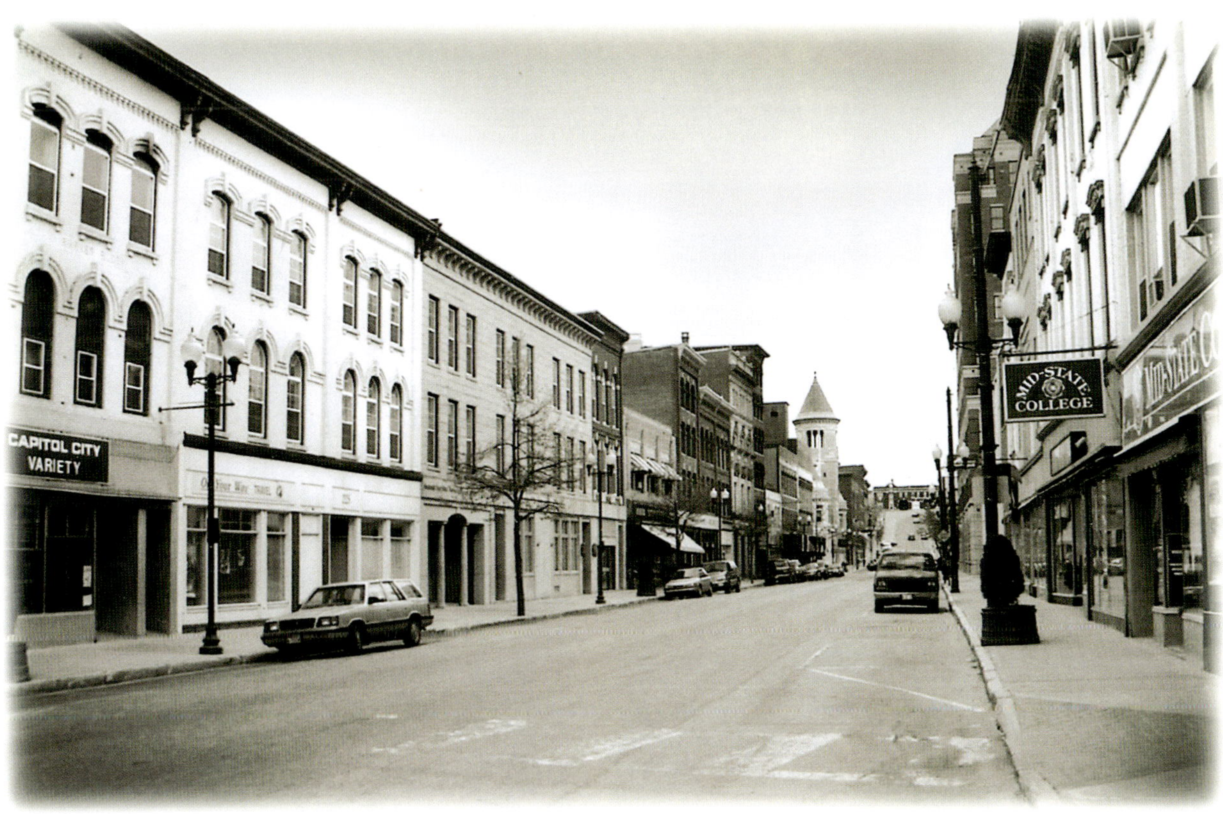
CAPITOL CITY
VARIETY
MID-STATE
COLLEGE

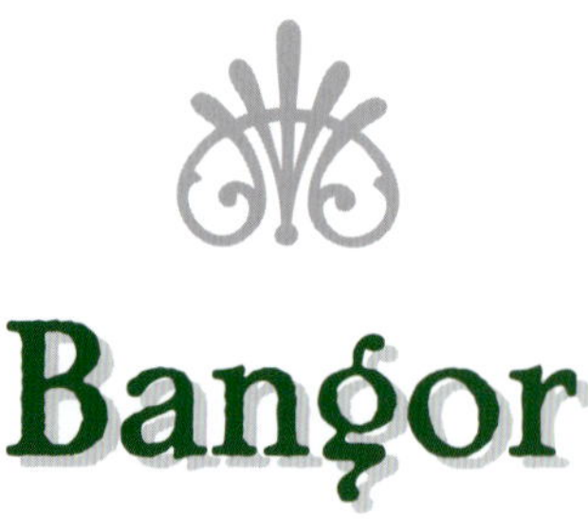

Bangor

INCORPORATED AS MAINE'S 73RD TOWN ON FEBRUARY 25, 1791

INCORPORATED AS MAINE'S 2ND CITY ON FEBRUARY 12, 1834

POPULATION IN 1900: 21,850

POPULATION IN 2000: 31,473

It's hard to know the true story of how things are named. Even if facts are embellished or contrived, the myth often becomes a nearly legitimate truth. For instance, settlers in the Kenduskeag Plantation sent the Reverend Seth Noble to petition the Massachusetts General Court for incorporation of their town, to be named Sunbury; but during the proceedings, he whistled a favorite tune, titled *Bangor*, a Welsh hymn quite popular in New England at the time. When asked for the name of the town, he thought they were asking for the name of the song—and thus Bangor was incorporated. Another researcher believes Noble changed the name after dining with John Hancock, who particularly admired the hymn, and that whistling had nothing to do with it. (It is a rather pleasant tune; to hear it, visit the *WhiteHouseInnBangor.com* Web site, under "Area Attractions.")

The town rapidly became the "Lumber Capital of the World" for the prodigious haste in which surrounding forests were cut. Henry David Thoreau wrote that the town was "like a star on the edge of night, still hewing at the forests of which it is built." By the mid-1830s there were more than three hundred sawmills turning virgin forest into lumber for new towns and schooners. Lumberjacks working in the northern Maine woods floated logs down the Penobscot River, which was often so swollen with logs that the men could walk from shore to shore upon them. Once in town the lumberjacks cut loose on drink, brawling and patronizing the local ladies of

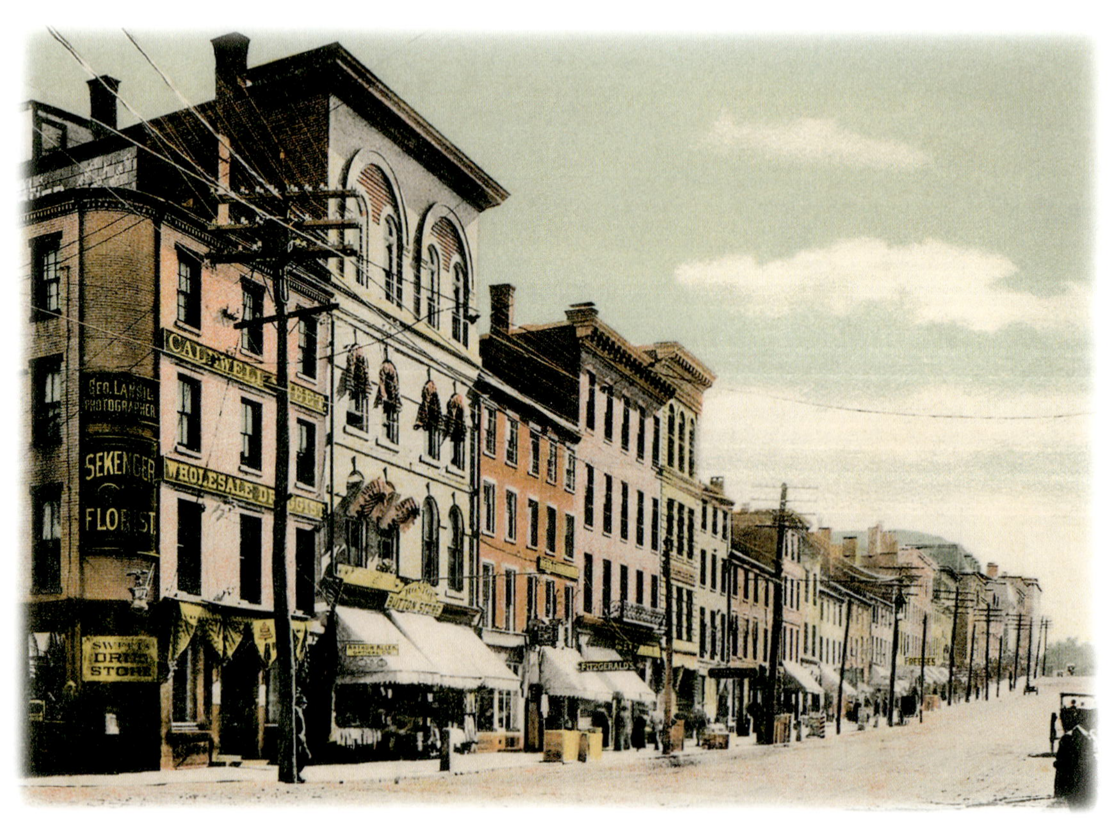

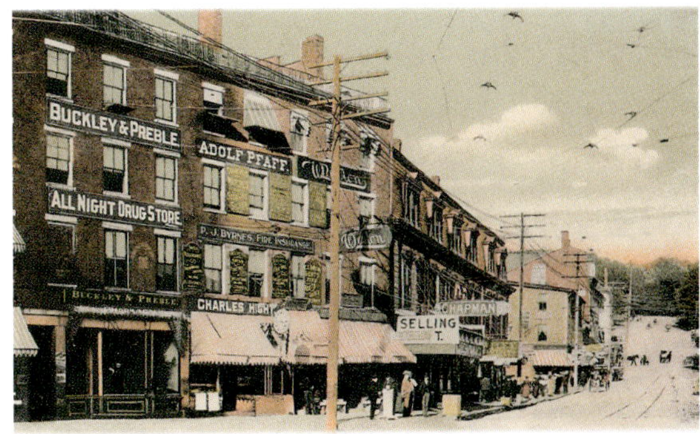

Kenduskeag Bridge, before the 1911 Fire.

the evening, giving Bangor its rough and rollicking reputation.

By the end of the nineteenth century, Minnesota and Oregon had entered the lumber market, and Bangor's fortunes began to fade. Bangor still honors the lumberjack era and its legendary glory with an enormous statue of Paul Bunyan. (Whether the fabled creator of the Grand Canyon and the Great Lakes was born in Bangor or in Minnesota is a matter of some dispute; he was evidently the invention of a newspaper reporter in Detroit who first published the tall tales in 1910.)

In 1911, after these postcards were made, a great fire reshaped the city's landscape, burning 55 acres and more than 300 buildings. Half the town and nearly the entire business district were destroyed, but Main Street remained unscathed. Its merchants offered a 25 percent discount to customers who purchased supplies for those left destitute by the blaze.

Urban renewal in the 1960s claimed many other edifices in the shiretown of Penobscot County. The beautiful Union Station at the end of Exchange Street was replaced with a strip mall. The old City Hall with its highly visible clock tower was torn down for a two-level parking garage. Indeed, parking lots seemed more important than the small businesses forced out by eminent domain. As in so many cities caught in the urban renewal craze, historically significant buildings were replaced with modern structures devoid of architectural style, and developments such as the Bangor Mall—located in a former cow pasture in 1978—drew business away from the downtown area.

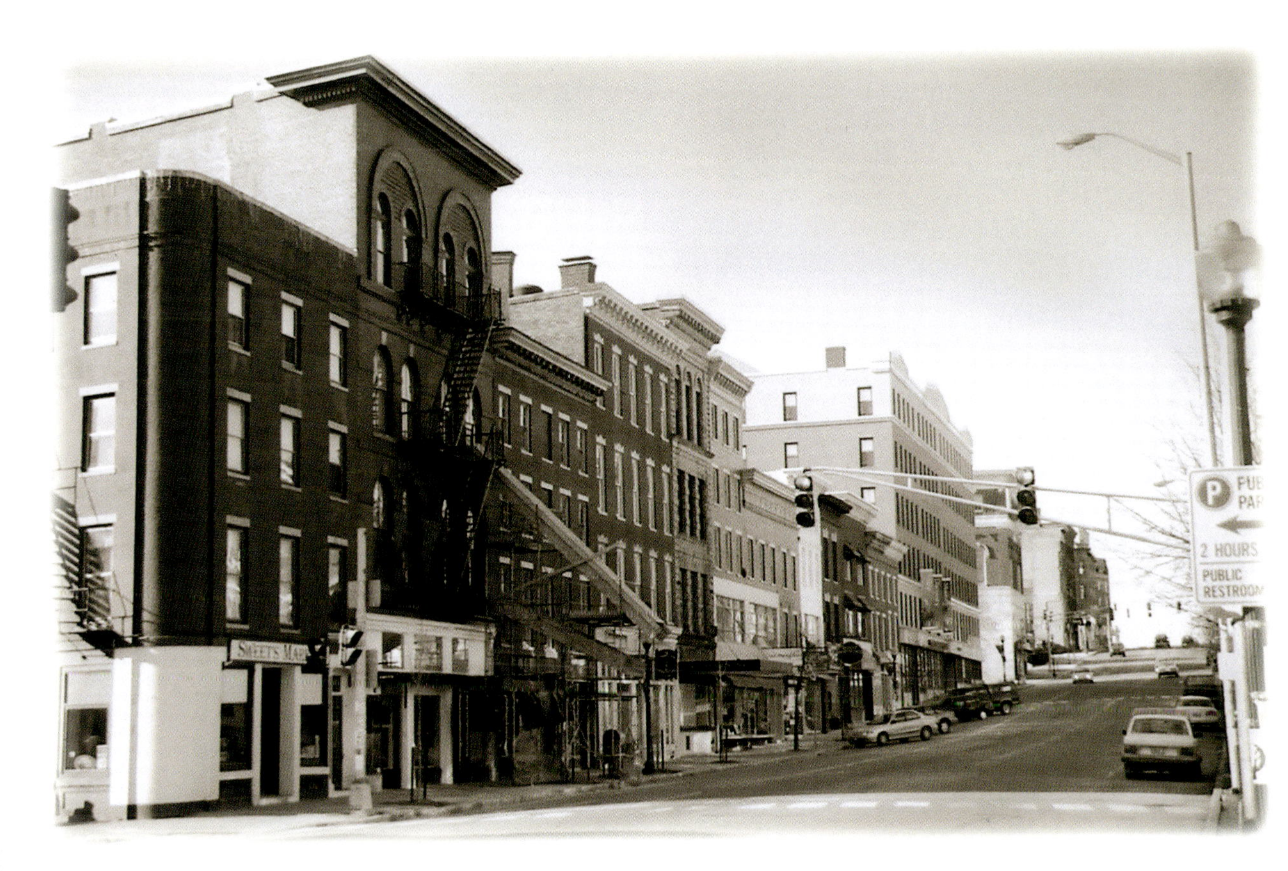

However, many of the historic buildings are today being renovated and the downtown revitalized. Instead of "magnet" department stores, the focus is on cultural anchors such as the new Maine Discovery Museum, located in the long-vacant Freese's Department Store, and the relocation of the University of Maine Museum of Art into the former Sears Roebuck building.

After the deactivation of Dow Air Force Base in 1968, the city developed the base into an international airport and industrial park. Stephen King set one of his spooky stories, "The Langoliers," at the Bangor International Airport.

In recent years, Bangor has hosted the traveling National Folk Festival (2002, 2003, and 2004), bringing 200,000 people and national attention to the city. Set on the banks of the Penobscot, the festival proved the city had come a long way, cleaning up what author Bill Caldwell two decades earlier had called "a sad, sleazy, deserted slum of what is left of the port of Bangor." Bangor has now revamped its plans for the waterfront to include performance space, and private developers are giving it another look, with an eye toward high-end condos and restaurants. There's even talk of establishing its own annual folk festival.

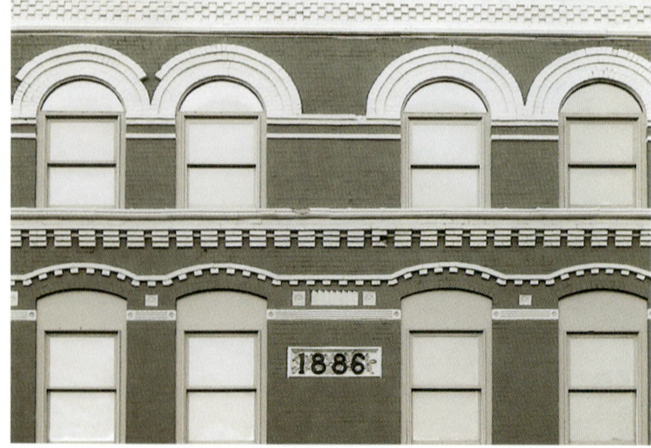

One of the lovely buildings on Main Street

The postcard of Main Street on page 28 shows many of the distinctive buildings that remain outwardly unchanged. On the left corner, now Sweet's Market, are signs for Sweet's Drug Store; George Lansil, photographer; and Sekenger Florist, as well as the phone company. The four-story building adjacent

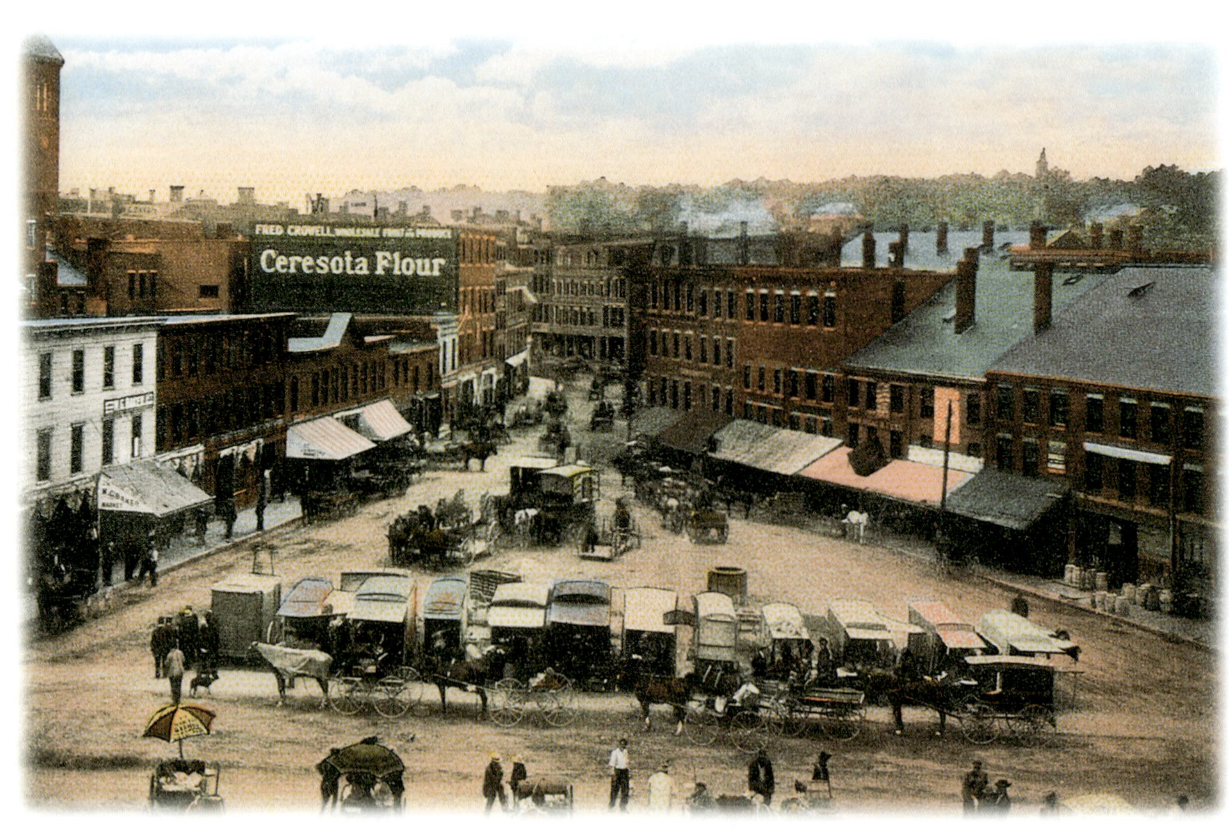

housed Arthur Allen Optical and the Boston Button Store (later the Boston Shoe Store), and Stephen C. Smith, Attorney at Law. It now houses Ireland's Furniture. Next was Fitzgerald's. The four-story building in the middle of the block, with an odd fifth-story section, had been the Standard Shoe Shop, which closed in the 1990s. The shop's lettering is still visible in the cement entryway. The six-story building in today's photograph is the Maine Discovery Museum. Just across Water Street in the distance is the 1868 Masonic Hall. In 1984 a six-block portion of the downtown area was placed on the National Register of Historic Places.

The view from the Market Place at Pickering Square on page 30 has changed more significantly. On the far left was the City Hall, no longer there, and the white building just below it was M. C. Baker's bakery. The prominent store advertising Ceresota Flour was the Fred Crowell Wholesale Fruit and Produce. Today's photograph shows the Phenix Block with the arched tower in the center background, flanked by the long-vacant Dakins Sporting Goods building in the historic district known as West Market Square. Built in 1900, the Dakins building is undergoing a facelift in anticipation of tenancy. Although no longer held in Pickering Square, the market has operated continuously for a century and is now located in Brewer.

INTERESTING TIDBITS:

- A town in Michigan was named Bangor in 1853 by a member of the board of supervisors who had lived in Bangor, Maine.
- The long-handled log-moving tool known as the *peavey* was invented in 1858 by Joe and Daniel Peavey from nearby Stillwater Village.
- A 600-pound moose wandering the streets of Bangor in 2002 had to be shot by a game warden.
- In April 1997, *Reader's Digest* named Bangor as one of the top fifty places to live in the United States.

REMARKABLE RESIDENT:

Stephen King, monarch of the horror novel, was born in Portland and has lived in Bangor since 1980.

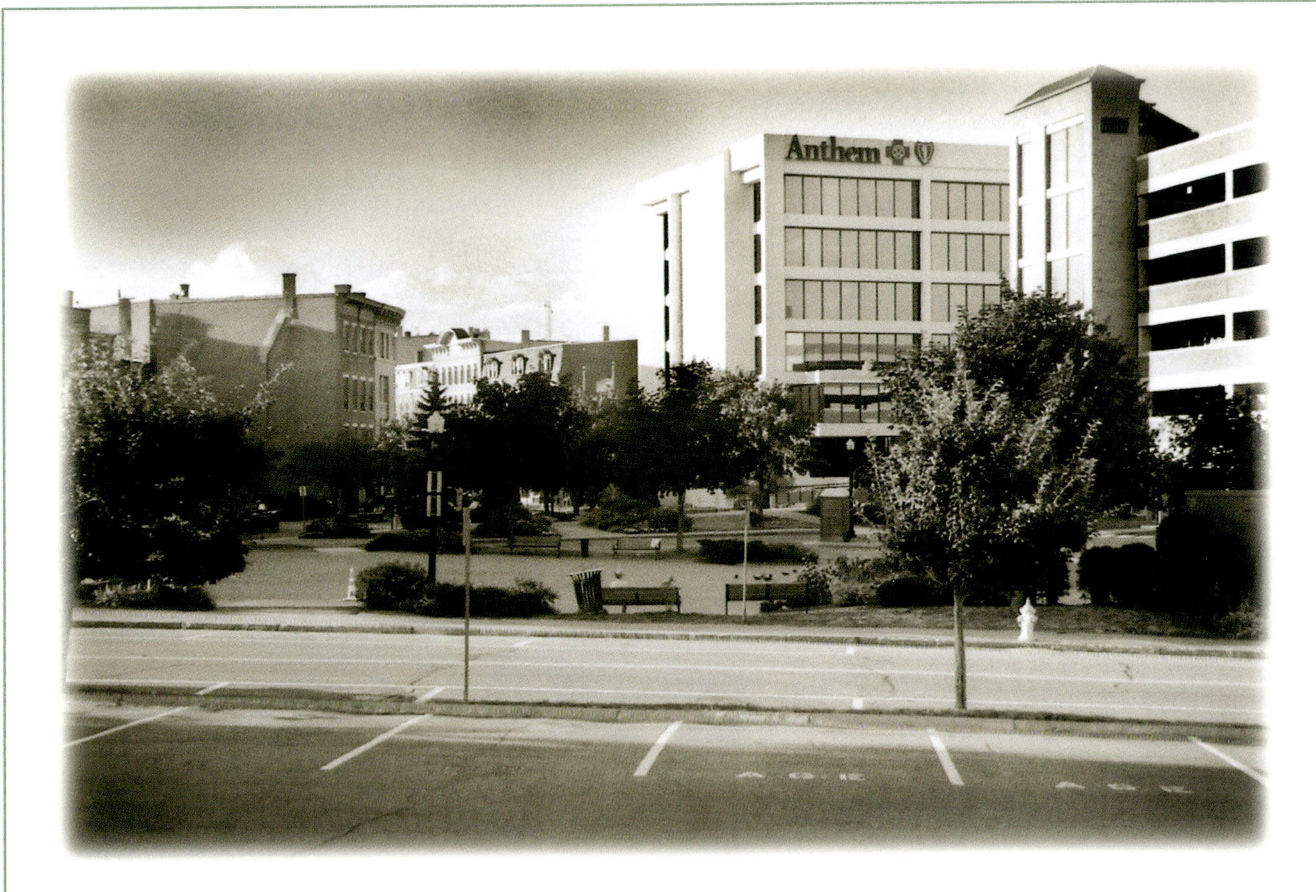

Bar Harbor

INCORPORATED AS MAINE'S 107TH TOWN ON FEBRUARY 23, 1796

POPULATION IN 1900: 4,379

POPULATION IN 2000: 4,820

Originally called Eden, the little settlement around Hulls and Salisbury Coves would later find its center of commerce relocated to where it is today. One early historian believes it was named for Richard Eden, a British statesman, but it is more widely thought to have been named for its scenic beauty. However, the later village known as East Eden was set smack onto a field scoured of trees. William Cullen Bryant wrote in *Picturesque America* (1872) that the village "is without one feature of beauty. . . . Every structure, with the exception of a few cottages erected by wealthy gentlemen of Boston, stands without trees, garden, or any other pleasant surroundings." The ugly duckling eventually grew up to be a swan.

As in many coastal villages of Maine, but particularly in Bar Harbor, rusticators were the first tourists. Often artists or educators, they preferred a more rustic enjoyment of the landscape, and boarded with locals or in simple lodges. They blended in with the townspeople and appreciated the local culture, finding pleasure in hiking or studying nature. In 1844, Hudson River School landscape painter Thomas Cole summered in the area, and soon others in the school, including Frederic Church, followed. Word soon got out that Bar Harbor was the place to be. Eventually, hotels had to be built, but by then the clientele was becoming more gentrified.

By 1888 there were eighteen grand hotels in the area of the summer colony, which was known as Bar Harbor because of the sand bar that connected it to Bar Island. Visitors arrived via the Maine Central Railroad at its terminus at Hancock Point, and they were ferried eight miles across Frenchman Bay. Soon the rusticators were outnumbered by the cottagers, the enormously wealthy set who built lavish mansions called "cottages" and gave them elegant names like Clovercroft, Chatwold, Talleyrand, Elsinore, and Llangollen. People named Rockefeller, Morgan, Ford, Astor, Vanderbilt, and Pulitzer set themselves apart with high-society airs, and the Mount Desert Island summer colony was born. "Luxury, refinement and ostentatious gatherings replaced buckboard rides, picnics, and day-long hikes," said one writer.

The impending war in Europe in 1914 was putting a damper on social life in the Bar Harbor summer colony, until the unexpected arrival of a German ocean liner one August morning. While in mid-sail from New York to Bremen, Germany, the captain of the luxury liner *Kronprinzessin Cecilie* received a message that Germany, Austria, France, and England were at war and that he was to turn back to the U.S. The ship was already being hunted by French and German boats because of the shipment of gold and silver ingots located in the hold.

Aware that all major ports from Halifax to the British West Indies were being patrolled, the captain took the advice of a New York investment banker familiar with the deep waters of a little-known port called Bar Harbor. The ship sailed in under the cover of fog, and an astonished town awoke to see a looming ship in the harbor that dwarfed the ferries and fishing boats. Once the passengers were unloaded and sent to Boston and New York by train, the locals and summer people alike took a proprietary interest in "their" ship. No cotillion or gala party was complete without the handsomely attired German officers in attendance. Though the town resisted it, the ship was later escorted to Boston, and after America entered the war, the ship was rechristened the USS *Mount Vernon* and served as a troop transport ship.

The village known as Bar Harbor had become widely known in the early 1900s, thanks to its summer colony, and it overshadowed the town that had birthed it. Historian Richard Walden Hale Jr. wrote, "It was becoming more and more of a nuisance to have a nationally known village, Bar Harbor, go under another name in legal use." Residents of Eden weren't too anxious to change their century-old name, but on

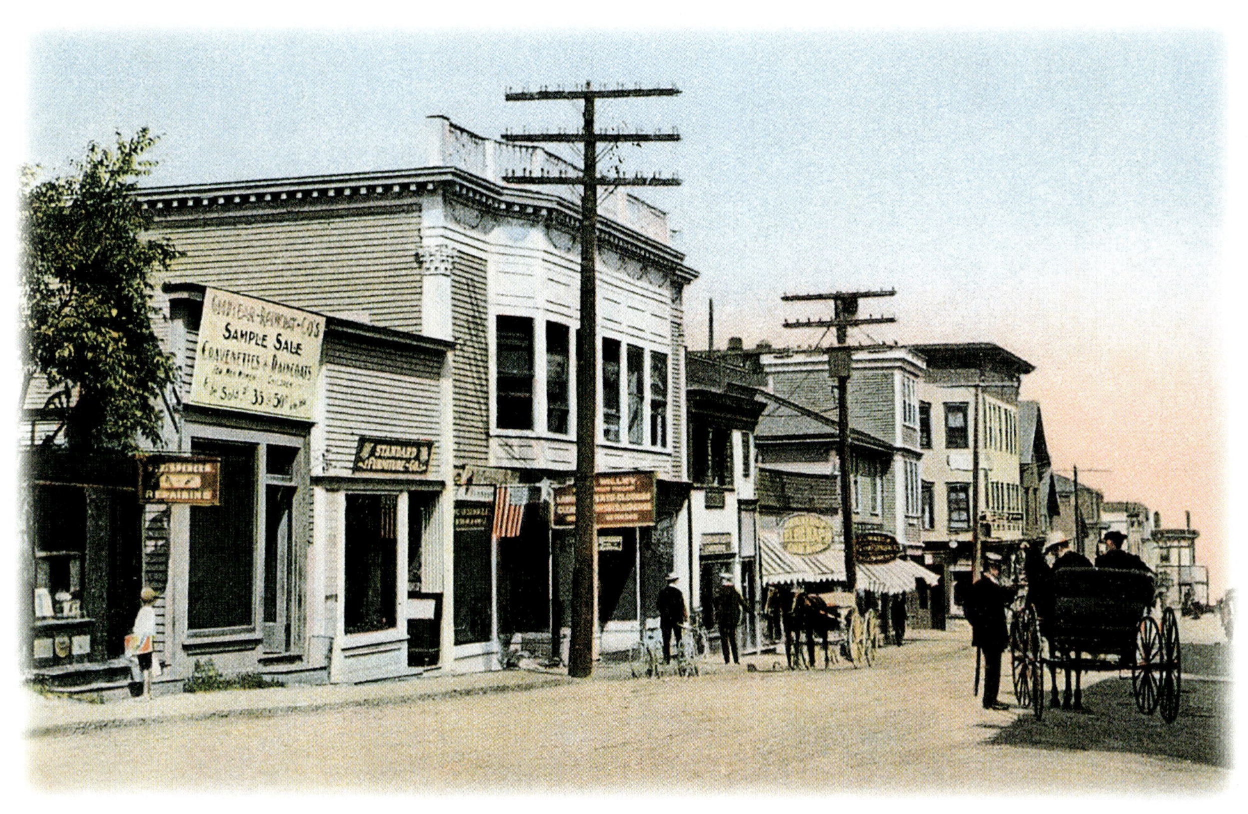
SAMPLE SALE
STANDARD
FURNITURE CO.
REPAIRING

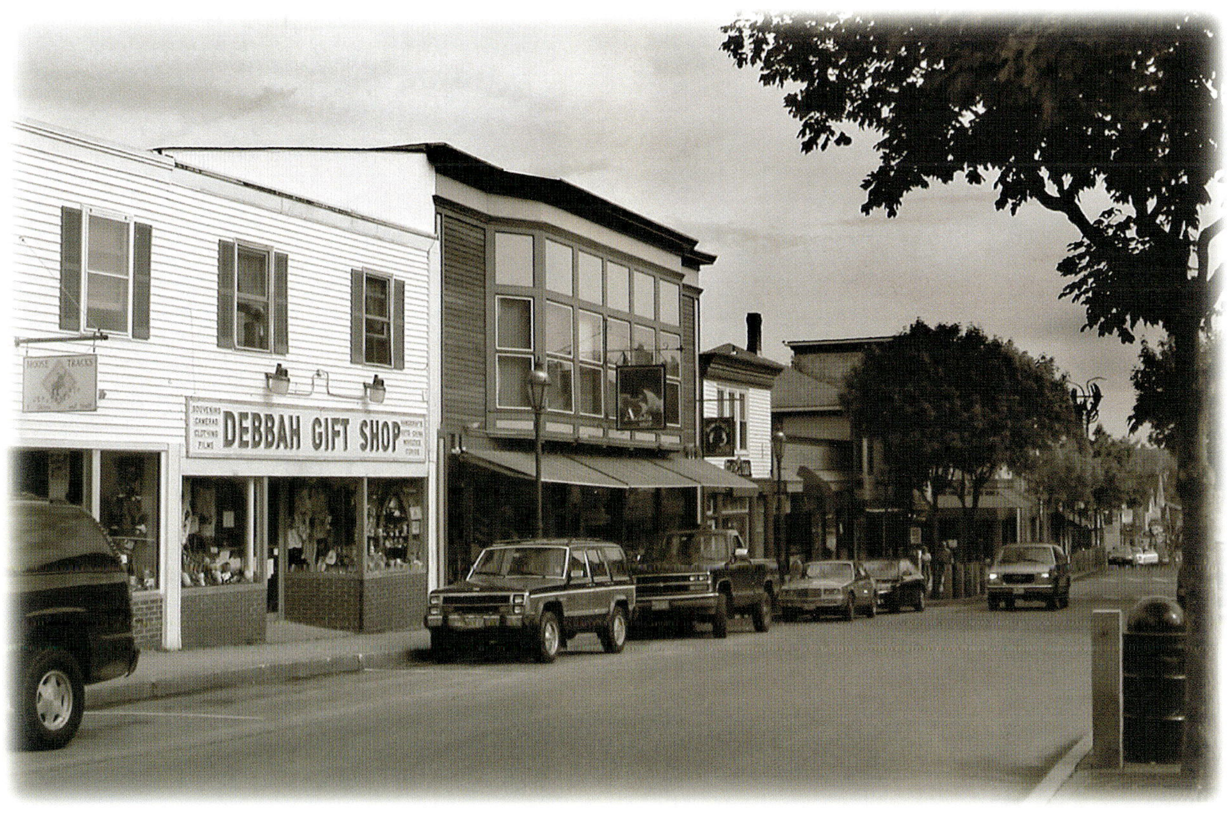
MOOSE TRACKS
SOUVENIRS
CAMERAS
CLOTHING
FILMS
DEBBAH GIFT SHOP

March 4, 1918, they voted to change the town's name to Bar Harbor.

The cottage era was already in decline when a 1947 fire swept through "Millionaire's Row," destroying dozens of lavish estates, along with 170 year-round homes and five historic hotels. The Mount Desert fire raged for ten days in October, and smoldered underground for more than two weeks after that. The business district was spared, but the exodus was terrifying. The roads were blocked at one point, and fishermen had to help 400 people off the island. When Route 3 was reopened, a caravan of 700 cars ran a gauntlet of roaring flames and raining sparks to arrive safely in Ellsworth.

More than 17,000 acres burned on Mount Desert Island in an abnormally dry year that had sparked fires throughout the state. Many of Bar Harbor's cottages were not rebuilt, eventually replaced by the motels that now line Route 3. Statewide, 850 homes and 400 seasonal cottages succumbed in the 200,000-acre devastation "the year that Maine burned." Bar Harbor today is more proletarian, geared less for refined elegance than for hordes of tourists.

The Main Street postcard on page 33 was published by Raphael Tuck & Sons, based in England. Many of the fine resort hotels were on Main Street, though none are pictured in this postcard. The Hotel Florence, which burned in 1918, was located where the current row of retail shops is now, across from the Village Green, which itself was occupied by the Grand Central Hotel. That 1873 grand dame was torn down before the turn of the twentieth century. Visible in the postcard, a repair shop of some sort, as well as the Goodyear Raincoat Shop and Standard Furniture Company, were located where Debbah Gift Shop is now. The building with the lovely bay window, now the Acadia Shop, had been a clothing store. The oval sign two shops down reads TELEGRAPH.

The postcard of the docks at right looks west from the present town pier. The Clark Coal Company sign is quite visible in the background. Today's view may not be the same, but it is indicative of how the public landing has changed. Another well-known launch site is that of the Canadian-operated passenger ferry to Nova Scotia. Introduced in May 1998, *The Cat* (a high-speed catamaran) cuts the traditional six-hour ferry crossing in half. It accommodates 900 passengers and 240 cars and is billed as the fastest car ferry in North America. It replaced the *Bluenose*, a ferry that began operation in 1956 carrying 150 cars and 500 passengers, later upgrading to a capacity in line with that of *The Cat*.

One of the island's largest employers with 1,300 on the payroll, the Jackson Laboratory has been working on cures for human diseases over the last seventy years. It supplies two million laboratory mice each year to universities and research institutions around the world, and maintains seventy different strains of mice used in breast cancer research.

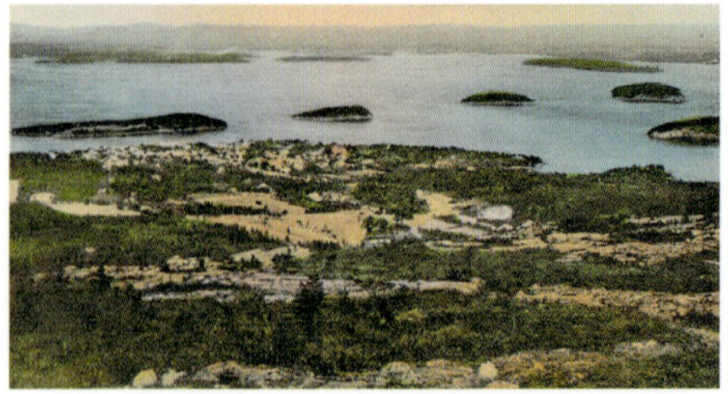

Bar Harbor and Frenchman Bay from Summit of Cadillac Mountain.

Bar Harbor seen from Bar Island, 1920s.

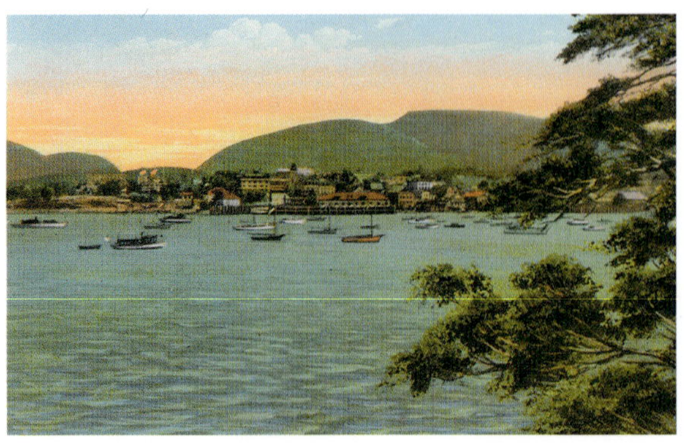

NOTABLE NATIVE:

Nelson Rockefeller, vice president to Gerald Ford (1974–1977), and son of John D., was born in Bar Harbor in 1908.

INTERESTING TIDBIT:

Ben and Bill's Chocolate Emporium sells ice cream with—*gulp!*—real lobster meat in it. They even have repeat customers.

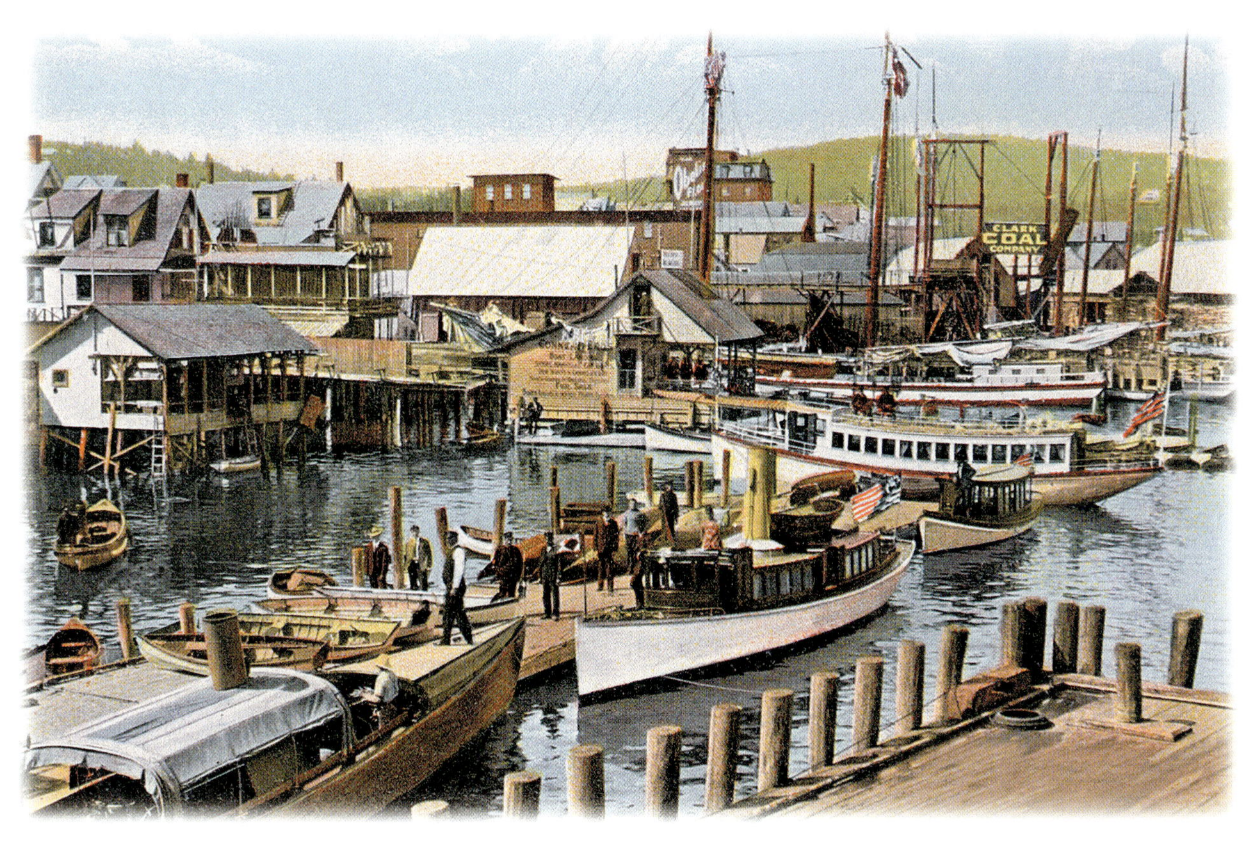
CLARK
COAL
COMPANY

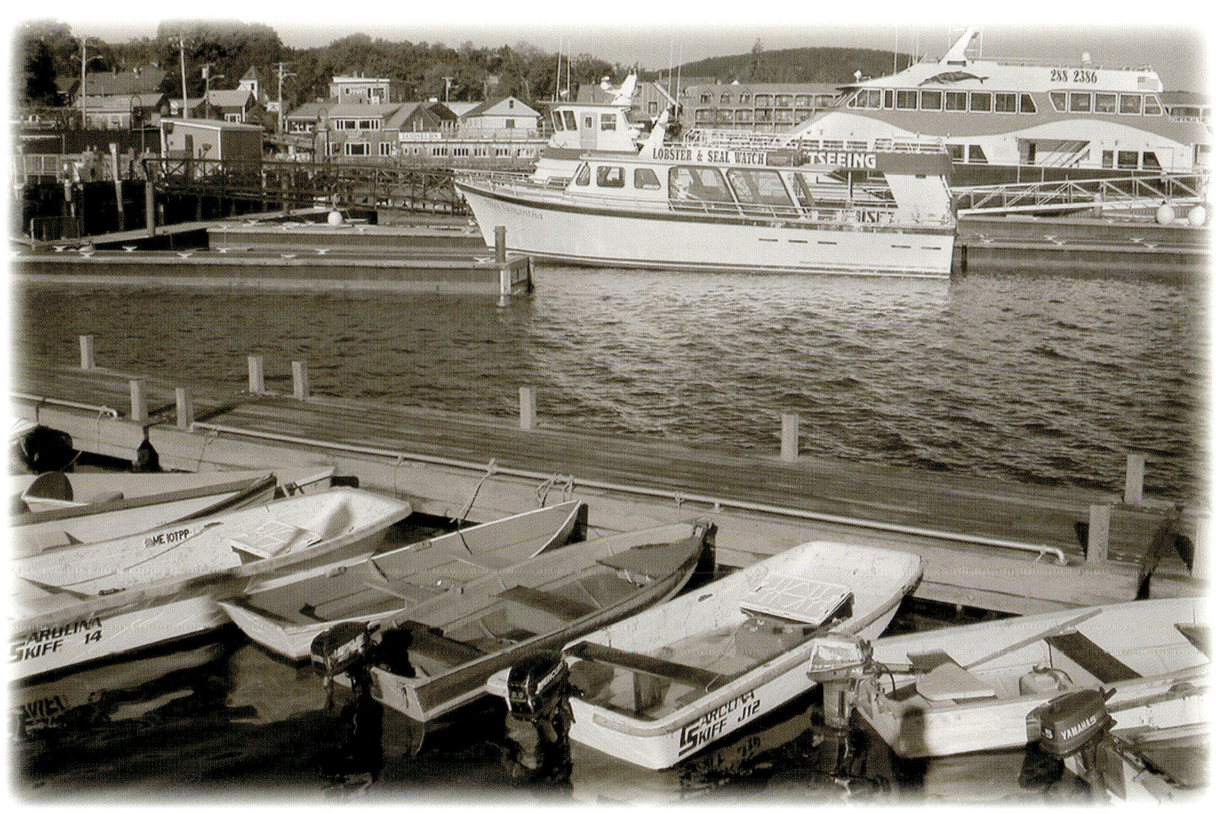
LOBSTER & SEAL WATCH
288 2386
CAROLINA SKIFF 14
CAROLINA SKIFF J12
YAMAHA

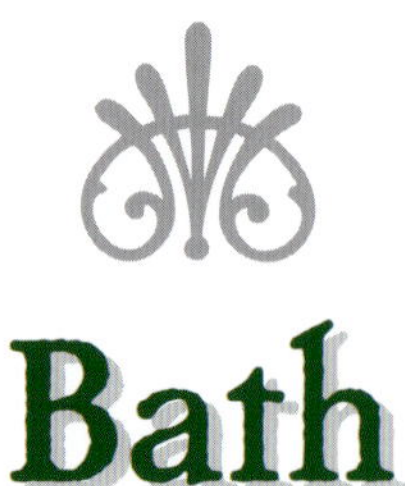

Bath

INCORPORATED AS MAINE'S
41ST TOWN ON FEBRUARY 17, 1781

INCORPORATED AS MAINE'S
3RD CITY ON JUNE 14, 1847

POPULATION IN 1900: 10,477

POPULATION IN 2000: 9,266

Maine towns and cities are, for the most part, blessed with downtown facades that have remained the same for a century or more. Resisting the lure of modernity, Bath said no to an urban renewal plan that would have torn down half of the city's 187 buildings—38 of them on Front and Centre streets alone. In the fashion of the 1960s, a tree-dotted pedestrian mall was slated for this area of irreplaceable architecture. Federal, Greek Revival, and Victorian-style buildings, many still sound, were to be replaced with functional, modernist (read *ugly*) buildings that are the much-lamented hallmark of urban renewal.

Despite the closure of dozens of businesses and the flight to Cook's Corner Mall, in 1965 the public voted two to one against the controversial razing of their city. The heightened interest in historic preservation brought about a new vision for revitalization—one that will use historic character to its full advantage. Though Sears, Grant's, and Newberry's department stores have left downtown for good, the storefronts now house specialty shops, restaurants, and a grocery store vital to a thriving downtown.

Bath was originally a part of Georgetown called Long Reach, and was eventually named for the lovely English resort town where many New England sailors found rest and relaxation. In the mid-1800s the Maine city was fifth among American ports in tonnage of ships registered. Bath-built ships sailed the globe, and a ship's maiden voyage could often pay for the entire cost of its construction. Shipyards once

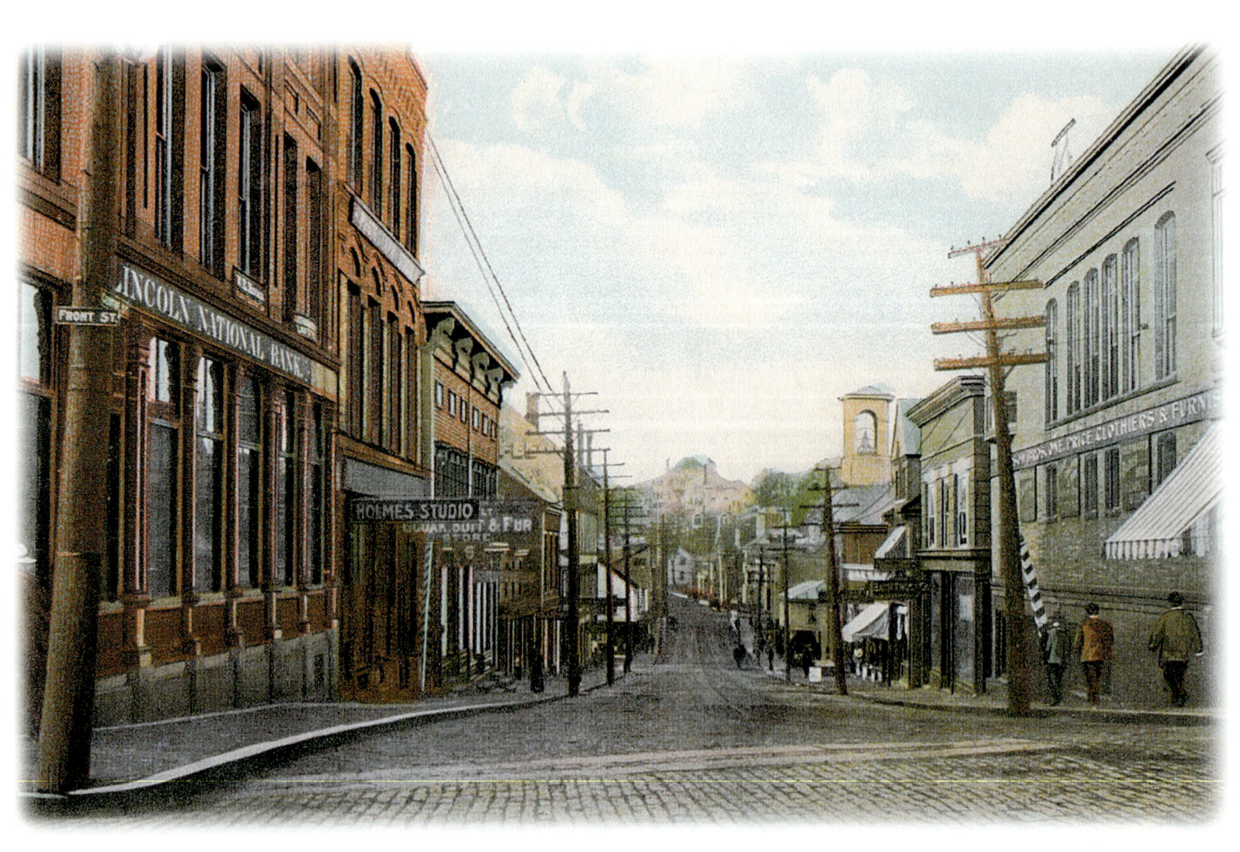

lined the banks of the Kennebec; now the industry is mainly confined to Bath Iron Works, which employs nearly 8,000 people and is one of the leading builders of vessels for today's U.S. Navy.

The Carlton Bridge that spanned the Kennebec was finished in 1927, named in honor of a Woolwich legislator who pushed hard for its construction. Prior to that, even the trains came across on a ferry. It was replaced by the Sagadahoc Bridge in 1999. In 1947 a four-lane highway divided the city in two and re-routed Route 1 traffic from Centre Street. In 1959, the Route 1 viaduct opened, carrying traffic over Bath as it exited the bridge. Passenger train service ceased at that time as well.

The postcard is looking down Centre Street from Front Street. On the left is the Lincoln National Bank built in 1878. It failed in 1910 and became the First National Bank, and is now a café. Adjacent in the Braggs Block were the Hatch Photographic Studio (Lucius Holmes, proprietor), and the Cloak, Suit, and Fur Store. The gambrel-roofed Ledyard Block of 1851 housed Stetson Furniture and the Masonic Hall in 1900; now a handmade furniture store stands beside a health food store.

On the right in the Sagadahock Block was the Thompson Brothers Clothiers and Furnishings store, built on the site of the Sagadahock House hotel, which burned in 1894. From 1931 to 1966 it was occupied by the J. J. Newberry Co. five-and-ten. It is now the Full Spectrum art and frame shop. The first City Hall tower is in the background, built in 1837 as the town hall. The belfry was added in 1861 to house a Paul Revere bell that was previously found in the old Universalist Church. Up on Centre Street Hill was the Sagadahoc County Courthouse, built in 1869. It was remodeled over the years and is still used as a courthouse today. The Sedgwick Hotel was located nearby but burned in 1973, to be replaced by the Sedgwick Medical Building.

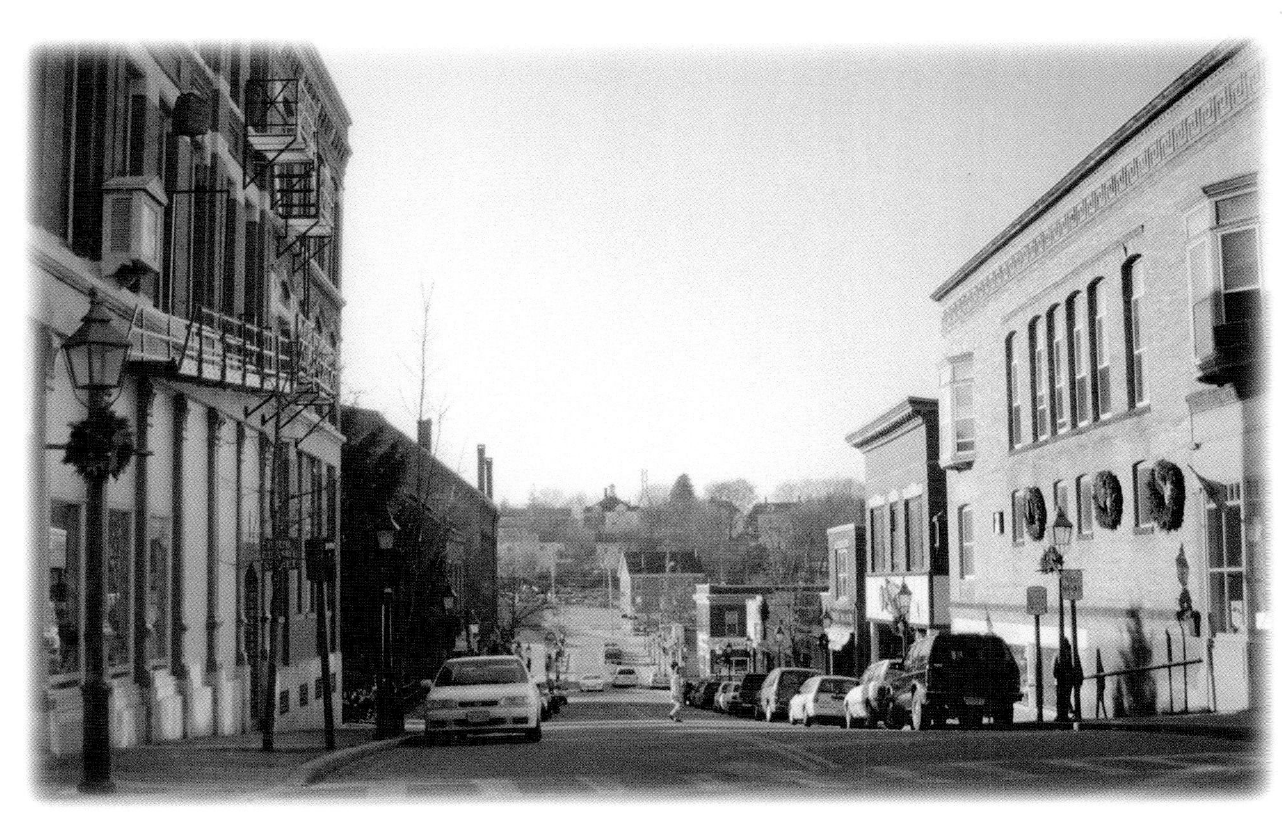

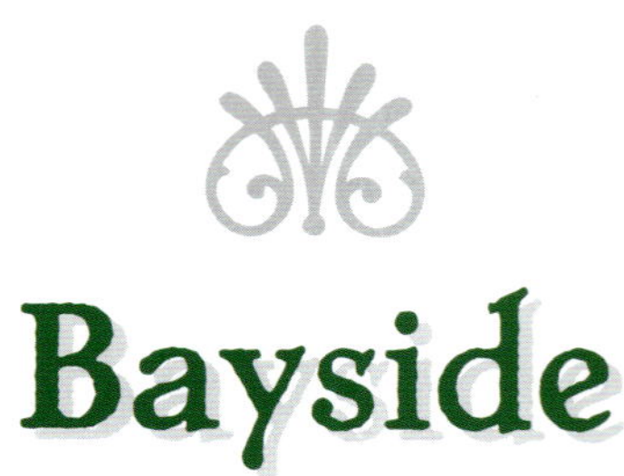

Bayside

A VILLAGE OF THE TOWN OF NORTHPORT, WHICH WAS INCORPORATED AS MAINE'S 106TH TOWN ON FEBRUARY 13, 1796

POPULATION IN 1900: 545

POPULATION IN 2000: 1,331

When people think of Northport, they probably think of Bayside, the charmingly picturesque village of tiny Victorian cottages with gingerbread trim, many having been in the same family for generations.

Bayside was established as a Methodist Episcopal Church camp in 1849. Open-air summer meetings were held there each year, with attendees pitching a little circle of tents. Eventually, wooden platforms made tenting somewhat more comfortable, and in the 1880s, tiny cottages were built on the platforms.

Before the advent of the individual cottages, some families stayed in big Society Cottages built cooperatively by each town's church society. Each family would have their own room (and maybe even a cupboard for storage), and there was a chapel in each cottage. Most are still standing in Auditorium Park, with names such as Brewer, Belfast, and Eddington still visible. The auditorium was where the green is now, and attendees adhered to a rigorous schedule of church meetings. "Conversion was a big part of it," said Beverly Crofoot, coordinator of the Bayside History Book Project.

The Northport Wesleyan Grove Campmeeting Association was chartered in 1873 to oversee the camp's activities. Acreage was eventually added to the property, and lots were sold for between five and fifteen dollars each. Apparently the setup was modeled after a similar camp-meeting site in Oak Bluffs on Martha's Vineyard. Thousands attended, many arriving for the day on carriages, trains, or steamers.

The association built the Wesleyan Grove House

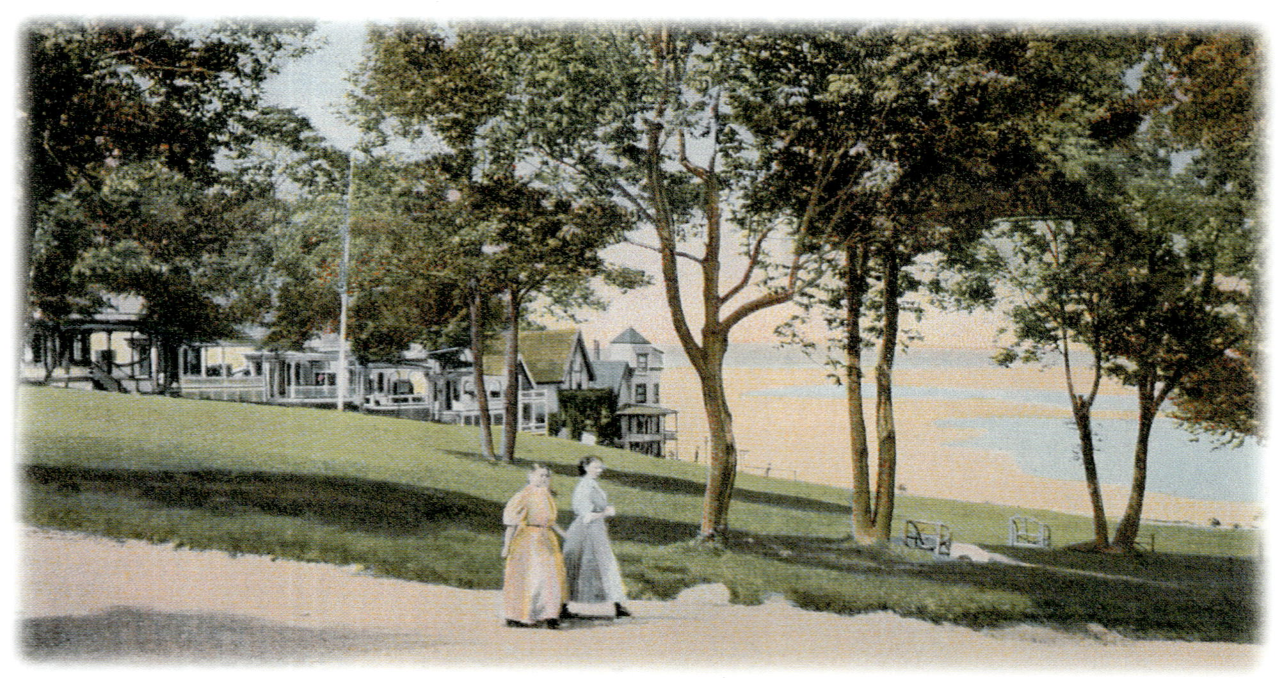

hotel in 1875. More private cottages (many with charming gingerbread trim) were built and named by the families who owned them. By the 1880s steamships from Boston and other ports were bringing fashionably dressed resort guests to enjoy clambakes, hayrides, firemen's musters, band concerts, and excursions.

The original hotel burned and was replaced by a larger one. Although the camp meeting still took place, the atmosphere was changing to one of more secular pleasures. Indeed, the association felt impelled to erect a fence and charge ten cents admission since so many of the heathens failed to attend church services. A stink was made over paying the toll . . . er, *admission*. A skipper of one of the excursion boats put an end to the matter. As historian G. H. Reed tells it, he "took an axe and converted the fence across the wharf to kindling wood, at the same time filling the air with a lot of words not at all in keeping with the religious surroundings."

Bayside in summer was a relatively self-sufficient colony. There were the grocery stores of C. O. Dickey and Chester Perkins (later, Hastings's store), the Tuttle photography studio, a newspaper, a justice of the peace, and a police force to weed out any intemperate revelry. There was also a pool table in one of the shops, a bowling alley, and a baseball diamond. In 1916 a nine-hole golf course was built by Ira Cobe and other private parties, and is still open to the public today.

By 1936, the Northport Campmeeting Week was no more. The Bayside Historic District is on the National Register of Historic Places, and encompasses 140 buildings on 300 acres. Of the 350 cottages listed in the late 1800s, most remain today. "People came originally for religious reasons," said Crofoot. "And every summer there is a great burst of new blood, an infusion of new perspectives."

The postcard is of Park Row bordering Ruggles Park, named for Hiram Ruggles who ran the campmeeting association at one time. This street of lovely cottages was once known as Paradise Row, probably for its association with the church and its focus on the eternal paradise, says Crofoot.

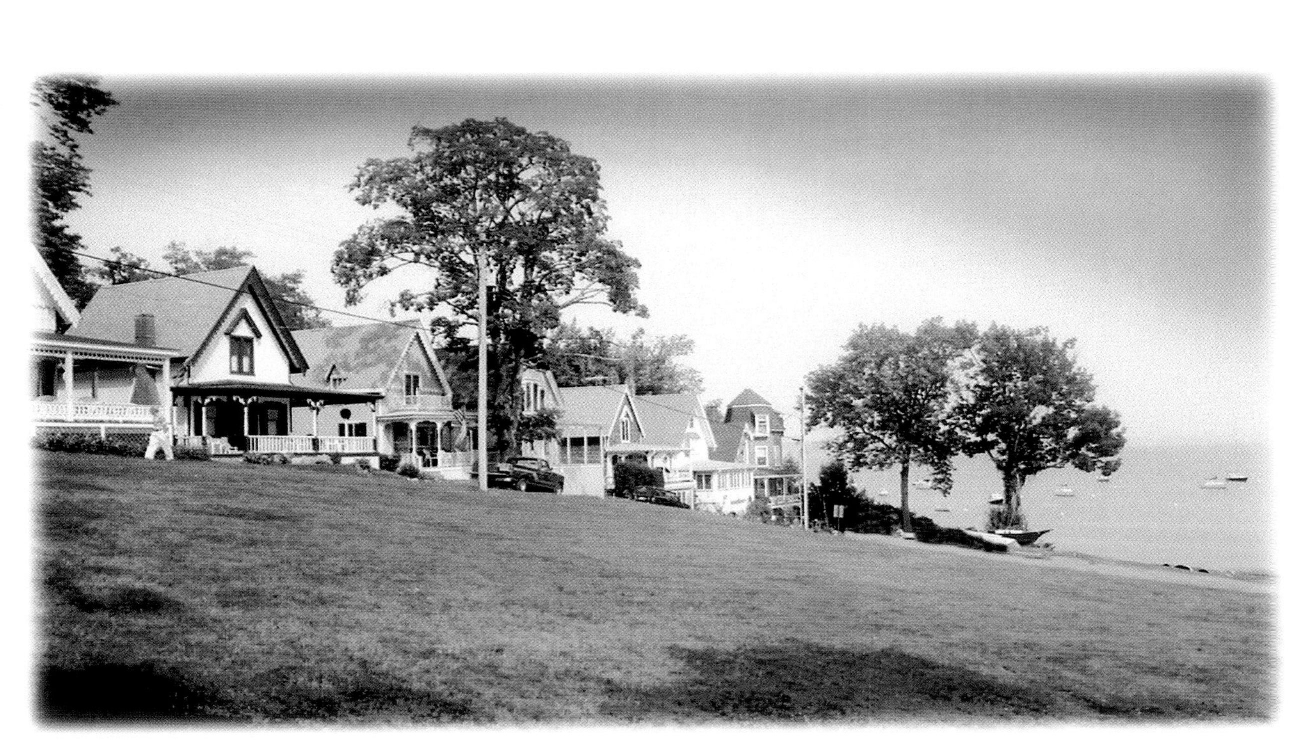

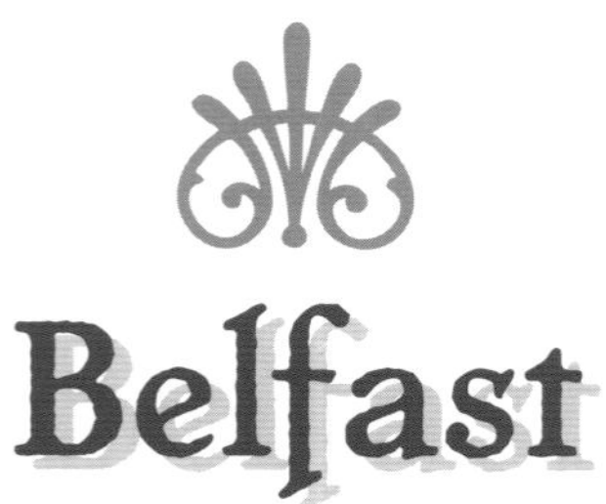

Belfast

INCORPORATED AS MAINE'S
26TH TOWN ON JUNE 29, 1773

INCORPORATED AS MAINE'S
6TH CITY ON AUGUST 7, 1850

POPULATION IN 1900: 4,615

POPULATION IN 2000: 6,381

This distinctive view of Belfast shows one of the least-changed Main Streets in the state, looking almost exactly as it did one hundred years ago. Spared from serious fire, which changed so many towns, and overlooked by urban renewal, which tore the soul out of many, Belfast weathered hardscrabble times before its current renaissance. It has the atmosphere of a college town, without the college. Like many towns with cheap rents, it was discovered by artists, and was named one of the hundred best small art towns in America in a national guidebook.

The shiretown of Waldo County was a railroading and seafaring hub at the turn of the twentieth century, and later became known for shoes, sardines, and chickens. The last shoe factory closed in 1989 and is now the Belfast Center. Sardine canning began in 1911 with the Lubec Packing Company, and ended in 2001 with the closing of Stinson Seafoods.

By the 1950s Belfast was the Broiler Capital of New England, celebrated with an annual Broiler Festival that fed 10,000 visitors with 10 tons of chicken. By the 1970s the two poultry-processing plants employed nearly 2,000 people. Scores of farmers raised hundreds of millions of chickens, and grain mills and other businesses supported the industry. But the town stank, feathers blew for blocks, and processing waste polluted the harbor and bay, earning the sneer "Schmaltzport" from *Newsweek* magazine in 1972. Maplewood Poultry closed in 1981, and Penobscot Poultry shut its doors in 1988, leaving Belfast one of the poorest communities in the East.

In the 1990s the economy began a reversal, and several diverse businesses set up shop. The arrival of credit-card giant MBNA solidified the trend. Two years after establishing its first Maine call center in Camden in 1993, MBNA expanded to Belfast. Today Belfast is the company's regional headquarters, and two thousand people—about half of the company's statewide workforce—work there in two large office complexes. The gently aging sea captains' homes are now being remodeled, and the downtown is thriving and robust with specialty stores, a hardware store, and the landmark Belfast Co-op, which specializes in organic foods.

The vintage postcard shows the triangular Belfast National Bank building built in 1878. When the bank moved to its new building across the street, a hole had to be made in the old structure to bring out the safe. An antiques store now occupies the building. To the far right is the 1866 Hayford Block, which was once the Opera House. To the left of the bank are three buildings that now house specialty shops, and the 1888 Oddfellows Block. An artist's cooperative, Artfellows, began on the second floor of the building in 1980. Early member Lucy Carver remembers that the Belfast Café was the meeting place for artists in the 1970s. Artfellows eventually moved to the old location of the Belfast Co-op, a few doors up the hill, before they closed in 1998.

The distinctive steeple at the end of the street belongs to the 1878 Masonic building. People's National Bank opened there in 1893, reorganized in 1904 as Waldo Trust, and eventually went bankrupt in 1927 after a scandal. Merrill Bank moved into the spot in that same year.

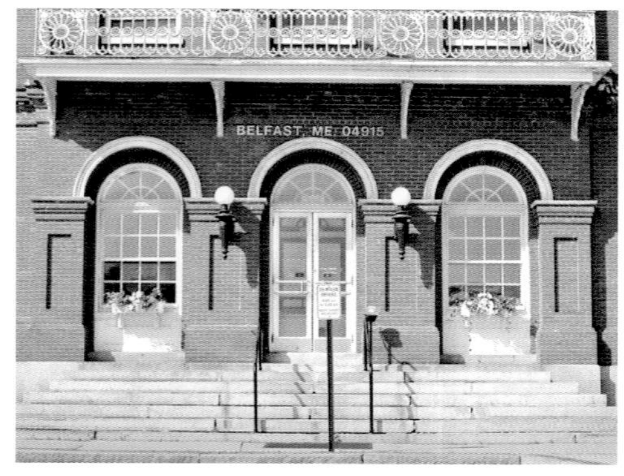

Belfast Post Office today.

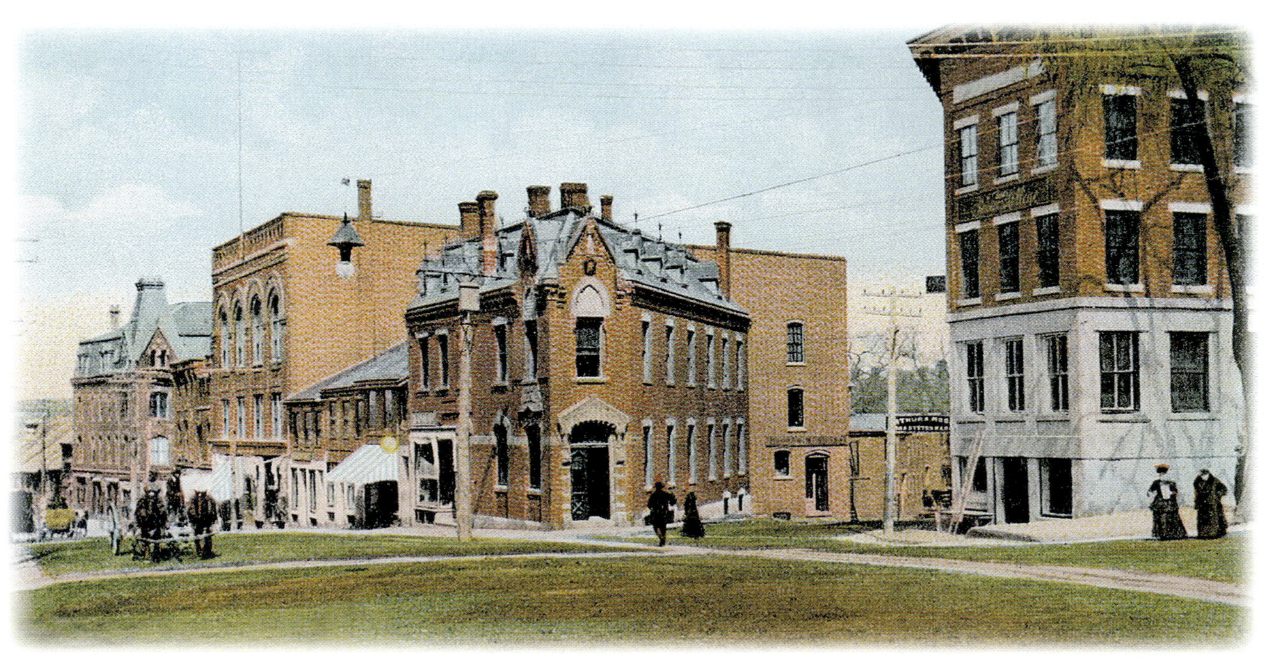

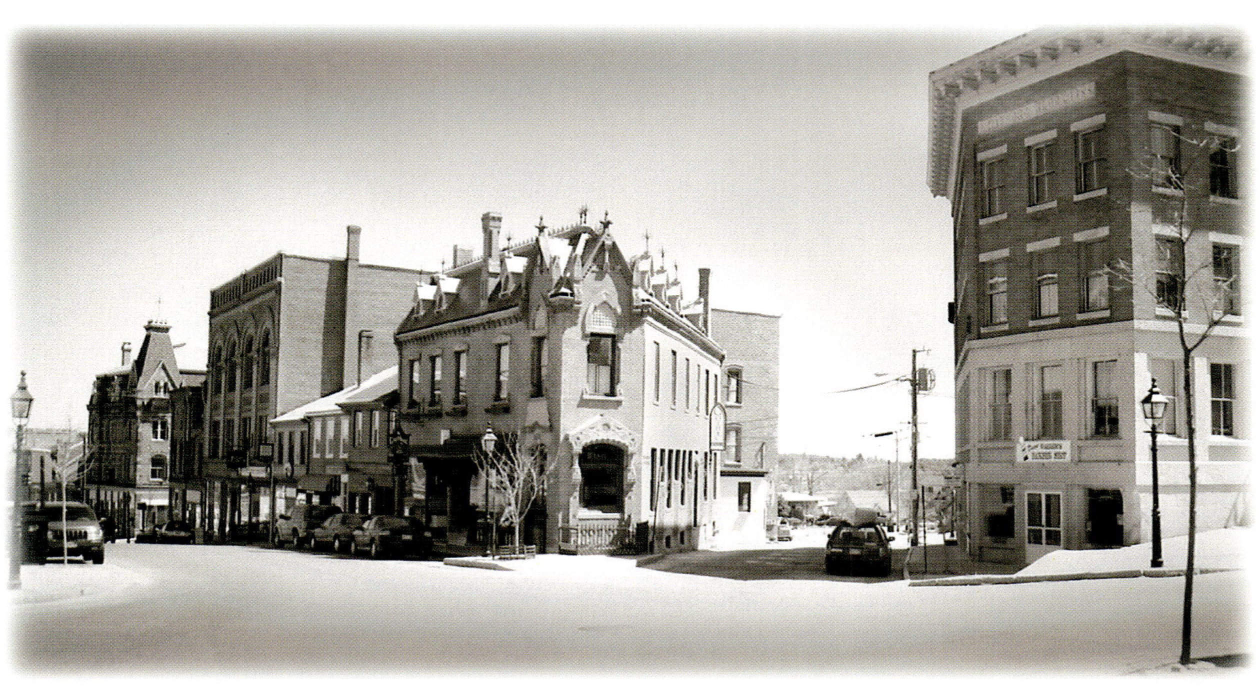

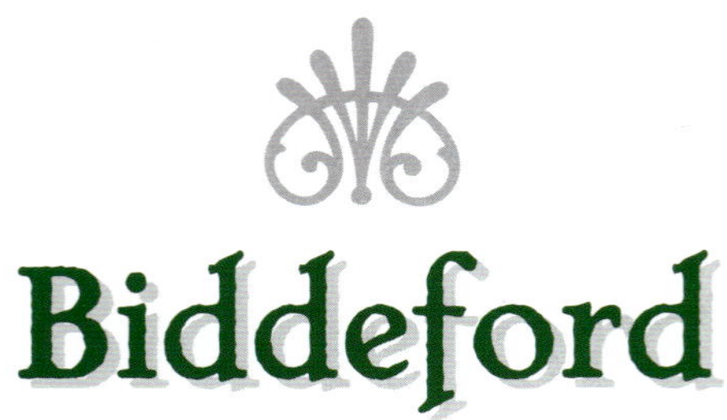

Biddeford

INCORPORATED AS MAINE'S
13TH TOWN ON NOVEMBER 17, 1718

INCORPORATED AS MAINE'S
10TH CITY ON FEBRUARY 10, 1855

POPULATION IN 1900: 16,145

POPULATION IN 2000: 20,942

Originally part of Saco, Biddeford shared that city's history as one of the nation's top textile manufacturers by the end of the nineteenth century. Named after a town in Devonshire, England, it occupies the banks of the Saco River in York County.

Among the mills were the Pepperell cotton mill, which merged with the Laconia mill in 1899 to become the state's largest. Bates Manufacturing was located on Factory Island in Saco, and closed in 1956. These two mills accounted for 25 percent of Biddeford's manufacturing jobs. Biddeford Textiles later occupied the old Laconia Division of the Pepperell mills, and was bought by a Taiwan-based manufacturer that upgraded the mill, renamed it Biddeford Blankets, then closed it a year later, in 2003, due to overseas competition. The mill had made four million electric blankets for Sunbeam in 1996. WestPoint Stevens, Inc., which makes Vellux blankets in the Pepperell mill on Main Street, filed for bankruptcy in 2003 but kept its 325 workers on the job.

The Pepperell mill is seen in both the 1930s-era postcard and today's photograph of Main Street. Established before the Civil War, it produced, among other things, fabrics of a specific shade of blue for the Chinese and East Indian markets, and heavy drill canvas for ship sails. The one-story Pepperell Hall was a gathering place for the workers and now houses the offices of the *Biddeford-Saco-Old Orchard Beach Courier*. The store on the far right was the F. W. Woolworth 5 and 10 Cent Store, which opened in 1928 in the

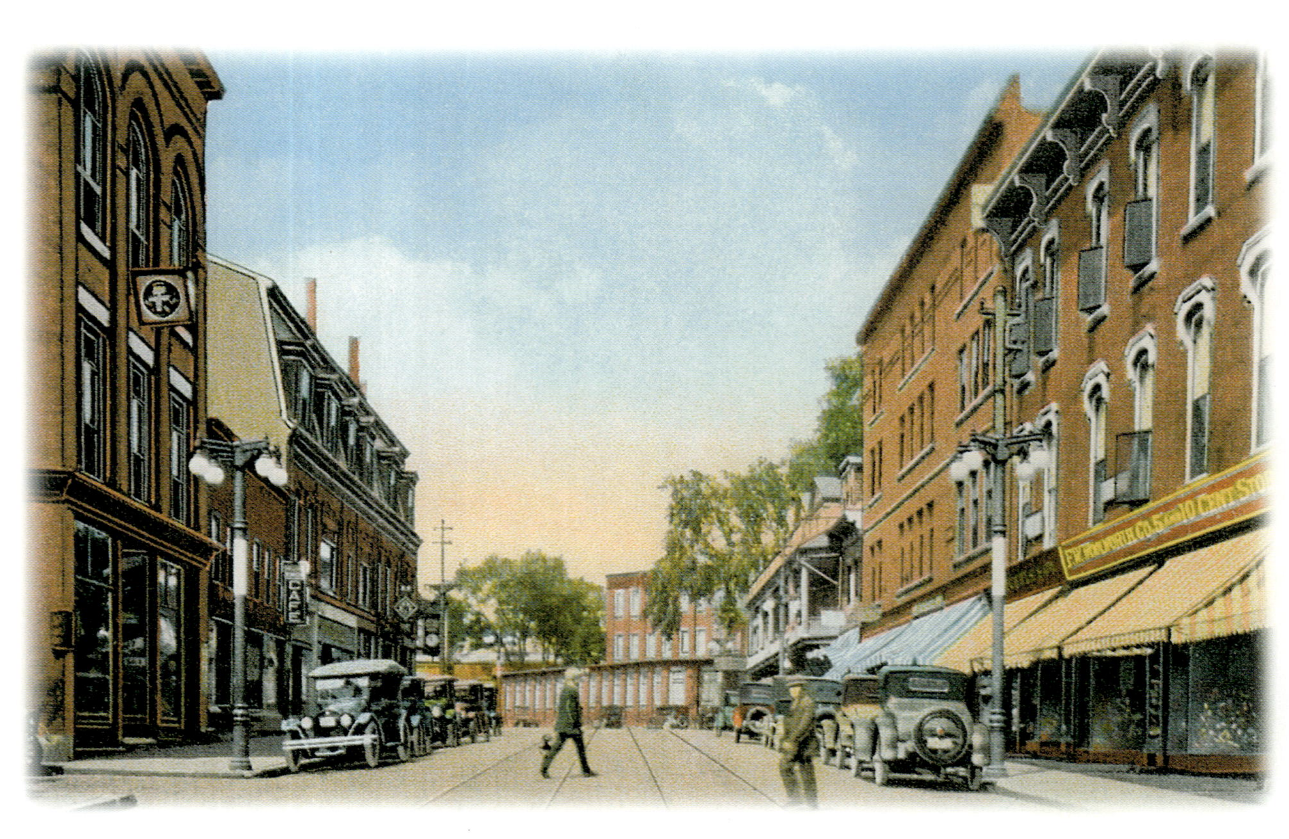

1857 Union Block. The taller building adjacent was Butler's Department Store. The Crystal Arcade with the white balcony at the end of the street housed a collection of stores, and in 1930 became Nichols Department Store. It was remodeled along with the small Gothic Block in 1937 in the current tawny brick.

On the right corner was the Smith Building, built around 1905 to replace the Smith Dry Goods store. It was bought by J. C. Penney in 1931. Green's Shoe Store operated for most of the twentieth century out of the two-story building adjacent, with the café sign. It is now the Shevenell Mini Park. The distinctive "Napoleon III"-style Pepperell Trust Co., built in 1872, anchors the end of the street.

By 1890 Biddeford had one of the highest concentrations of French-Canadians in New England, and by 1970 it shared with Lewiston the largest percentage of Franco-Americans—60 percent—for Maine's large cities.

In Biddeford the Pepperell mill workers maintained a strictly Quebecois identification up through the 1920s, studying Quebec history and singing the national anthem, "O Canada," at school graduations. French was the primary language of instruction as late as the 1950s, and it wasn't until the 1930s that English-language articles began appearing in the local French newspaper, *La Justice*. Indeed, the newspaper—which operated from 1896 to 1950—was one of the strongest promoters of *la survivance* (ethnic survival) among Biddeford's Francos. But gradually, assimilation changed the French in Biddeford, as it had elsewhere in the state.

Work in the Pepperell mill was hard and the hours long. Children as young as nine were sent to work there. Wages were low, and even with several family members working, the Francos often found it difficult to escape their impoverished lifestyle. There was a large out-migration from Biddeford between 1910 and 1920, as mill work slacked off, but more often than not, word of mouth brought more Francos in to replace those who had left. By the end of the 1950s, the bloom was off the rose, and the Pepperell mill closed most of its operations in 1968.

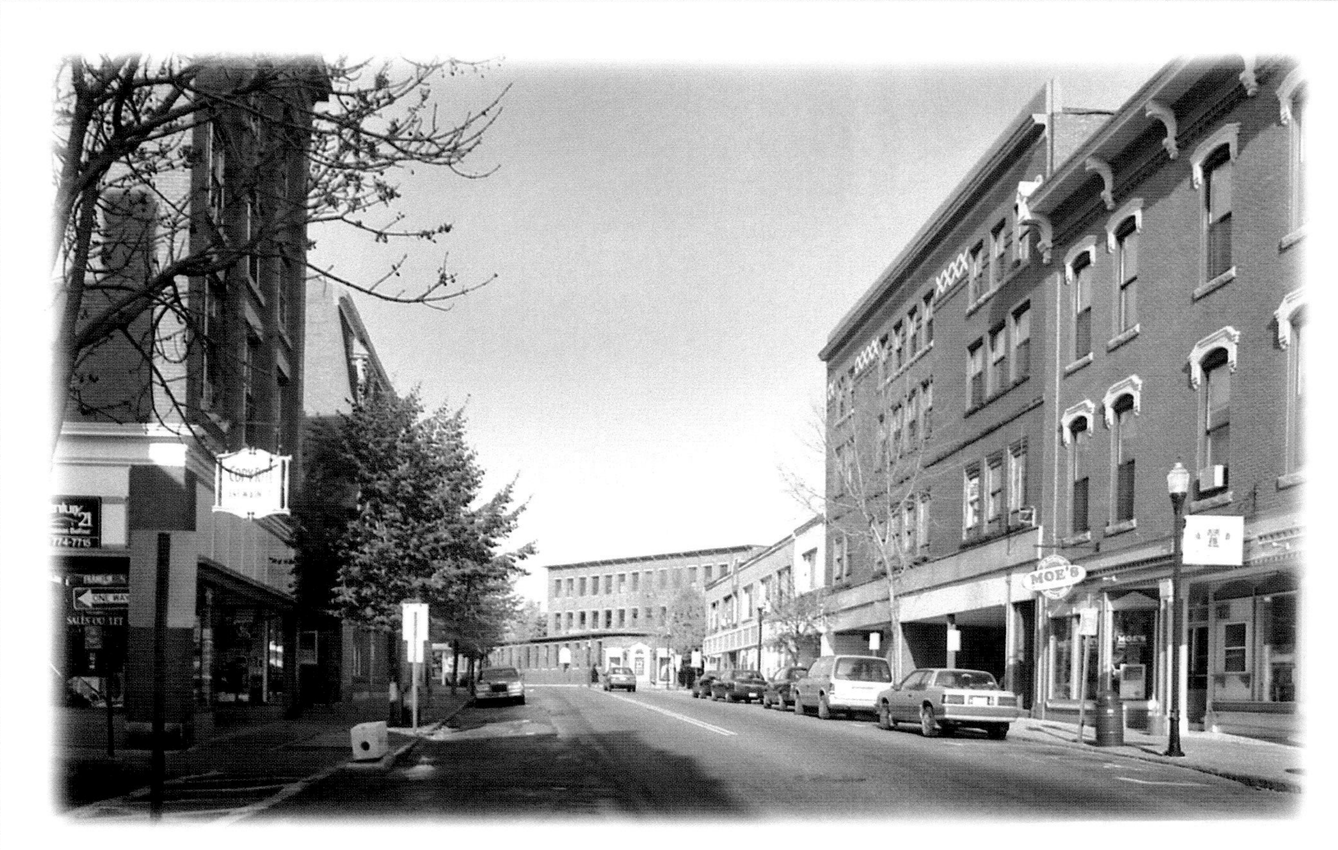

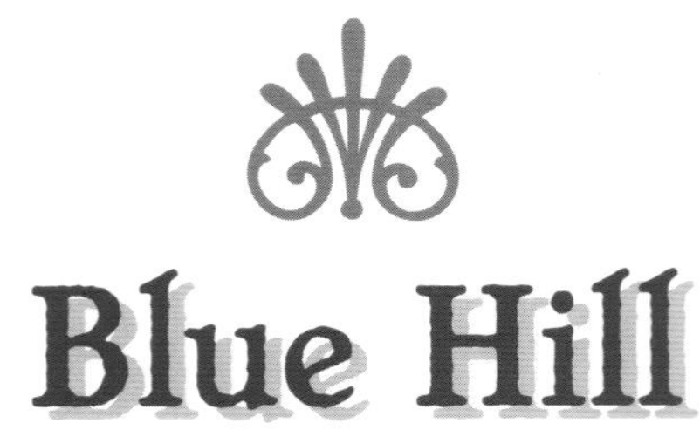

Blue Hill

INCORPORATED AS MAINE'S
62ND TOWN ON JANUARY 30, 1789

POPULATION IN 1900: 1,828

POPULATION IN 2000: 2,390

The Algonquian word for the mountain that rises above the village of Blue Hill is *Awanadjo*, meaning "small, misty mountain." It presides over a town of stately homes, a lively arts scene, and a few remaining pampered elms. Initially the name was spelled *Bluehill*, and for years the single- and double-word versions were used interchangeably, causing some confusion and controversy.

There had been a bit of silver, gold, and copper mining in the area, and granite quarrying had its heyday from 1875 to 1907, when six quarries prospered. Structures built with Blue Hill granite include the Brooklyn Bridge, the Pittsburgh post office, and the New York Stock Exchange. During World War I a copper mine produced ore that was taken in horse-drawn carts to be shipped for processing. The mine was reopened briefly in the 1960s and 1970s.

As in many coastal communities, there is a large summer population that began with the rusticators in the 1880s; by the 1960s, some of them began winterizing their cottages and staying year-round. The new residents brought along their appreciation for music, creating several structures devoted to celebrating the arts. Notable buildings included Kneisel Hall, the Bagaduce Music Lending Library—with 150,000 titles of sheet music—and the now-defunct Left Bank Café, which provided an intimate coffeehouse setting for folk singers of national repute. Kneisel Hall, devoted to teaching and performing chamber music, was founded by Dr. Franz Kneisel in 1902. The twenty-acre campus offers one of the most significant chamber music programs in the country.

In 1988 Blue Hill Mountain sprouted an antenna on its 940-foot summit. Noel Paul Stookey (of Peter, Paul, and Mary folk-trio fame) had moved to town a decade earlier. He later started a radio station in a former henhouse he was using as a recording studio. WERU community radio station began broadcasting at 89.9-FM, and became known far and wide as "that Blue Hill station." Staffed by mostly volunteer programmers, the station's success led to the building of its new digs in East Orland in 1997, though its antenna remains on the mountain.

One of its favorite commentators, Rob McCall, brings the Awanadjo Almanac to listeners twice a week. Part essay, part prayer, part satirical commentary on the human doings (or undoings) of the natural community, the Almanac is what he calls "a collection of natural and unnatural events, rank opinion, and wild speculation."

The elms that line the village streets are some of the few that survived the Dutch elm disease catastrophe, which claimed most of the country's elms in the 1960s and '70s. A town that once had five hundred elms now has fewer than five dozen left. Like its neighbor, Castine, the town began an aggressive campaign in the 1970s to save them.

The town's retail section had begun a shift from Main Street to South Street in the late 1980s. But Merrill & Hinckley grocery store, across from the town hall, has been in its downtown location for more than 110 years. It features old-fashioned touches such as home delivery, monthly credit, and a wooden floor that's survived several remodelings.

During the last decade, most of the region has experienced a 20 percent growth in population, adding strain to this "service-center" town that has the only hospital and banks on the peninsula.

INTERESTING TIDBIT:

The Blue Hill Fair was the model for the country fair depicted in *Charlotte's Web*, the beloved 1952 children's book by E. B. White about a pig named Wilbur and his friend, Charlotte, the spider. Held on Labor Day weekend, it has the requisite oxen pulls, livestock competitions, amusement rides, and performances by nationally known musicians.

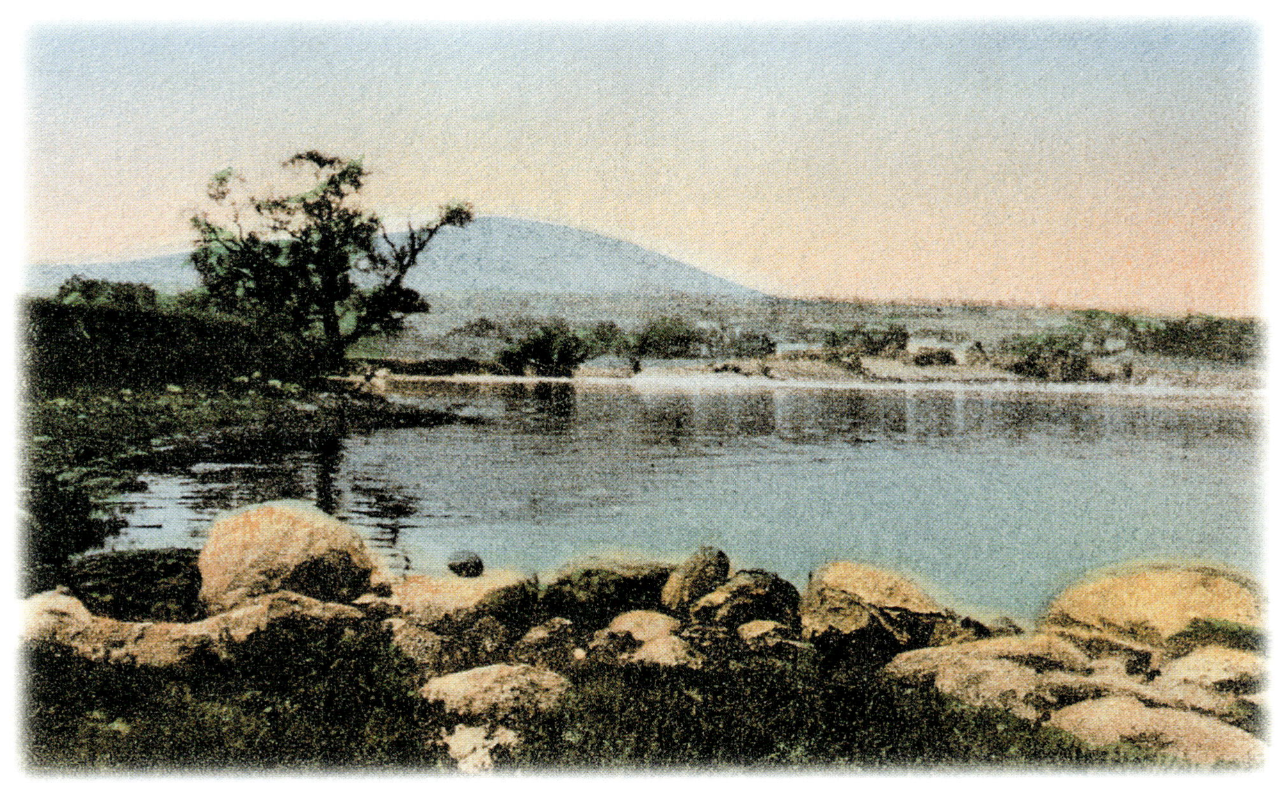

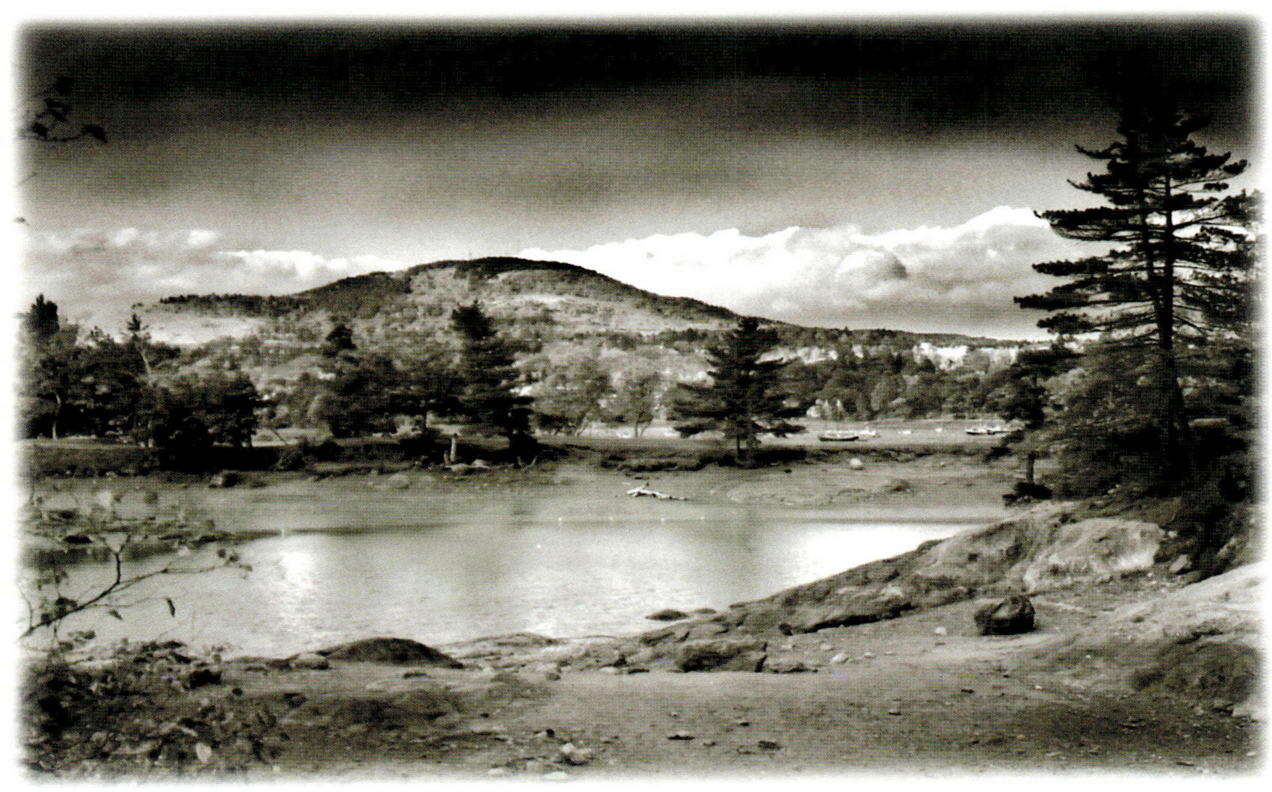

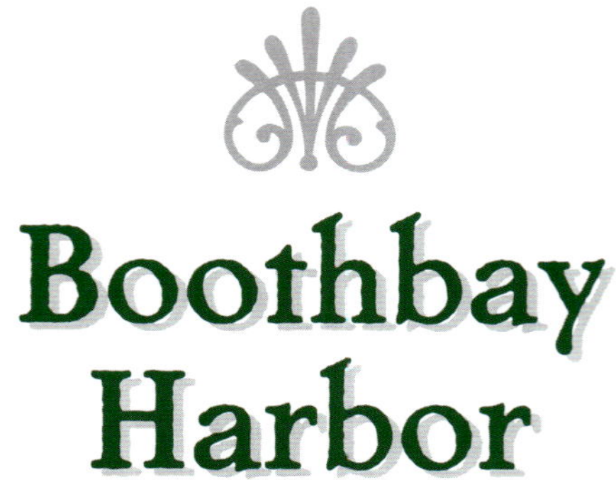

Boothbay Harbor

INCORPORATED AS MAINE'S
452ND TOWN ON FEBRUARY 16, 1889

POPULATION IN 1900: 1,926

POPULATION IN 2000: 2,334

Boothbay Harbor was in many respects like Bar Harbor—rusticators, then cottagers, then just plain tourists slowly changed the economy from fishing and shipbuilding to recreation. The 1880s were the flowering era of leisure travel among the wealthy classes. There was no income tax to reduce one's fun money, and because traveling from Boston or New York entailed long journeys by train or steamer, the wealthy tended to stay in one place for the entire season. The many summer colonies and old resort hotels that were built in this era helped to define Boothbay Harbor for decades to come.

Three art colonies, each with their own teachers and stylistic emphasis, were also an important part of the area. These schools offered more than mere art classes; students were taught by premier artists and often stayed for several weeks at a time during the summer. The Commonwealth Art Colony began in 1906 on Mount Pisgah, and some of its students became influential artists. The Boothbay Studios—one of the largest private art schools in America—opened in East Boothbay in 1921. It was located on and around a wharf, and the hundreds of students enrolled each year roomed in village homes. The Commonwealth ended its tenure in 1930, and teacher Anson Cross started his own school the following year. The Boothbay Studios closed in 1942.

The town was originally part of Boothbay, but separation came after an argument over the creation

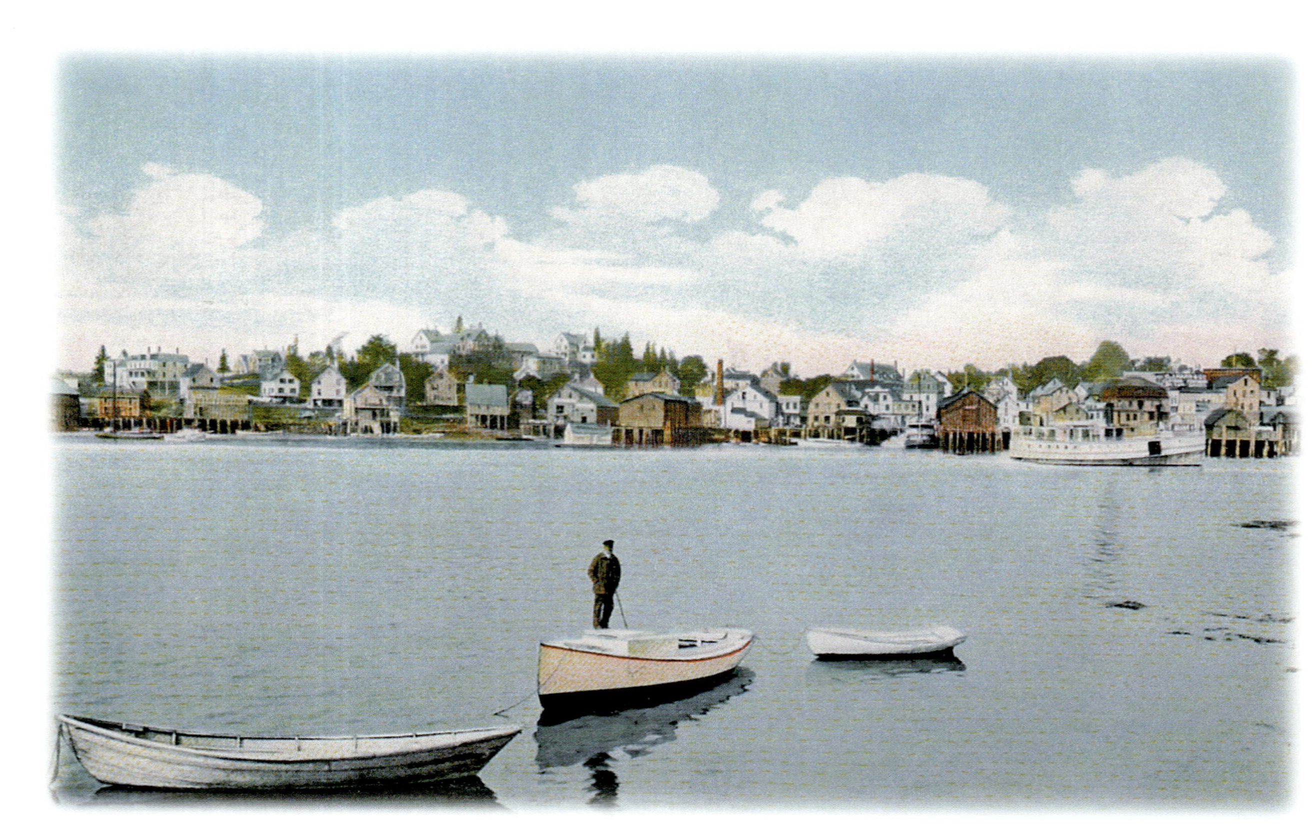

of a water supply following a disastrous 1886 harbor fire. Reunification of the two towns has been discussed now and then over the past century, without success—once in the 1970s, and most recently, in 1999.

Of course, the town has always relied heavily on the ocean for its livelihood, whether for its bounty or its beauty. At the turn of the twentieth century, the tiny herring was king fish. By 1906 four sardine canneries were operating in the area. A cold storage plant on the east side of the harbor was built in 1919, adding to the west side's plant built in 1892. Fisherman's Wharf had just been remodeled in 1958 when it was leveled by a fire. In the 1960s most of the fishing income in the region came from lobstering, but up to twenty-six boatloads of shrimp a day kept three shrimp-processing plants humming. Most of the delectable crustaceans were exported to Sweden before the fishery declined during the following decade. However, lobster landings have actually increased, perhaps because there are fewer groundfish to eat the baby lobsters.

A Fishermen's Festival was instituted in the mid-1970s, but it has the odd distinction of taking place in April, when it's still basically wintertime. Among the highlights are the Cod Fish Relay through the center of town, and the trap-hauling contest. A Shrimp Princess is crowned, and the festival culminates in an adults-only "Tall Tales" event that features fishermen's wild stories. In the more reasonable month of June, Boothbay Harbor hosts its Windjammer Days, which include parades on both land and water. Around four dozen antique boats usually participate in this tribute to the town's maritime heritage. The Friendship Sloop Society moved its regatta from Friendship to Boothbay in 1985, but then moved it again to Rockland ten years later.

A U.S. Fish Hatchery was built at McKown Point in 1905. It hatched and released lobsters, cod, haddock, and other fishes with mixed success. Hatchery operations gave way to research, with another try at raising lobsters in 1938, ending a decade later when young lobster mortality was too high. In 1974 it transferred to state ownership, and the Maine Department

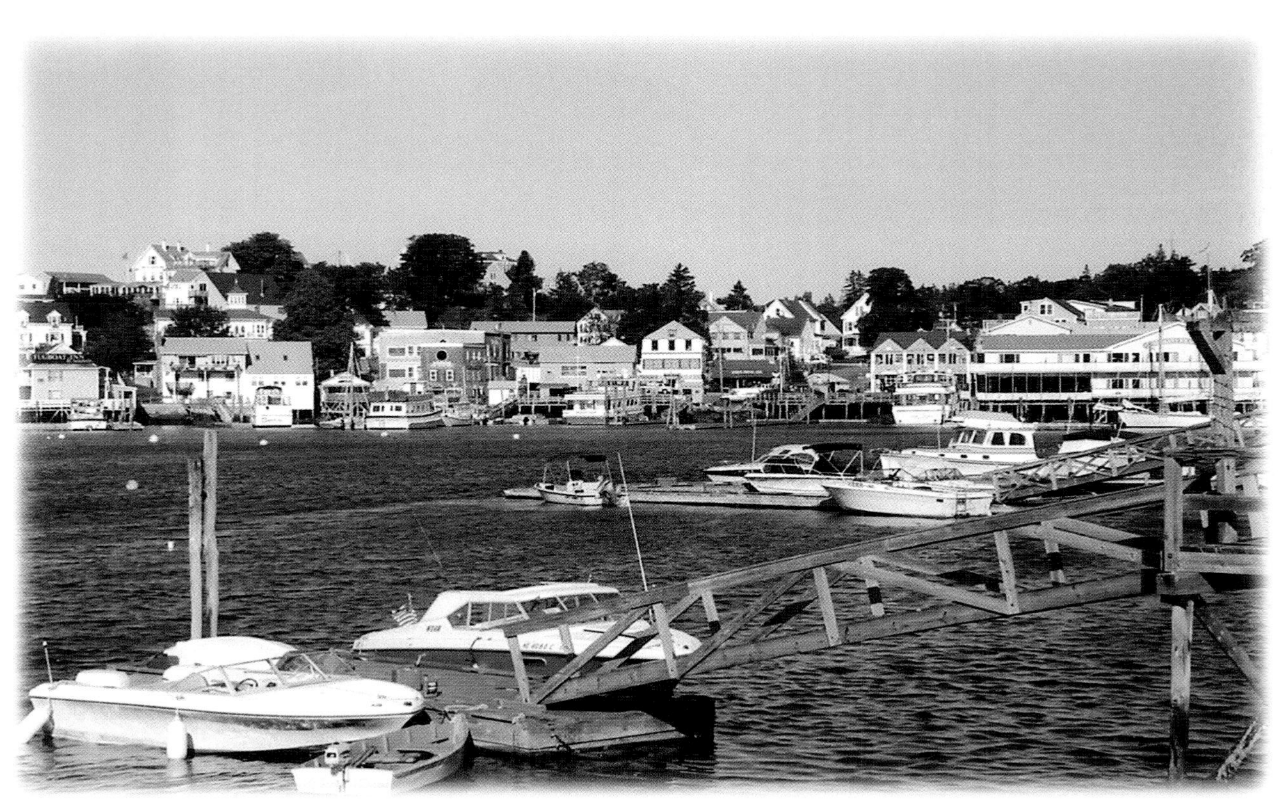

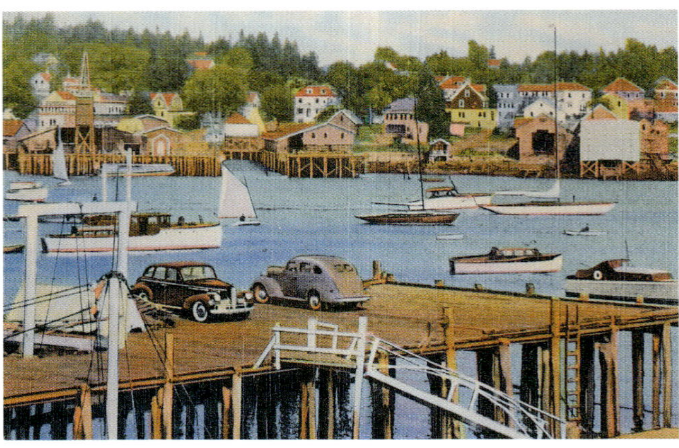

The east side of the harbor, 1940s linen postcard.

of Marine Resources laboratory continues to conduct research there on commercially important marine resources. The Bigelow Laboratory for Ocean Sciences also moved onto the point in 1974. This internationally renowned marine research institution studies ocean currents and productivity, oil spills, paralytic shellfish poisoning (red tide), and more, often with the aid of satellite technology. One of its most significant discoveries is the role of marine bacteria as building blocks in the ocean's food chain. It is building a new facility on a 67-acre site in East Boothbay, due to open in 2006, doubling the current number of employees to 100.

Naturalist Rachel Carson had a summer cottage on nearby Southport Island. Her books, *The Sea Around Us* and *The Edge of the Sea*, were written in part about the landscape and seascape outside her door. Her most famous book, *Silent Spring*, was published in 1962, two years before she died. That book was credited with helping to ban the pesticide DDT and subsequently fueling the environmental movement.

The waterfront postcard on page 46 shows a steamer, perhaps the *May Archer*, at dock, with fishing boats in the harbor. Today the working waterfront has been transformed by condominiums, sailing yachts, and motorboats. In the postcard two seafaring-family homes are visible on the highest point. Today they are the 1873 Welch House Inn and the Topside Inn. On the far left at the water's edge was Montgomery Boat Storage. The sign on the far right reads

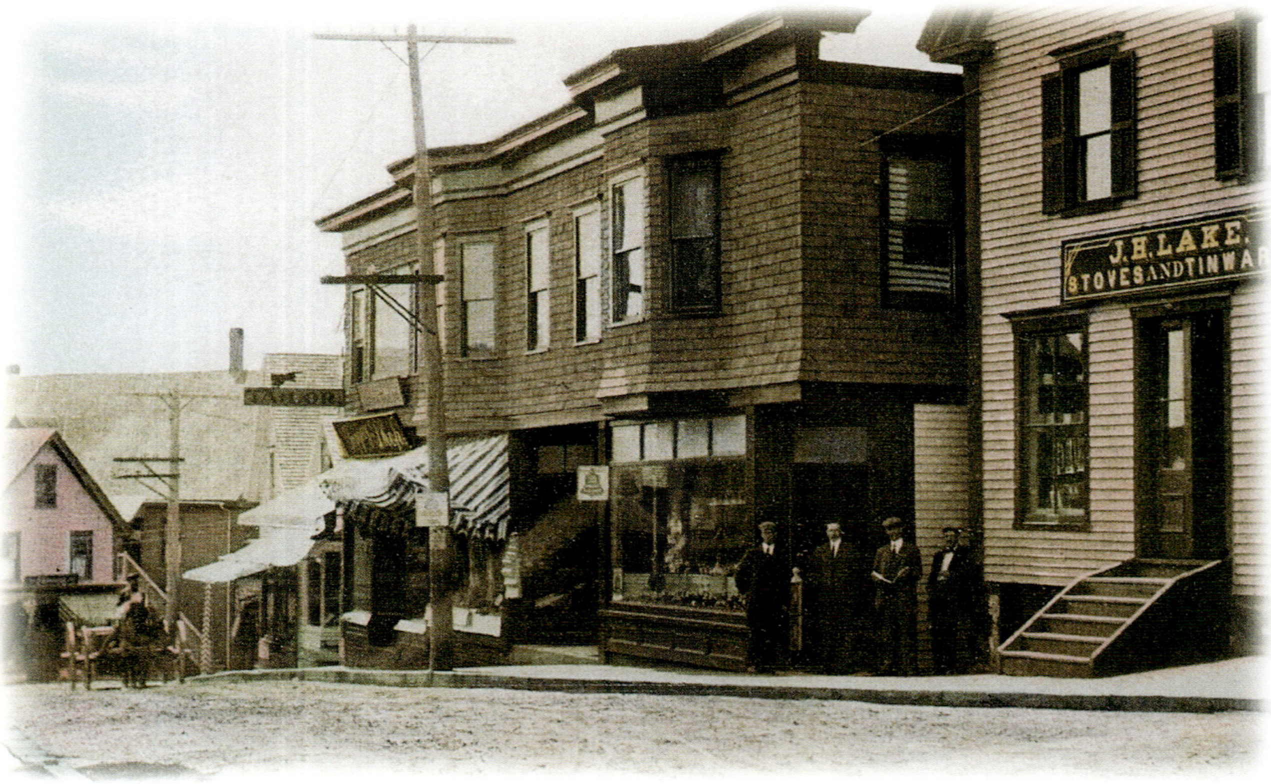

C. J. MARR & CO., a clothing and shoe store. It is now Paine's Clothing Store on Commercial Street. The chimney marks the site of the cold storage plant that burned in January 1934, leaving a chimney that remained long after the buildings were gone. The new photograph is a telephoto view of the harbor with the Welch House in the background.

Several fires changed the makeup of Boothbay Harbor over the years. On a bitterly cold day in January 1945, a number of buildings along the west side of the harbor went up in flames, including two dozen boats in storage and the Campbell Products Sail Loft. In March 1978 the Boothbay Region Fish and Cold Storage plant on the east side of the harbor burned, threatening to explode a 5,000-gallon storage tank of ammonia. Residents were evacuated and firemen stayed on the property for twelve days to be sure all was safe. From 1980 to 1981, a rash of over twenty major arson fires kept the town and its firefighters on edge. Although there were several convictions, some of the cases remain unsolved.

The postcard of Commercial Street on page 48 shows the E. L. Porter store, next to the J. H. Lake stove and tinsmith shop. Known as the "lower" of the two stores in Boothbay Harbor, it burned in April 1942 and was rebuilt as a one-story brick A & P grocery store. Sherman's Bookstore bought it in the late 1980s and later added the second story.

REMARKABLE RESIDENT:

Radio comic George Rockwell lived in Southport and Boothbay Harbor. He appeared on Fred Allen's radio show and for many years contributed humor columns to *Down East* magazine.

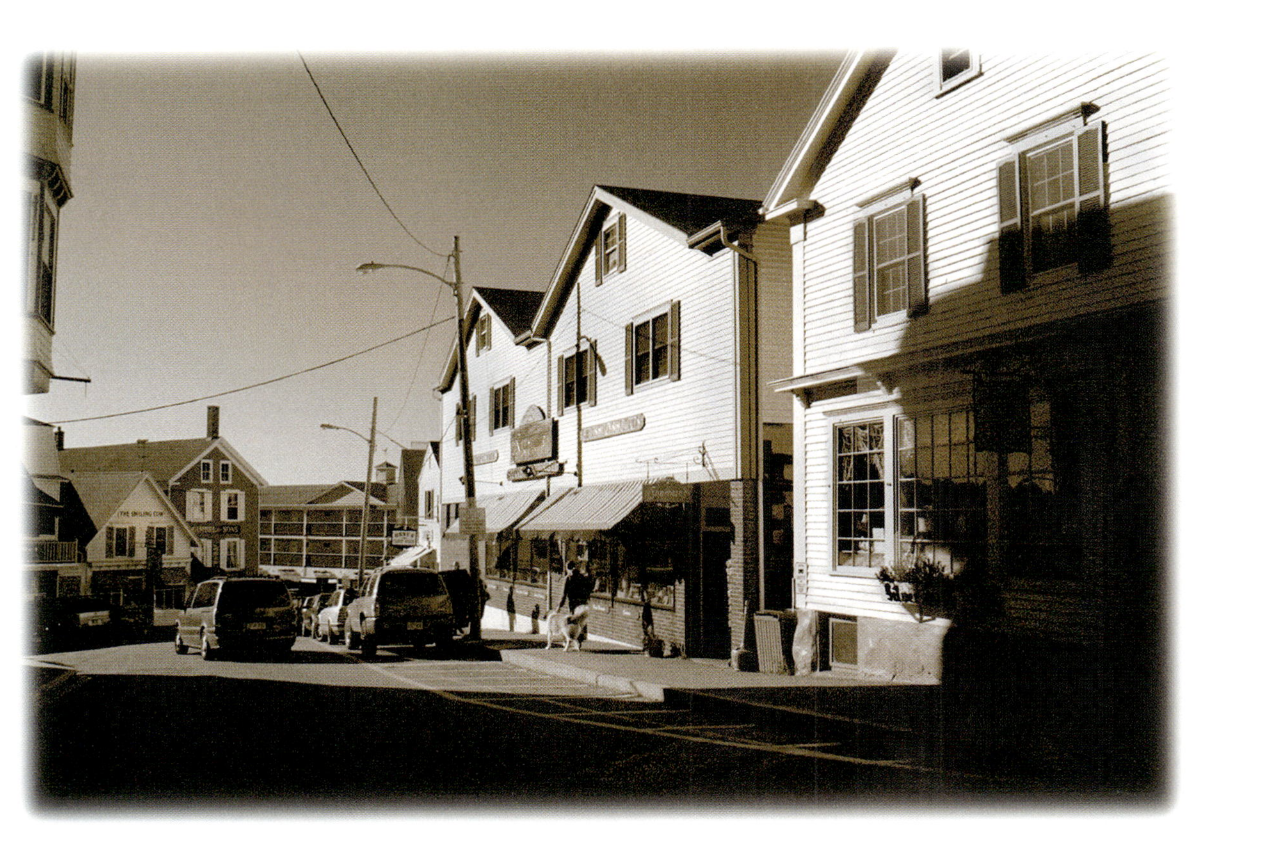

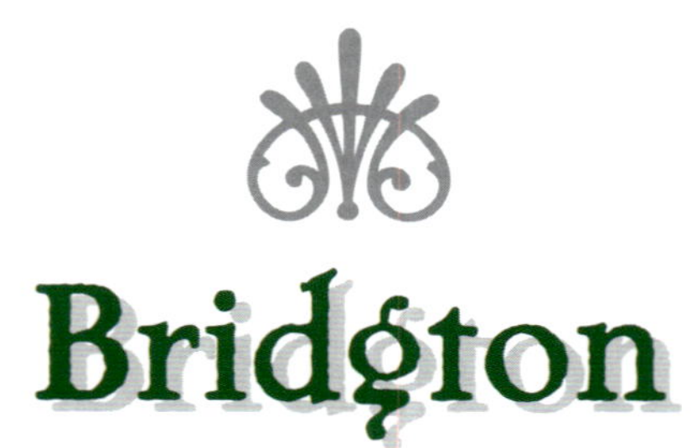

Bridgton

INCORPORATED AS MAINE'S
84TH TOWN ON FEBRUARY 7, 1794

POPULATION IN 1900: 2,868

POPULATION IN 2000: 4,883

It is not known for certain why Bridgton was originally called *Pondicherry*. One historian says it was named for a territory on the Coromandel Coast in India, which is known as the French Riviera of the East for its beauty. The town was later called *Bridges Town*, in honor of proprietor Colonel Moody Bridges. Today, Bridgton is known for its all-season recreation and antiques shops.

Lumber and textile mills helped define the economy of early Bridgton. Forest Mills Co., established during the Civil War, manufactured fine woolens, including cashmere. It was later operated by American Woolen Co. and closed in 1929. The Pondicherry Mill was also active at the turn of the twentieth century, changing hands several times before the building was razed in 1965. The Sebago, Inc., shoe factory, which recently closed, once had 300 employees. Malden Mills, Inc., which made Polartec fabrics, closed its Bridgton Knitting Mills in 1998. At the time it was the town's largest employer, and when it shut down, 350 workers lost their jobs. The building later became the Bridgton Commerce Center and has attracted many new, smaller industries.

The postcard shows Pondicherry Square and Main Street. The buildings in the background on Flint Street were removed in 1968 for the reconstruction of Route 117. The one on the left was the Dunn Brothers Druggists before the turn of the century. The building burned in 1916, but it was rebuilt and continued as a drugstore under different ownership before being remodeled as a restaurant. Before it was razed it was the Discount Center. The building to its right was the oldest continuously operating grocery store in town under a succession of various owners. In 1953 it was Curt's IGA, and then Larry's IGA when it was razed in 1968. The nearby Food City supermarket sits on the site of the old Pondicherry Mill.

The building with the bay window was a photography studio in the early 1900s. By 1919 it was a gift shop, which added women's clothing to the lineup in the 1950s. It is now Bridgton House of Pizza. To the left was the Andersen Abbott dry goods store, now the parking lot between the florist/bakery building and pharmacy. It burned in 1914 and was replaced by another grocery which burned five years later. Beyond the center tree was the Wales & Hamblen store, which carried hardware, appliances, and dry goods. The Oddfellows Hall was on the second floor. Built in 1882, it was listed on the National Register of Historic Places a century later. In later years it served as a self-service laundry, grocery, restaurant, and discount store, and today is Wales & Hamblen Antiques.

The tall building at the end of the street is the Masonic Hall, erected in 1867 with a grocery and dry goods store located on the ground floor and in the basement. The hall itself was on the second floor, now occupied by the Big Kahuna Café folk-and-blues club. In 1946 two men bought out a local estate and opened a furniture store in the building to sell the items. It was still a furniture store in 1968, with the self-service laundry in the basement. In the spirit of ever-changing storefronts, the Bridgton A.G. Supermarket photographed in 2002 is now an unfinished-furniture shop.

Main Street in the 1940s, looking north.

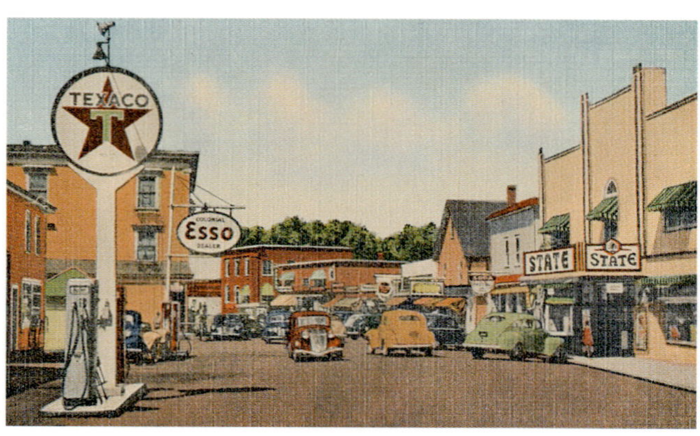

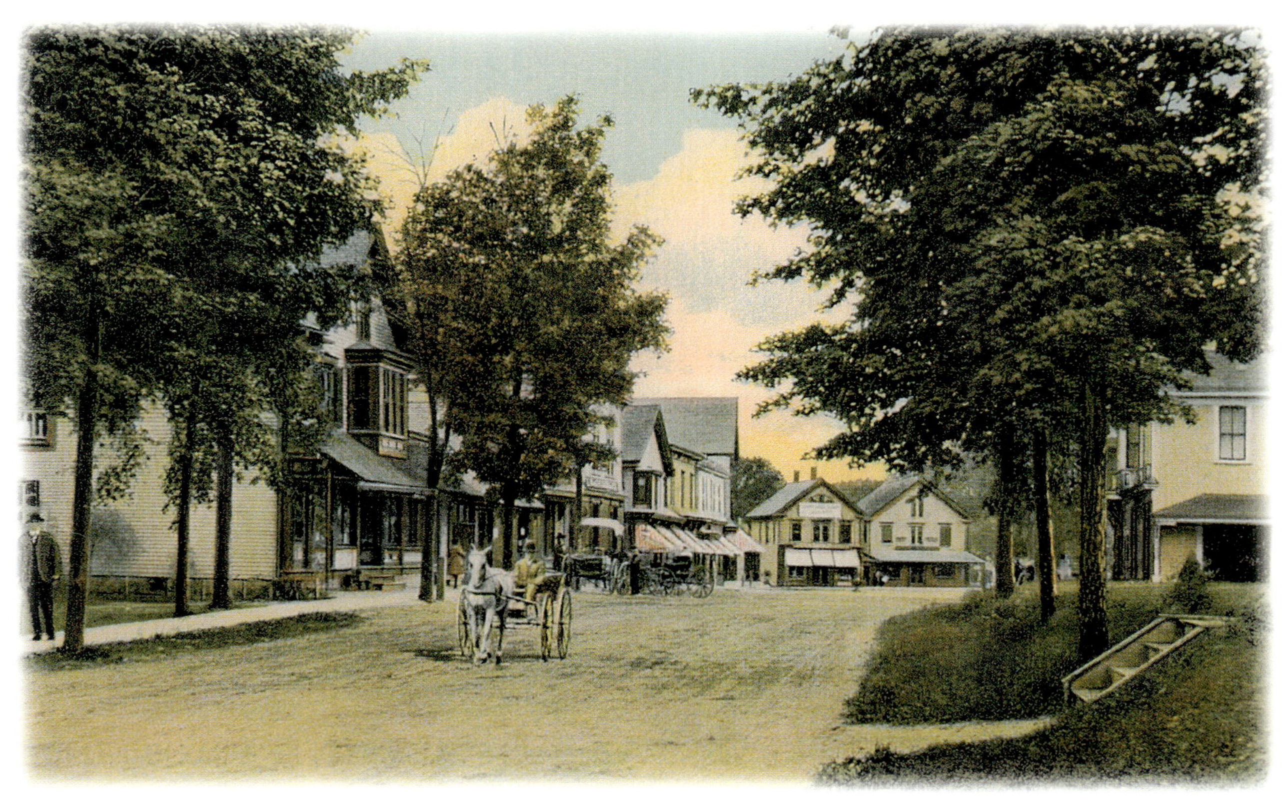

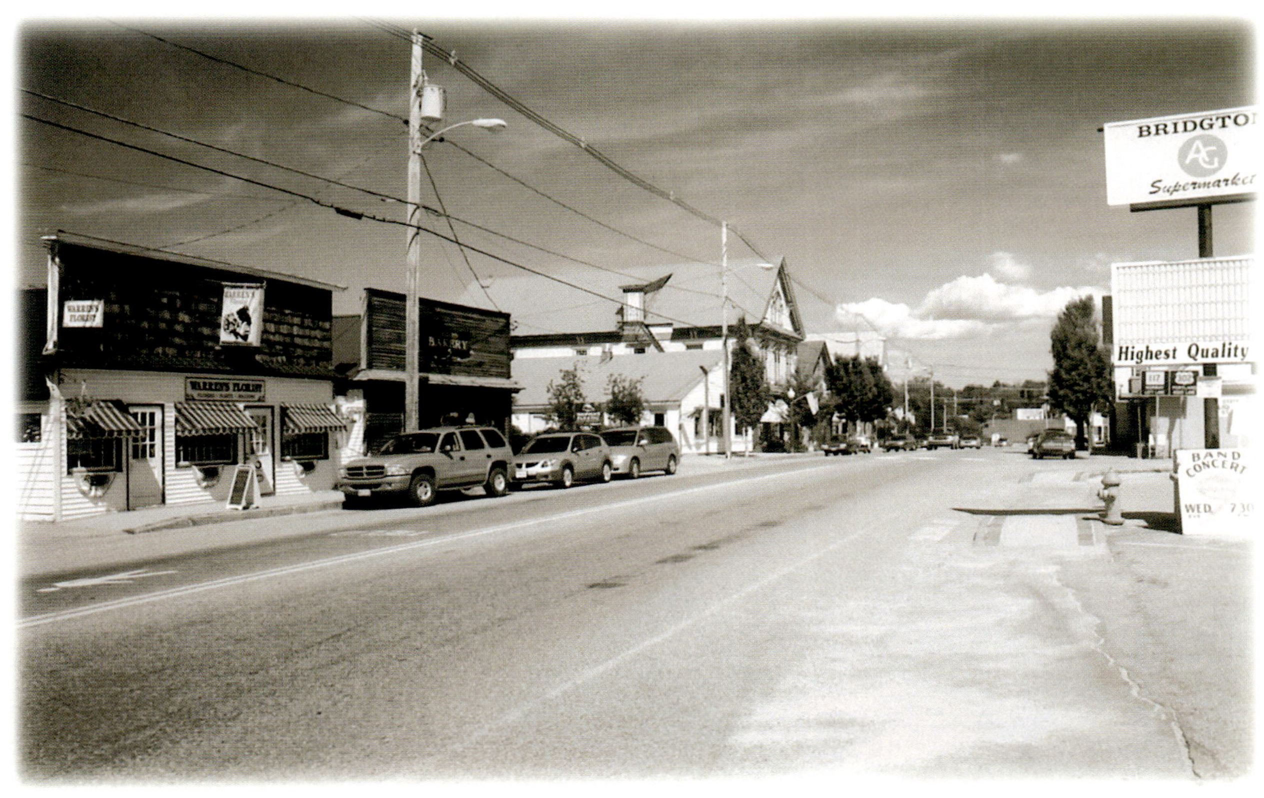
BRIDGTON
AG
Supermarket
Highest Quality
WARREN'S FLORIST
BAKERY
BAND CONCERT
WED.

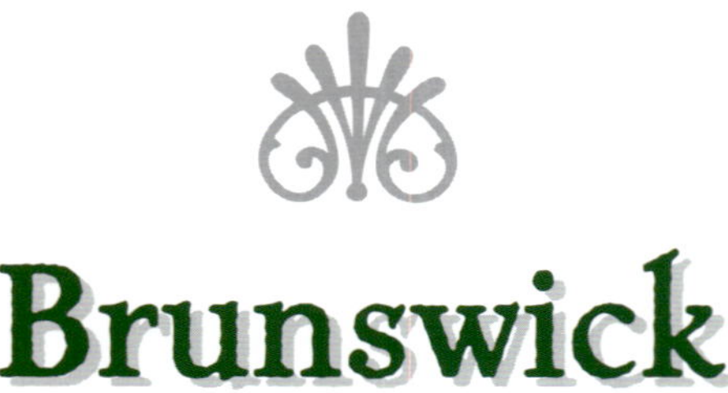

Brunswick

INCORPORATED AS MAINE'S
11TH TOWN ON JANUARY 26, 1739

POPULATION IN 1900: 6,806

POPULATION IN 2000: 21,172

It is said that the Civil War began and ended in Brunswick, if one credits *Uncle Tom's Cabin* with helping to instigate the conflict. Harriet Beecher Stowe wrote the groundbreaking book while she was living on Federal Street in 1851, and Bowdoin professor and Civil War hero Joshua Chamberlain accepted the Confederate surrender at Appomattox in 1865.

In its early days, mills along the Androscoggin River Falls, between Brunswick and Topsham, produced lumber, cotton, paper, and other products. By 1904, more than half the area's population was French-Canadian, having arrived to work in the mills. Cabot Manufacturing Co. was once the town's largest employer, producing cotton textiles for more than one hundred years.

Bowdoin College, more than two centuries old, counts among its alumni Henry Wadsworth Longfellow, Nathaniel Hawthorne, and U.S. President Franklin Pierce. From 1820 until 1921 it also contained the Maine Medical School, which trained more than two thousand doctors. Today, both the college and Brunswick Naval Air Station provide an influx of transient residents from all cultural backgrounds. The air base was established in the 1940s on what had once been blueberry barrens, and the routine training flights of its P-3 submarine hunters are now part of the landscape.

Maine Street—named in honor of the new state in 1821—is extraordinarily wide for a small town. In 1717, the Pejepscot proprietors laid it out at a width of 12 rods (198 feet) to keep travelers well clear of the forest on either side, and thus safe from Indian am-

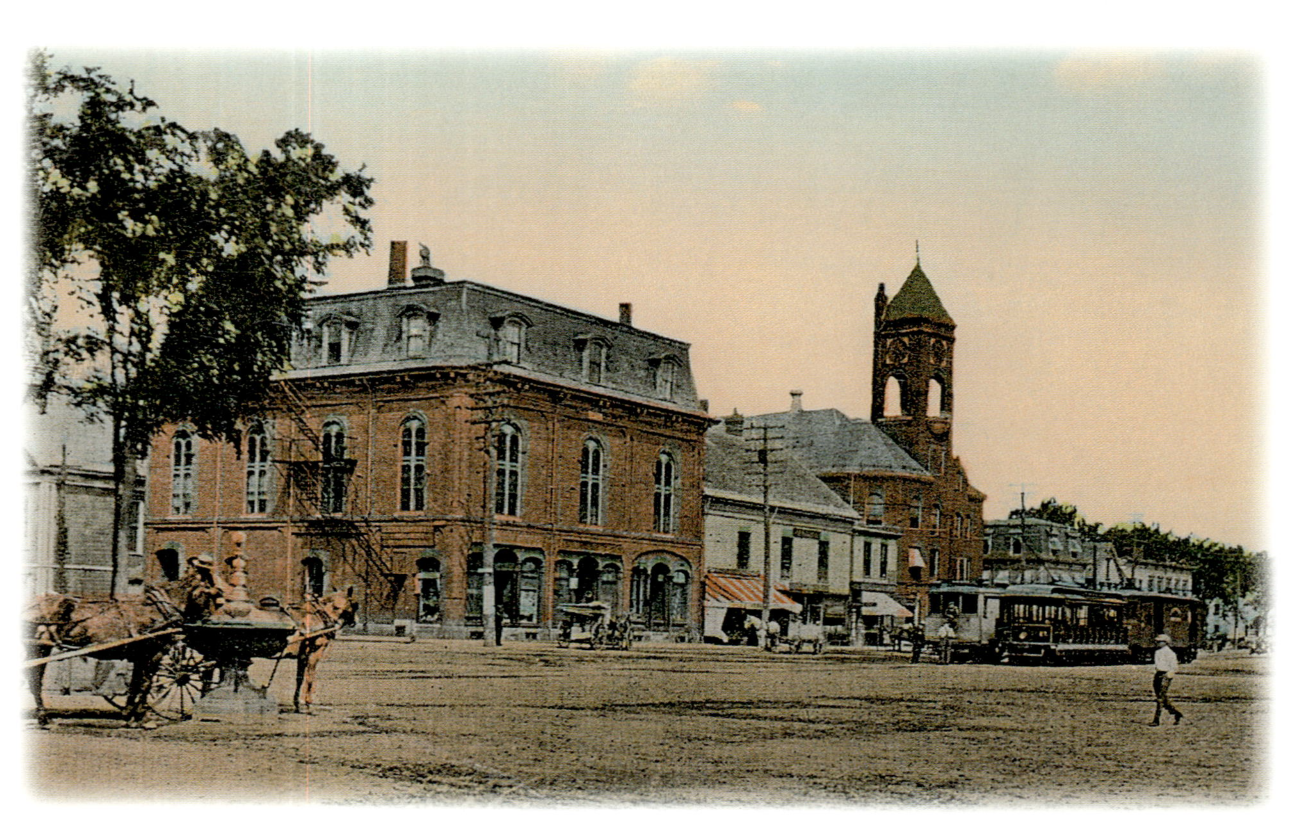

bush. It skirted a swamp which was filled in 1827, creating the Mall Park.

In the vintage postcard, the Knights of Pythias Building, built by the Fort George Lodge #37, is prominent on the corner of Maine and Pleasant Streets. Loring, Short, and Harmon Office Supplies occupied the lower floor for many years, closing in the 1990s. Bowdoin Pharmacy occupied the center storefront at one time. The former United Methodist Church to its left now houses a pizza place and a pool hall.

The Town Building, pictured with its magnificent clock tower, was torn down with mixed emotions in 1961, replaced by the J. J. Newberry Department Store. In 1994, it became the Grand City Department Store, which still occupies the spot today. Built in 1884, the Town Building contained the town offices, post office, and telephone exchange, as well as the Brunswick Club and Printing Office, according to a message written on the card in the early 1900s. Grace Lane worked for seven years on the first floor at the New England Telephone switchboard; in 1946, she made $23 a week. Upstairs in the meeting hall was a country music show. "We used to race upstairs after work to go to the show," said Ms. Lane.

Brunswick resident Linda Tetreault recalled, "There was quite a controversy when they tore down the Town Hall. When they started, the wrecking ball kept bouncing off. It just wouldn't come down. The town has since regretted it. That building wasn't meant to die." The new town hall was built on Federal Street, and the clock sat in the town garage for several years before Dr. Maurice J. Dionne bought it. It now sits in a cupola on the Dionnes' white barn on Pleasant Hill Road. For years it kept accurate time, and people would come by to set their watches by it, said Dr. Dionne's daughter, Carmen Dionne Morris.

Next door to Newberry's was Senter's Department Store, which went out of business in 1992 and is now Senter Place, a collection of shops and offices. Maine Bank and Trust currently resides next door, with Fleet Bank on the next block.

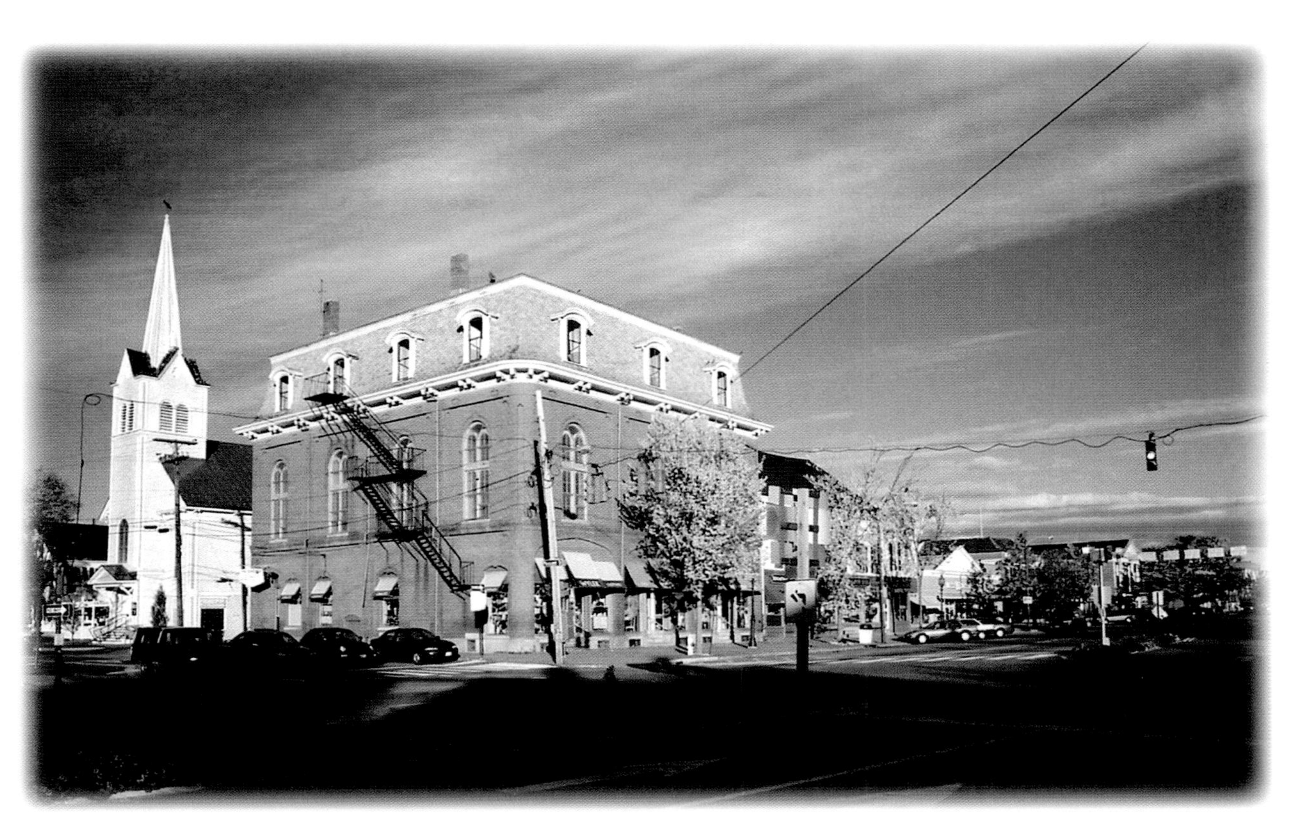

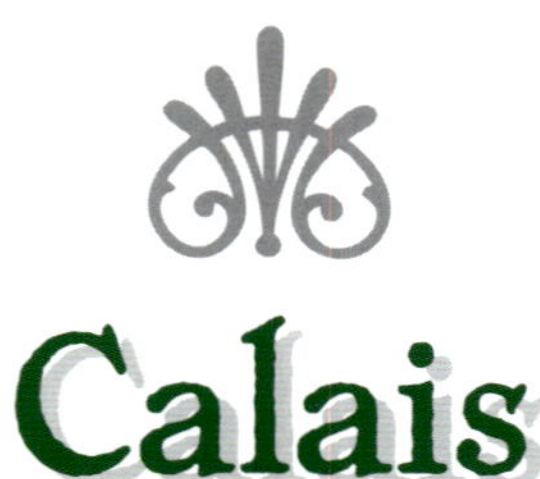

Calais

INCORPORATED AS MAINE'S
176TH TOWN ON JUNE 16, 1809

INCORPORATED AS MAINE'S
7TH CITY ON AUGUST 24, 1850

POPULATION IN 1900: 7,655

POPULATION IN 2000: 3,447

A city truly "on the edge of Maine," Calais shares a border down the middle of the St. Croix River with New Brunswick, Canada. Indeed, Calais depends on Canadians for much of its business, and has close ties with St. Stephen, New Brunswick, just across the river. Many residents have married Canadians, and there are cooperative efforts by both cities' fire departments, water districts, and other organizations to render service across the border. A brochure from the 1960s stated, "We help celebrate the Queen's Birthday on the 24th of May. . . ." and the Canadians likewise celebrated Independence Day on July 4. It was out of gratitude to France for its help during the American Revolution that the new settlement was named for the French port city.

Calais has one of the top-ten busiest ports of entry along the U.S.-Canadian border, and the two countries are now cooperating in the construction of a third bridge to help ease traffic congestion. The U.S. end of the bridge will be near the Calais Industrial Park, and the planned completion date is 2007.

When Canada tightened regulations in 1993 on what its citizens could bring back from the U.S., the city's economy suffered. It saw a 14 percent drop in population in the last decade, and more than a third of the stores on Main Street are now vacant.

Efforts to boost tourism are seen as a vital way to revive the economy. The new Down East Heritage Center was built in the old train station along the banks of the St. Croix River. It opened in May 2004 on the four hundredth anniversary of the settlement of St. Croix (Holy Cross) Island by Samuel de Champlain and Sieur de Monts. Although it was abandoned the following year, after a harsh winter, it is the site of the second-oldest European settlement in North America, after St. Augustine, Florida. It is as important to people of French descent as Plymouth Rock is to those of English ancestry, since the exploration eventually led to the founding of the Acadian colony in Nova Scotia. The city is promoting the site as a tourist destination in Europe, particularly in France (although the Americanized pronunciation of Calais—*KAL-iss*—may be a little hard on French ears).

A front-page article in the *Calais Advertiser* in 1962 depicted a montage of old buildings that showed "the extent to which BLIGHT has eaten into the city of Calais. They show how the business section is shot through with outworn houses and warehouses . . . how a potentially beautiful waterfront is made ugly by dumps and rotting buildings on its banks." Today, those buildings are gone, replaced by a lovely park. A one-mile trail through the downtown area follows the route of the former Maine Central Line nearly to the International Bridge, and many beautiful Victorian homes with gingerbread trim line Main Street.

The North Street postcard shows a three-and-a-half-story lodging house on the right-hand corner. The sign on the neighboring building says DEPARTMENT STORE GOODS. The small red building on the bank of the St. Croix River is a hardware store, and a printing shop is visible on the left-hand edge of the postcard.

Calais Waterfront
from the International Bridge

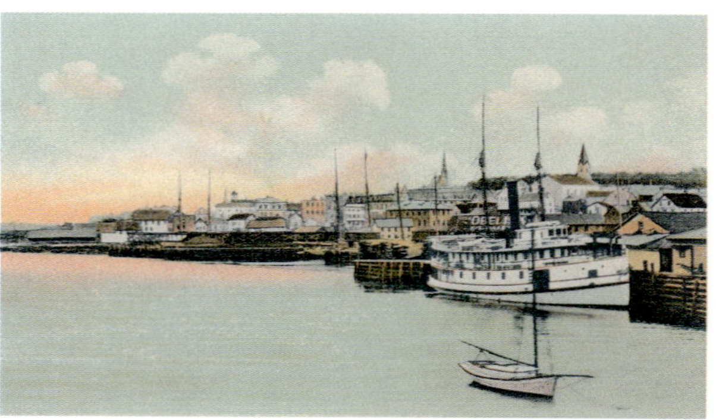

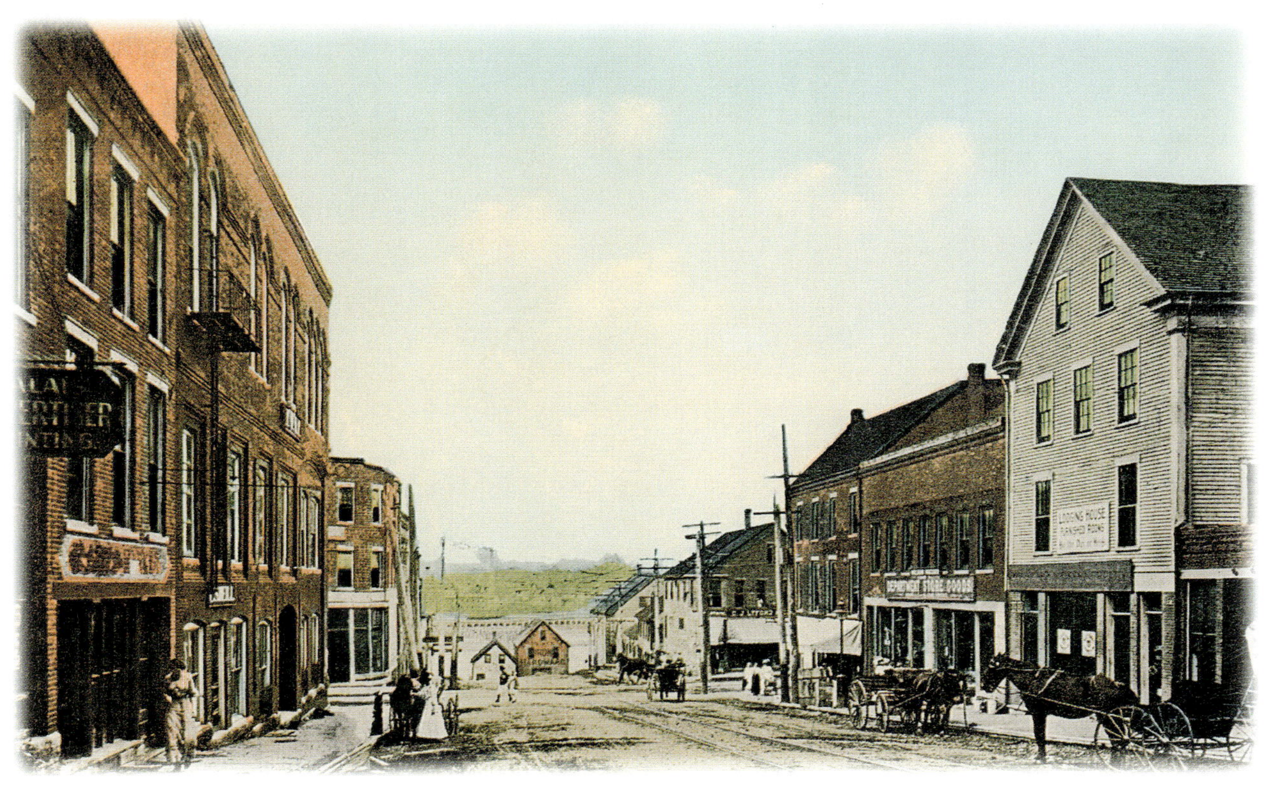

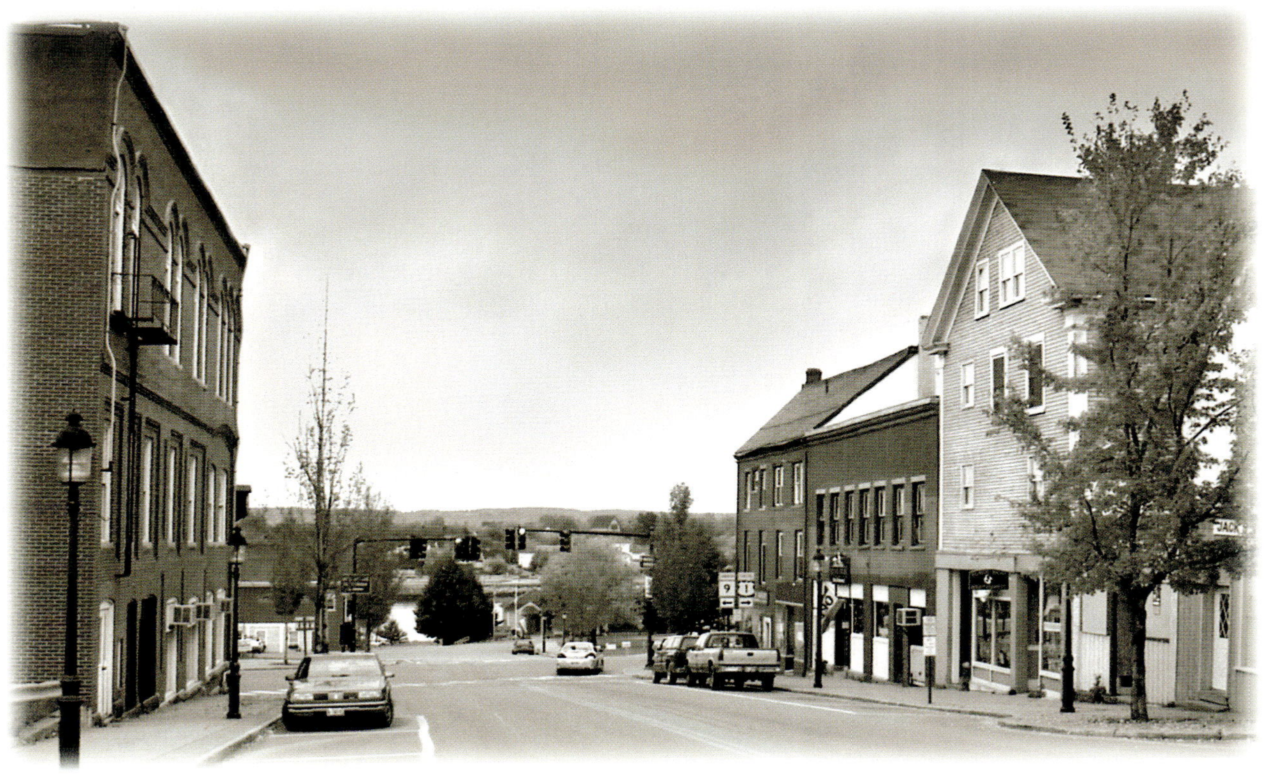

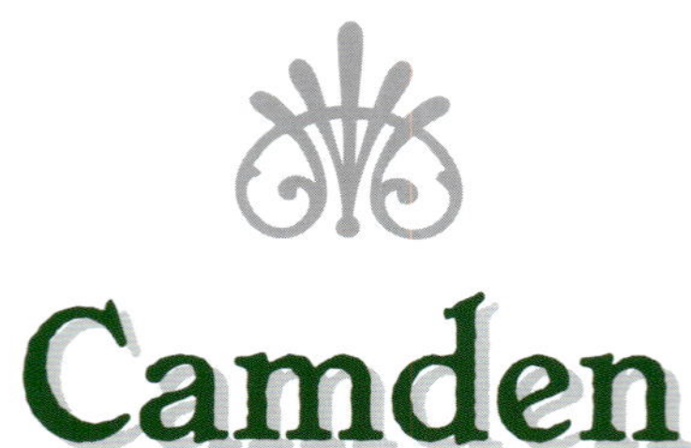

Camden

INCORPORATED AS MAINE'S
72ND TOWN ON FEBRUARY 17, 1791

POPULATION IN 1900: 2,825

POPULATION IN 2000: 5,254

All I could see from where I stood
was three long mountains and a wood . . .

Edna St. Vincent Millay's poem "Renascence" opens with this view from Mount Battie, which towers over the picturesque town of Camden. Named for Lord Camden, a friend of the colonists prior to the American Revolution, it was originally spelled *Cambden*, but that seems to be an error. Known for its summertime traffic bottleneck on U.S. Route 1—as well as its charming specialty shops, restaurants, and its schooner fleet—Camden is a quintessential Maine coast tourist destination.

Like many coastal towns, housing prices are high and the sensibilities upscale. Even the old Knox Woolen Mill was gentrified in 1993 when the credit-card giant MBNA moved in. The mill was built 130 years earlier to produce the country's first endless felts used in paper-making machines. Blankets were the by-product of this endeavor, and in 1941 the mill had nearly three hundred employees. When it closed in 1988, it was the last operating mill in Camden. In 2004, MBNA closed its doors at the Knox Mill and moved the 360 employees to its Rockland and Belfast call centers. It is leasing the Knox Mill building to smaller enterprises. The first tenant was the Owl and Turtle Bookshop, which relocated there from its long-time Bay View Street address.

Maine's first lobster festival was held here in 1947, but the next year it moved to a more spacious location in Rockland, where it has thrived since. In

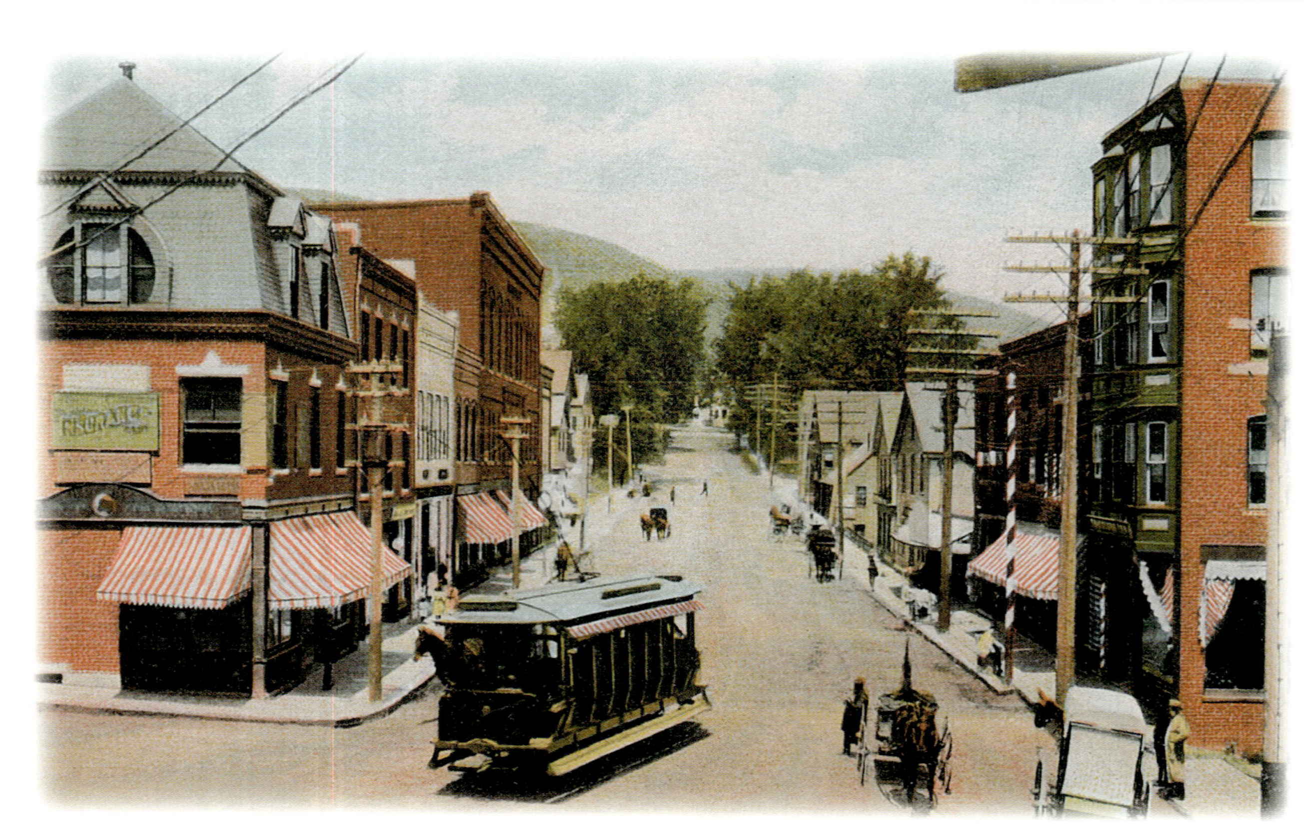

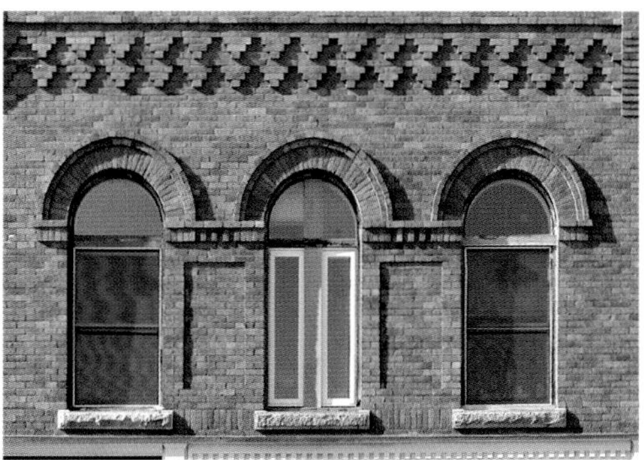

Arches on the Huse Building

1957 the movie *Peyton Place*, starring Lana Turner, was filmed in Camden.

The postcard with the trolley shows Main Street facades that remain pretty much unchanged today. After a fire in November 1892 destroyed sixty businesses and eighteen homes on Main, Elm, and Washington streets, most of the buildings were understandably rebuilt in brick. Thanks to tireless research by Barbara Dyer and others, much is known about the previous occupants.

On the left, the Adams Block (1893) with its unique side window is at the corner of Mechanic Street and Main Street, where Wiley Brothers had a market on the first floor and in the basement. There is an insurance company sign on the second floor. Ora Brown's market occupied it in the 1930s and '40s, and today it is the home of Camden Embroidery. Next door is the Cleveland Block, now occupied by the Foreside Company.

Planet Emporium occupies both the 1903 Huse Block and the two-story Russell Block with three arched windows. The three-story Masonic Block was built in 1893. The Lodge was on the top floor, and retail stores occupied the bottom two floors, including Follansbee & Wood Dry Goods, G. W. Achorn Dry Goods, Colson & Staples Milliners, and Fred Lewis's jewelry store and newsstand. There is now a fourth floor with distinctive blue awnings, and the top three floors are occupied by the Lord Camden Inn, with Russell's of Camden jewelers and Rockport Blueprint on the ground floor.

Barely visible next door in the postcard is the

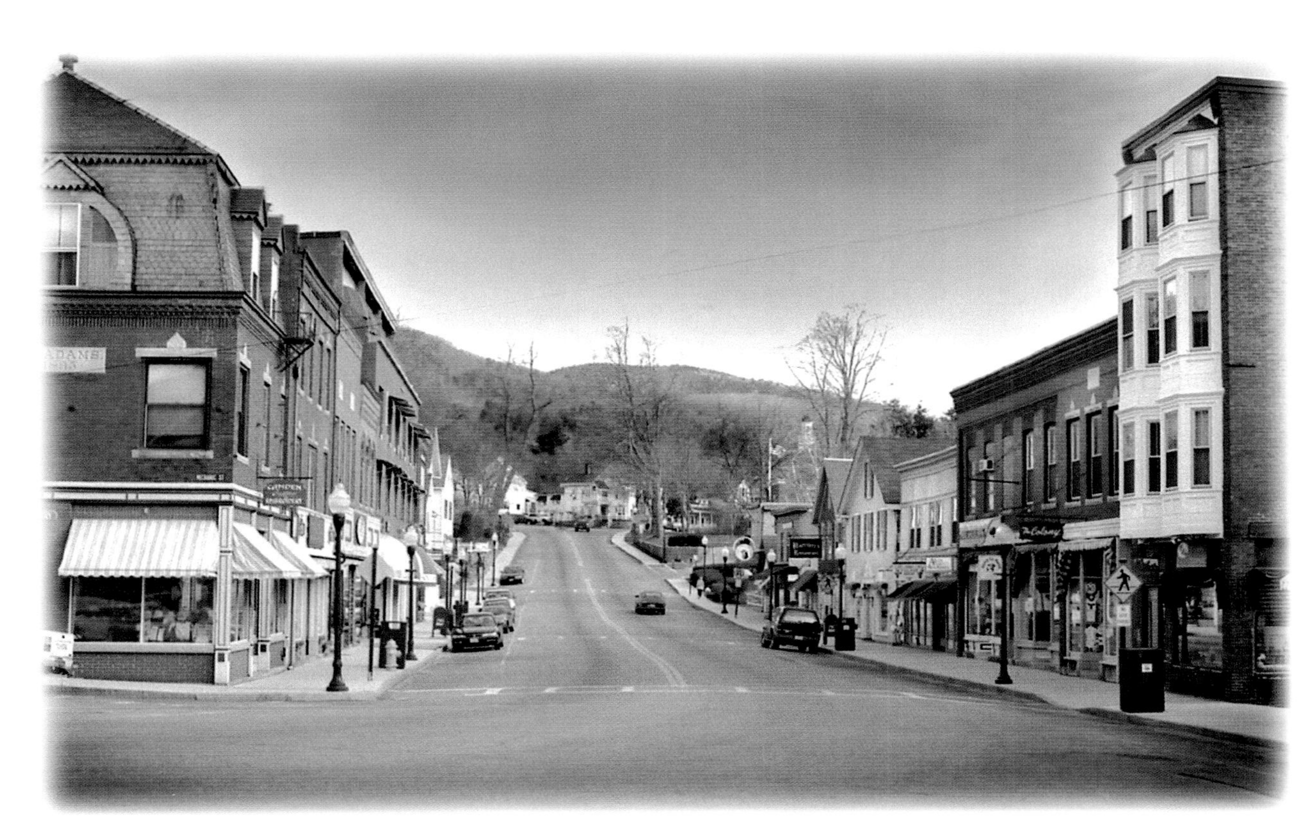

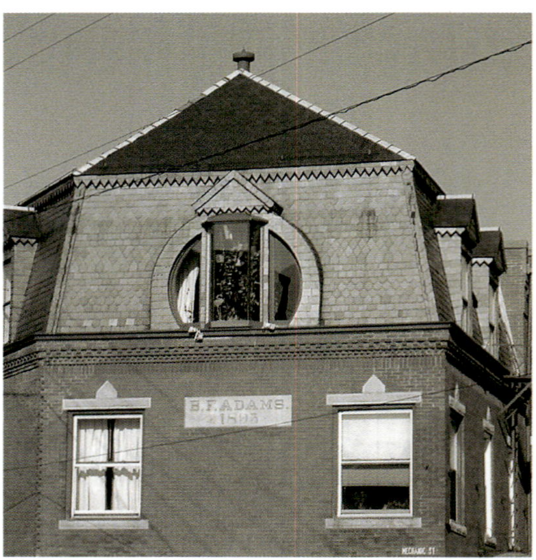

The Adams Block today

1893 Fletcher Building. Boynton's pharmacy was there, later becoming Boynton-McKay. It closed in the mid-1990s, but owners of two other local businesses bought it and reopened it as a coffee and ice-cream parlor. The old druggist's bottles and furnishings have remained, along with the gorgeous tin ceilings, bird's-eye maple showcases, and shelving. Dyer writes, "The art-tile soda fountain of milk glass and black glass was said to have cost as much as a small farm at the time." French's Café occupied the second floor in the old days.

The building on the right edge was the Traveler's Inn, built in 1894. It is occupied on the ground floor today by Camden Pottery, which makes its trademark blueberry-patterned pots. Next down the street is the Arau Block (1893) built by Sylvester Arau, a local barber who liked to tell people he was descended from royalty, according to Dyer. A collection of specialty shops and eateries occupy the buildings that continue down the street. Trolley service began in 1892, and the line eventually ran for seventeen miles from Camden to Warren. The last trolley clattered by on the tracks in 1931.

The 1920s postcard of the waterfront (below) shows steamers at dock. Several shipbuilding and chandlery firms occupied the far shore of the inner harbor, including the H. M. Bean Yard, which be-

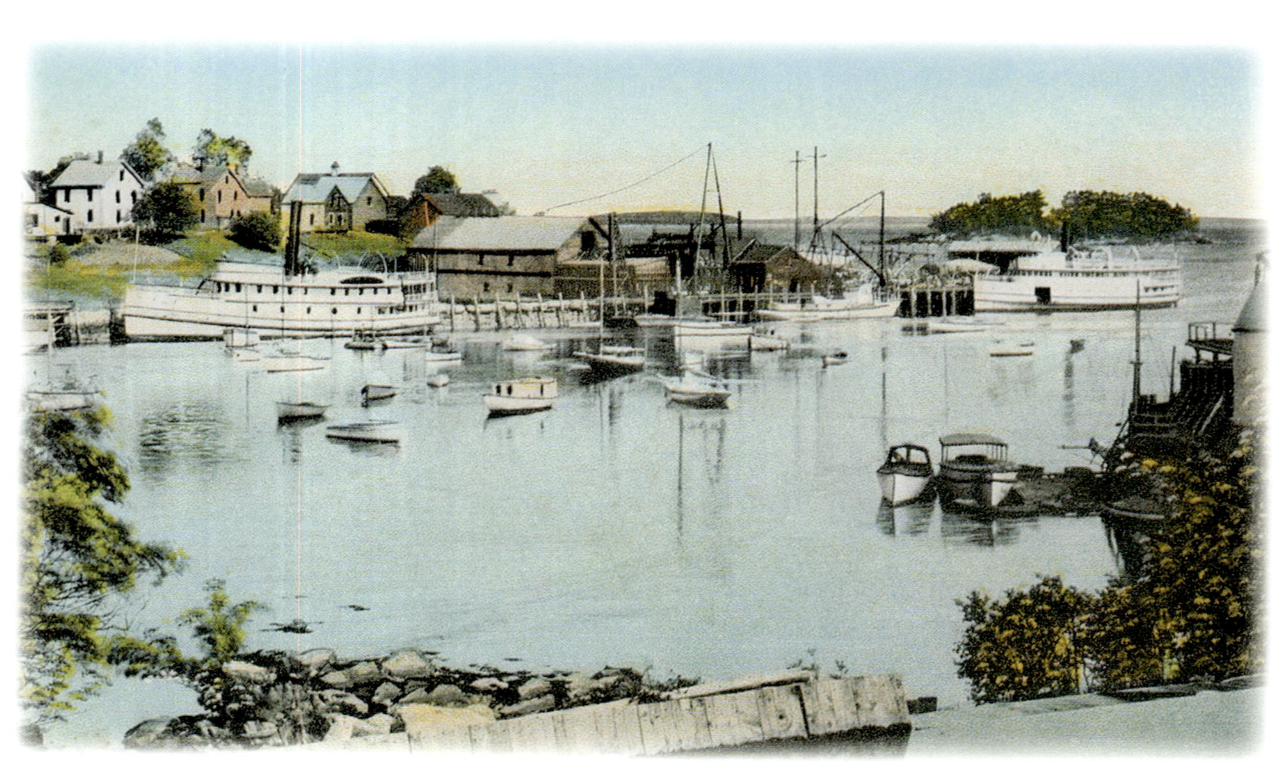

came one of the most well-known shipbuilders on the Atlantic. Later, it became the Camden Shipbuilding and Marine Railways Company. Dyer went to work for them in 1942, and the section by the launching yard was known then (and for some old-timers, still is today) as "the Bean Yard."

Dyer said she had answered an ad in the *Camden Herald* for painters and caulkers. "The ad said they'd *even* hire women, but not to expect a glamorous job because you'd be outdoors wearing a mackinaw and getting your nose red from the cold." She had been a top student and hoped to be a math teacher someday, but the Depression and the war put the kibosh on those dreams. When her academic and math skills were discovered they moved her into the office, where she stayed for forty-four years, eventually being named office manager.

During the war the shipyard built two minesweepers, twelve rescue salvage tugs, four coal barges, and several troop transports. As a matter of fact, the coal barge was President Franklin Roosevelt's idea, since New Englanders were concerned about how the war would affect their ability to get fuel. First Lady Eleanor Roosevelt was on hand in 1943 to christen one of them, says Dyer. "That was an exciting day." Up to 1,500 people worked in two shifts during the war. The enterprise later became Camden Shipbuilding, making wooden yachts and fishing boats. In 1963 the yard was sold, and is now Wayfarer Marine, providing yacht storage, repairs, and supplies for the busy harbor.

It was Dyer's inveterate collecting of news clippings and photos of the shipyard that led her to research Camden's shipbuilding history in the 1980s. Her first book, *Grog Ho*, was published in 1984, and she now has a total of eight books on Camden history to her credit. She has been a lifelong Camden resident, but can't technically claim to have been born there; there was no hospital in Camden then, "so I had to be born in Rockland," she says wryly.

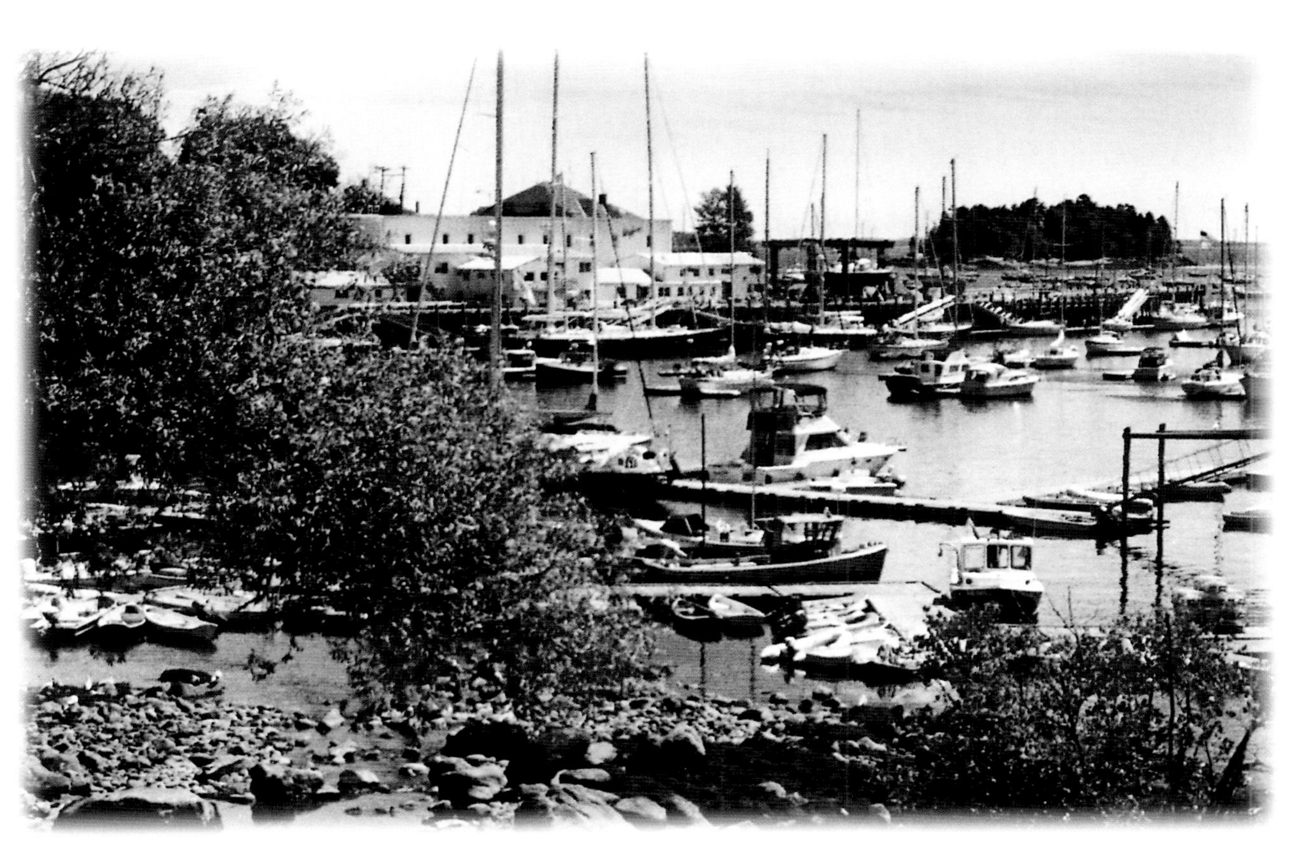

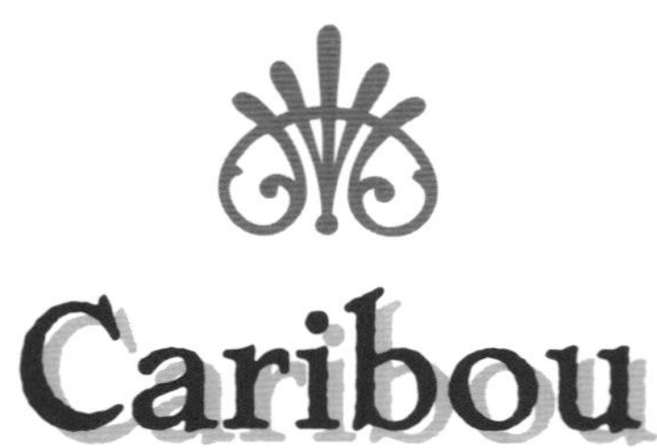

Caribou

INCORPORATED AS MAINE'S 405TH TOWN ON APRIL 5, 1859

INCORPORATED AS MAINE'S 22ND CITY ON JANUARY 1, 1968

POPULATION IN 1900: 4,758

POPULATION IN 2000: 8,312

Located in a narrow strip from Caribou to Houlton, the soil of eastern Aroostook County provides perfect nourishment for the potatoes that helped define the city. In 1909 the county's potato production was more than twenty-four million bushels, many of them from Caribou. Maine also ranks third in the nation in broccoli production, with Aroostook being the largest grower on the East Coast.

Most of the potatoes are processed into frozen foods and potato chips. It's common to see bags of potatoes for sale using the "honor system" at little roadside stands in the area. Starch was once made from potatoes, and in the 1920s the R. L. Pitcher Co. operated the largest starch factory in the Eastern states. The last of the factories closed in the 1980s.

In 1859 Township H was incorporated as the town of Lyndon, and a decade later two plantations were added to its boundaries. The name was changed to Caribou in 1877. Many of the early settlers had come from Canada, and even today one may occasionally hear "Valley French" being spoken, a mixture that includes Old French, Quebecois, and English—sometimes all in one sentence. America's most northeastern city is only ten minutes from the border and still has close ties with Canada.

The postcard shows Sweden Street before urban renewal. On the left corner is the Hackett Block, built in 1932 on the site of the O'Regan Block after it burned. J. A. Clark had operated a store in the earlier three-story wooden structure, and there was also a drugstore, law offices, and an entertainment hall. A drugstore still operated there at the time the postcard photo was taken.

Town assessor Claire Randolph said that one of the buildings in the Hackett Block burned in 1963, and the remaining old wooden buildings were removed during urban renewal. "A bypass went through in 1970 and that changed the configuration of the town," she said, moving the major business area today to Bennett Drive northeast of the city. In the 1970s the street was reconfigured and replaced with a "mall," where People's Heritage Bank and H&R Block are now located.

The National Weather Service began operating at the Caribou Municipal Airport in 1937. In 1958 it became one of six stations in the country measuring ozone levels, and forty years later became a full-fledged Forecast Office. The average January temperature in Caribou is 9.5 degrees Fahrenheit, with an average high of less than 20 degrees. The average snowfall in "the County" is nearly ten feet.

Thanks to that white stuff, Caribou has become a popular destination for winter sports. Its snowmobile trails are "second to none," says Randolph. "You can get on a trail and go to Quebec or Millinocket if you wanted to," she said of the 1,600-mile system. There are also local trails for cross-country skiing, and two world-class Nordic ski centers have recently been built in nearby Fort Kent and Presque Isle. Randolph says that children are once again learning the tradition of cross-country skiing, thanks to the Maine Winter Sports Center. The Center is supported by the Libra Foundation, which was established by philanthropist Elizabeth Noyce.

When Caribou was declared a city, the ten-day celebration began with a bonfire of discarded Christmas trees on New Year's Day 1968. A live caribou, en route to the Chicago Zoo from Newfoundland, lent an arctic air to the festivities when it was put on display for a day in a parking lot opposite the Hotel Caribou.

INTERESTING TIDBIT:

In 1897 Caribou residents voted in town meeting to stop horse racing on Sweden Street.

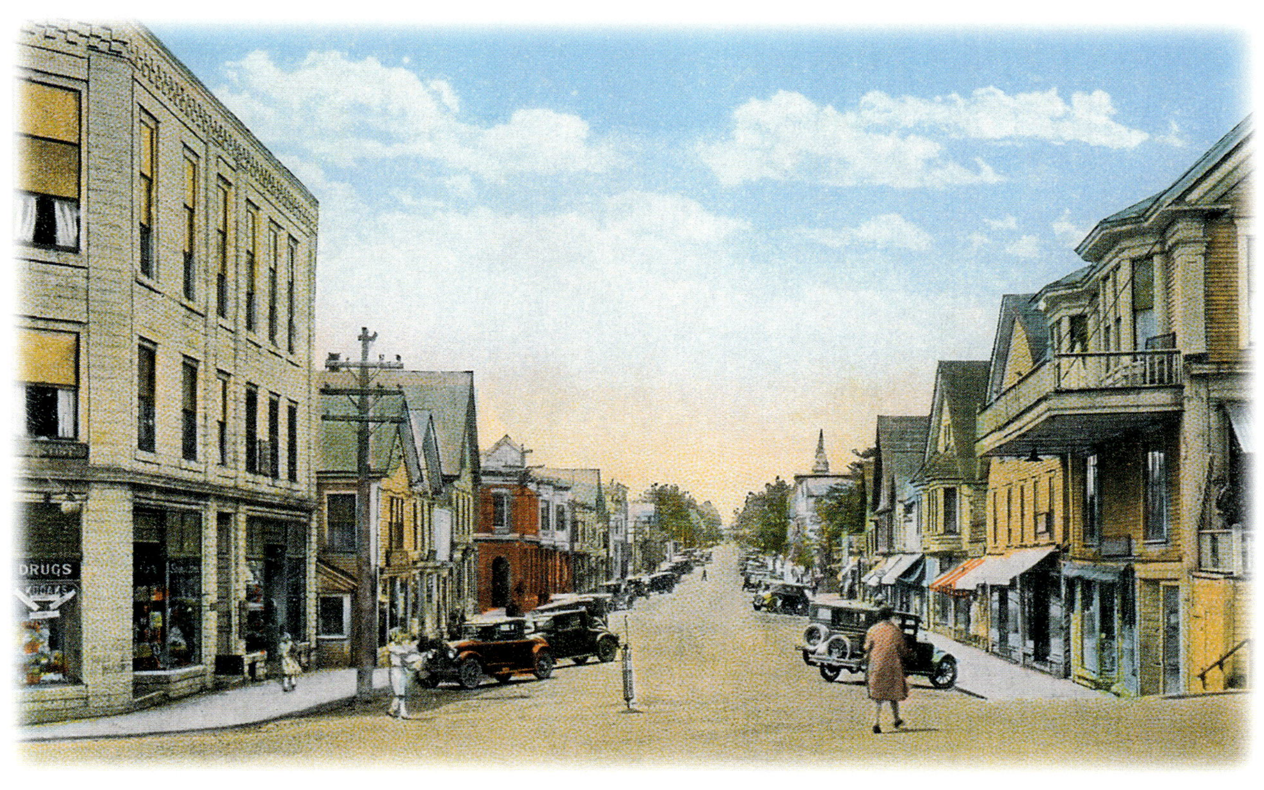
DRUGS

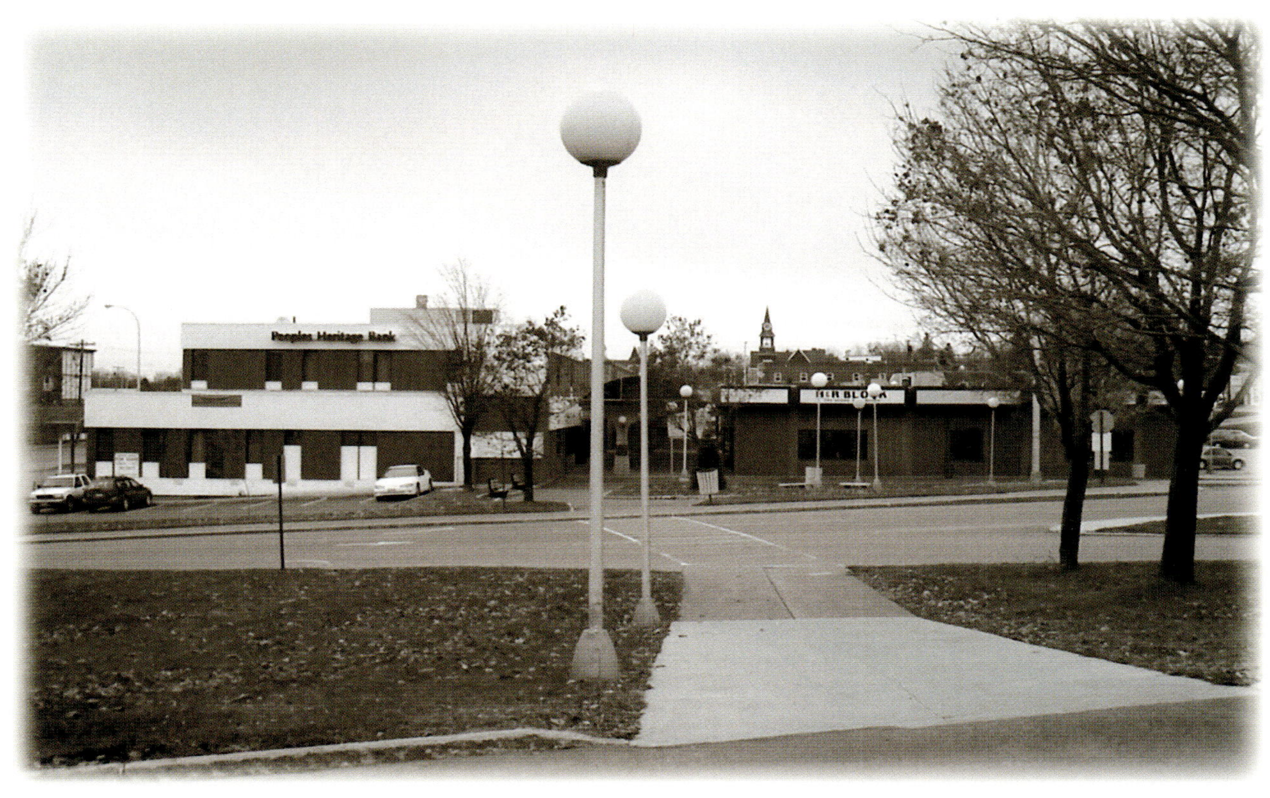
Peoples Heritage Bank

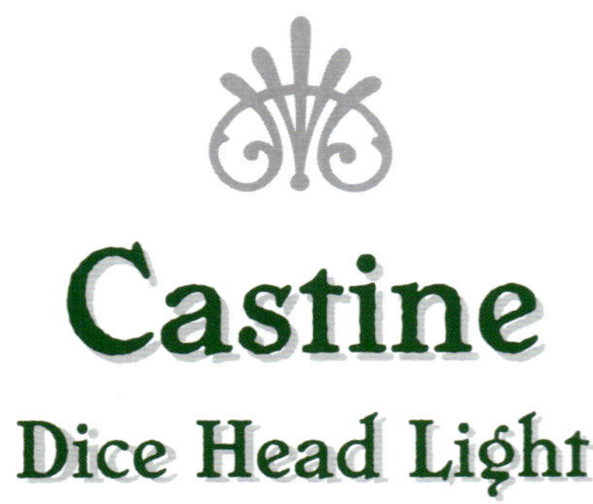

Castine

Dice Head Light

INCORPORATED AS MAINE'S 104TH TOWN ON FEBRUARY 10, 1796

POPULATION IN 1900: 925

POPULATION IN 2000: 1,343

The "Flying Santa" tradition was born at Dice (sometimes Dyce) Head in 1929. Maine floatplane pilot Bill Wincapaw, of Friendship, often flew sick and injured islanders to the mainland. Once, during a snowstorm, he ran low on fuel, and the beam of Dice Head Light guided him to safety. That Christmas, he flew over the light station and dropped presents for the keeper and his family. He then brought the tradition to other Maine and New England lighthouse keepers, dropping packages of newspapers, magazines, coffee, candy, and other items. Since 1978, pilots in the Flying Santa program have continued to visit the lighthouses by helicopter rather than by plane.

First lit in 1829, the light sat atop a tower built of stone with brick lining. The headland was named for John Jacob Dyce, who owned the lower portion of the peninsula, yet journal writers of the era often spelled it *Dice's* or *Dice* Head. In 1858 the tower was surrounded by an angled wooden frame, the reason for which is unclear. The covering had been removed by 1907, according to the National Park Service. The postcard dates from earlier than that, for it clearly shows the frame still in place.

The lantern is 51 feet above the ground. The original Winslow Lewis system of lamps and parabolic reflectors was replaced in 1858 with a fourth-order Fresnel lens that projected a fixed beam visible seventeen miles out to sea. That beacon was discontinued

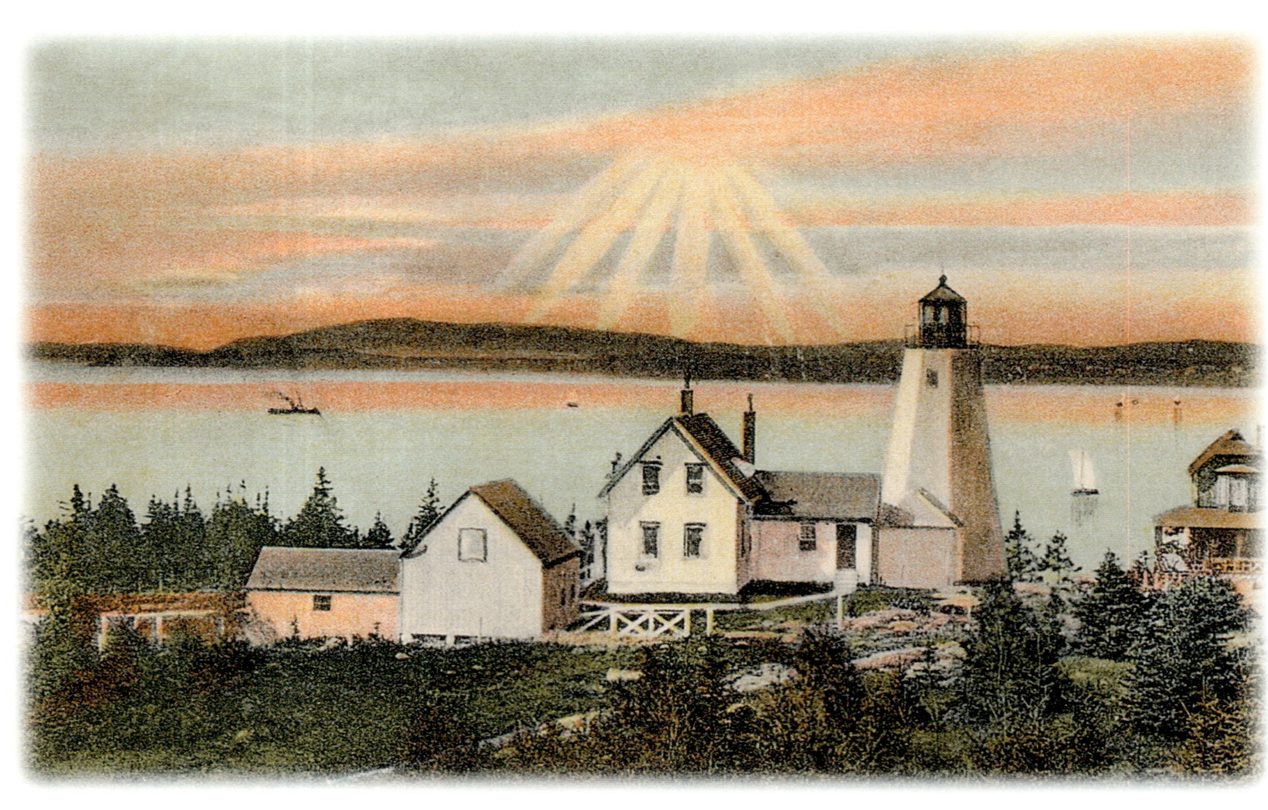

in 1935 and replaced with a white skeleton tower on the north side of the harbor entrance. The 1829 keeper's house was destroyed by fire in April 1999 and restored the following year. Today, the town of Castine maintains the old light, the keeper's house (which has been rented by an artist for more than thirty years), and the grounds.

A Castine Historical Society writer says the lighthouse's history is rather uneventful: "Shipwrecks and heroic rescues performed by lighthouse keepers, their families, and even their dogs have no part in the stories surrounding Dice's Head Lighthouse."

The entire town of Castine, one of America's oldest communities, is listed on the National Register of Historic Places. Occupied continuously since the early 1600s by the French, Dutch, and British, it was part of the town of Penobscot until its incorporation in 1796. In the mid-1800s Castine was the second-wealthiest town per capita in the nation, primarily due to the six shipyards and the wealth generated by shipping. More than a hundred historic markers denote special places or events in the village, or "off neck"—a narrow strip of land that separates the Bagaduce River from the Penobscot River.

Most of the Maine coast was almost treeless two centuries ago, the forests having been cleared for farmland and to fuel lime kilns, yet today large elms are still a hallmark of this coastal town, which allocates $10,000 a year for care and maintenance of the trees to prevent their loss to Dutch elm disease and for purchasing new disease-resistant trees. About fifty trees have been planted in the past few years.

The Maine Maritime Academy has been a public institution in Castine for more than sixty years. It trains seven hundred students a year for careers in the merchant marine trades and marine sciences. Several training vessels, including the schooner *Bowdoin*, berth in the harbor.

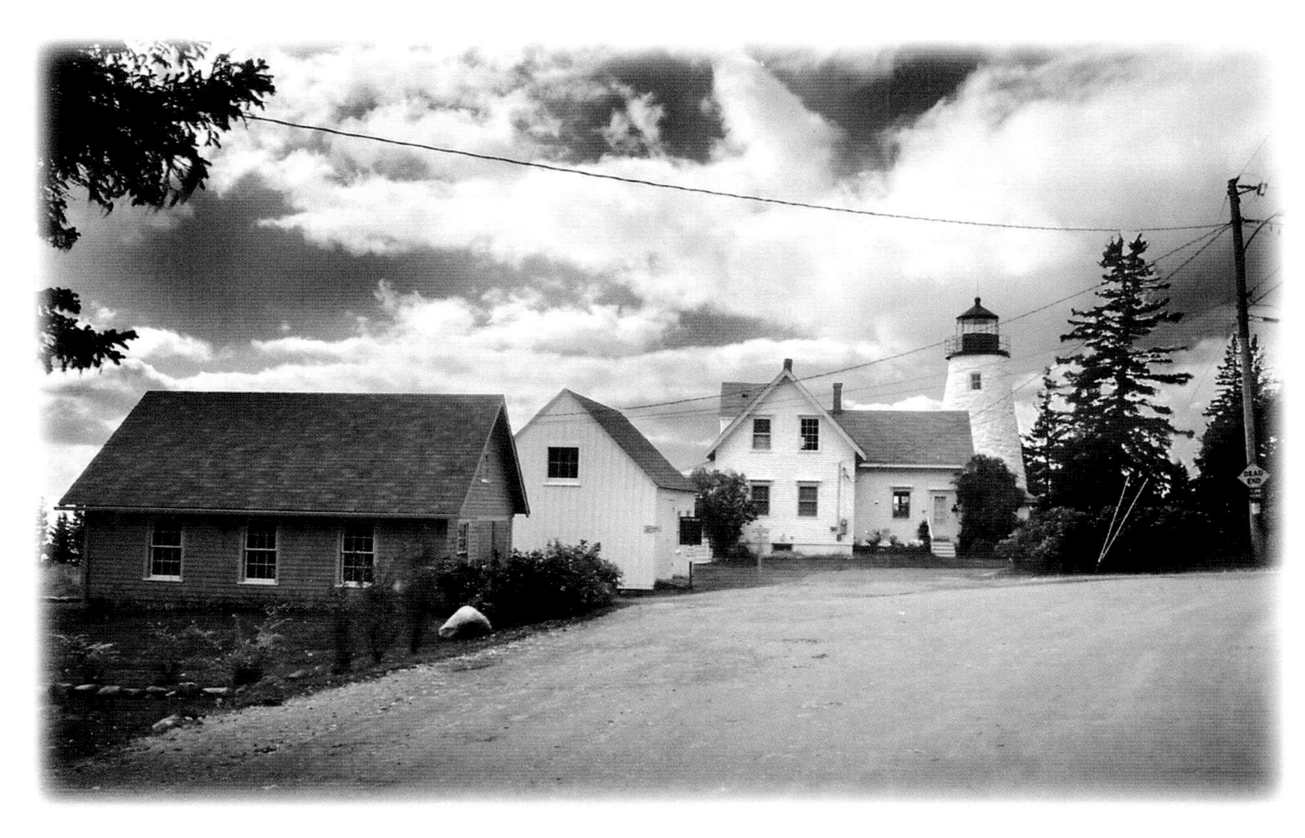

Damariscotta

INCORPORATED AS MAINE'S
373RD TOWN ON MARCH 15, 1848

POPULATION IN 1900: 876

POPULATION IN 2000: 2,041

Known as "the place of many fishes" to Native Americans, Damariscotta was originally part of Nobleboro. Alewives—the "many fishes" the name refers to—still migrate upstream each spring to spawn, congregating in the picturesque hamlet of Damariscotta Mills just up the river.

Native peoples gathered on the banks of the river for thousands of years before the arrival of the Europeans, feasting on oysters and other shellfish. They left some of the world's largest shell heaps, encompassing five million cubic feet of shells, on both banks of the river. Enterprising businessmen "mined" the heaps for many years, grinding the shells for use as chicken feed, fertilizer, and building materials. These native oysters were extinct long before the arrival of the Europeans due to changes in seawater level and temperatures. The middens were placed on the National Register of Historic Places in 1969.

Damariscotta's Main Street business district, as well as numerous homes, is also in the Historic District. In the postcard, the 1875 Lincoln Hall Theater on the far right was dedicated with a fancy ball and concert. Throughout the Gay '90s, it was the social center of the community, and in the early 1900s the wooden floor was adapted for a roller-skating rink. The Lincoln County Community Theater now owns the building, and continues to stage productions there. The Maine Coast Book Shop and Café currently occupies the ground floor.

Next down the street is the 1850 Day's Block, built by shipbuilder Joseph Day Jr. On the first floor in 1925 were the offices of the First National Bank, a barbershop, and the post office, after it moved from the other side of the street. Originally, the top two floors were the Maine Hotel, with twenty rooms and a billiard room, but by 1925 they were converted into apartments. By the 1940s the bank had expanded to occupy most of the first floor. The smaller Isaac Genther Block is attached, and the building was restored in 1962.

Down the street, the Dr. Robert Dixon and Asa Snow buildings at one time housed an A & P store and a shoe store, with a millinery shop on the second floor. Both buildings are currently occupied by Renys Department Store, which has been an area institution since 1949. Robert H. Reny opened the first of a dozen Maine stores in this location. The adjacent Henry Mellus Block, housing Chapman and Chapman Insurance, was built in 1846 and was formerly the First National grocery store.

The left side shows a yard where Perley Waltz constructed the clapboard-and-brick building in 1949. A bowling alley was in the basement until Renys Underground took over the spot in the mid-1960s. The First National grocery store occupied the ground floor here as well, and now Renys and Waltz Pharmacy are in that space. The dormered brick building next to it housed Senter's Dry Goods Store from the early 1900s through at least the 1960s.

The three-story Stetson-Metcalf building toward the end of that side of the street in the postcard became Gay's Grocery Store in 1882, and operated until 1972. It still has the sign that reads GILBERT E. GAY on the front. The post office was next door until 1916, and separated Gay's Grocery from the C. M. Jones Cash Grocery.

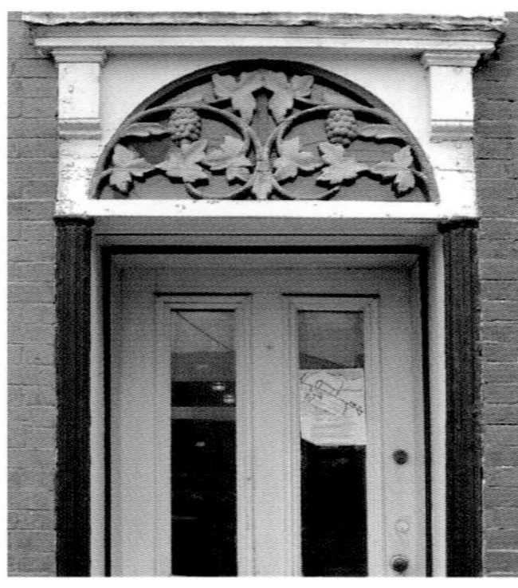

Modern view of an ornamented doorway in the Henry Mellus block on Main Street.

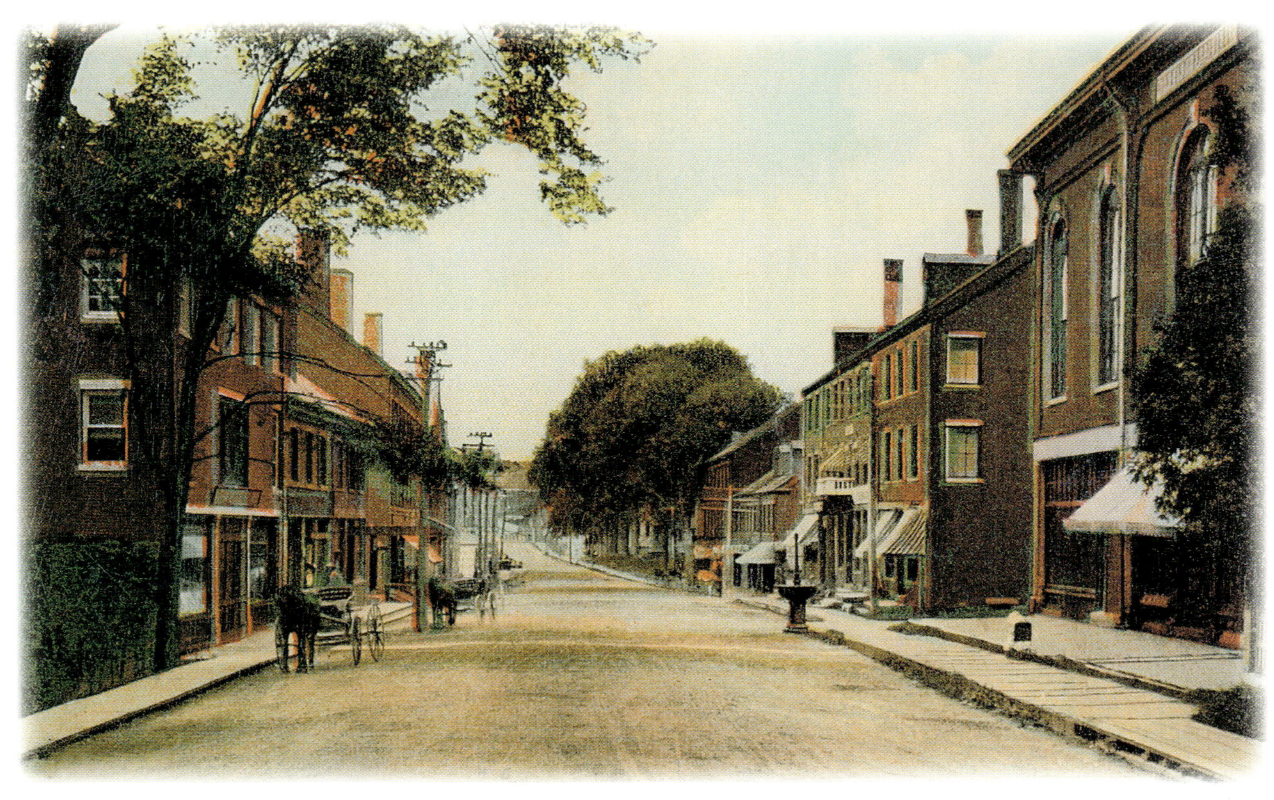

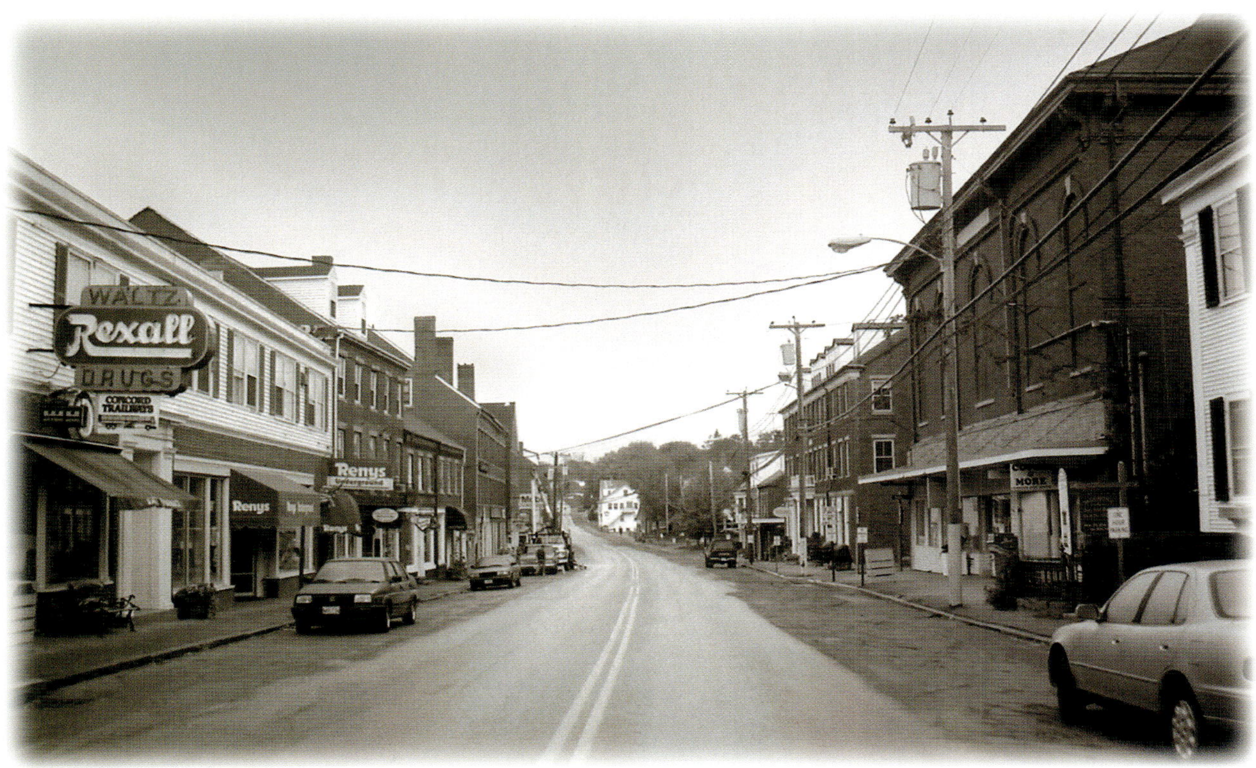
WALTZ
Rexall
DRUGS
CONCORD TRAILWAYS
Renys
Renys

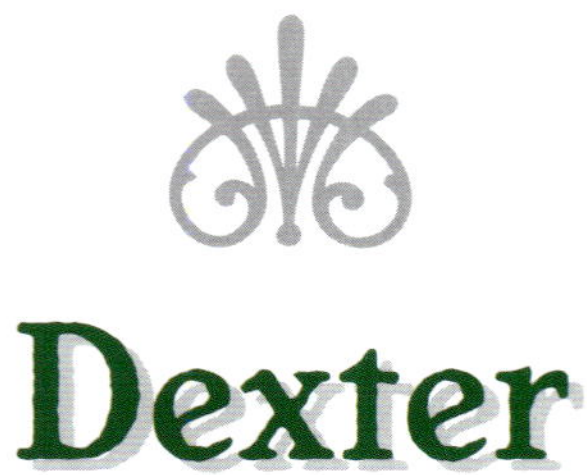

Dexter

INCORPORATED AS MAINE'S 217TH TOWN ON JUNE 17, 1816

POPULATION IN 1900: 2,914

POPULATION IN 2000: 3,890

Dexter was named for Samuel Dexter, a respected lawyer from Boston. Henry Paine Dexter (no relation) was responsible for the construction of up to eighty dwellings, building or renovating four churches and many of the Main Street businesses. Between 1830 and 1860 there were six woolen mills in town, including the Amos Abbott Co., which made heavy mackinaw cloth known as "Abbott grays." It closed in 1975 after 155 years of operation. In the 1950s, the Dexter Shoe Company picked up the slack left by the closing of the woolen mills. The venerable manufacturer, which in its heyday employed 1,500 people, closed its three local plants in 2001, putting nearly 500 out of work. It still maintains a warehouse and a corporate headquarters in Dexter, but its manufacturing is now done overseas. With little economic base, Dexter is becoming a bedroom community for other towns, and is in the midst of developing ways to restore its vitality.

As shown in today's photograph, "Nancy the Clock"—erected by John L. Morrison in 1925 in memory of his wife, Nancy—wasn't even around when the old postcard was made. The town offices now occupy the building, which was built after the Dexter House was moved in 1906 to a site across from the Methodist Church.

The clock stopped working in the 1970s, and in the 1980s, Doug Pooler decided to fix it. "I didn't know how it worked," he said. "I just went up and watched it until I figured it out." Though it runs by electricity, he adjusts the pendulum's length by hand

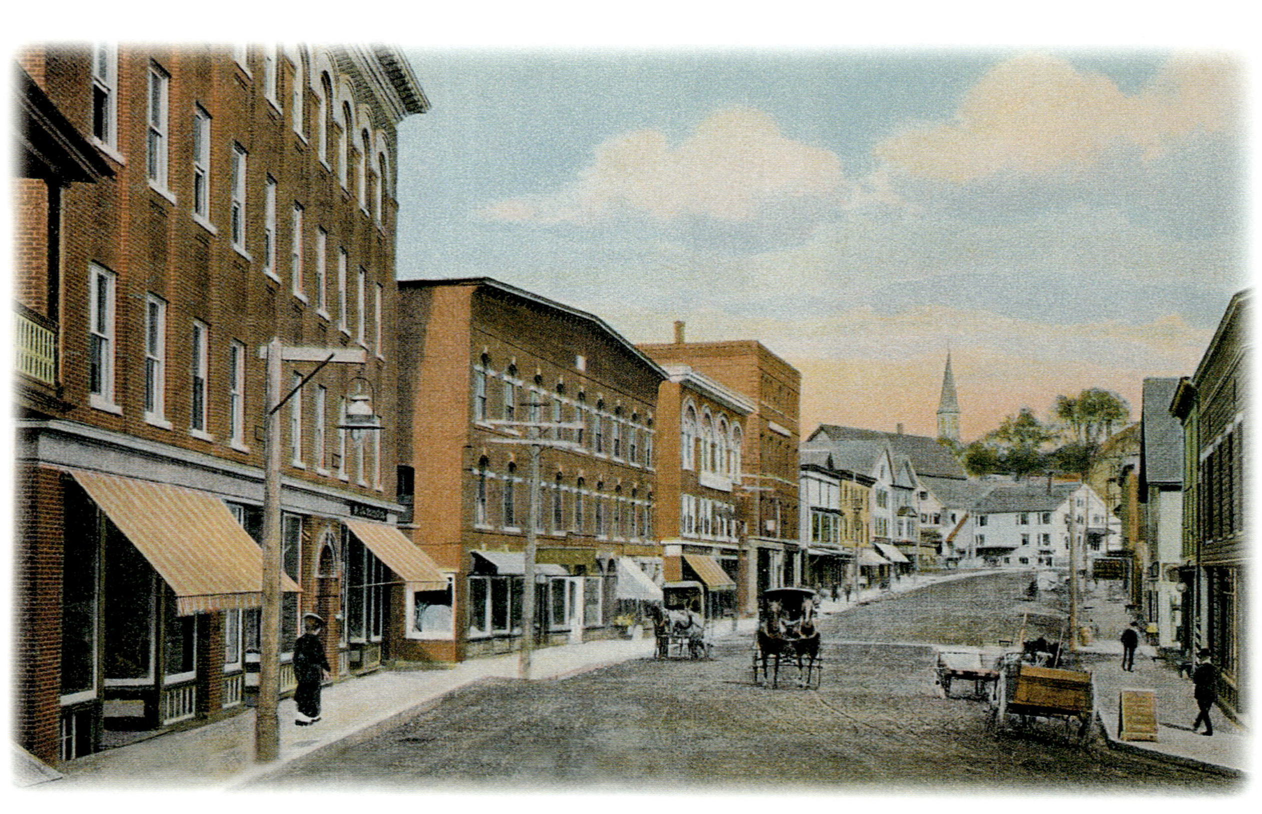

to speed up or slow it down, making many trips back and forth to get it just right.

In the postcard, the building on the left where Renys is now was once occupied by the Dexter Meat Market. It was known as the Gerry Block and was built in 1905 by F. J. Gerry & Co. on the site of an old tavern. It was a creamery and a grocery until 1911, and at one point Gordon's Shoe Store and the post office occupied the building. The top floor was demolished in a fire on October 12, 1931, in which a fireman was killed. In 1937 the building housed Koritsky's Department Store, then Dexter Hardware. Renys bought it in 1973.

Next down the block is the 1884 Dustin Block, which was originally a hardware store. It was later Dexter Pharmacy and then Berry's Rexall before Renys bought it in 1986 and added the connector between the Dustin and Gerry blocks two years later. The roof on the Dustin building collapsed under snow on January 30, 1990.

Next is the Morrison Memorial Building, and the last four-story brick building is the Bank Block, which had a mansard roof until 1896 when a fire burned the top stories. At the end of the block today is Tillson True Value Hardware and the offices of the Maine School Administrative District 46. Since this photo was taken in 1999, the Dexter Oil Company (formerly a Texaco station) at the street's end became the Dexter Police Department. Behind it are the old Grange and the steeple of the First Universalist Church.

REMARKABLE RESIDENT:

Hiram Maxim patented more than 270 inventions, including the machine gun. In England in 1884, years before the Wright brothers' famous flight at Kitty Hawk on December 1903, he flew an airplane of his own, with two eighteen-foot propellers. It stayed airborne for two hundred feet.

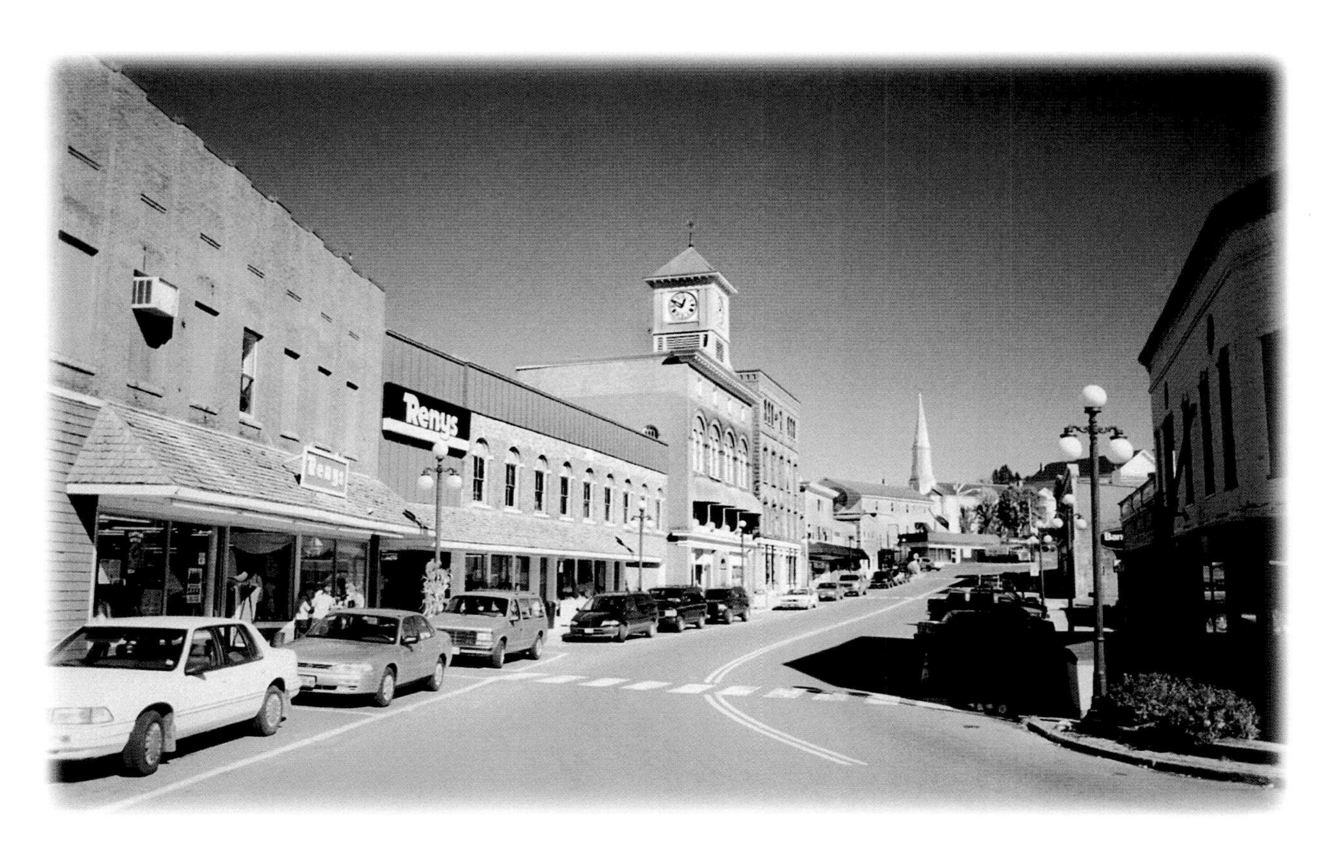

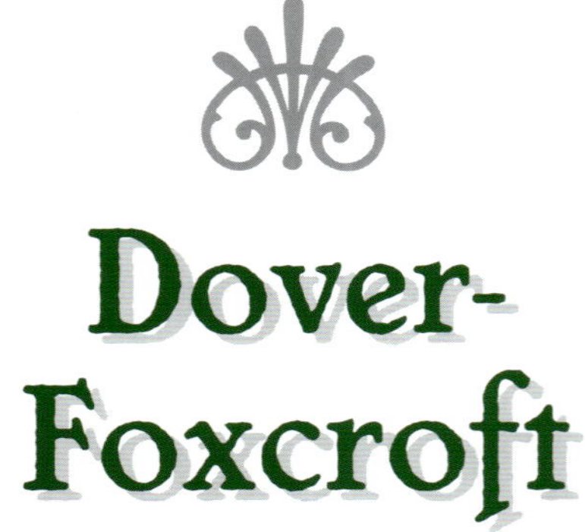

Dover-Foxcroft

INCORPORATED AS MAINE'S
485TH TOWN ON MARCH 1, 1922

POPULATION IN 1900:
DOVER 1,889; FOXCROFT 1,629

POPULATION (COMBINED) IN 2000: 4,211

When the towns of Dover and Foxcroft joined as one in 1922, the event was celebrated with a symbolic marriage ceremony performed by the Piscataquis Club, a men's party club. "Miss Dover" was gowned in white satin and attended by four maids as she married "Mr. Foxcroft." Although the legislature in 1915 had authorized the union of the towns, and although Foxcroft in town meeting promptly agreed to accept the provisions of the union, it took Dover townspeople several more years of indecision before it was finally consummated. A local historian believes it was the women, who had recently been granted the right to vote, that made the difference.

There must have been an informal union long before 1915, because the postcard, dated 1907, is titled DOVER-FOXCROFT. Foxcroft was incorporated in 1812 and named for one of the proprietors, Colonel Joseph Ellery Foxcroft. Dover, incorporated in 1822, was named for the town in England that the proprietors had once called home. Dover-Foxcroft is now the shiretown of Piscataquis County.

Industries operating at the turn of the twentieth century included the American Woolen Company at the former Brown's Mill (1899 to 1953) and the Mayo and Sons, Inc., Woolen Mill, which was later bought by American Woolen. In the 1950s they were bought by Textron, which sold the machinery. In 1976 it became Moosehead Manufacturing, a furniture company, and is today one of the town's major employers. The Cushing Perfection Dyes Co., a small company that started in 1897, was one of the nation's largest dye manufacturers by 1964, and even produced dye for Navajo rugs.

The postcard shows Union Square from the Dover side. The three buildings on the left burned on February 2, 1962. At the time they housed Collette's Restaurant and a Western Auto Store. The covered bridge in the center, which spans the Piscataquis River, was replaced by a concrete bridge in 1911. To the immediate left of the bridge is the Mayo Mill, erected in 1844. Behind the bridge was the Foxcroft Exchange hotel, which was demolished in 1951; there is now a Texaco station on the site. Today the spire of the Congregational Church, built in 1876, is visible in the distance.

On the right side of the street from the bridge is the Masonic Temple with the mansard roof, built in 1871. In the late 1950s the ground floor was occupied by Haskell & Corthell Co. Clothing Store. The boundary of the two towns actually goes through the center of the Masonic Temple. Next to it (not shown in the postcard) in the 1950s was the IGA Store, and in between was a tiny little building the width of a door and its sidelights. In 1963 it was a business selling cottage lots on Sebec Lake. Today, the two-story brick building is the Union Square Mall, and houses several offices. The three buildings to the right were combined into a single storefront, and were recently renovated for a café and gallery. In 1957, Fred Peters opened Peters' Pharmacy in that location. On the Foxcroft side was a drinking trough for livestock, with a lower drinking bowl for dogs. Cattle and sheep frequently passed through town en route to market.

Dover, showing Foxcroft Falls, around 1908.

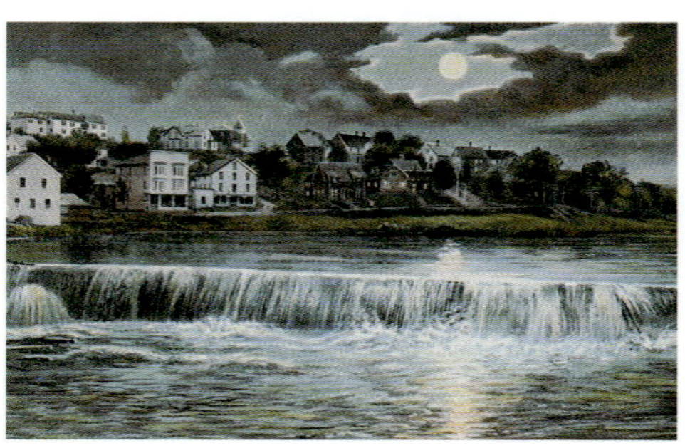

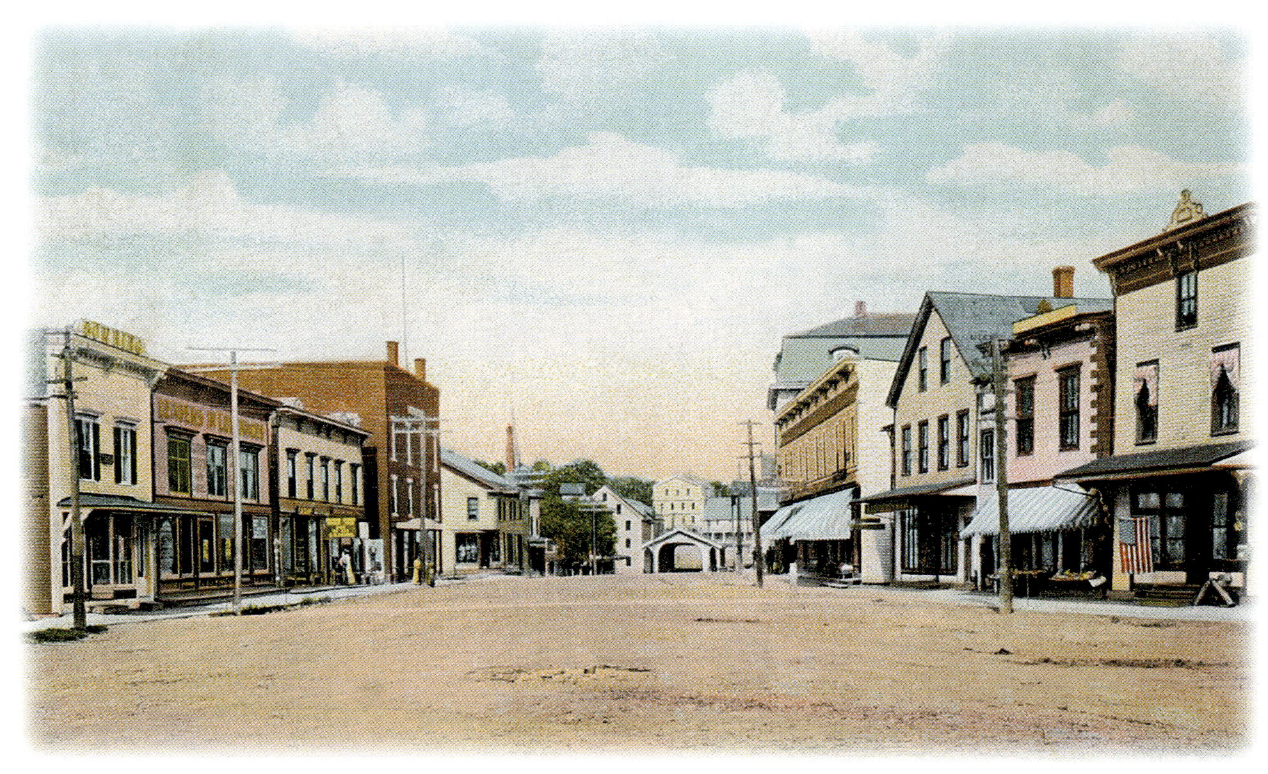

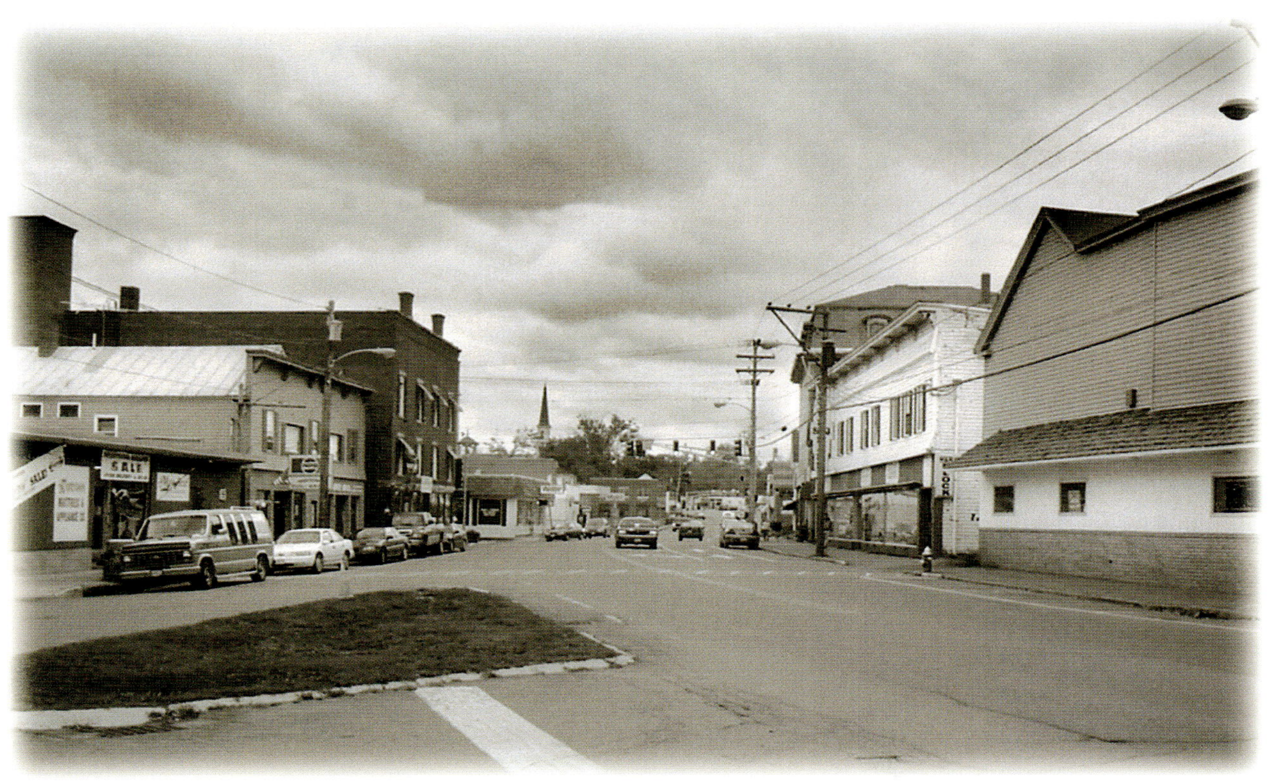

Eastport

INCORPORATED AS MAINE'S
115TH TOWN ON FEBRUARY 24, 1798

INCORPORATED AS MAINE'S
19TH CITY ON MARCH 3, 1893

POPULATION IN 1900: 5,311

POPULATION IN 2000: 1,640

Eastport is home to many superlatives. It was so named because it is America's easternmost city. Maine's first sardine-canning business began here in 1875. And the 45th parallel crosses through its boundaries, marking the spot where one could stand halfway between the equator and the North Pole. It also has the greatest span of tides in the United States, up to 28 feet from high to low tides (leaving boats resting crazily on their keels in some places).

It is also an island city in a collection of islands. Moose Island is the largest, connected to Carlow Island by a tidal-dam causeway. The other islands are Dog, Treat, Burial, Spectacle, Matthews, Goose, and Dyer. The town itself was originally known as Moose Island, and Lubec was set off from it in 1811.

During the nineteenth century it was a major shipping center, rivaling the port of New York in the 1850s. It is the closest U.S. port to Europe by one day, and the

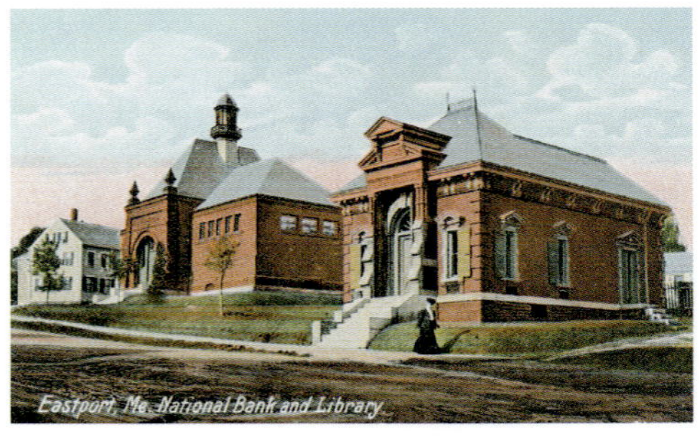

National Bank and Library

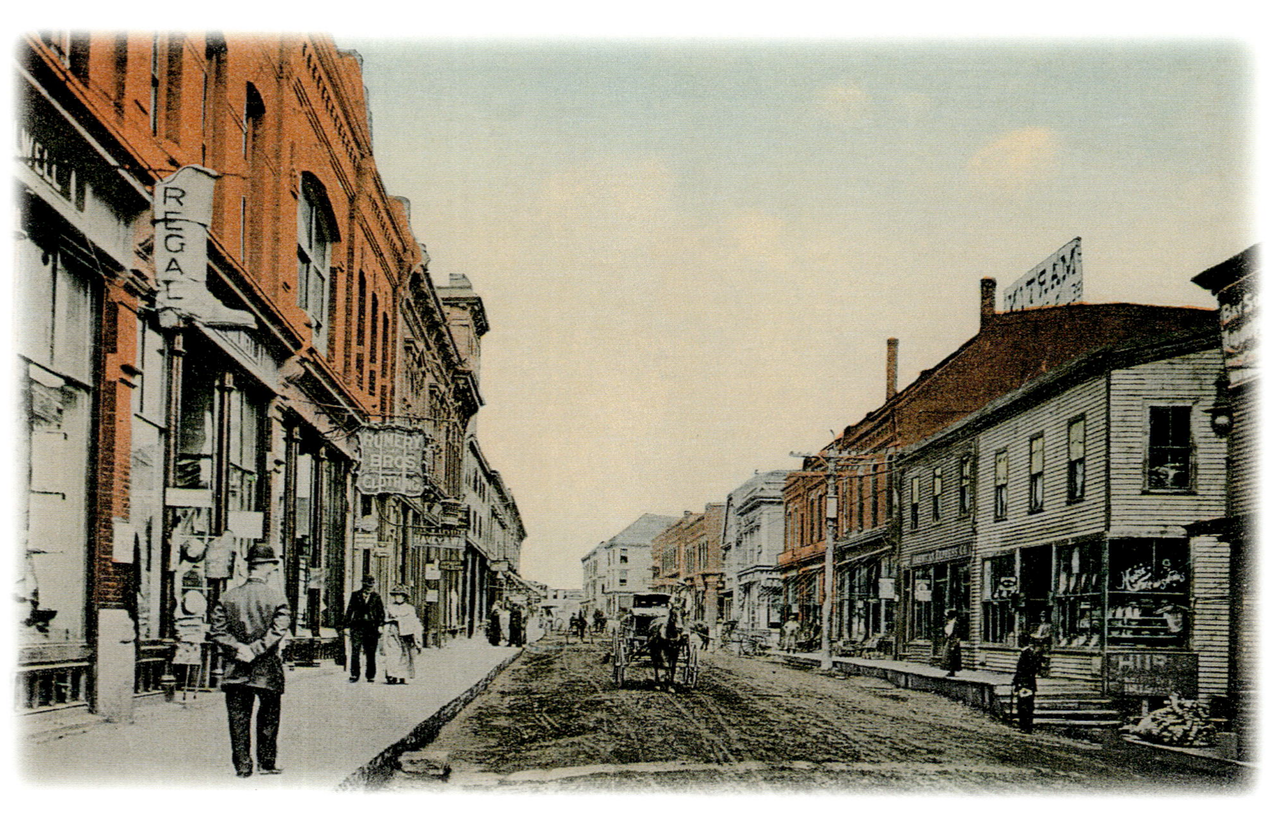

vast majority of products shipped today are forest products such as paper and pulp. In 1900 there were approximately three dozen sardine canneries in the Eastport-Lubec area, and by 1905 Maine produced nearly all of the country's sardines. But as the fishery dwindled, so did the factories, and the last cannery closed in the 1980s. Fading, too, are the memories of sardine factory whistles that called people to work—two blasts for processors, three for flakers, and four for packers. Raye's Mustard Mill, which formerly made mustard sauces for the sardine industry, is America's only remaining mill producing stone-ground mustard.

A new fish-based industry has emerged in recent years: aquaculture. Now Eastport and the surrounding Maine and New Brunswick communities are the North American capital for farming Atlantic salmon in sea pens. There's even a Salmon Festival held in September to celebrate the industry. The first commercial nori seaweed production and processing facility in North America also began here. (Nori is used in sushi and other dishes.)

After a devastating fire in 1886, downtown Eastport was rebuilt with masonry in a mostly Italianate style. Most buildings were designed by Boston architect Henry Black and share a harmony of style and consistency of design. The entire downtown area is on the National Register of Historic Places.

Today Eastport is one of the last outposts of the Maine coast not overrun with summer tourists. It has had vacant storefronts for many years, but as the value of coastal Maine real estate continues to skyrocket, more people are finding Eastport an affordable community. On its Web site, the Chamber of Commerce urges potential visitors, saying, "If you feel diagonally parked in a parallel-parking world, maybe a trip to Eastport is just what you need!"

On the left of the postcard view of Water Street is a sign shaped like a giant boot with the word REGAL on it. A few doors down was the Rumery Brothers Clothing store, and on the opposite side of the street was the American Express Company office. A sign on the tall building faces the water and spells MARTIN backward—evidently so people on incoming ships could read it.

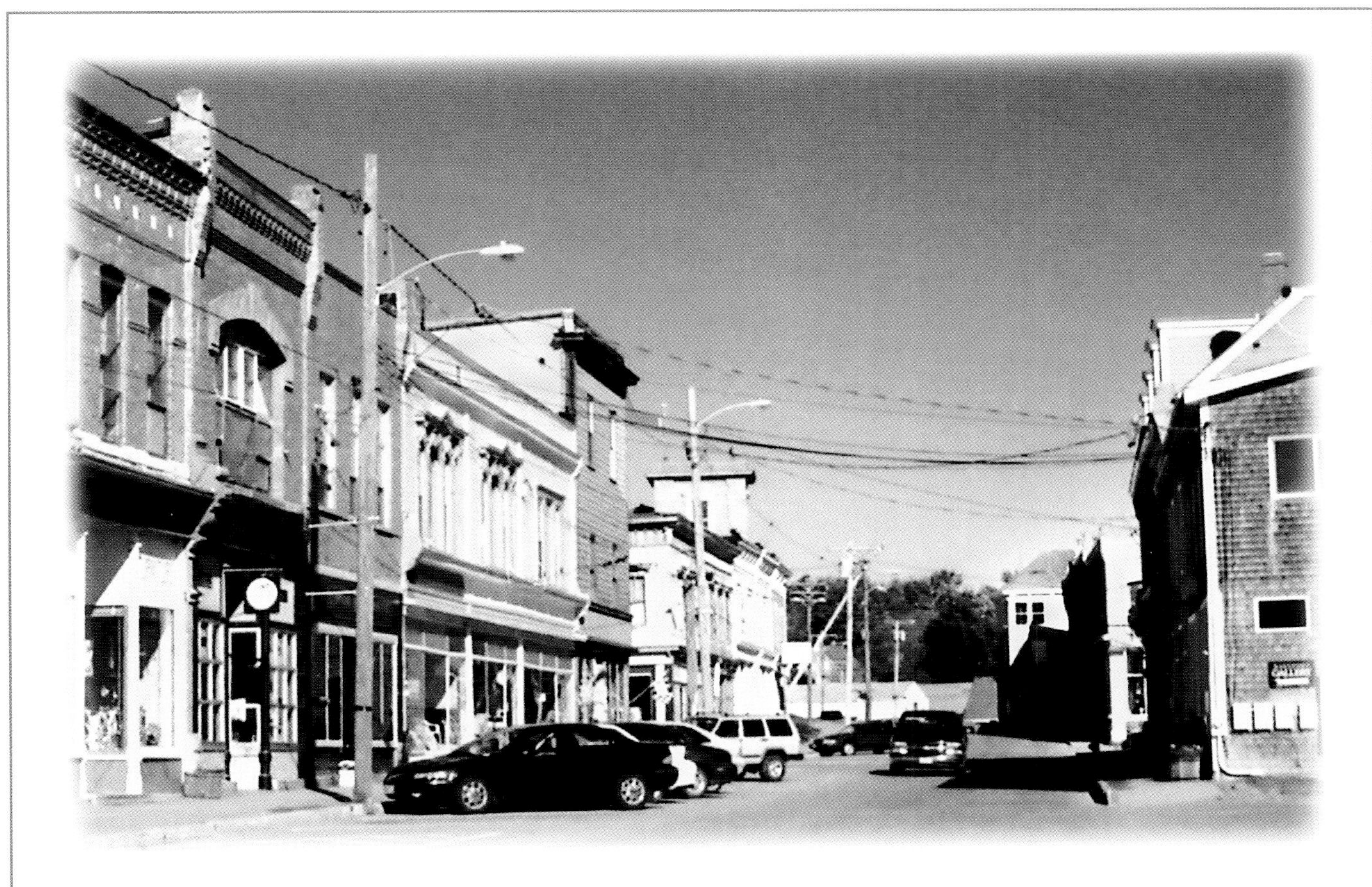

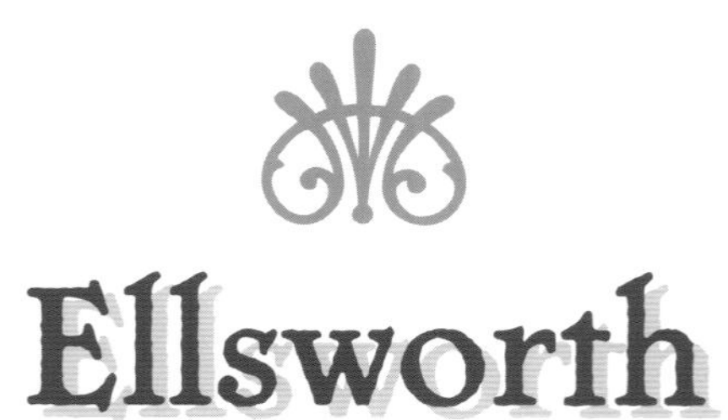

Ellsworth

INCORPORATED AS MAINE'S
124TH TOWN ON FEBRUARY 26, 1800

INCORPORATED AS MAINE'S
14TH CITY ON FEBRUARY 6, 1869

POPULATION IN 1900: 4,297

POPULATION IN 2000: 6,456

Like many Maine towns, Ellsworth was cobbled together from parts of several early-day townships that lay alongside the Union River (first named the Mount Desert River). It was named for Oliver Ellsworth, the third chief justice of the U.S. Supreme Court, who never even visited his namesake.

The river, dammed along its seven falls, was lined with wharves for building ships and mills for sawing lumber at the turn of the twentieth century, making Ellsworth the barrel-stave capital of Maine. Now the mills and wharves are gone, and over time the river silted in, no longer a powerhouse for industry. Today the river is lined with shops, car dealerships, vacant lots, and the city's waste-treatment plant. However, a recent dredging project restored the five-foot depth at low tide, which has resulted in increased boat traffic for the city dock, and planners are developing further changes to make the riverfront a more viable and accessible asset.

Fire and water reshaped the face of Ellsworth in the twentieth century. In 1923 the new Graham Lake Dam was breached by heavy spring runoff, destroying the Route 1 bridge and most of the buildings on the east side of the river. An even greater tragedy occurred a decade later, almost to the day. More than 130 buildings—three-quarters of the city's businesses—were destroyed by fire in May 1933, including the City Hall and most of the town's records. Many Main Street stores were rebuilt later that year.

Mary Laury, executive director for Schoodic Arts for All, said it was the resurrection of the Grand Theatre that spurred the rejuvenation of Main Street. Built in 1938, the Grand closed in the early 1960s and was scheduled for demolition before a citizens' group saved it. "There was a time when the town was kind of dying. Small stores were closing, there were a lot of vacancies," said Laury. "Now Main Street's gotten a lot more artsy." The Grand now hosts fifty concerts and performances a year, featuring both local and internationally known personalities.

Although Main Street retains its vitality, Ellsworth's gateway location to Bar Harbor has given it a split personality. Just around the corner on High Street is big-time sprawl. Tourists heading to Acadia National Park must first run the gauntlet of fast-food and department store chains, not to mention the many "tourist traps" all along the way. Fortunately, the downtown area retains a distinct charm and identity despite this influx.

In the postcard of Main Street, the foreground buildings, built in the 1830s, were evidently untouched by the fire of 1933. However, most of the buildings down the block are dated the year of the fire. The Granite Block in the middle of the postcard was built in the early 1850s from Sullivan granite. The foreground building on the corner of Water Street was occupied by Wiggin and Moore Druggists at the turn of the century. By 1927 it was Moore's Pharmacy, and has been occupied by the *Ellsworth American* and other businesses. In a 1963 photograph, it was Moore's Drug Store, and the adjacent building was Kane's Cut Rate, selling tobacco, cosmetics, perfumes, vitamins, and sundries. A barbershop was upstairs. In the middle of the street are the Adams and Joy blocks, built in 1933, and at the end is the 1933 Austin Block, now Harry C. Austin & Co. Furniture. New streetlights evoking an earlier era were installed in 2000.

INTERESTING TIDBIT:

President William Howard Taft visited Ellsworth on July 23, 1910.

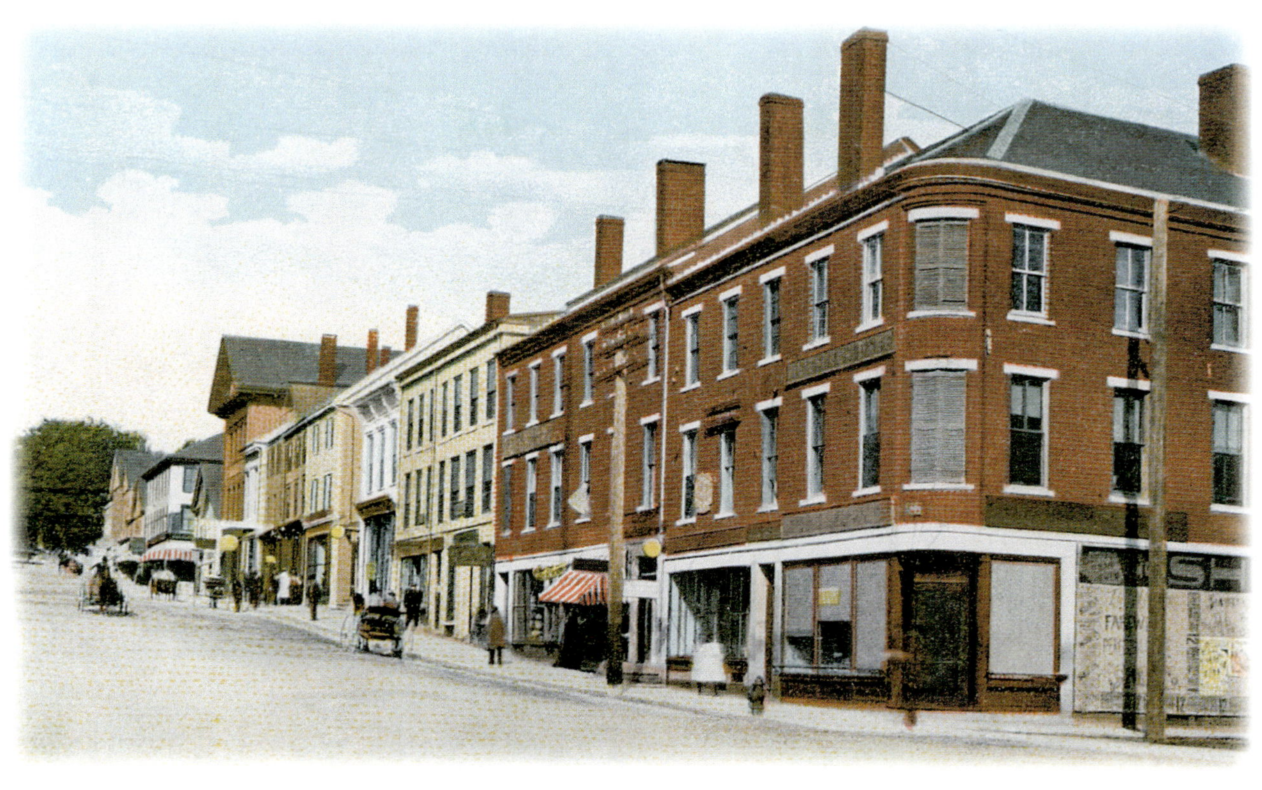

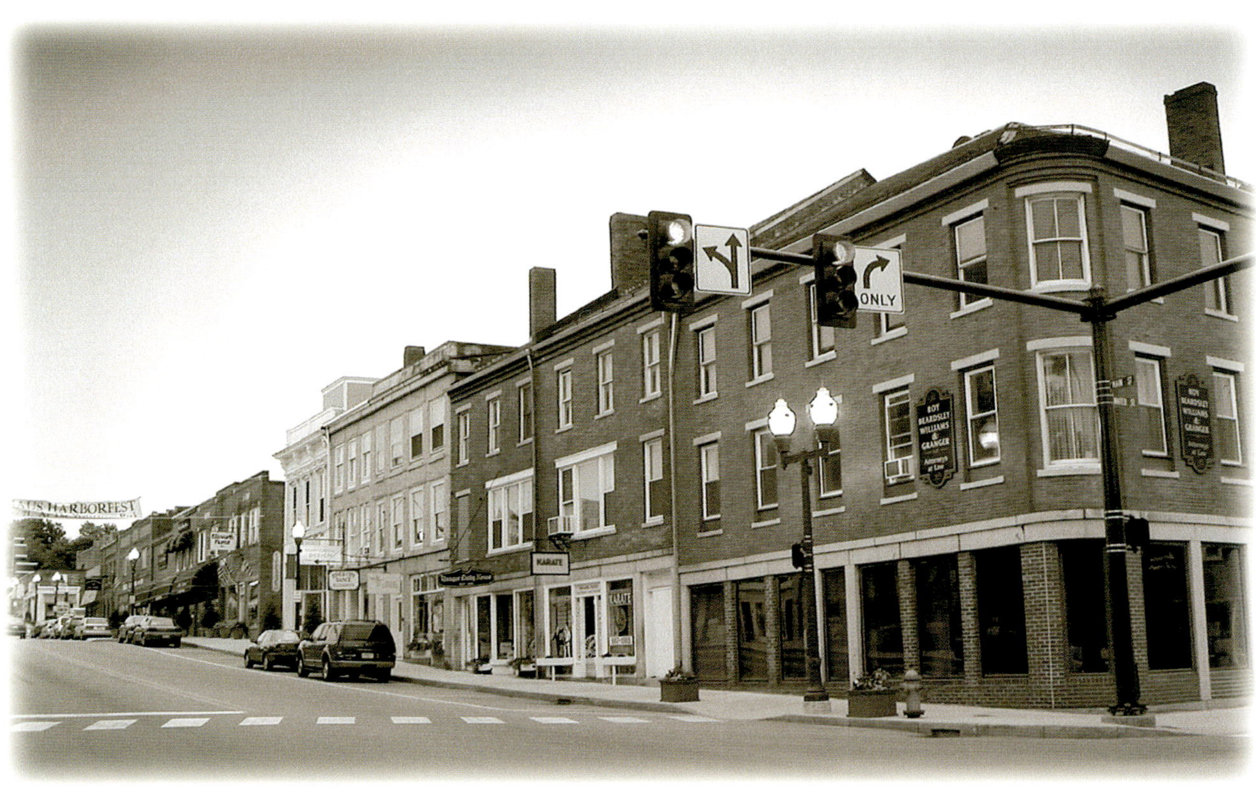
ONLY
KARATE
ROY BEARDSLEY WILLIAMS & GRANGER

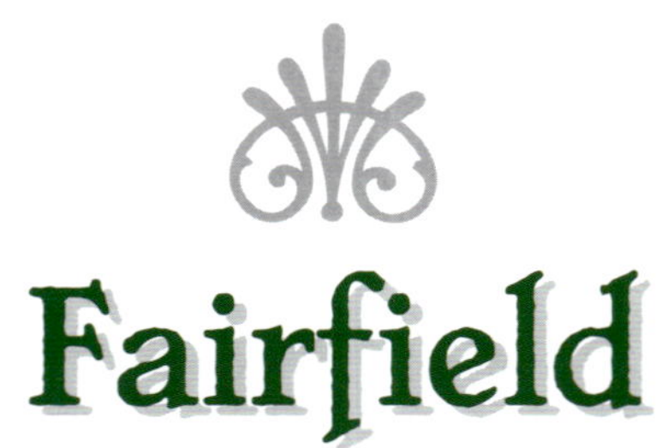

Fairfield

INCORPORATED AS MAINE'S 56TH TOWN ON JUNE 18, 1788

POPULATION IN 1900: 3,878

POPULATION IN 2000: 6,573

It was a town named for its "fair" appearance, but it took more than a hundred years after the town's incorporation before the extraordinary Gerald Hotel, would turn *fair* into *grand* (shown on the left in the postcard below). The highly ornamented hotel with its German helmet-style domes was built in 1900, and hosted its last guest in 1937. It was one of the most elegant hotels in the state, made of pressed brick with large plate-glass windows and a roof garden. The nine-by-nineteen-foot threshold is made from the largest single piece of cut granite ever quarried in Maine, weighing sixteen tons.

Amos F. Gerald, who built the first electric railroad in Maine, devoted himself to various enterprises designed to increase ridership on the trolleys. Since he built the hotel, he considered it within his right not only to name it after himself, but also to include his bust on the center dome. It was topped with a sculpture of Mercury, the god of speed. Many prominent men, including presidential candidate William Jennings Bryan and Franklin D. Roosevelt, spoke from its ornate balconies.

The ground floor at the right of the entrance was occupied during its hotel days by the Lawry Brothers Furniture Store, which like many furniture stores of the day served as undertakers on the side to facilitate the selling of coffins. The building has been extensively remodeled by its new owners, the Northern Mattress and Furniture Galleries. The gorgeous relief figures, Renaissance-style paintings, tin ceilings, stained glass, and woodwork make this a fabulous setting for any shop.

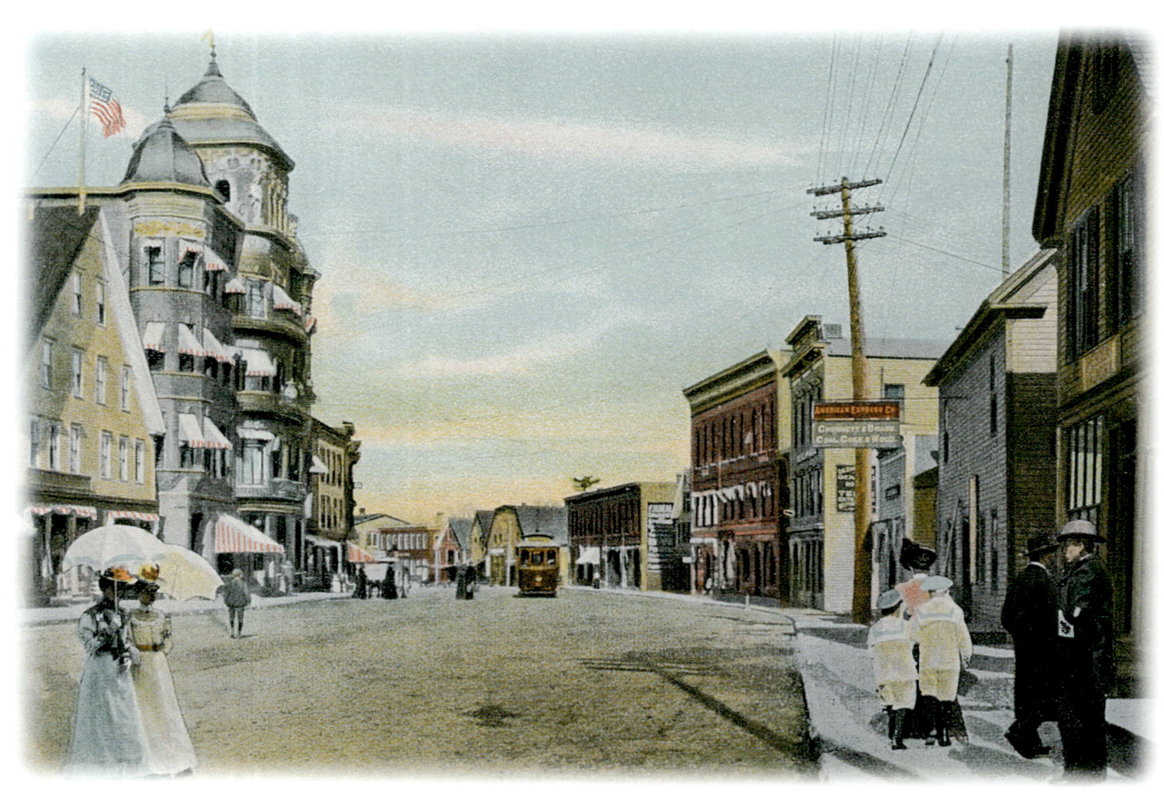

At the turn of the twentieth century, Fairfield was dominated by lumber mills and forest-products factories such as Shawmut Manufacturing Company, which cut dimension lumber and pine clapboards. The Keyes Fibre Company made disposable wood-fiber containers, and Somerset Fibre Company later became United Boxboard and Paper Company, which consolidated with Kennebec Fiber Company in 1902. The S. A. Nye Manufacturing Company's fifty employees made famous Steinbach novelties, including desks, chiffoniers, chairs, and other wooden furniture.

One of the more interesting enterprises was started by a man who witnessed an injustice as a child and wanted to do his part to improve the moral fabric of society. The Reverend George W. Hinckley saw a classmate arrested for stealing food because his widowed mother had no money to feed him. He later established the Good Will–Hinckley Home in East Fairfield (now Hinckley) in 1889 to house and educate homeless boys.

To the left of Northern Mattress in today's photograph is a tiny little building which at one time was a sports shop. On the cornerstone is inscribed JOSEPH 1956. Joseph's Golf Shop is now on the other side of the old hotel. Since the photograph was taken in October 2001, the buildings in the background were removed so the conjunction of three bridges over the Kennebec could be made into one. Three trolley lines once terminated here as well. The Waterville, Fairfield and Oakland line lasted the longest, operating until 1937.

On the right side of the street in the postcard was the Crescent Laundry, now the post office. The signs on the telephone pole say AMERICAN EXPRESS and CRUMMETT AND BRAGG, COAL COKE AND WOOD. The three-story brick building in the middle is the Masonic Hall, and the front of the building bears the names of E. Kelley and E. F. Files.

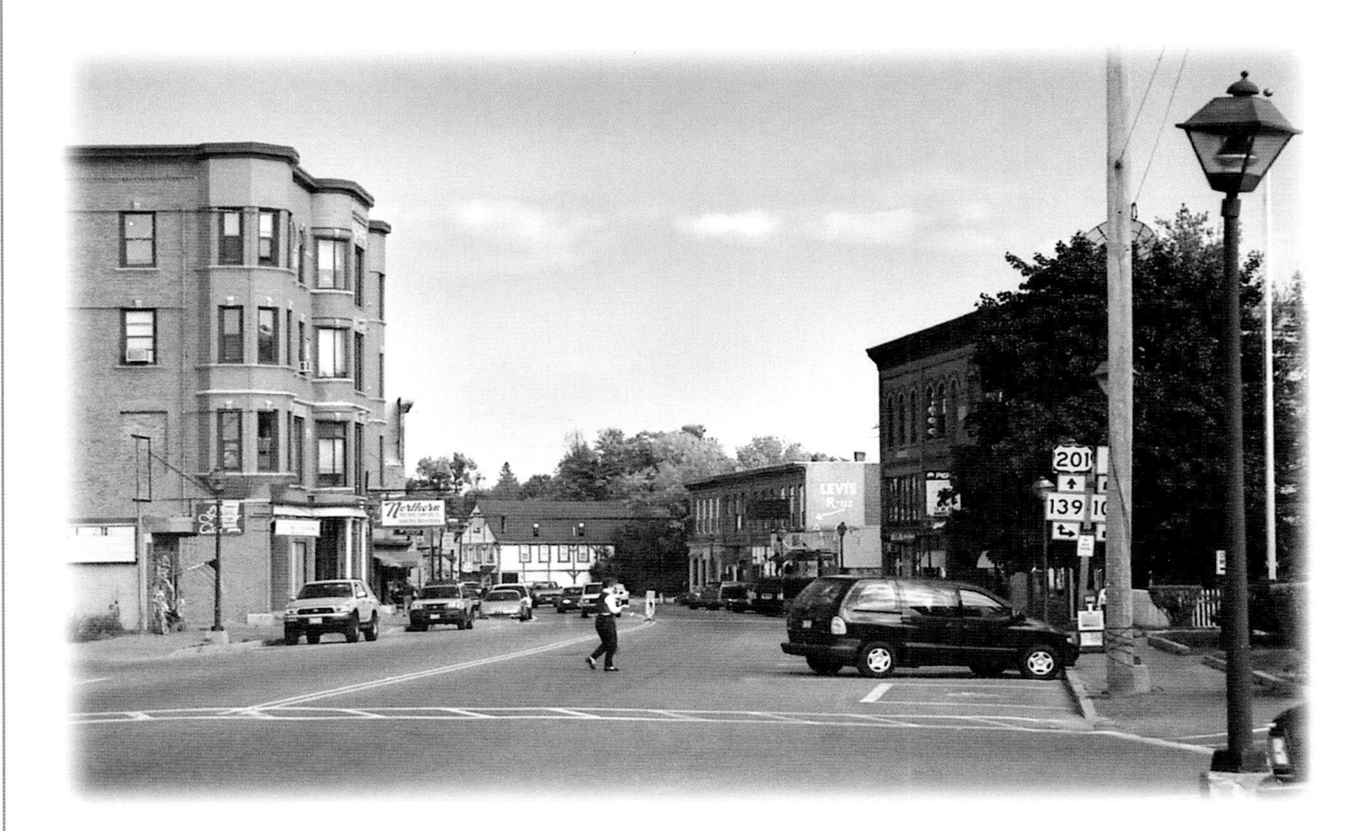

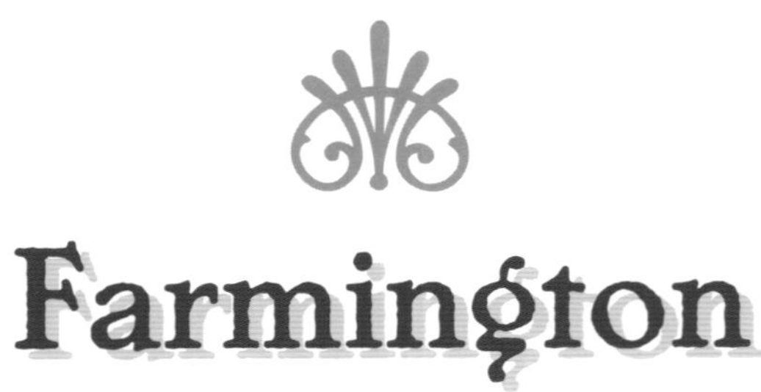

Farmington

INCORPORATED AS MAINE'S
83RD TOWN ON FEBRUARY 1, 1794

POPULATION IN 1900: 3,288

POPULATION IN 2000: 7,410

Originally known as the Sandy River Township, Farmington has several claims to fame: earmuffs, a college, a singer, and a photographer. Well, maybe not too many people know that Charles H. Sawyer spent the early years—from 1904 to 1920—establishing his Sawyer Pictures Company in Farmington before he moved operations to Concord, New Hampshire. A protégé of Wallace Nutting, Sawyer photographed New England landscapes and tinted them with colored paints.

In 1857, opera singer Lillian Nordica was born as Lillian Norton in Farmington. She performed at some of the world's greatest musical centers: St. Petersburg, Paris, London, and the Metropolitan Opera in New York. In the 1930s her birthplace was converted into "a shrine for music lovers," (according to the July 1930 *Sun-Up* magazine) with some of her extravagant costumes and personal effects on display.

The University of Maine at Farmington has been consistently listed in *U.S. News and World Report* as one of the top one hundred colleges in the country. It began as the Western State Normal School in 1864, when Maine leaders lobbied for passage of the Normal School Act. After many incarnations, it merged with the University of Maine System in 1968 and continues its emphasis on producing teachers, with about half the graduates receiving education degrees. Enrollment today numbers around 2,000 students.

So now on to earmuffs, which are cause for yearly celebration even though hardly any are made today. Fifteen-year-old Chester Greenwood, a Farmington native, couldn't wear woolen scarves because they made him itch, so in 1873 he bent some baling wire to form two ear-shaped loops and had his grandmother sew fur pads on them. At the age of nineteen, he patented a better model, and Greenwood's Ear Protector Factory made a fortune supplying Ear Protectors (he never called them earmuffs) to American soldiers in World War I. That's when Farmington became the Earmuff Capital of the World. A parade every December features people and animals wearing earmuffs, or decorations that look like them.

Another industry that kept Farmington humming was the Franklin Shoe Company. It made a hundred different styles of shoes that could be dyed any color. In later years, the company started importing shoes from Asia, and in 2000, the plant closed, putting more than 200 people out of work. A year later, however, Dyeables, Inc., moved its headquarters from Auburn to the Farmington factory, where it will handle sales, distribution, and dyeing of shoes and handbags.

In the postcard of Broadway Street looking west, the corner building on the left was the First National Bank (today, Kyes Insurance). The center building just downhill, founded in 1892, reads W. W. SMALL CO.—FLOUR, GRAIN, FEED & GROCERIES, HARDWARE, FARMING TOOLS. On the right corner was the Red Store selling "Men's and Boy's Clothing." It was remodeled in the 1930s as Ferrari Brothers men's clothing, which continued through the 1970s. Today, a multicultural boutique called Liquid Sunshine occupies the space; its owners began by vending beads, crystals, and vintage clothing at Grateful Dead concerts. Next down the street was the Broadway Garage, followed by Spinney's Auto Garage.

Peoples Bank is on the left edge of today's photograph. An advertisement for People's National Bank (note that it still carried the apostrophe) in 1930 stated, "If you repeat the magic formula 'Deposit this, please!' with sufficient frequency, the deposit book becomes a talisman of great potency. It points the way to prosperity and independence."

INTERESTING TIDBIT:

In a 1969 supplement to the *Franklin Journal*, it was noted that "Farmington has been selected as the area for an emergency capital in case of nuclear attack."

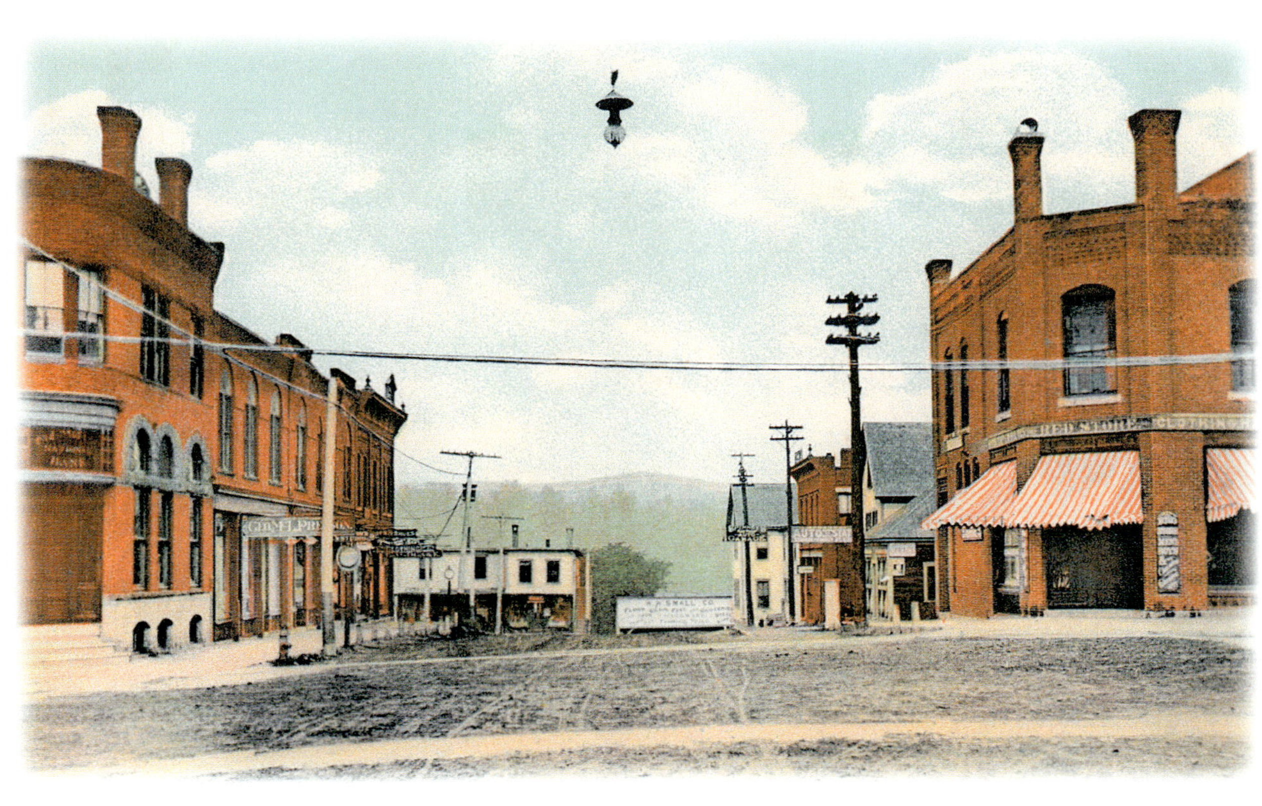
RED STORE

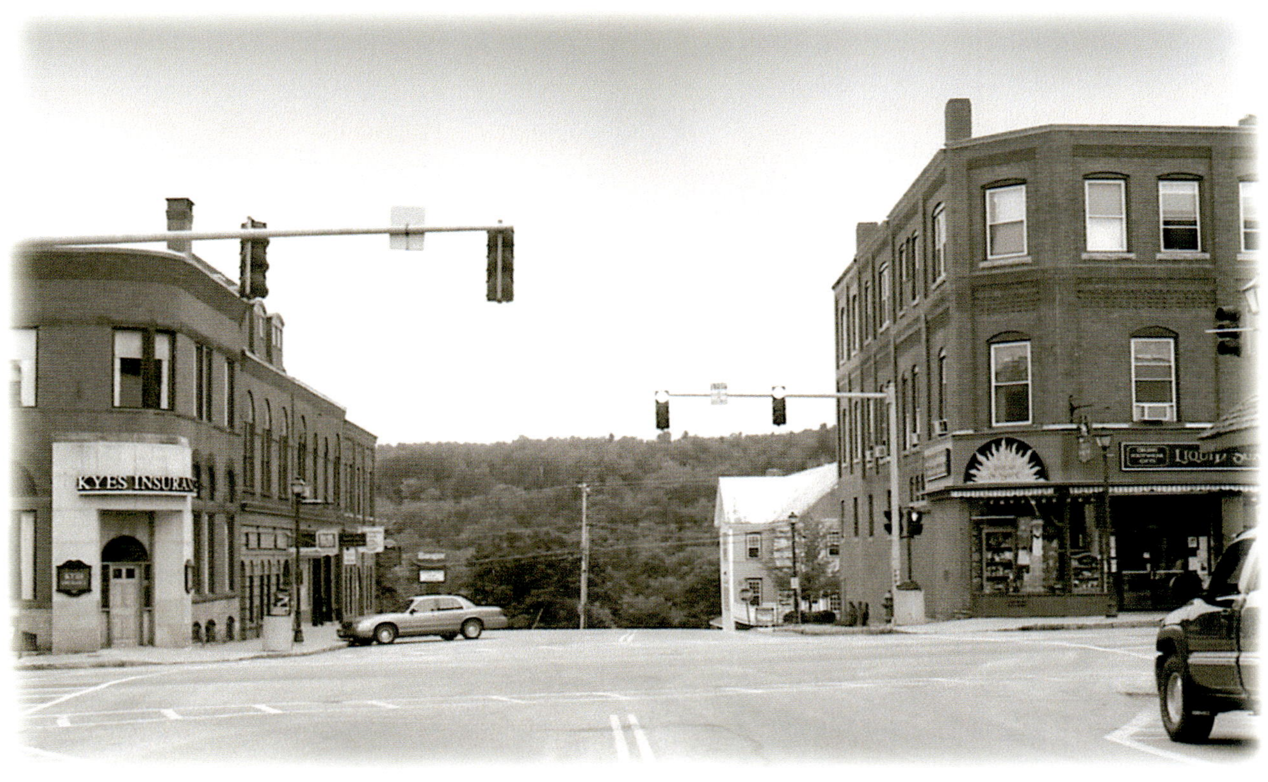
KYES INSURAN

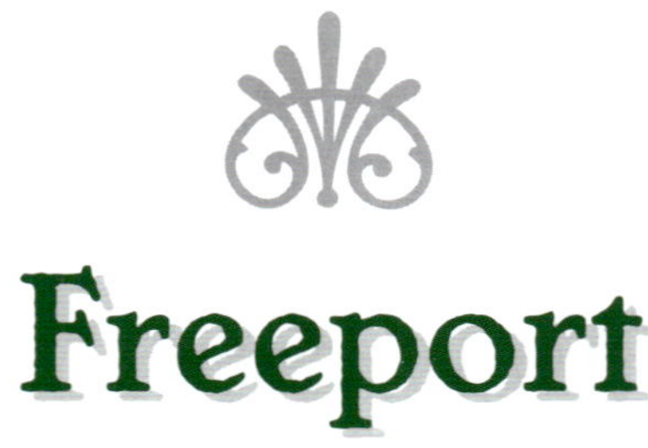

Freeport

INCORPORATED AS MAINE'S
64TH TOWN ON FEBRUARY 14, 1789

POPULATION IN 1900: 2,339

POPULATION IN 2000: 7,800

A mecca for factory-outlet shoppers, Freeport has a thriving Main Street, perhaps at some cost to its soul. Its wide Main Street turn was originally designed to accommodate the transport of huge ship masts from the forest to the wharves. The British Royal Navy was so adamant that pines of a certain height and diameter be reserved for the King that there were fines for unauthorized cutting. These tremendous poles were loaded at Mast Landing at the head of tide on the Harraseeket River.

Freeport was set off from North Yarmouth, and today the Harraseeket Historic District encompasses the villages of Mast Landing, Porter's Landing, and South Freeport. Shoe making was the major industry in the twentieth century. The Freeport Shoe Company operated until 1972, employing five hundred people. The building was razed in 1980. Eastland Shoe Manufacturing had been operating in Maine since 1955 when it closed its Freeport factory in 2001, going the way of most manufacturers by relocating its plants overseas.

Maine author John Gould wrote about the Congress boot, made by the H. E. Davis shoe factory in Freeport. This was an ankle-height, dressy sort of boot with no lacings and elastic sides, allowing the boot to be easily slipped on or off. They were quite popular among congressmen, sea captains, sailors, and average citizens alike. Gould wrote that they were, er, *provided* to customs inspectors when ships arrived from foreign ports of call to ease their way through customs.

A December 28, 1909, fire destroyed Main Street

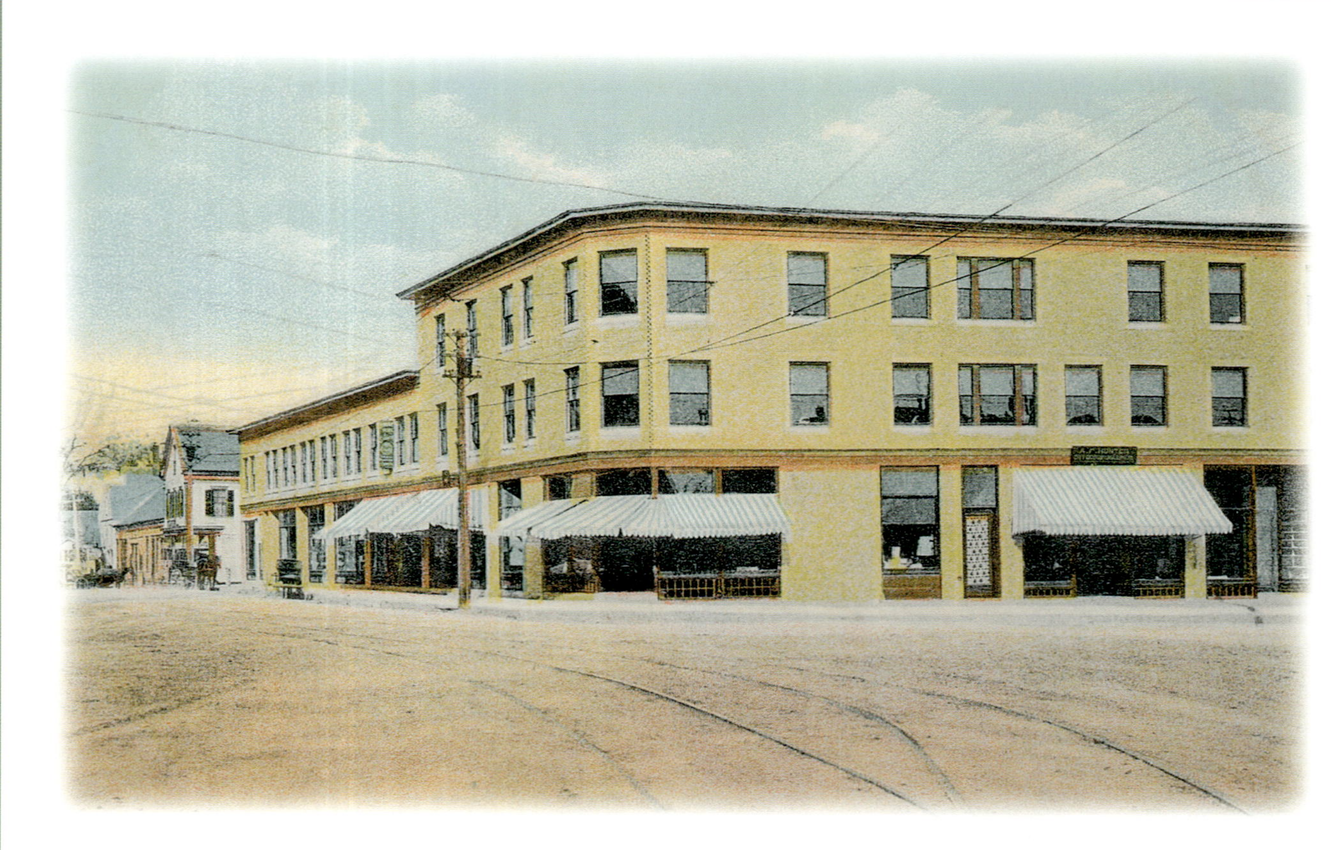

between Bow and Mechanic Streets, snuffing out more than a dozen businesses. In the postcard of Post Office Square, the Clark's Hotel replaced the Harraseeket House which burned in that blaze. It later became Leighton's Five-and-Ten, which burned due to arson on September 22, 1981. That left a gaping hole in an already dying downtown, and created opportunity for outside planners to develop the existing commercial mix of factory outlets and mom-and-pop stores. Of course, Freeport's strip is more upscale than most, thanks to detailed town design codes that govern renovations and new construction. Even McDonald's can't look too . . . *McDonald's-y*. After the fire, discounters, restaurants, and Maine and national-outlet stores alike began populating Main Street: Dansk, Hathaway Shirts, Cannon, Cole-Haan shoes, Frye boots. Tour buses now come by the hundreds, especially at holiday time, so consumers can shop till they drop.

Of course, this may not have happened if L.L. Bean hadn't been there. It was and still is *the* anchor store of Freeport. In 1911, Leon Leonwood Bean designed the rubber-and-leather Maine Hunting Shoe, which became wildly popular. He had a store first in a basement and then on Main Street above the post office. It focused on mail-order business, since visiting the retail shop entailed a circuitous trip up the outer staircase to the second floor, where the shoes were manufactured.

The store expanded to 36,000 square feet in 1939 when it began designing boots for the military. A women's department opened in 1954, and in 1962 the store expanded again when the post office moved out. A new store was built in 1969, remodeled fifteen years later, and now totals nearly 200,000 square feet. By 1976 the company was receiving so many orders it had to acquire its own zip code. L.L. Bean has become synonymous with Maine hardiness and success. It has long had a reputation for quality and a money-back guarantee, and is particularly distinguished by its twenty-four-hour-a-day accessibility (since 1951). Today its sales total more than $1 billion.

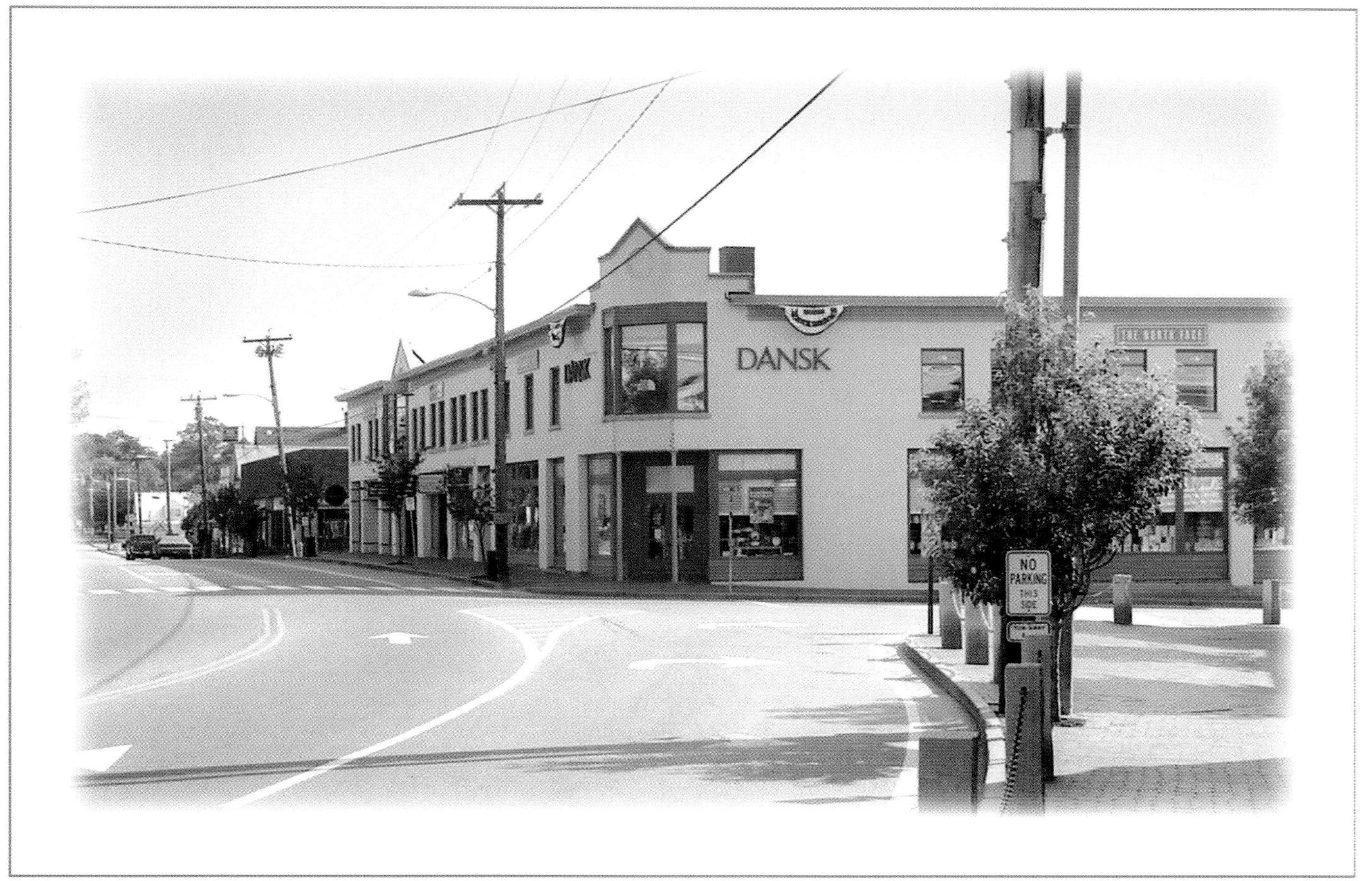

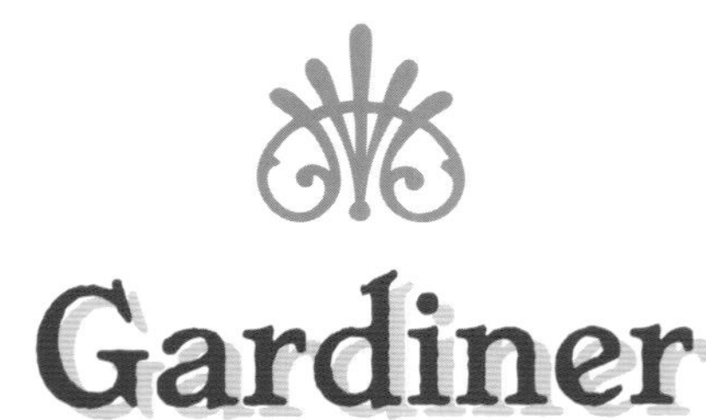

Gardiner

INCORPORATED AS MAINE'S
139TH TOWN ON FEBRUARY 17, 1803

INCORPORATED AS MAINE'S
5TH CITY ON AUGUST 11, 1849

POPULATION IN 1900: 5,501

POPULATION IN 2000: 6,198

Although credit is usually given to Dr. Silvester Gardiner for the city's name, there's a strange little twist to that. It was known after 1754 as Gardinerstown plantation, because the Boston physician developed mills and factories along the 130-foot drop of the Cobbossee Stream where it joins with the Kennebec River.

But Dr. Gardiner sided with the British during the American Revolution and was exiled to England. He returned to Rhode Island the year before his death, and willed his estate in Maine to his four-year-old grandson, Robert Hallowell—contingent upon the boy's agreement to change his surname to Gardiner. Until the boy reached legal age, nobody in Gardiner wanted to improve or develop land without clear title. (The town of Hallowell was named for the boy's other grandfather.) Robert Hallowell Gardiner claimed his title in due time, became the principal landowner, and the town blossomed. Pittston had been set off from Gardinerstown in 1779, and in 1803 the new town of Gardiner was set off from the area of Pittston on the west side of the Kennebec.

Ships, shoes, paper, and ice dominated the economy through the nineteenth and early twentieth centuries. By the time the shipping industry started to fade, ice harvesting from the Kennebec was becoming a mainstay, and would remain so through the 1920s. Shoe factories employed thousands. In 1947 the Commonwealth Shoe Company employed 450 people and produced 3,000 pairs of men's shoes a day, mostly the Bostonian and Mansfield national lines. The Gardiner Shoe Company's output was 2,400 pairs of men's Yorktowns a day. It later became the R. P. Hazzard Shoe Company, then Gardiner Shoe, before the building was razed in 1971.

There is little manufacturing in Gardiner today; it has become a bedroom community for state workers in Augusta and for employees of Bath Iron Works, as well as commuters to Portland.

There are forty-seven buildings included in the Gardiner Historic District along both sides of Water Street, as well as the railway station just behind Water Street. The postcard of Water Street shows five Romanesque Revival structures built in the 1890s. On the far left was Chester H. Beane's Drugstore, built in 1895. Gardiner Oil bought the building around 1960, and it was sold to Webber Oil in the 1980s. Dentists' offices were on the second floor. Next door is the block built by William Wood in 1896, the first tenant being H. M. Davis's clothing store. An 1896 newspaper described it as being "light and commodious, finished throughout in white pine, it is as nice as can be." It also housed P. F. Noyes Photography on the third floor. The Gosline-Murchie Insurance Agency occupies both buildings today. The 1896 Patten Block and its neighbor, formerly occupied by the post office and Oddfellows Hall, today house Renys Department Store. Renys also occupies the slightly bowed Masonic Block, built after the postcard was made.

On the right edge of the postcard is the 1903 Gardiner Real Estate Association Building. The Evans Hotel on the site had burned two years earlier. It also housed American Express on the first floor and the Maine Trust and Banking Company on the second. The Knights of Pythias Hall occupied the top two floors. At some point the top two floors were removed, and it later became the National Bank of Gardiner. In the 1980s the building housed Merrill Trust, before becoming Fleet Bank by the end of the decade. Gardiner Savings Institution, built in 1891, abuts the real estate building in the postcard. The bank building and adjacent commercial block were replaced in 1954 by Gardiner Savings Bank.

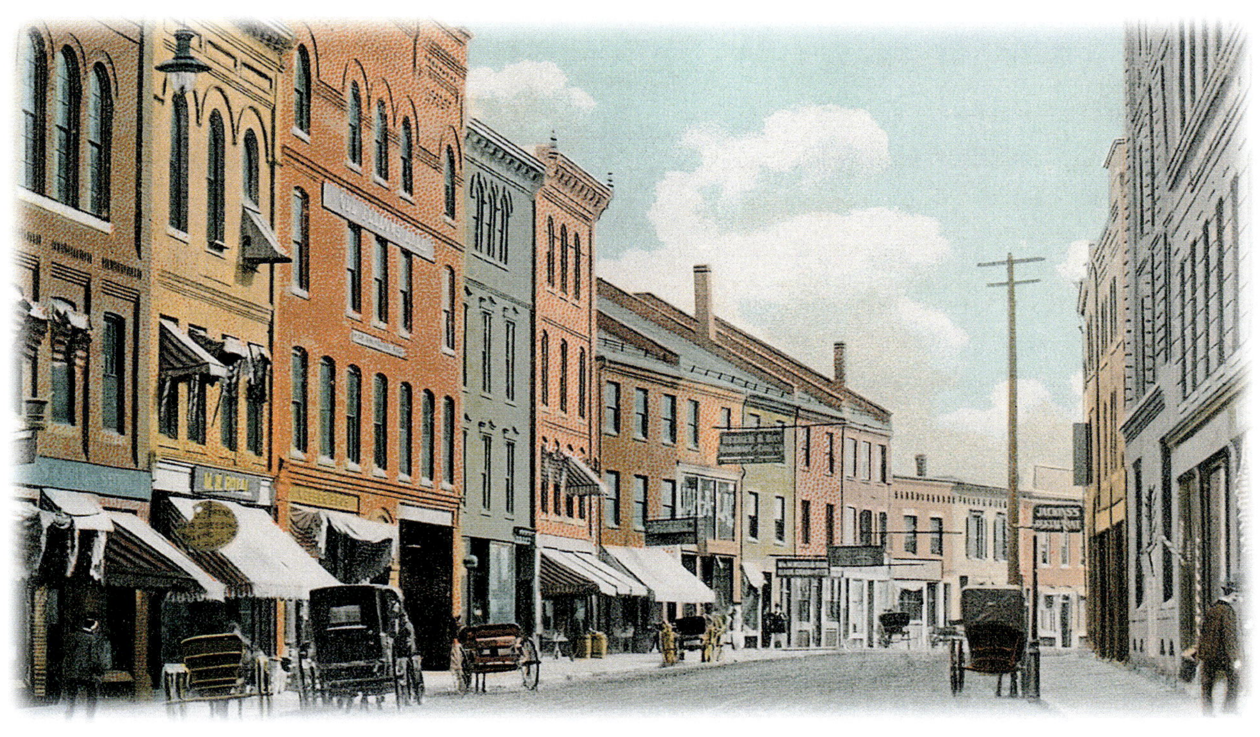

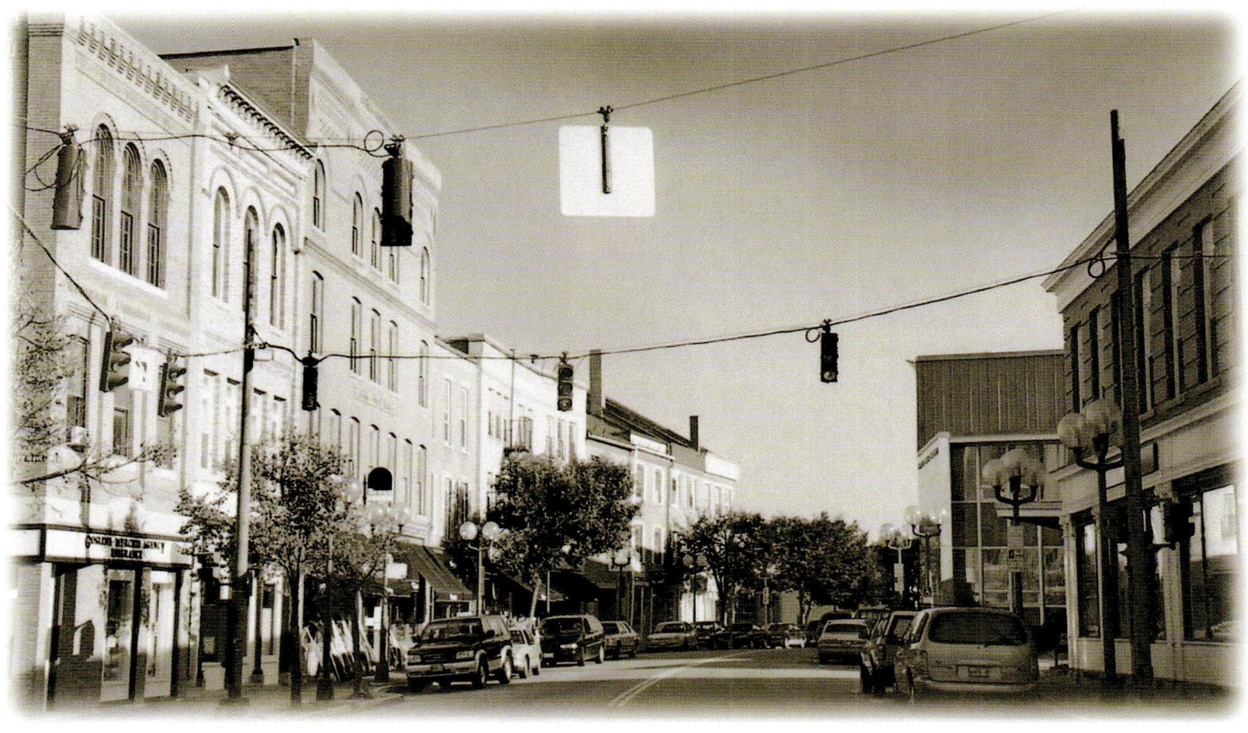

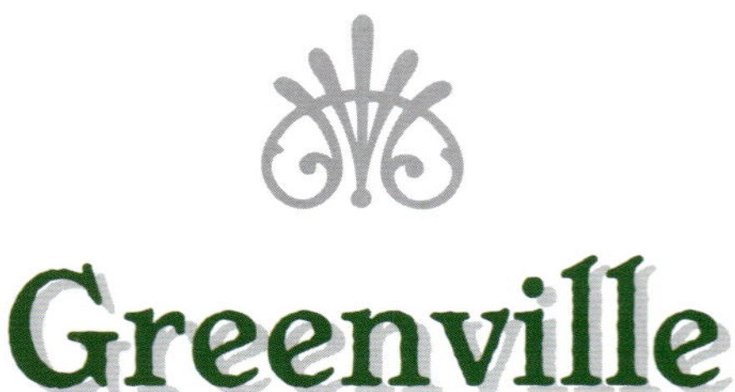

Greenville

INCORPORATED AS MAINE'S
329TH TOWN ON FEBRUARY 6, 1836

POPULATION IN 1900: 1,117

POPULATION IN 2000: 1,623

Greenville, located at the southern end of Moosehead Lake, is promoted by the town's Web site as being "perched at the wilderness edge of sparsely populated Piscataquis County." There's even a photo on the site with a caption that reads HIGH RATE OF MOOSE CRASHES NEXT 3.0 MILES. Not one to downplay its remoteness, Greenville instead capitalizes on its attributes as a recreation center. The summer population more than triples, and around a thousand lodging rooms in the general area are available for those wishing to partake of the Moosehead Lake experience. There are seaplanes, snowmobiles, skis, sled dogs, a steamer, and hiking trails to make it happen.

Originally part of Haskell plantation, the settlers voted to incorporate the new town as Cuba—nobody seems to know why—and then as New Saco, before finally settling on Greenville by the time incorporation papers went to the legislature.

Of course, lumbering has long played an important role in Greenville's economy. In 1900 the Great Northern Paper Company began operations on the east side of Moosehead Lake, cutting numerous roads into the wilderness. The Atlas Plywood Corporation mill employed around 120 men in 1936. In the 1930s the Hollingsworth and Whitney (H & W) lumbering company employed as many as 1,200 men. The H & W was bought by Scott Paper Company in 1954, which sold out to South Africa Paper & Pulp International (SAPPI) around 1990, and in 1998 was again sold to Plum Creek Timber Company, Inc.

Greenville Junction was known as West Cove

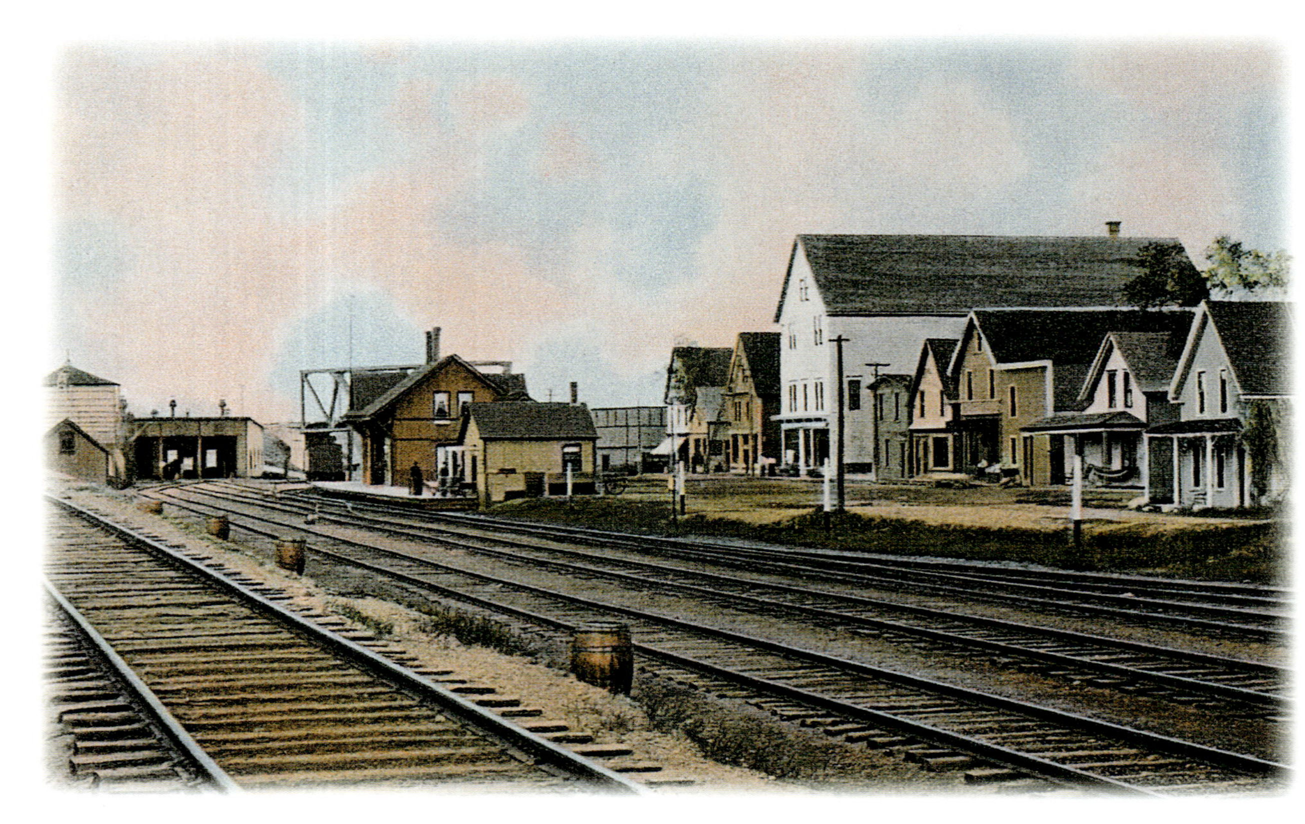

until the arrival of the Bangor and Piscataquis Railroad (later the Bangor and Aroostook) in 1884. The Canadian Pacific Railroad arrived four years later. The postcard shows the Canadian Pacific train station at the far end of the tracks, with the trestle behind it. The ground to the left had to be leveled to accommodate the additional tracks.

Beyond the station was the YMCA (not pictured), built by the H & W in 1911. This building also served as a ten-bed hospital, and was later used for furniture manufacturing before it burned in 1943. In its place today is Junction Wharf, the public parking lot across from Currier's Flying Service and its floatplanes dock. Incidentally, Currier's is where the Moosehead Inn was located before it burned in 1912.

The four-story building in the center was Arthur A. Crafts's store, which lost its top floor in a fire in 1913, and burned again in 1926. The top was repaired and is now The Depot, a small summer theater. The tracks were torn up in 1938 and the residential lane is now Depot Street.

For a town that bills itself as "a gateway community to the North Maine Woods," it seems anomalous that Greenville has a sixty-acre industrial park for a handful of businesses engaged in light industry and commercial building contracting. The largest is the Greenville Steam Company, producing electricity from biomass.

The annual seaplane fly-in over Labor Day weekend began in 1973, and hundreds of planes crowd the local airport and lake moorings, with concessions lining Main Street. Also berthed at Greenville is the 1914 steamer, *Katahdin*, affectionately known as Kate. She was the largest and last of the steamer fleet that carried visitors to the nearby Mount Kineo resort hotel.

REMARKABLE RESIDENT:

Henry Perley, "Chief Henry Red Eagle" (1885–1972), was a Penobscot Indian who earned his Maine Guide license at age fourteen, penned more than five hundred short stories, and was a silent film star. In some movies, he drew a higher billing than Mary Pickford.

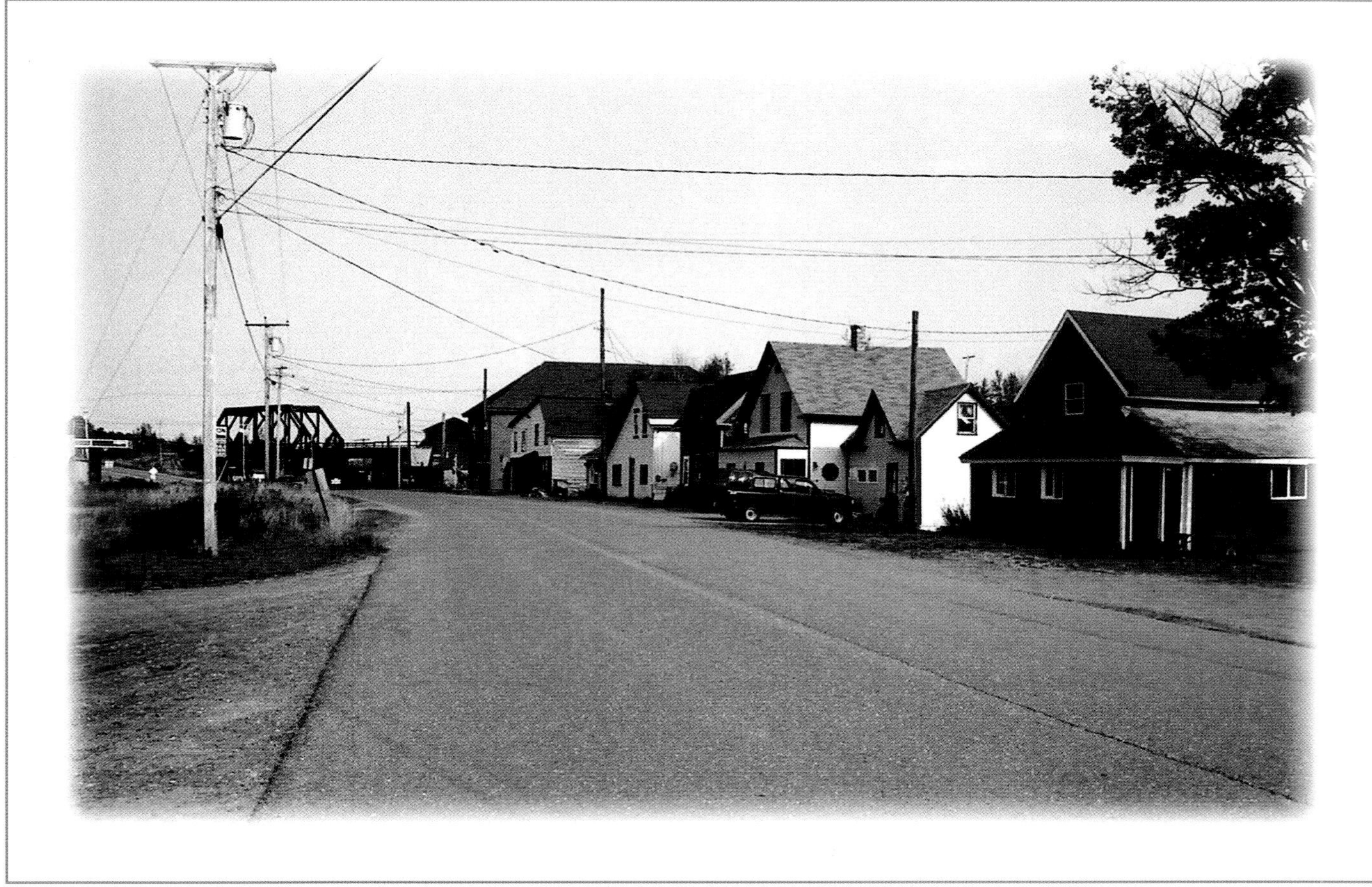

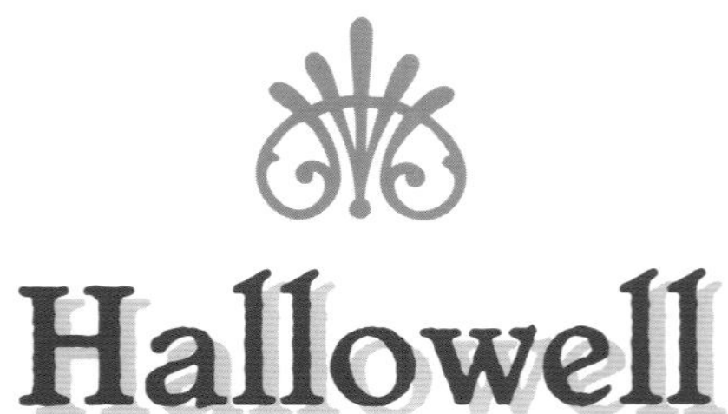

Hallowell

INCORPORATED AS MAINE'S
21ST TOWN ON APRIL 26, 1771

INCORPORATED AS MAINE'S
8TH CITY ON AUGUST 29, 1850

POPULATION IN 1900: 2,714

POPULATION IN 2000: 2,467

Early proprietor Benjamin Hallowell gave his name to the settlement known as *Bombahook*—or "the Hook" for short—an Indian word for a nearby stream. Originally, the township of Hallowell encompassed present-day Augusta, Chelsea, and parts of Manchester and Farmingdale.

Hallowell is probably best known for its granite. One of its first projects was quarrying all of the granite used in the Maine state capitol building a few miles upriver in Augusta. Hallowell's soft white stone was particularly suited for statuary, as it broke cleanly and carved easily. In the early 1900s artisans came from the British Isles, Scandinavia, Italy, France, and Portugal to carve statues that sold for $100 a foot.

Chockablock with antiques shops, cafés, and historic buildings, Hallowell's Water Street was once "a slum," according to Virginia Lathe Clark, a town resident since 1936. "There were a lot of bars, and a lot of stores had illegal gambling with card games and such." Now the entire city—one of the country's smallest—is a National Historic District, and "maintains a bohemian, mellow atmosphere," according to a *Boston Herald* writer. Live entertainment is hosted in several coffee shop and pub venues, and Slate's Restaurant is perhaps the most well known.

In 1975 the Maine Department of Transportation wanted to raze the old buildings on Water Street to widen the road, but citizens turned out en masse to protest. Sumner Webber, city historian, was one of the participants in the "Save Hallowell" campaign, which featured a parade led by the police chief, and the hanging in effigy of the DOT commissioner. Preservationists had already been actively pursuing Historic District designations for the old buildings in the city, and the DOT finally backed down.

In the postcard of Water Street, the prominent building on the left with the false-roof siding is now Boynton's Market. The building housed the post office and Ballard's Market when Arthur Boynton took it over in 1936. A beauty shop was located in the back. His employee, Charles "Jim" Whitten, developed a mincemeat pie recipe that made Boynton's Market famous. (Mincemeat ingredients include apples, beef, sugar, raisins, suet, molasses, vinegar, and spices.) An advertisement in 1991 said, "Still made the original way . . . by hand. Over a ton made yearly!" As Sumner Webber recalls, "Everybody got mincemeat from Boynton's at Christmastime."

To the left of Boynton's was a variety store. In the 1930s it was a Socony filling station, and now Slate's Bakery sits in back alongside an antiques store visible in today's photograph. Down the street was Dodge's Dollar Store in the 1950s, now Hallowell Printing Company, and upstairs was the Heart Cure Company, a patent-medicine company that mixed its concoction with huge paddles, in big vats. A new post office had to be built in 1931 to accommodate the amount of mail churned out by this business.

Farther down were Shea's Fish Market in the 1950s and Gardiner Savings Bank. Behind the telephone pole in the postcard was a bakery operated by the Hayes family for nearly a century. The big brick ovens that were used to bake both beans and bread were removed several decades ago, and an antiques store now occupies the building. Sumner Webber has vivid memories of his childhood trips to the Hayes Bakery during the World War II years, when he would pick up a loaf of warm bread just before noon. "Every Saturday we got baked beans from the oven, and on Easter there were hot cross buns for Good Friday. We got our birthday cakes there, too, and they'd put your cake in the window and everybody could see it was yours."

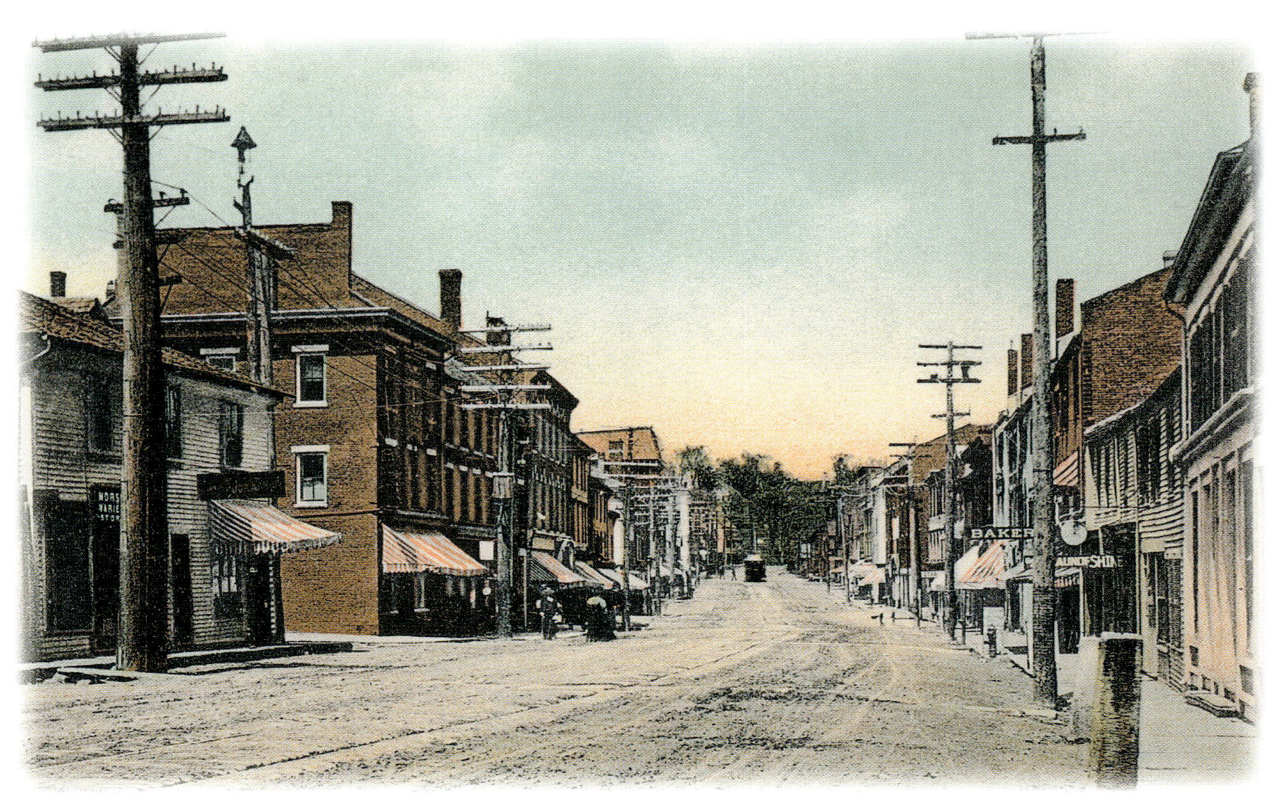
BAKER

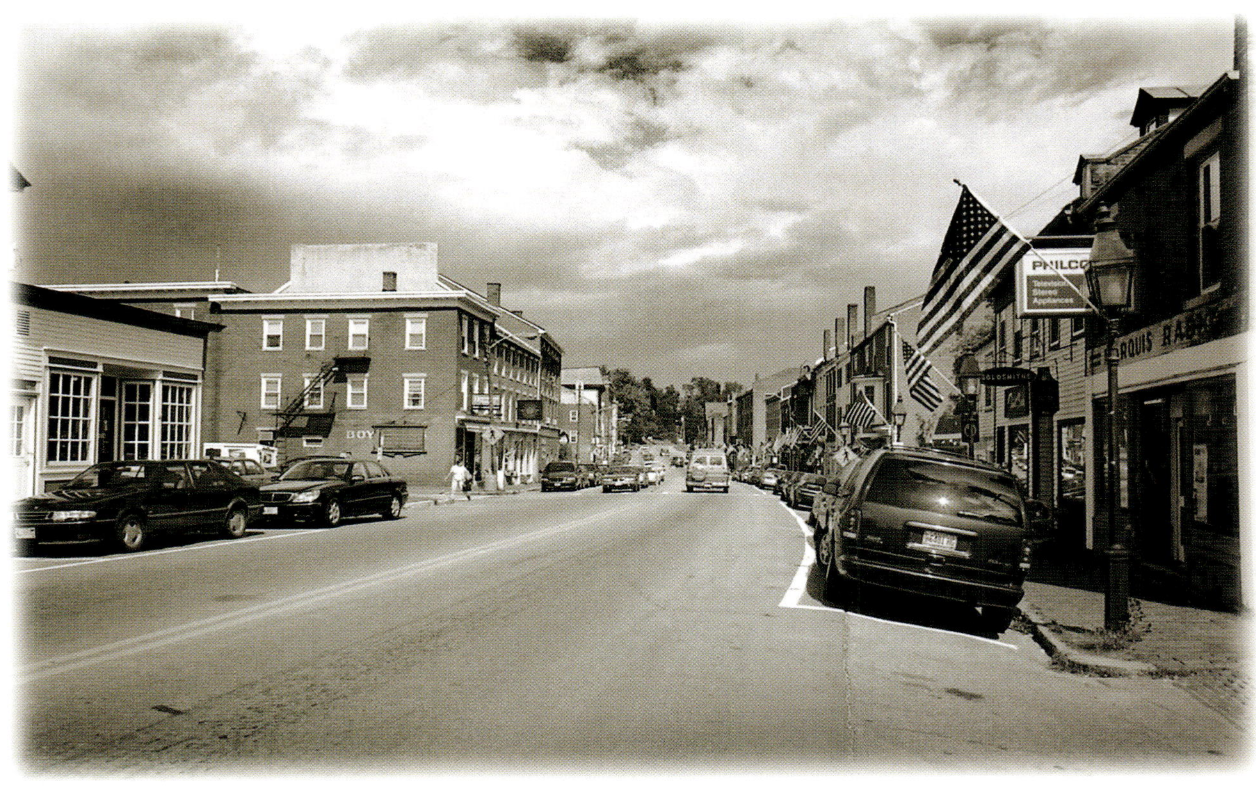
PHILCO
Television
Stereo
Appliances

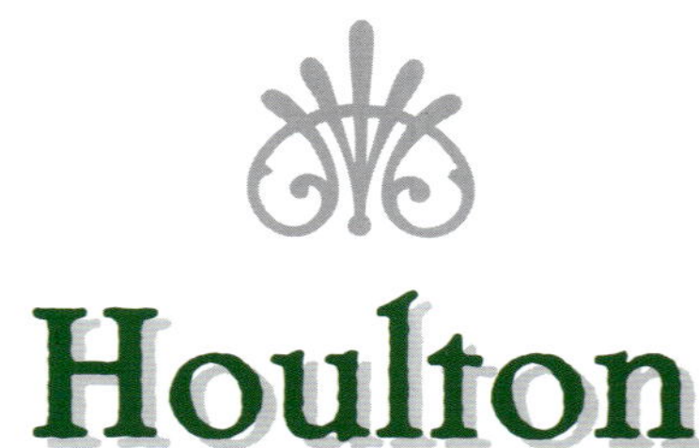

Houlton

INCORPORATED AS MAINE'S
291ST TOWN ON MARCH 8, 1831

POPULATION IN 1900: 4,686

POPULATION IN 2000: 6,476

In Aroostook County, potatoes define the changing of the seasons. In the old days the seasons were known as Planting, Summer, Digging, and Winter. Digging, of course, was the busiest, and even today high schools take a three-week recess to allow the kids to help with the harvest. Kay Bell, who grew up on a potato farm in nearby Monticello, said that before World War II, the schools didn't recess for harvest. "All of us farmers' kids just stayed home, and then we had to make up the work."

Potatoes were grown in the Houlton area from the time of the first white settlement in 1805, but when the New Brunswick Railroad opened a branch line in 1870, the tuber became a commercial crop. Thanks to the renowned "Caribou loam," Aroostook County is quite compatible with potato growing. In addition to fresh and processed potatoes, 90 percent of the country's potato starch once came from "the County." The burgeoning textile mills relied on the starch for sizing cloth.

In 1903 Houlton had twenty-two potato houses and shipped 1,032 carloads of potatoes. Figures for Houlton aren't kept these days, but by way of comparison, all of Aroostook County shipped 37,689 carloads in 2003. The starch plants operated through the 1950s, and A. E. Staley Manufacturing still operates in Houlton, producing food starch used to thicken gravies and processed foods. The 1950s saw several bad years in the potato industry, and as a result, the town lost around 2,000 people in that decade.

During World War II, the Houlton Army Airfield (Camp Houlton) became a prisoner-of-war camp for

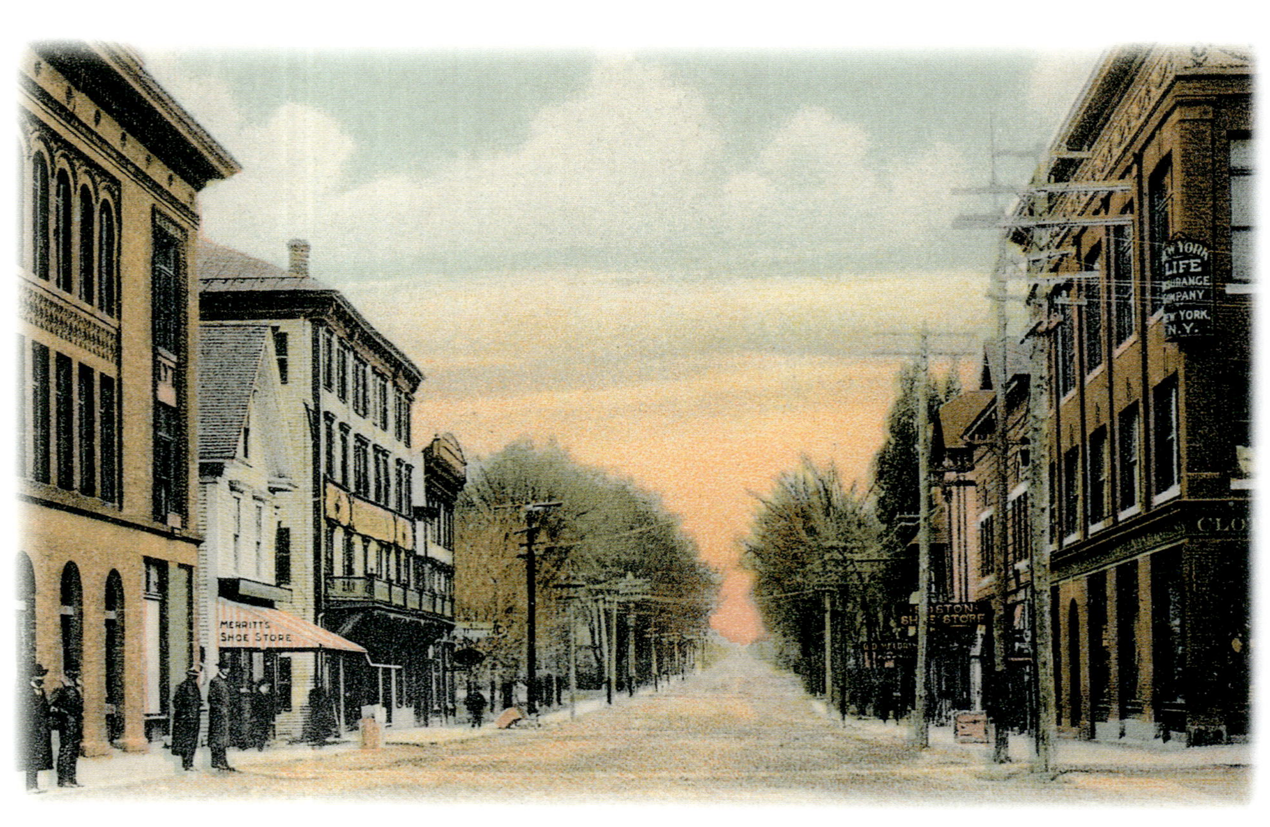

as many as 2,100 German prisoners. The fascinating aspect is that they weren't treated so much as prisoners, but as members of the community. The army needed food and pulpwood, and local men were off fighting the war, so the prisoners—many of them just kids—were put to work hand-picking potatoes and harvesting pulpwood. When the Germans left the U.S., they left as friends. In September 2003, four former POWs in their seventies and eighties returned to Houlton for a reunion, and a ceremony was held at the Houlton International Airport, site of Camp Houlton.

As in many towns, fire brought about its share of change. An inferno on May 17, 1902, which started in the Fogg Block on Main Street, destroyed seventy-five buildings, three churches, and nearly twenty business blocks. The Exchange Hotel and livery on Court Street was saved, preventing the fire from spreading further up the street.

The postcard shows Court Street at the corner of Main Street in Market Square. On the left, the building with arched windows was French's Drugstore, and remained so for many years, later becoming Bither's Clothing until around 1995 (it's vacant today). Merritt's Shoe Store with the red-striped awning is a secondhand shop today. The 1880 Hotel Exchange, which survived the fire four decades earlier, burned to the ground in May 1942. There was a livery stable adjacent to it. On the right side of the street, the New York Life Insurance Company took up the corner residence, with a clothing store on the ground floor. Adjacent was the John A. Millar's confectionary and fruit store, Houlton's first brick building. The Boston Shoe Store sign is prominent between the buildings, and the old Opera House was next door. The latter was renovated as the Heywood Apartments in the late 1920s. Not visible in the postcard but obvious in today's photograph is the steeple of the Court Street Baptist Church.

INTERESTING TIDBIT:

Interstate 95 was extended to Houlton in 1967, making it the end of the nearly 2,000-mile highway.

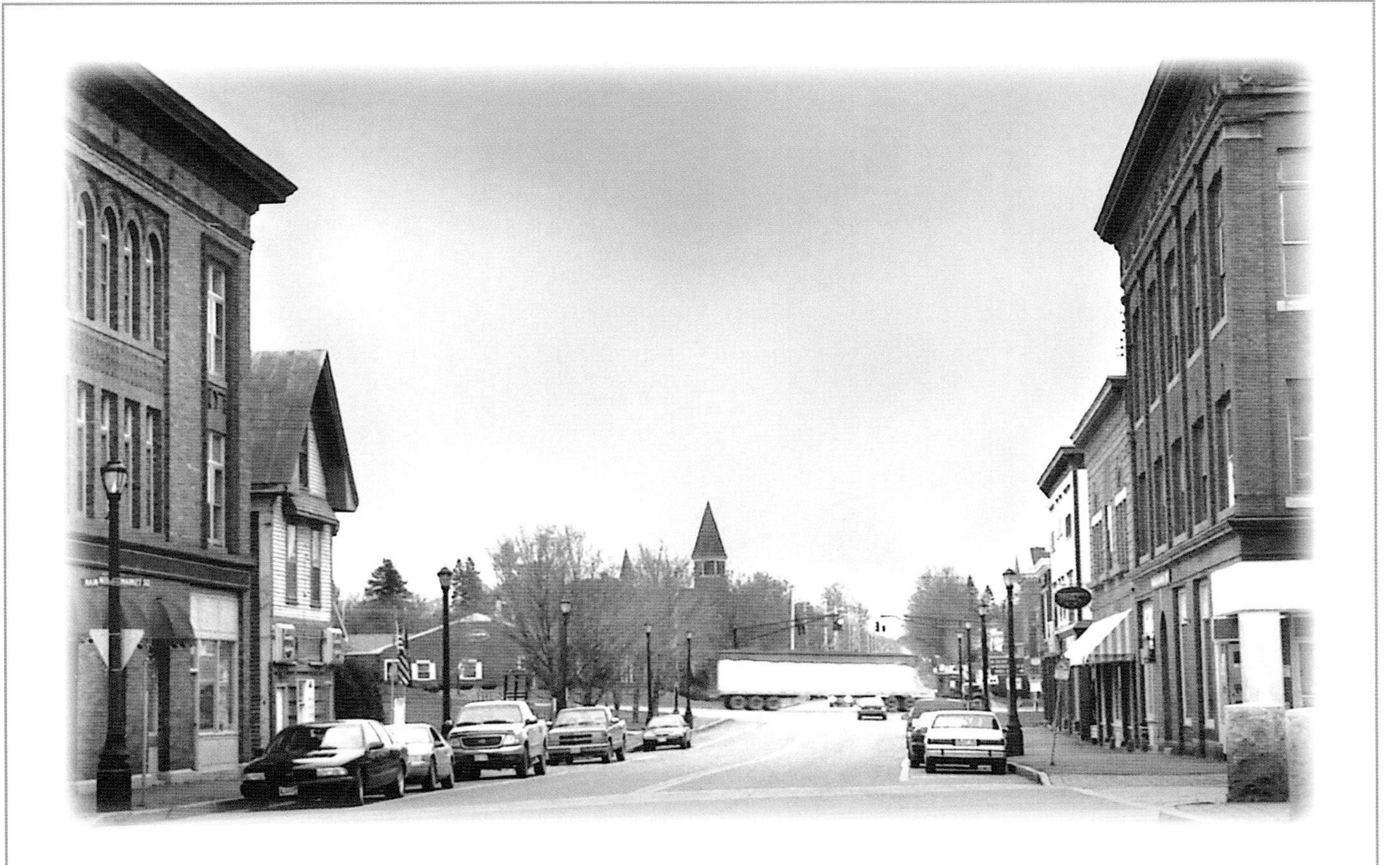

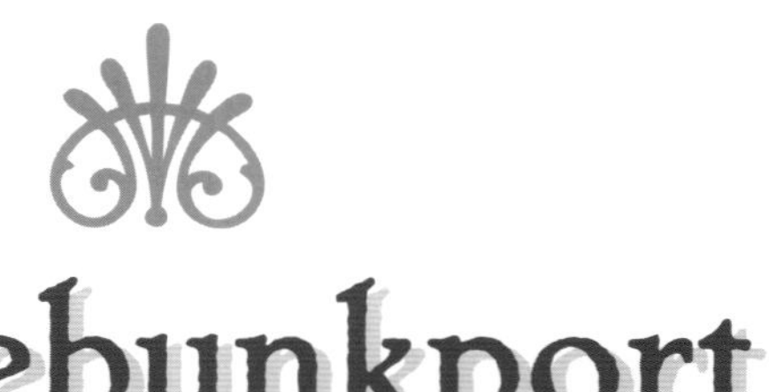

Kennebunkport

INCORPORATED AS MAINE'S
5TH TOWN ON JULY 5, 1653

POPULATION IN 1900: 2,193

POPULATION IN 2000: 3,720

Originally inaugurated as Cape Porpus, named for the graceful sea mammals seen offshore, this southern Maine settlement was renamed Arundel in 1719. By 1820 the nearby town of Kennebunk had garnered a good reputation in the business community, and, wanting to ride to success on its neighbor's coattails, Arundel changed its name to Kennebunkport in 1821.

In the nineteenth century the town was the state's second richest due to its maritime industry, with hundreds of vessels built on the Kennebunk River. The influx of summer people began in the 1870s, when four men from Arlington, Massachusetts, bought hundreds of rocky acres that the locals considered worthless for crops or pasture. Now Kennebunkport is a famous tourist destination and a retreat for third-generation summer resident George H. W. Bush and his family.

The postcard of Post Office Square (now Dock Square) shows Bonser's Bazar, which had previously been Miller's Drugstore in the Brown Block. Edward C. Miller opened the business in 1881, and his father Charles operated a competing drugstore across the street. They evidently prospered, and Charles sold his business in 1908 to George Weinstein, who sold fruit, vegetables, and gourmet foods there until 1971. In 1904 Kennebunk merchant George Bonser bought the Brown Block and added plate-glass windows on the Spring Street side. Edward continued operating the store until 1954, when Edward's pharmacist son Frank retired. It became the Colonial Pharmacy, and remains so today.

The post office, which oddly enough is not visible, was built in 1893 after operating out of an old building in Union Square. In 1911 Mrs. Alice Hodgkins rented the first floor as Hodgkins Variety Shop, selling sewing supplies and toys. In 1949 she sold the business to Adelaide Day. Alice holds the honor of being a storekeeper in Kennebunkport longer than any other woman. The building now houses Julia's Gift Shop.

The Soldier's and Sailor's Monument was hewn of Kennebunkport granite topped with a bronze eagle. It was erected in 1909 on the site of an old hay scale and wooden water pump, which by 1896 had been converted into an iron drinking fountain. A plaque added later on one side lists the Honor Roll for World War I.

From 1899 to 1927, the Atlantic Shore Line Railway trolley connected many points in York County. Today up to twenty tour buses may visit Kennebunkport during just one summer day, adding to the congestion of the small downtown shopping area. A $35 bus fee and an hourly quota were imposed in 2002 to cut down on bus traffic, but the merchants complained about the drop in business, so the fee was dropped a year later. As in many coastal areas, working-class families are concerned about whether they can afford to live in such a pricey community. In the 1980s land and home values quadrupled and congestion increased, causing many retirees and newcomers to wonder if they had brought with them the very thing they came to Maine to escape.

REMARKABLE RESIDENT:

Booth Tarkington, Pulitzer Prize–winning author, summered at his estate called Seawood in Kennebunkport, and wrote aboard his two-masted schooner, the *Regina*. His novel, *Mary's Neck*, was set in a fictionalized version of Kennebunkport. The book was number seven on the 1932 fiction best-seller list. *The Good Earth* by Pearl S. Buck was number one.

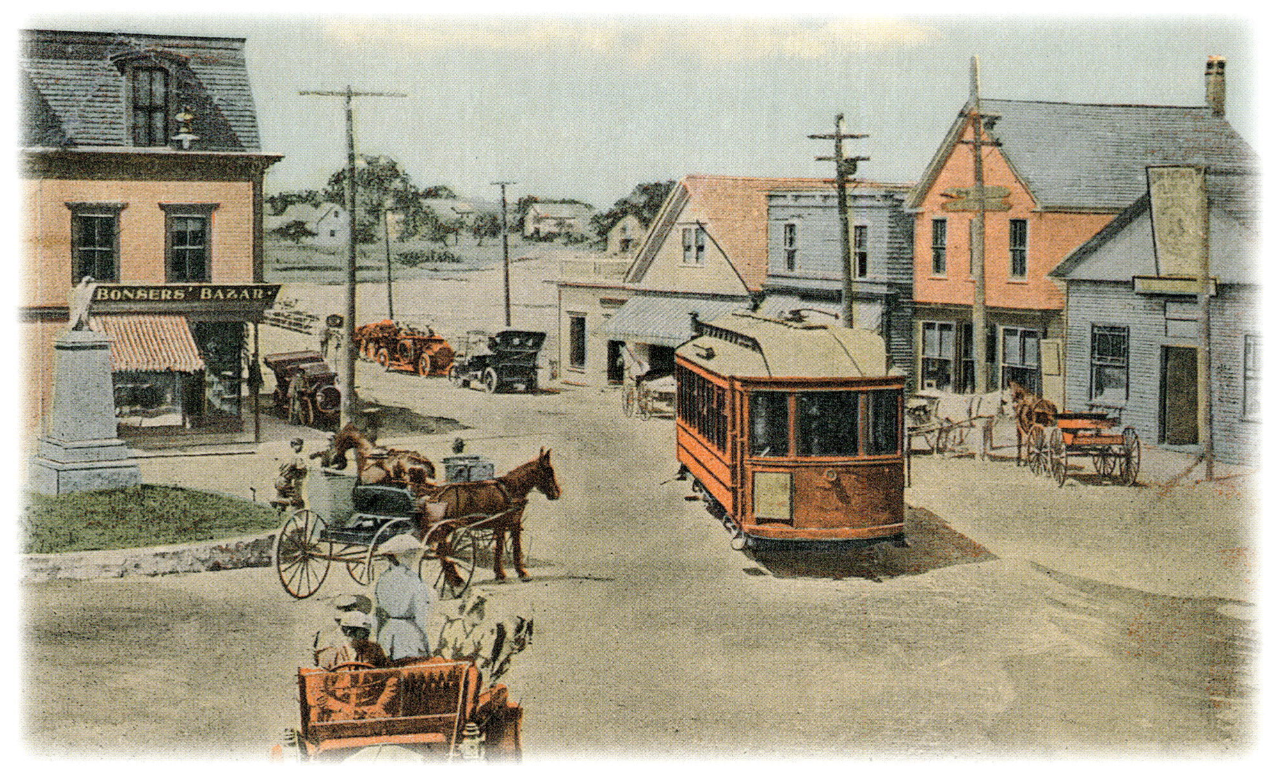
BONSERS' BAZAR

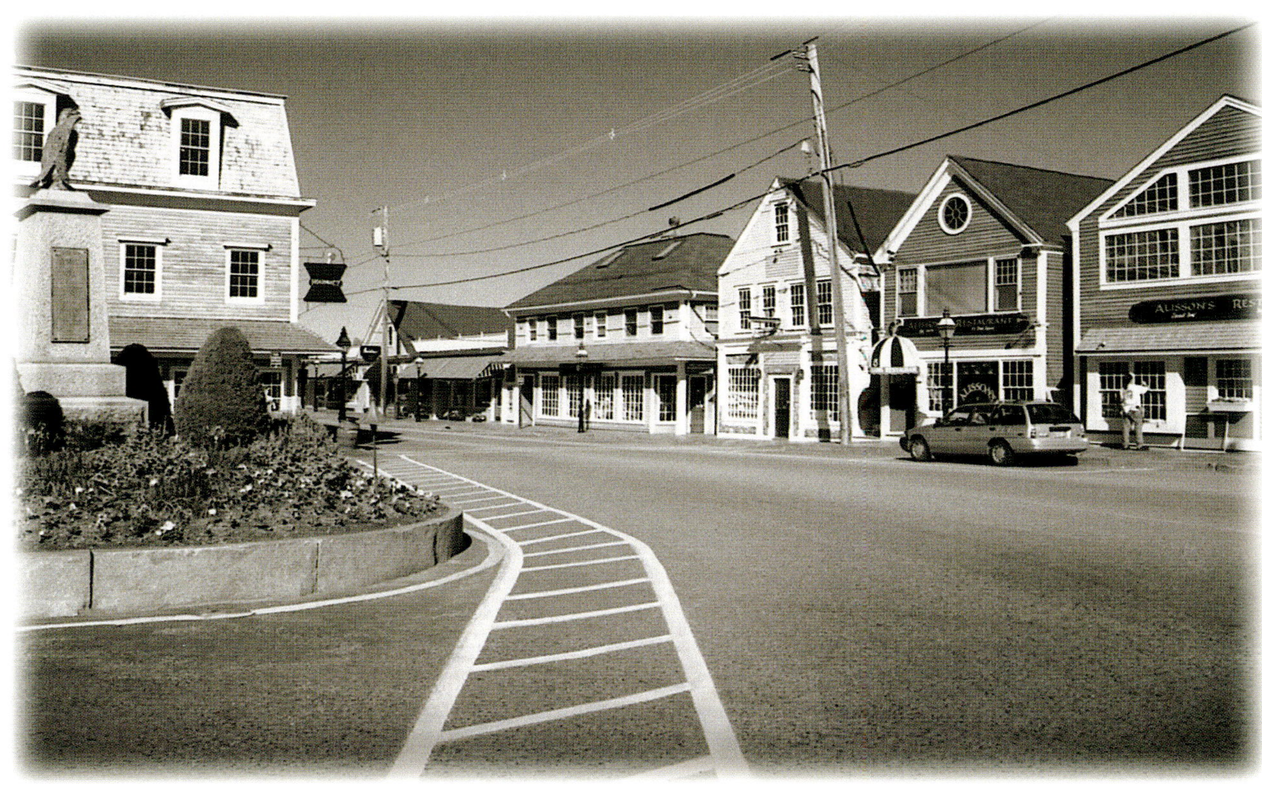
ALISSON'S RESTAURANT
ALISSON'S

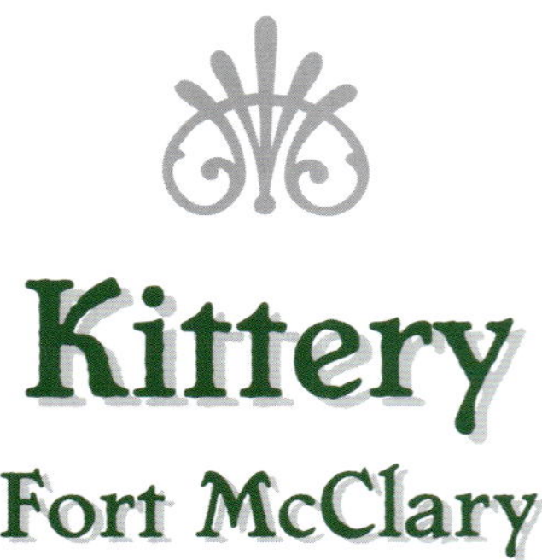

Kittery

Fort McClary

INCORPORATED AS MAINE'S
1ST TOWN ON NOVEMBER 20, 1652

POPULATION IN 1900: 2,872

POPULATION IN 2000: 9,543

War has been part of the history of every civilization, and old forts and monuments remind Mainers that life here wasn't always "the way it should be." Fort McClary's blockhouse was the last to be constructed in the state, and overlooks a particularly splendid view of the Atlantic. Like most military sites, it was used only in time of need, and spent many decades as a lonely, silent sentinel.

The land itself had been important for military defense since 1689, when William Pepperrell erected a small garrison adjacent to his house in Maine's oldest town. A permanent fort was constructed during the colonial period and was named Fort William, after Pepperrell, who wound up loyal to the British Crown during the American Revolution (and had his land confiscated by the local citizens as a result). In 1808 the federal government modified the fort and named it for Major Andrew McClary, the highest-ranking American officer killed at the Battle of Bunker Hill in 1775. The original breastwork was rebuilt into a large, semicircular granite wall. This lower battery had five 32-pound guns and four 8-inch howitzers in place. The current blockhouse was built on the site of the Upper Battery in 1844 with a foundation of mortared fieldstone. The first-story walls are cut granite, and the second and third stories are made of squared logs. A powder magazine was located in the center of the first floor, and the upper stories were officers' quarters. Two brick riflemen's houses were built on either side of the blockhouse.

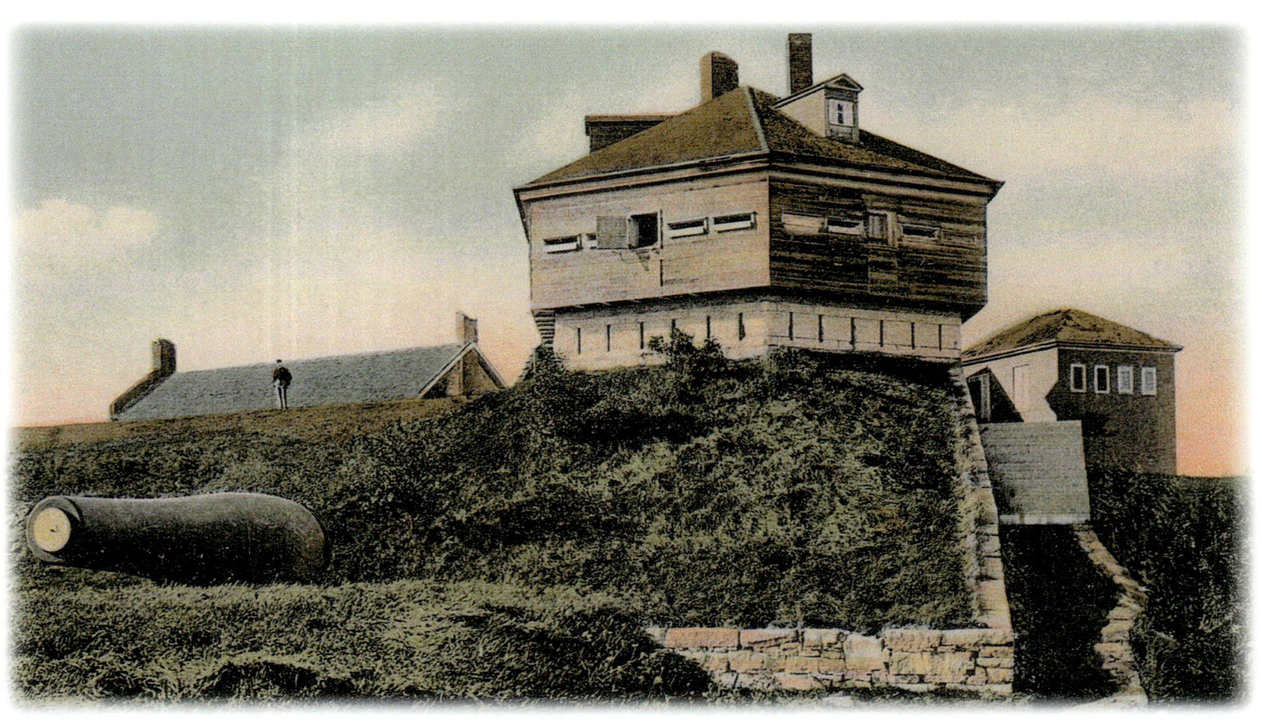

In 1846 the fort was deactivated, and later reoccupied during the Civil War. While he served as vice president to President Abraham Lincoln, Hannibal Hamlin was called to the Maine Coast Guards, Company A, in the summer of 1864, and served three months at Fort McClary as a private. Though he could have accepted an honorary role, he said, "I am the vice president of the United States, but I am also a private citizen, and as an enlisted member of your company, I am bound to do my duty." Promoted to corporal, he drilled and performed guard and kitchen duty with the rest of the enlisted men.

In 1874 the circular granite wall at the Lower Battery was modified again into a broad earthwork, which is how it remains today. Three Rodman cannons were emplaced there, one of which is visible in the postcard. A parrot gun (a type of cannon) from the fort currently resides in Prospect Park in Ypsilanti, Michigan, acquired by that town's mayor some time in the early 1900s. Most of Fort McClary's guns were sold or scrapped by 1910, and the fort fell into disrepair shortly thereafter.

During both World Wars the blockhouse was used as an observation post. In 1969 Fort McClary was placed on the National Register of Historic Places, and the blockhouse was refurbished in 1987. Kittery is still important to the nation's defense. For two centuries the Portsmouth Naval Shipyard has built vessels ranging from tall ships to nuclear submarines, and is currently engaged in overhauling the Los Angeles class of nuclear-powered submarines.

A sidelight to Kittery's military history is that the bloody Russo-Japanese War ended with the signing of a treaty at the Portsmouth Naval Shipyard in 1905. Russian troops had marched into Manchuria and Korea in 1904, threatening to invade Japan. In response, Japan launched a surprise attack on the Russian-occupied Port Arthur (now Lushun, China), starting the war. Although President Theodore Roosevelt was never present at the month-long peace-treaty negotiations, he won the Nobel Prize for coordinating the event as a neutral party.

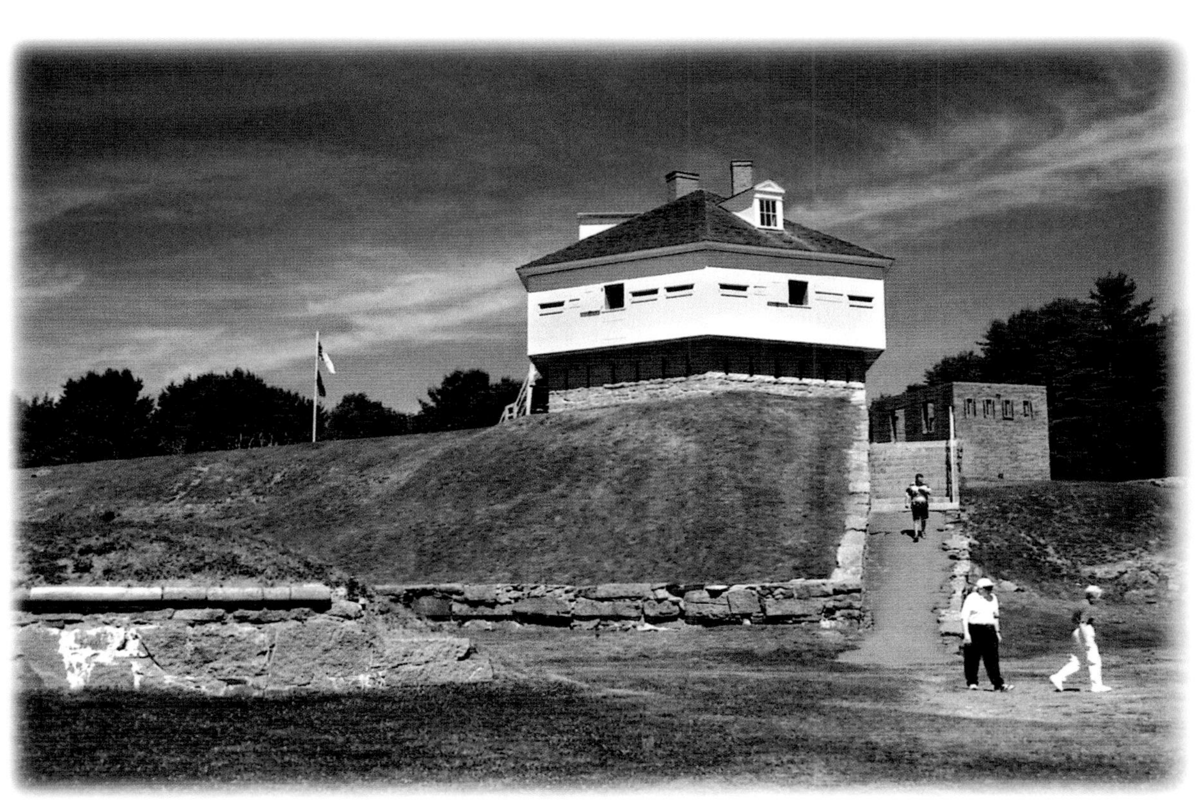

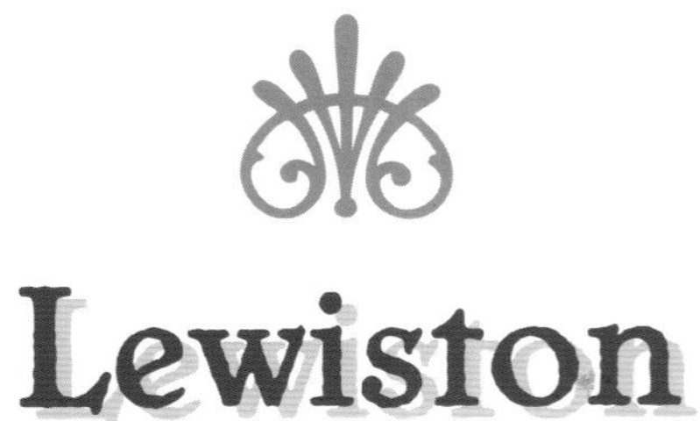

Lewiston

INCORPORATED AS MAINE'S 94TH TOWN ON FEBRUARY 18, 1795

INCORPORATED AS MAINE'S 11TH CITY ON MARCH 15, 1861

POPULATION IN 1900: 23,761

POPULATION IN 2000: 35,690

Lewiston was probably named after Pejepscot proprietor, Job Lewis, who had done a kind turn for one of the townsfolk years earlier. The settlement was developed in 1850 by Boston investors anxious to harness the energy of the Androscoggin River for textile production. The Lewiston Water Power Company (later the Franklin Company) owned much of present-day Lewiston and Auburn land and had nearly exclusive control of the water resources of the Androscoggin. Lewiston's canals and streets were laid out with the mills in mind, and for many years the LWPC and the Franklin Company dominated the town's financial, political, and cultural life.

While some of Lewiston's most prominent mills still line the 800-foot-long canal, they no longer produce the fabrics and goods that defined Lewiston's economic strength in the early twentieth century. Instead, the health-care industry is now the largest employer in the area. Central Maine Health Care even converted the Knapp shoe factory into a medical office complex and nursing school. Smaller, more high-tech manufacturers and retail shops have also taken up residence, some in converted buildings such as the Hill Mill and Bates Mill Complex.

In 1905 Lewiston boasted four woolen mills and seven cotton mills. (Auburn also had a cotton mill.) At least half the workers were women and children, and many were immigrants, mostly from French-speaking Canada. About 70 percent of Lewiston's population at the turn of the twentieth century worked in the mills. By 1970, the textile firms employed about 10 percent of the city's workers.

In the 1920s the 1860 Androscoggin Mill was one of the largest producers of rayon products in the world. In its heyday, the 1852 Bates Mill manufactured tenting and cotton goods for the Civil War, and later, parachutes and camouflage during World War II. It became one of the greatest producers of woven bedspreads in the world, but eventually operations were scaled back, and the mill finally closed in 2001, putting a hundred employees out of work. A restoration project had already begun on the unused portions of the mill in 1992, with the goal of bringing in new and diverse businesses. Today a courtyard with a water fountain and ornate metal benches provides an attractive ambience, and tenants include People's Bank customer-service operations, the Creative Photographic Arts Center of Maine, and dozens of other businesses.

The highly regarded Bates College, with an enrollment of 1,700 students, began as a Baptist seminary in the mid-1800s. Today the campus has more than 80 buildings on 109 acres, many added within the last fifteen years, and its museum boasts a collection of paintings by native son Marsden Hartley.

Continuing its heritage of attracting immigrants, in 2001 Lewiston became the home of more than one thousand Somali refugees fleeing strife in their homeland. This influx caused some controversy at a time when Lewiston was experiencing relatively high unemployment, but the Somalis now seem to be an accepted part of the community.

Lewiston is proud of its many historic buildings, and when the Continental Mill and its distinctive tower were abruptly demolished recently, the city passed an ordinance that will give historic-preservation groups more time to save such architecture. Many of the historic buildings are on Lisbon Street, as seen in the postcards and modern photographs on pages 93 and 95.

In the postcard on the facing page, looking back from Main Street, the 1902 Gateway Building on the right features Italianate details. It was originally the site of the First Baptist Church. While a fire in 1977 gutted the interior and destroyed the copper roof, the

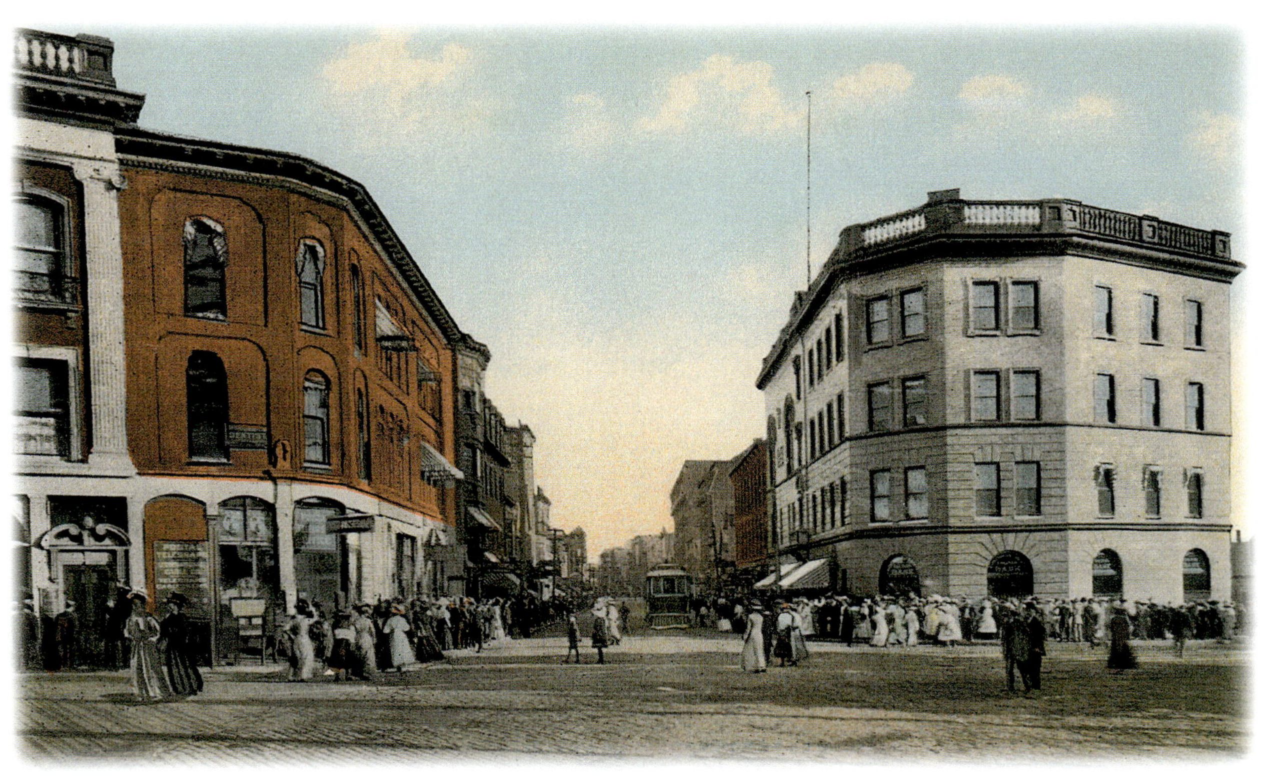

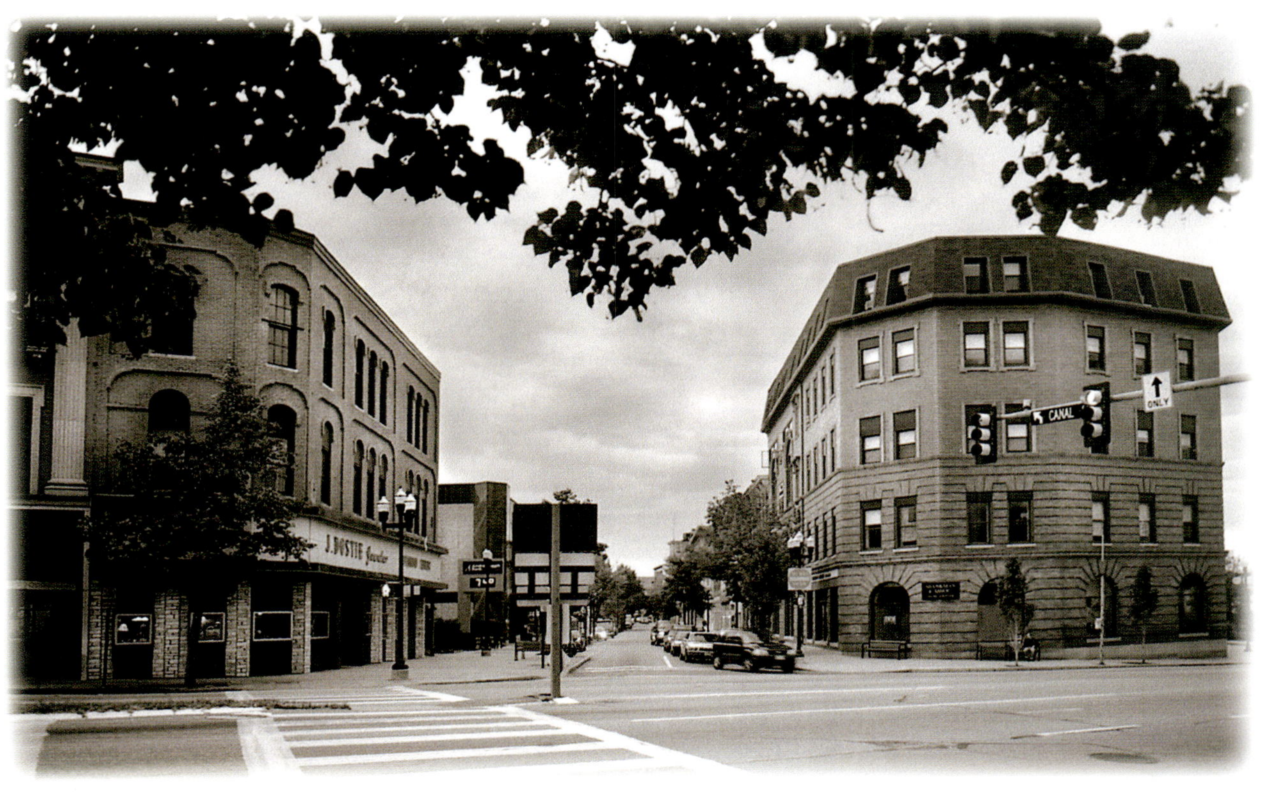
CANAL
ONLY

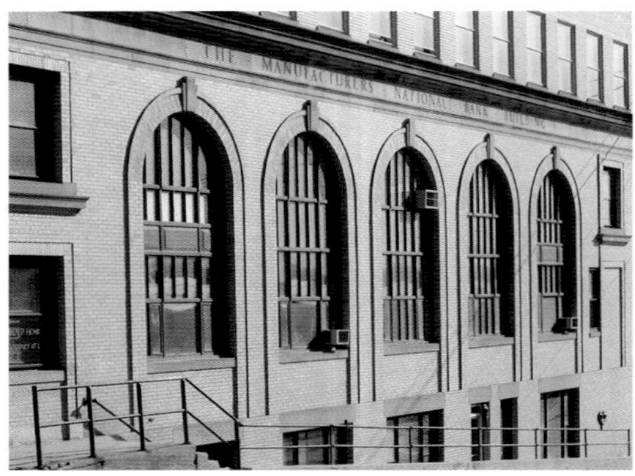

The Lewiston Manufacturers National Bank Building today.

building's shell survived. Although it was later earmarked for demolition, it was restored instead, with the addition of a fifth-floor mansard roof. It now houses the Masonic Hall, commercial space, and apartments. The stone looks white in the postcard, but it is actually a light-red brick color.

On the left is the First National Bank Building. At the turn of the twentieth century, this building and the one adjacent housed a drugstore, a dentist's office, the New York Life Insurance Company, and a telegraph office.

The 1940s postcard of Lisbon Street looking toward Main Street on page 95 is of later vintage than most in this book, but is too attractive and informative to omit. On the far left is the seven-story Manufacturers National Bank building of neoclassical design, now called the Professional Building, flanked by the New England Furniture Company. Across Ash Street on the left is the distinctive 1895 McGillicuddy Block, built by state legislator and mayor, Daniel McGillicuddy. It is interesting to note that the third-floor arched window has a sharper profile today.

Adjacent is the 1893 Osgood Building, which features contrasting white brick imported from Leeds, England. The crosses and pitched roofline no longer exist today. It now houses the Berman & Simmons law offices, and in the 1940s was owned by the American Hellenic Greek Social Club. WLAM Radio occupied the top floor in that era, says Martin Berman, whose father opened a law office in the building in 1914, moved out, and then moved back in with his uncle in 1941.

Next down the block are the Supovitz Brothers building and the old Grant's Department Store, originally built for the Lewiston Trust Company in 1898. Grant's remodeled it in 1926 and sold clothing there until 1985. The 1,300-seat Music Hall was built in 1877 and billed as "the best opera house east of Boston." U.S. Representative William Frye contributed much of the construction funds, and his name is carved in stone on the building. The Music Hall went out of business in the 1930s, and by the 1960s it had become rather derelict, but the exterior was recently renovated to its former glory now that the building houses the District Court.

The B. Peck Company in the 1898 building on Main Street facing Lisbon billed itself as "The Great Department Store Company." Its entrance is dominated by an elaborate terra-cotta arch, and since 1988 has housed one of three L.L. Bean telephone-order centers and a law office.

On the right side of the street, Peoples Savings Bank in 1938 had leased the Cronin and Root building. (Sometime between 1930 and 1938 the apostrophe was dropped from the name.) Lisbon Street today is the focus of the city's Downtown Urban Center Master Plan, adopted in 1999. In an attempt to reverse the 32 percent vacancy rate in the commercial district and to enhance livability, plans are afoot to restore the southern gateway into the downtown area, including restoration of two historic buildings—the Public Theatre and the Androscoggin Mill Block.

NOTABLE NATIVE:

Expressionist painter Marsden Hartley (1877–1943) was born in Lewiston.

REMARKABLE RESIDENT:

James Longley, elected in 1974 as Maine's first independent governor.

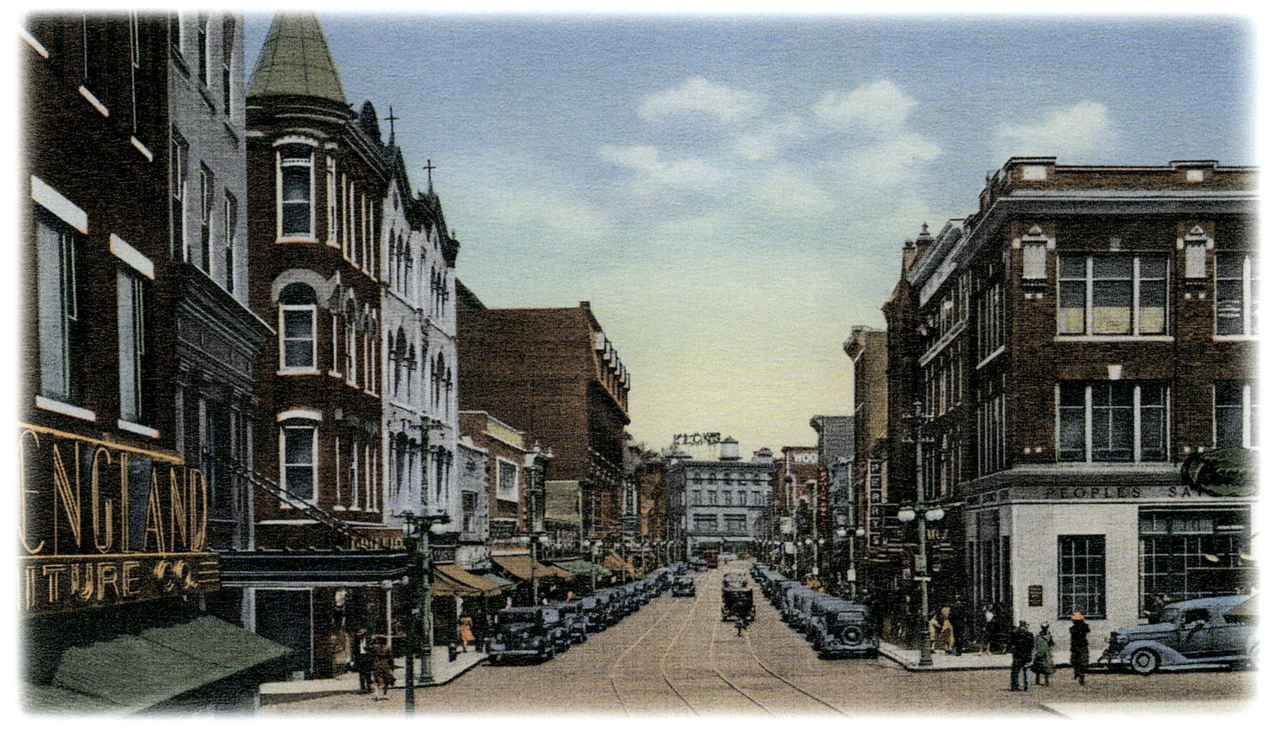
ENGLAND
PEOPLES

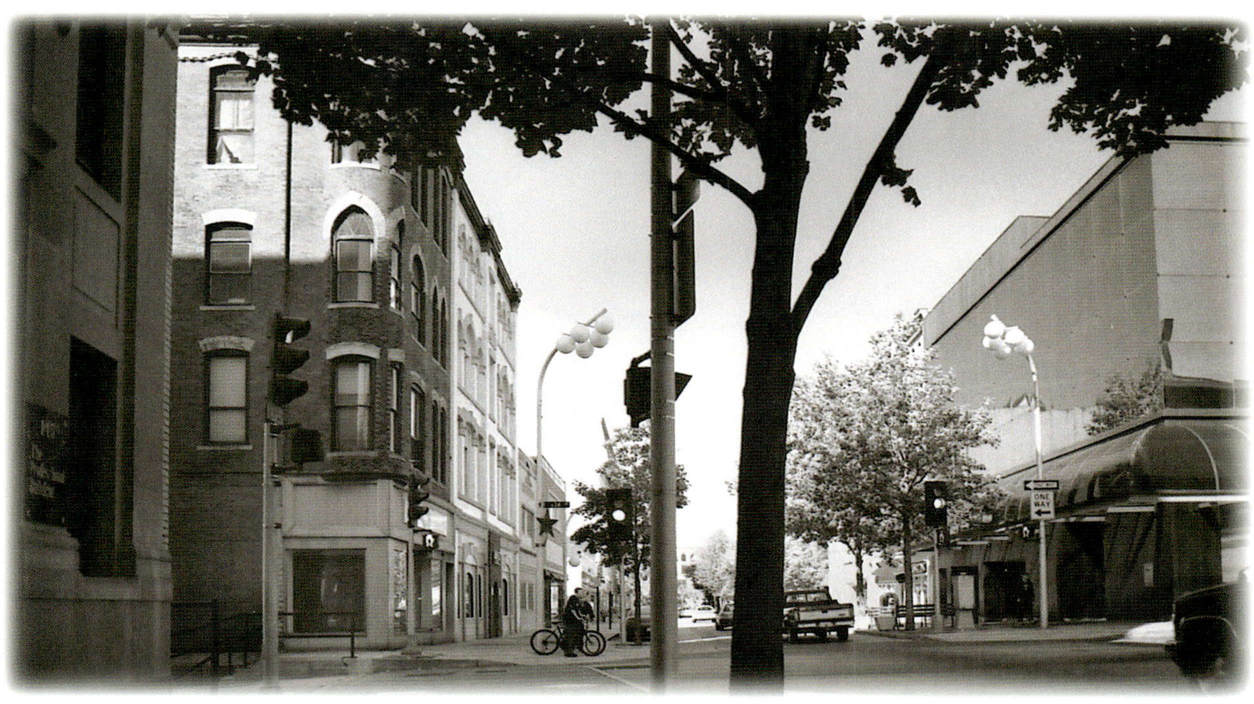

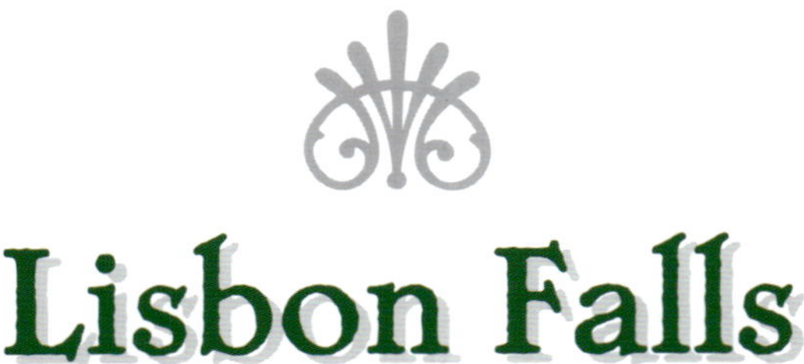

Lisbon Falls

A VILLAGE OF THE TOWN OF LISBON

INCORPORATED AS MAINE'S 121ST TOWN ON JUNE 22, 1799

POPULATION IN 1900: 3,603

POPULATION IN 2000: 9,077

Although the distinctive soft drink called Moxie was never manufactured in Lisbon Falls, and nothing of real significance in Moxie's more than 125-year history actually took place in this town, it is still the unofficial headquarters of Moxie fandom, with a three-day summer Moxie Festival to prove it. Spearheaded by Frank Anicetti, owner of the Kennebec Fruit Company, the festival draws an estimated 25,000 people each year.

Incorporated under the name of Thompsonborough in 1799, the town became Lisbon in 1802, after residents objected to "the inconveniency in the length of the name." It is unknown whether it was named after Portugal's capital; however, it was fashionable in that era for American towns to be named for European countries and cities. It encompasses three villages: Lisbon, Lisbon Center, and Lisbon Falls, which was known as Little River Village until 1865.

The Worumbo Manufacturing Company woolen mill at the end of the street in the vintage postcard was established in 1864, and employed 600 at its peak. It processed animal fibers of all sorts, ranging from mohair, camel hair, chinchilla, and the extremely expensive vicuña. It also manufactured peacoats for the troops during World War II.

The mill closed in the mid-1960s and went through several owners before Miller Industries bought it. In July 1987, during renovations following a flood, a spark from a construction worker's torch set off the conflagration that claimed the mill. Around 75 people were temporarily jobless, and resi-

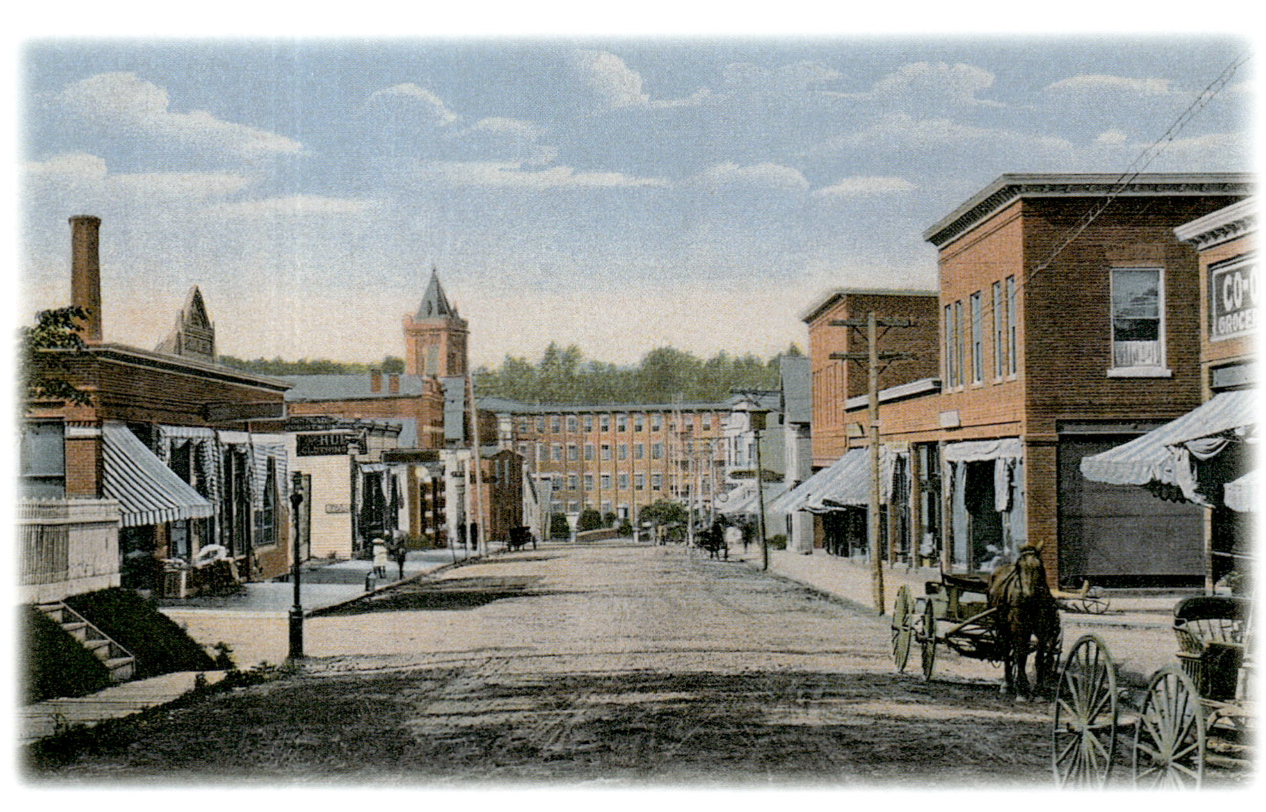

dents whose mothers and grandmothers had worked in the mill watched as it went down. Buildings on Main Street were soaked with water to keep sparks from setting them aflame, and town records were moved in case the fire spread.

Anicetti said, "In his graciousness, Mr. Miller transferred employees to his other mills in Lewiston or Augusta, or to the white section." That section, built in 1921 and made of cement—hence the name—survived the fire, and it still produces cotton, wool, and chenille blankets today.

The postcard photograph was taken after the town was rebuilt following a fire in 1901, which destroyed most of Main Street and left fifty families homeless. Only the Worumbo Mill and two stores survived.

The grocery store on the far right was the Lisbon Falls Co-Operative Association (now the home of the Lisbon Falls Library). The Co-Op was organized in 1885 by a group of Worumbo employees who had taken part in a similar enterprise near Rochdale, England. Members purchased shares of stock at $5 each (with a maximum of $200), earning 6 percent interest each year. After the original wooden building on Union Street burned in 1901, the brick one in the postcard was built.

An ad in the 1889 *Lisbon Observer* listed prices for the Co-Op's goods, which included California prunes, sardines, sugar-cured dates, raw Rio coffee, Sicily canary seed, dried currants, fresh fish every Friday, and oysters every Saturday. "No flies are allowed to stand on our Meat Benches . . . our Goods are all new and fresh, and are sold 16 ounces to the pound, 4 quarts to the gallon." The Co-Op lasted about thirty-five years, and the faded imprint of the sign can still be read on the bricks.

Up the street from the Co-Op building is the University of Maine Cooperative Extension Service office, which had been the site of the town office from the 1960s until 1999. Prior to that, Crosman's Furniture store occupied the main floor. Typical of many furniture stores of the day, it also offered burial services, with an embalming room in the basement and caskets displayed on the top floor.

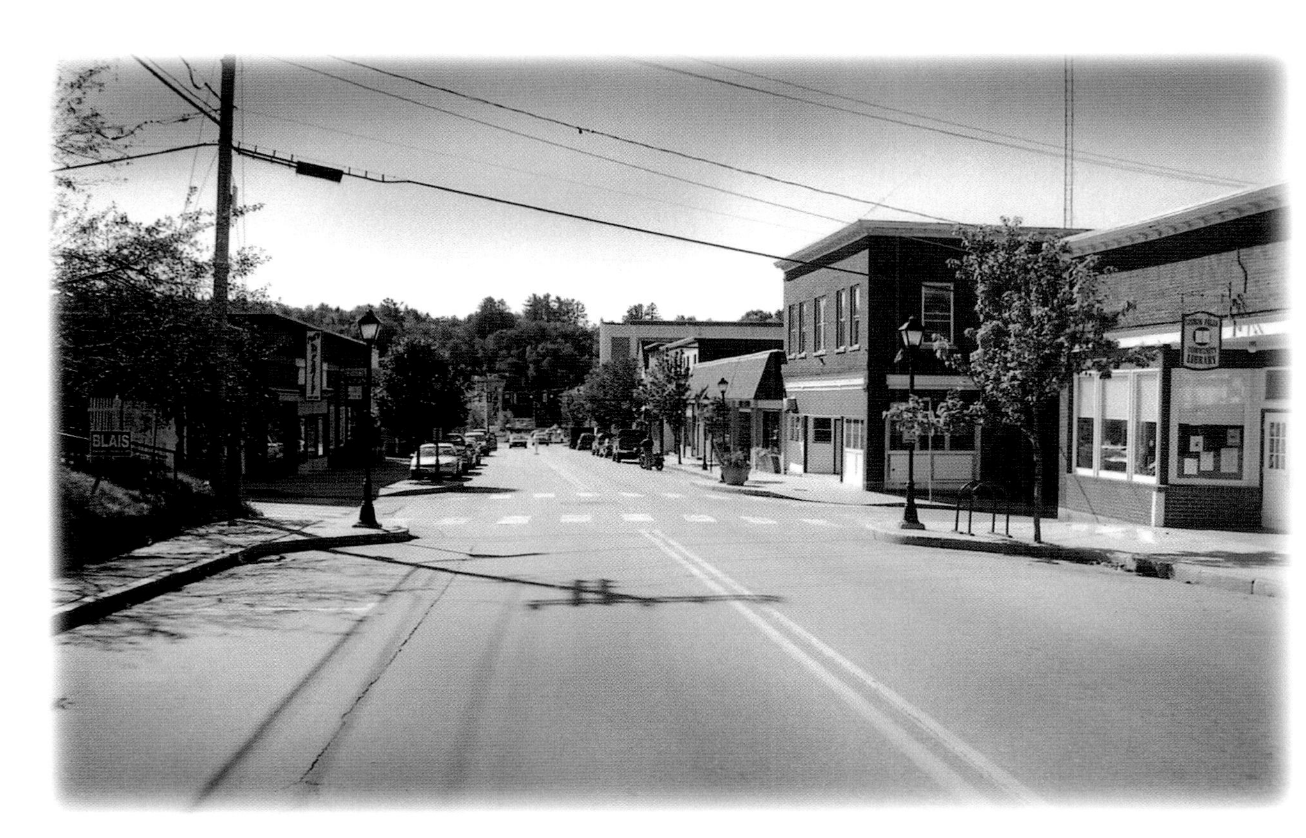

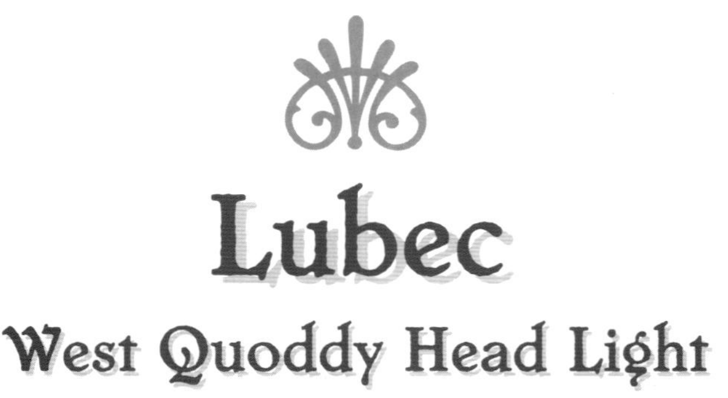

Lubec

West Quoddy Head Light

INCORPORATED AS MAINE'S
187TH TOWN ON JUNE 21, 1811

POPULATION IN 1900: 3,005

POPULATION IN 2000: 1,652

Lubec's West Quoddy Head Light stands on the easternmost point of the U.S. mainland, looking across to Canada's Campobello and Grand Manan islands. The current tower has eight red and seven white stripes, making it one of Maine's most recognizable lights. (There seems to be no specific reason for the varying number of stripes over the years. A twenty-five-cent commemorative stamp issued by the U. S. Post Office in 1990 depicted it with twelve stripes.)

Construction of the light was authorized in 1806 by Thomas Jefferson, and the original wooden tower was replaced in 1830 by one made of rubblestone. In 1858 the tower was replaced again with the current brick structure, and the keeper's house was built. A third-order Fresnel lens, still in use today, was placed in the 49-foot tower at that time. It sits on a 34-foot cliff, placing the lens at 83 feet above sea level. The brick foghorn building was built in 1887 and still stands today.

The light once had a fog cannon to warn mariners of dangerous Sail Rock just offshore, and it received one of the nation's first fog bells in 1820. The 500-pound bell had to be struck by hand, sometimes for days on end during a spell of fog. It was replaced several times because it was difficult to hear offshore. A Daboll trumpet steam whistle was installed in 1869, sounding much like the call of a steam locomotive. A keeper in the 1920s was once asked if the foghorn ever kept him awake. "Only when it stops," was the reply. In 1988 the light itself was automated. Still an active aid to navigation, it has two white flashes every fifteen seconds, and can be seen for eighteen nautical miles.

The keepers' children attended school in Lubec, which meant a two-mile walk each way. Originally spelled *Lubeck*, the town was named for the port city in Germany, which today is the largest port on the Baltic Sea. Beginning in the twelfth century, that namesake was a prime economic force in the Hanseatic League of merchant cities, and undoubtedly the founders of the town in the New World wanted the same success for their settlement. The tiny herring was first smoked here in 1797, then canned as sardines beginning in 1875, and for a while Lubec was the sardine capital of the United States. The last sardine-packing plant, Lubec Packing, ceased operations in 2001, and today Lubec is struggling to restore its once vigorous economy.

The West Quoddy Head Light Keepers' Association of Lubec operates a museum in the keeper's house. The light is in the 500-acre Quoddy Head State Park, which is a prime spot for watching whales and dolphins. The last keeper of the West Quoddy Light was Malcolm "Mac" Rouse of the Coast Guard, who took up the post in 1986 with his wife and three children, ages five, fifteen, and sixteen. His responsibilities included the usual: shining the lens, testing the fog signal and the radio beacon, and every three hours sending out the weather conditions via radio to Jonesport for the National Weather Service.

Automation of the light "stirred up a big hornet's nest," said Rouse, who is now a real estate agent in Buckfield. "The local people and fishermen wanted eyes out there. Those are dangerous waters in the Bay of Fundy, and they knew if someone broke down, a keeper might see them." Rouse wound up on national TV when the media descended to cover the controversy; despite the protest, the light was closed on June 30, 1988. Four months later, he said, two fishermen drowned within view of the light.

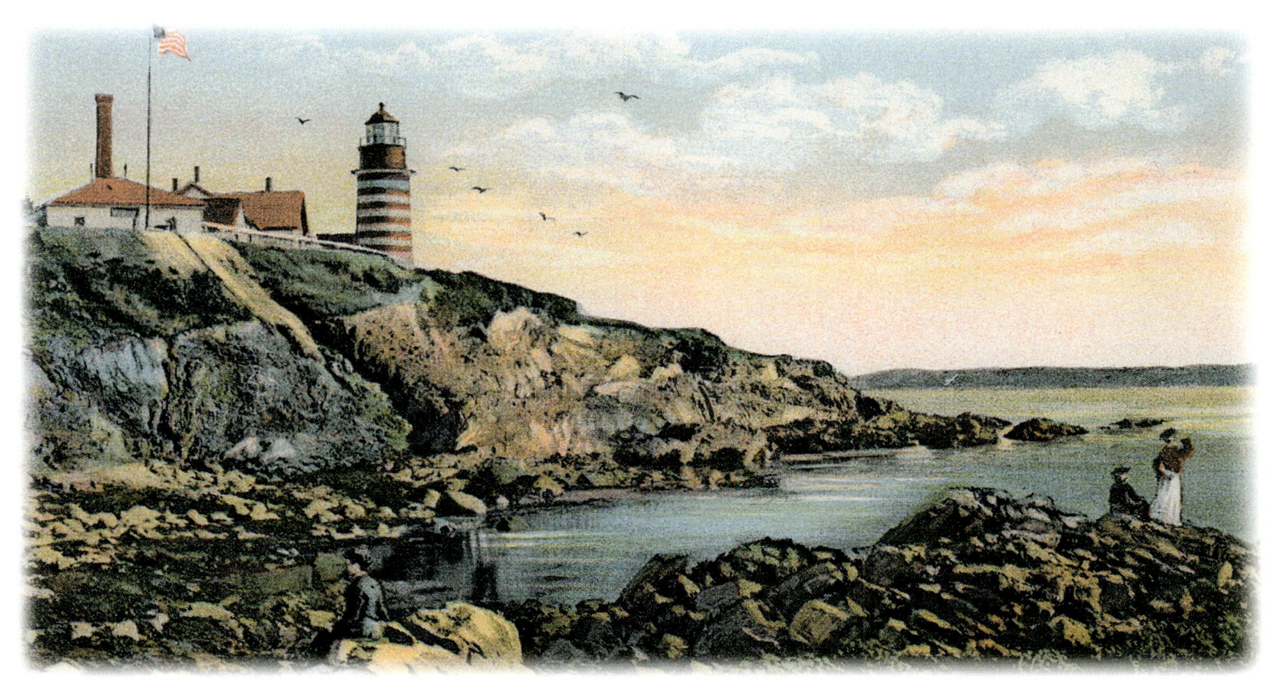

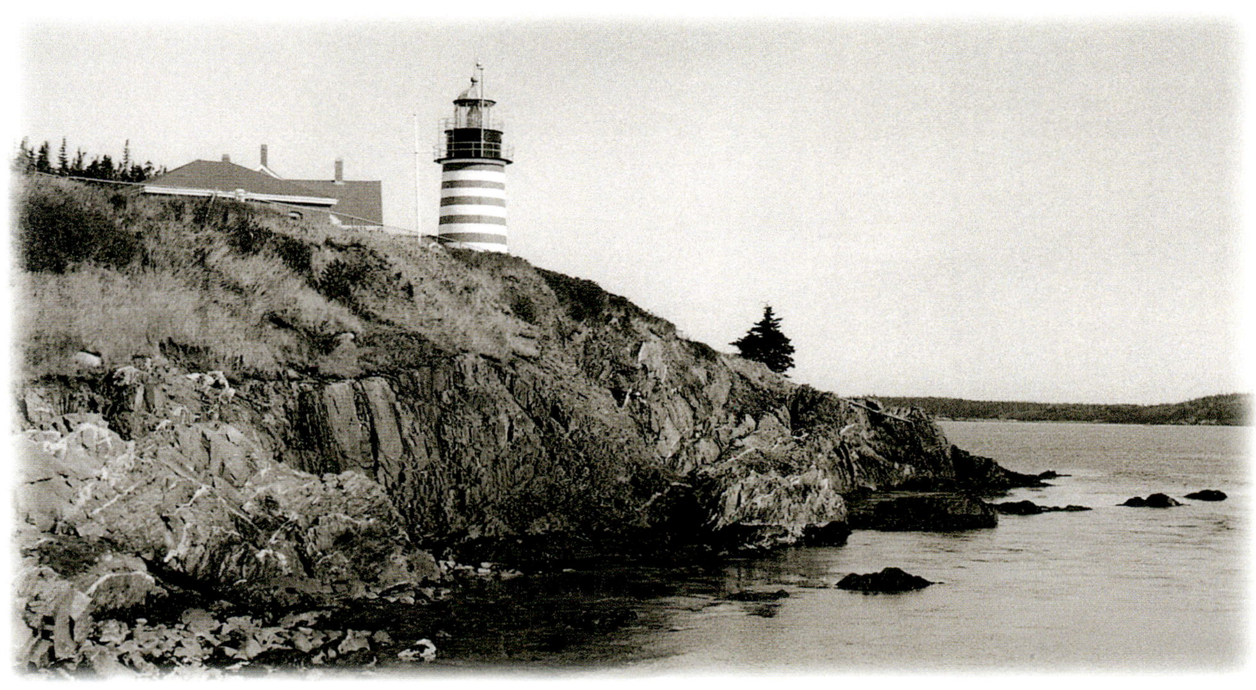

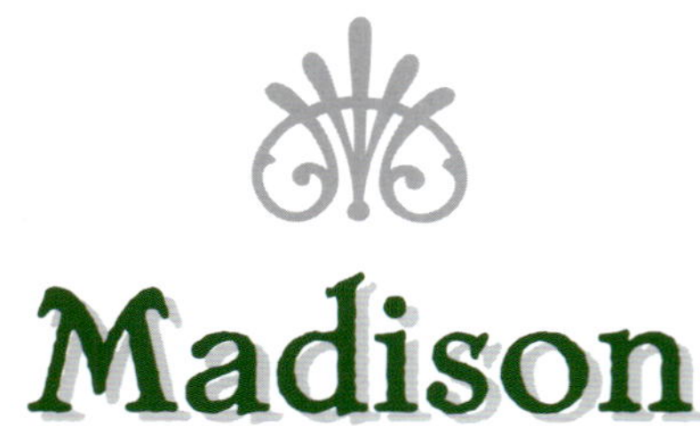

Madison

INCORPORATED AS MAINE'S 150TH TOWN ON MARCH 7, 1804

POPULATION IN 1900: 2,764

POPULATION IN 2000: 4,523

The 1903 town register described Madison as one of the state's leading towns "in amount and importance of her manufactured goods." About forty new buildings were erected or under construction that year in a veritable blitzkrieg of industry. This new construction was in addition to the huge mills already in operation along the Kennebec River, such as the 1881 Madison Woolen Mill, the 1887 Indian Spring Woolen Company, and Somerset Woolen in East Madison. There was also a 900-foot "chemical pulp" mill that used a top-secret, patented German papermaking process. The mill was later taken over by Great Northern Paper, and is presently occupied by Madison Paper Industries (owned by Finland's Myllykoski Corporation and the *New York Times* Company).

Originally known as Barnardstown after the principal landowner, Moses Barnard, Madison was later named for James Madison, who became the president of the United States in 1809.

In the postcard of Main Street, the 1899 Oddfellows Block is prominent on the left. At the turn of the twentieth century, the ground floor was occupied by the Davis and Miller men's clothing store and by the post office. The post office moved in the 1960s and Campbell's Hardware took its place. The second floor for many years housed a beauty shop, optometrist, and dentist, with the Oddfellows Meeting Room on the third floor. The Madison Electric Company had its home offices in the basement. In the early 1980s the Oddfellows building was sold to

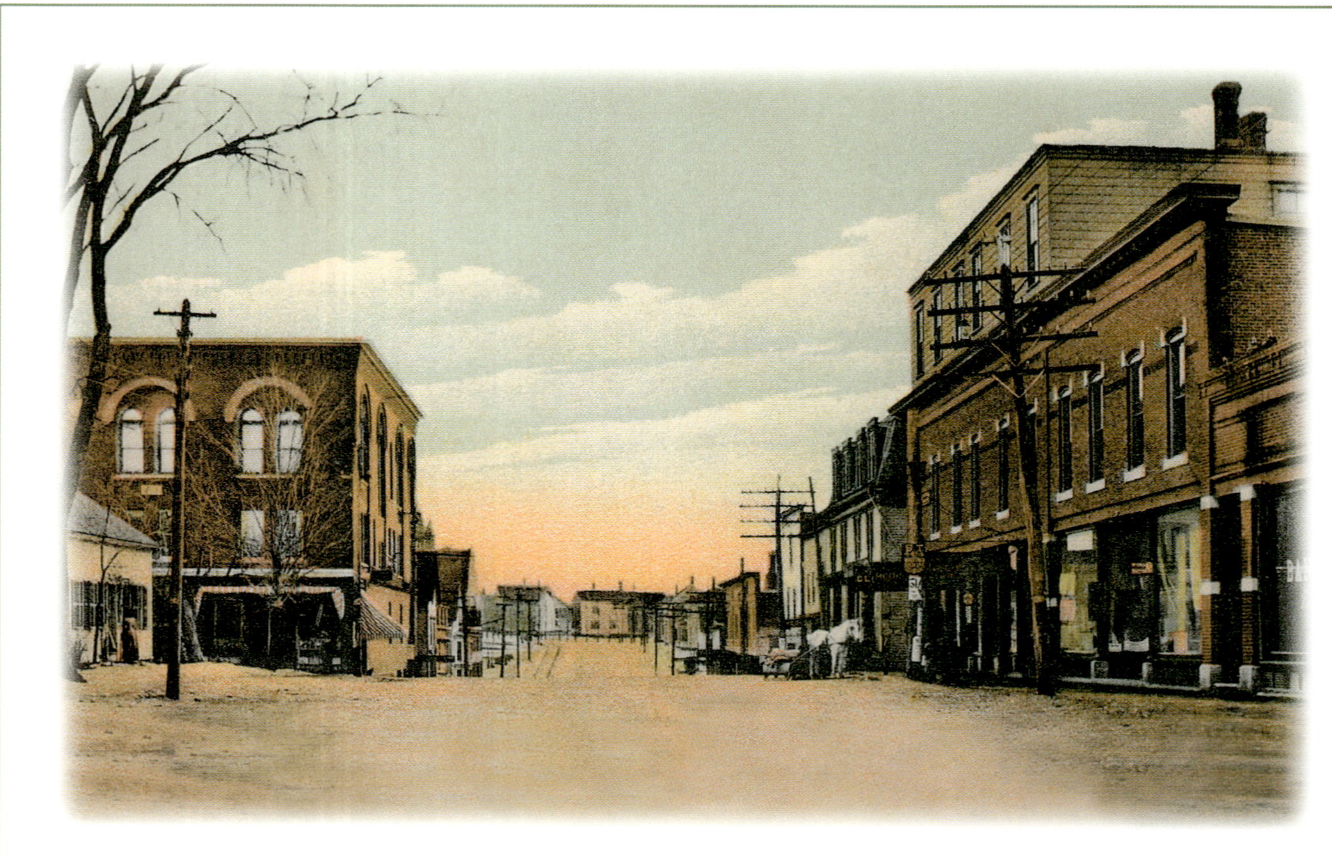

an apartment developer and is now One Madison Avenue Apartments for the Elderly.

The small building just to the left of the Oddfellows Block was a drugstore owned by Harold Porter, complete with a soda fountain and notions. In the early 1900s, Amadeo Christopher started his wholesale business in the back half. A bowling alley and poolroom in the basement closed in the 1960s. The A & P store also occupied the front half of the building, and when it closed, Christopher took over the whole building. Leo Demchak, a Madison native, worked for Christopher Wholesalers from 1946 to 1965. He told of visiting the small stores and filling stations to sell cigarettes, candies, and other items. The business still continues there today. The Congregational Church, barely visible in the postcard, is in the background on the left.

On the right-hand edge of the postcard was the First National Bank. The bank remained in that location for three decades. It became a branch of the Augusta Trust Company and moved to a new building on the corner of Main and South Maple in 1922. The original bank building is now the home of Weber's Insurance.

Next to it is Union Hall, which was the Madison Clothing House in 1882. Demchak remembers that it used to house the J. E. Cannon haberdashery, and after a fire in 1941 the First National Grocery occupied the spot for around two decades, before the Ben Franklin five-and-ten moved in. The Wright Brothers Drugstore occupied a long, narrow space in the building. Renys department store took over much of the ground floor around 1960, and by the 1970s, it occupied the entire building.

The tall building adjacent had been the Exchange Hotel, which was moved there in 1891. In 1916 it was destroyed by fire and rebuilt with a shoe store on the ground level and rooms on the second and third floors. The false-fronted store located most of the way down the block is the 1902 Blackwell Block, formerly a tannery and now a Casey's Buzzard Breath Saloon. Jim Spence ran a jewelry and watch repair shop there until the 1950s, when it became the Spence & Company women's clothing store.

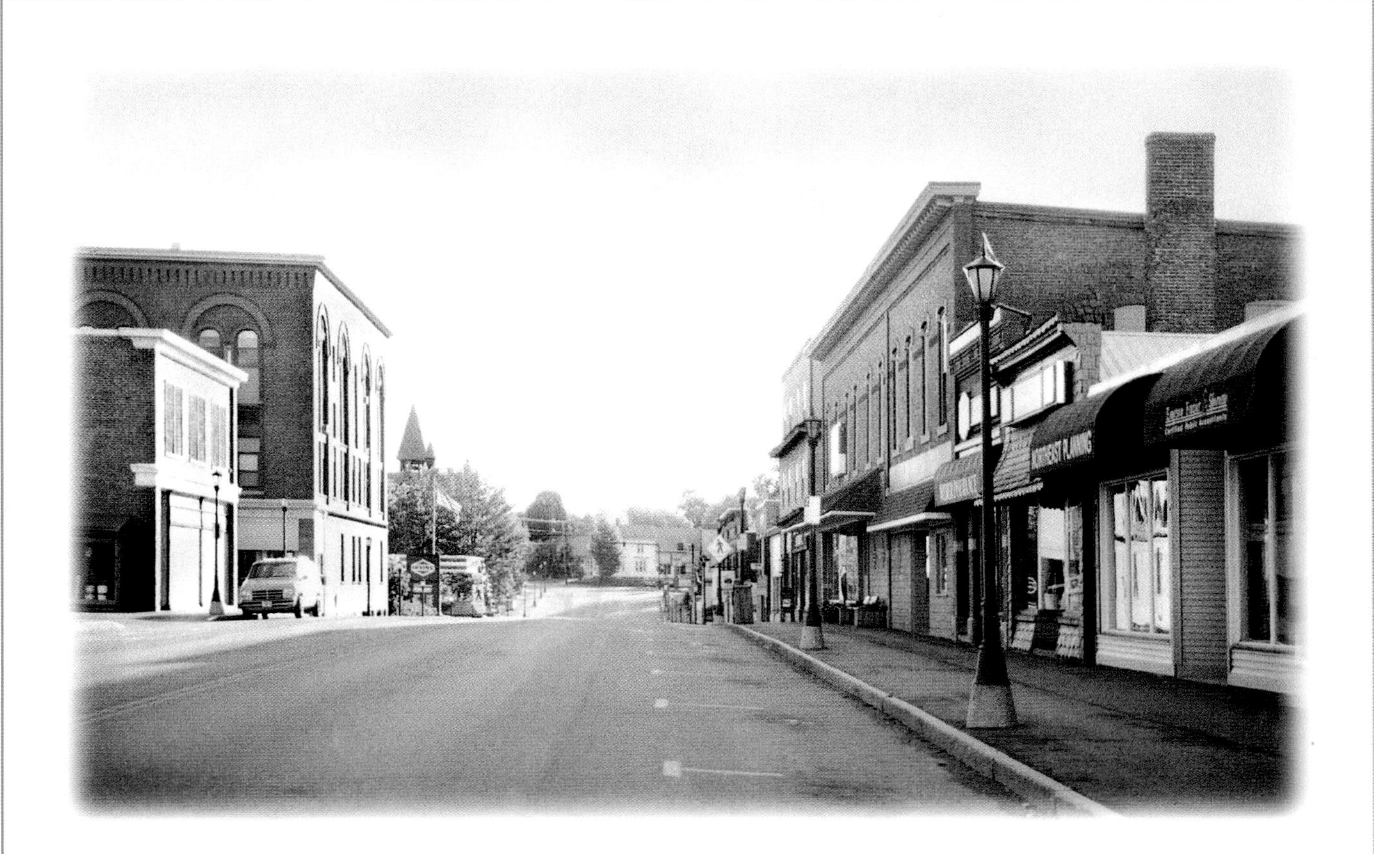

Mechanic Falls

INCORPORATED AS MAINE'S
456TH TOWN ON MARCH 22, 1893

POPULATION IN 1900: 1,687

POPULATION IN 2000: 3,138

"Mechanic Falls is not a designed town. It happened by chance. For many years it had no name," wrote Charles Waterman in his 1894 historical sketch. Before the post office was established in 1841, it was called Jericho, Groggy Harbor, and Bog Falls. The postmaster suggested it be named Mechanics' Falls in recognition of the workingman's nature of the local industry. In 1887 the possessive apostrophe was dropped.

Originally part of the Bakerstown Grant, the town was formed from equal parts of Poland and Minot. Paper, shoe, and clothing factories employed over a thousand people by 1894. Some of the companies were Eagle Mill Paper Works, Colonial Mill, and the Diamond Mill. Industry continued to fuel the economic engine well into the twentieth century. "Town fathers . . . believe Mechanic Falls may be on the road to the most prosperous era, in cold cash, since the township was formed in 1893. . . ," gushed an article in the 1948 *Lewiston Daily Sun*. But it had to end sometime.

The Marcal Paper Mill in 1981 was the last major mill to close, laying off 250 workers and leaving the town financially devastated. Like most mill towns, Mechanic Falls found it necessary to reinvent itself.

Nearly every aspect of life and business in a mill town traditionally revolved around the mill. Families may have worked there for several generations, and restaurants and support businesses catered to the employees or the mill itself. When the sole employer closes shop, a town is left with two choices: to wither and die, or to adapt.

The Mechanic Falls Development Commission was organized the year after the paper mill closed and sought state funding to attract smaller, more diversified businesses. Modernizing infrastructure, such as new water and sewer pipes and sidewalks, also helped make the town more appealing to new industries. The Little Androscoggin River was cleaned of trash, and the townspeople's mindset slowly began to change. This was no longer and would never again be a mill town. For a while, the old mill building was used by Great Northern Recycling and employed forty people, but the company was recently sold and has since moved out. Maine Waste Management now owns the former mill, but its dispatch operations may not be there much longer.

Skills acquired at the mill were transferable to some of the new, smaller shops, such as metal fabrication, engineering, and machining. One of those, now a primary employer, is Auburn Manufacturing, Inc., specializing in heat- and flame-resistant textiles for industrial and military applications. The Depot Square Transportation Center was recently completed in the heart of the downtown area. It provides off-street parking to reduce congestion, and features a park-and-ride area for the shuttle bus to Lewiston-Auburn.

The postcard shows the picturesque bridge over the Little Androscoggin River. It was probably replaced during the 1950s when the road was redirected to feed onto Pleasant Street instead of onto Main Street. The sign on the bridge says THREE DOLLARS FINE FOR RIDING OR DRIVING ON THE BRIDGE FASTER THAN A WALK.

The four-story building partially hidden by the bridge is Perry's Block, which had been the Lewiston Trust building (later taken over by a succession of other banks). It had a fourth floor with a mansard roof before a fire destroyed it in the 1950s. Adjacent to the left is the J. A. Bucknam building, which housed the Home Insurance Company. The first-floor windows were arched at one time. The ground floor today is occupied by Sheila's Hair and Tanning Salon. Both buildings were rehabilitated by the Mechanic Falls Development Commission as apartments.

The low white building to the right was a general store and later became the Manchester Market, with a post office downstairs. It burned at the same time the bank building did and was rebuilt. Since the 1970s it has housed Russ Day's Barber Shop and Charlene's Cut and Curl.

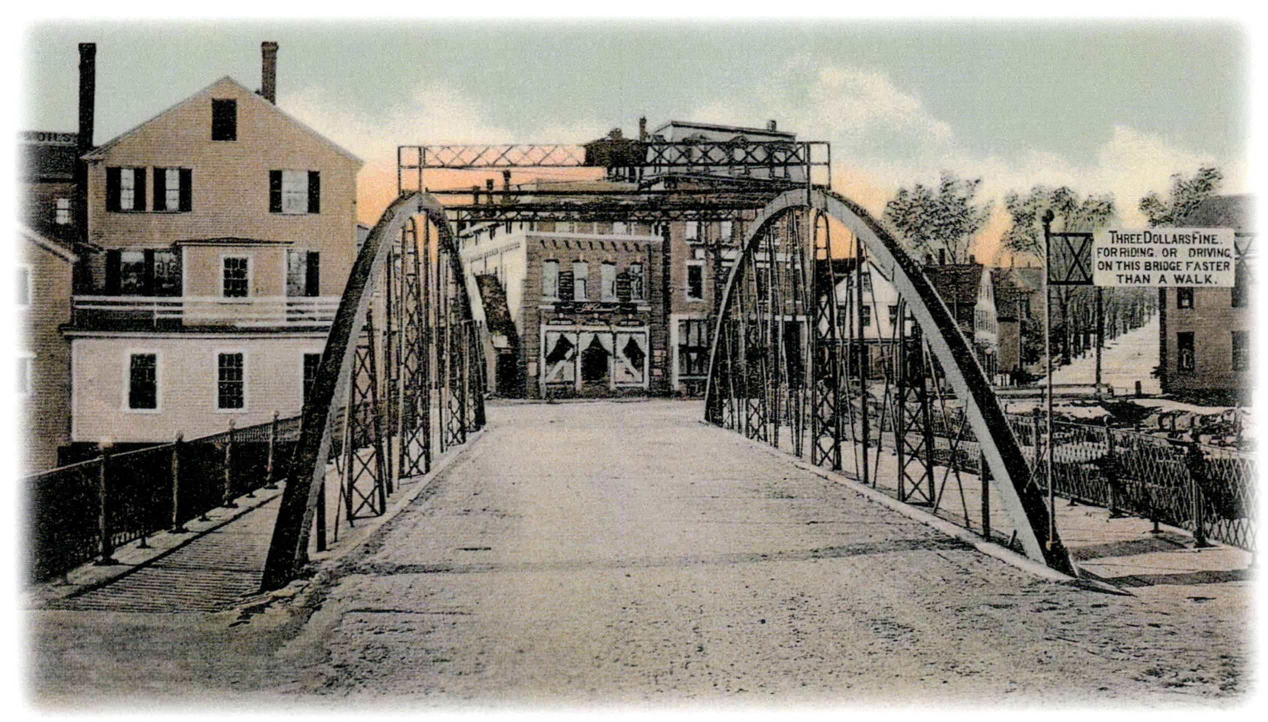
THREE DOLLARS FINE.
FOR RIDING, OR DRIVING,
ON THIS BRIDGE FASTER
THAN A WALK.

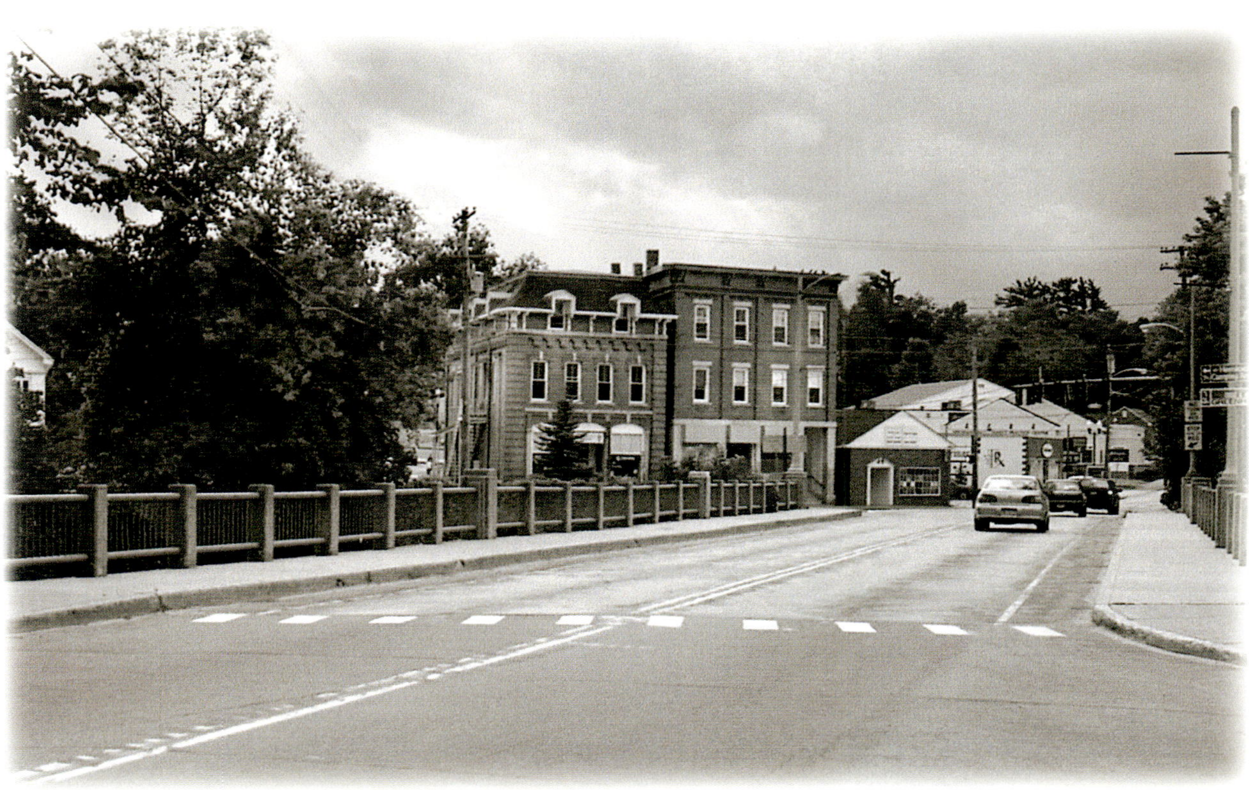

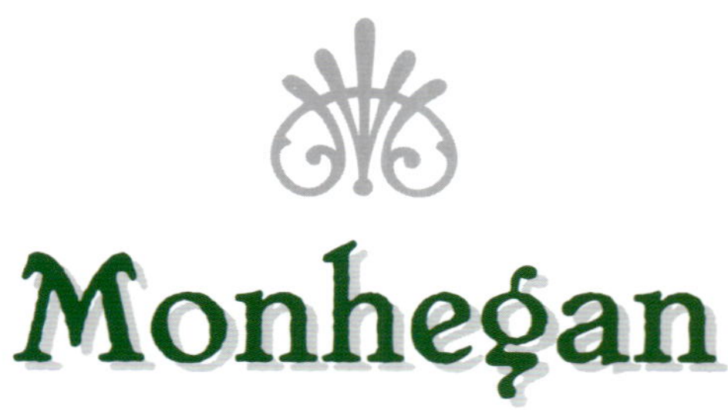

Monhegan

INCORPORATED AS A PLANTATION
ON SEPTEMBER 4, 1839

POPULATION IN 1900: 94

POPULATION IN 2000: 75

As resort communities go, Monhegan is primitive, which is precisely its appeal. Eleven miles offshore from the fishing village of Port Clyde, Monhegan has around seventy year-round residents, although the population quadruples in the summer. The village never bothered to get itself made into a town. Most of the island is undeveloped and held in a land trust, and the picturesque village is nestled on the harbor side. There are few motorized vehicles. Who needs them? There's not even a stitch of asphalt.

The Island Inn—formerly the Pink House, built in 1816 by Josiah Starling—became lodging for rusticators in 1906. It was expanded over the years as the tourist trade grew, and is now a principal landmark overlooking the harbor. The Monhegan House is perhaps the largest of a handful of inns. Of course, such an island attracts artists of international repute. Rockwell Kent built a cottage on the island in 1906, and helped others build theirs, including his mother, Sarah. Jamie Wyeth bought Sarah's cottage in 1968, initiating "the rapid acceleration of property values on Monhegan," according to a local author.

Until 1987 there was no electrical service. Most islanders relied on generators or solar panels. Water flows through above-ground pipes in summer, but those staying through the winter rely on wells or on rainwater captured in cisterns. Three boat lines keep islanders linked to the mainland. The *Balmy Days* sails out of Boothbay and the *Hardy III* out of New Harbor (in the summer months), but the most important has been the *Laura B* out of Port Clyde, shown in the photograph.

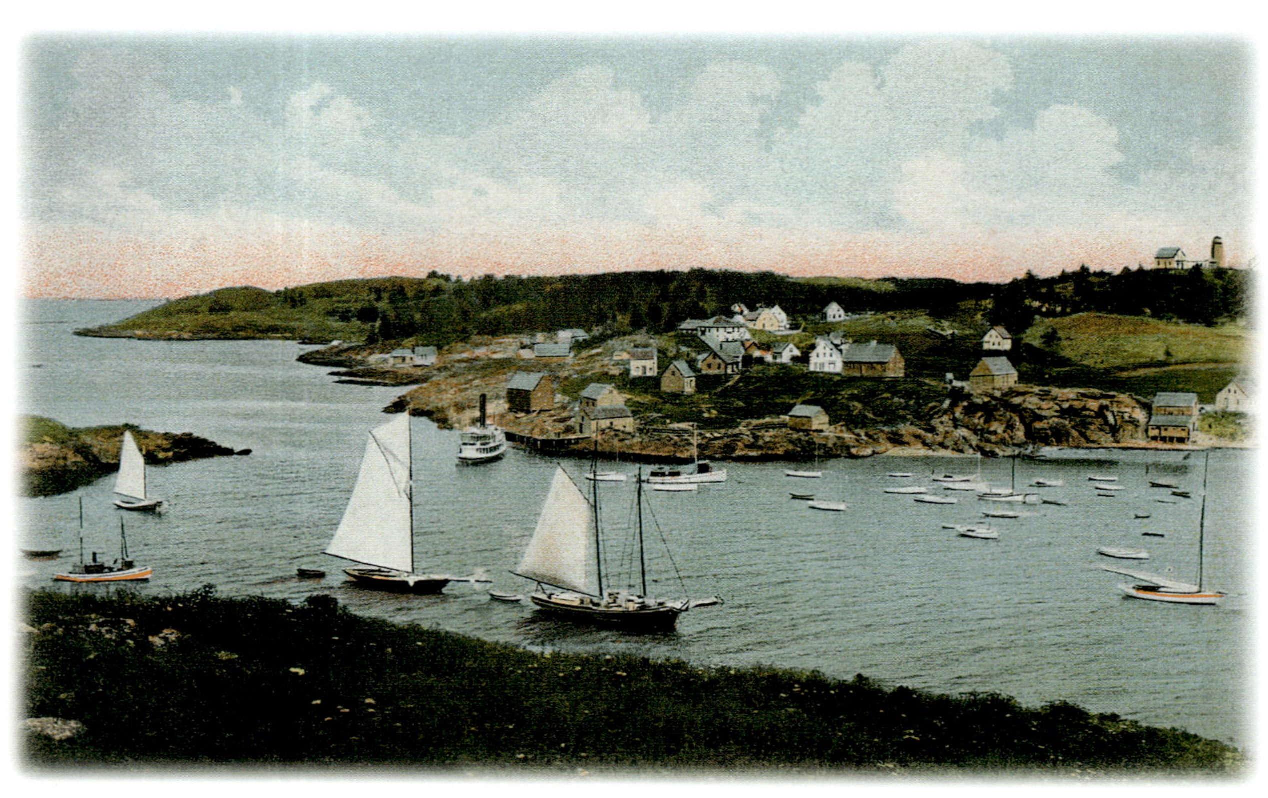

Built in 1943, the 65-foot vessel spent World War II in the Pacific as an army patrol boat. She carried two 50-caliber machine guns on deck and had to use them on occasion. In 1946 she was brought to Maine and spent her days carrying lobsters from Vinalhaven to Boston and New York City, until pressed into service as the Monhegan mailboat. After a half century, the Monhegan Boat Line added a more modern yet not *too* sleek sister vessel, the *Elizabeth Ann*. Summer trips on the *Laura B* usually mean sharing deck space with firewood, crates of fruit, and equipment needed for island living.

The small fleet of lobstermen on Monhegan has established a unique tradition. First of all, their season is exactly opposite that of most Maine fishermen. Since the early 1900s, the first day of January (December 1 as of the mid-1990s) is Trap Day, when all the traps are set at the same time. Tradition has it that no one goes out until every person's boat is loaded. When Monhegan's lobster-fishing season ends, in June, the rest of Maine's lobstermen are just beginning their busy season.

The postcard shows the Monhegan Island Light in the upper right. The first tower was established in 1824 and razed in 1850. The current tower was built that year, and new lamps and clockwork were installed. The Island Inn had not yet been built on the site of the Pink House. In the contemporary photograph, the *Laura B*, captained by Jimmy Barstow since 1974, makes a smooth turn in the harbor before returning to Port Clyde with passengers and mail. In winter she travels to Monhegan three times a week in her official capacity as mailboat. Regular mail service was established in 1883 with the *Goldsmith Maid* sailing from Port Clyde. Before the mailboats, fishermen took turns getting the mail and sorting it on Fish Beach.

REMARKABLE NATIVE:

Zoe Zanidakis, ninth-generation lobsterman (they don't like to be called lobster*women)* appeared on CBS's "Survivor Marquesas' in 2002. When she was voted off *that* island she returned to Monhegan and resumed fishing from her 40-foot *Equinox*.

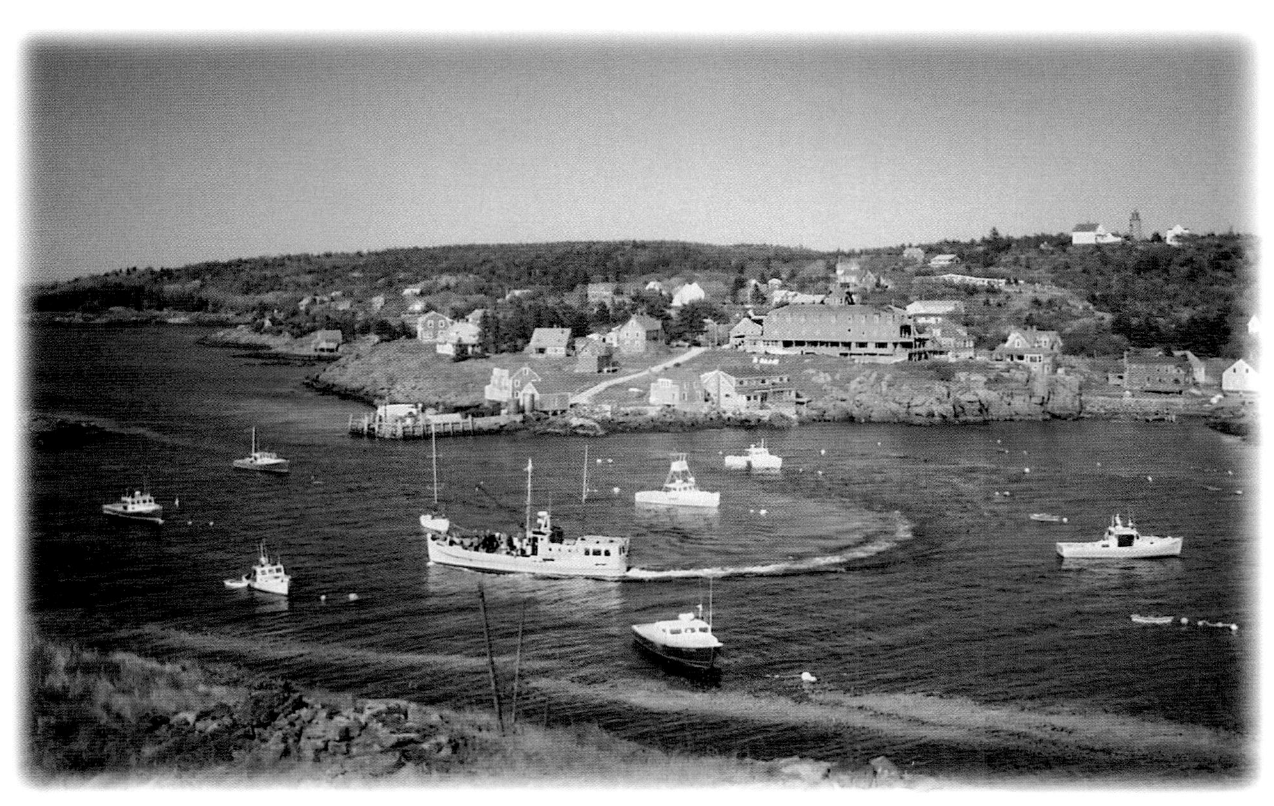

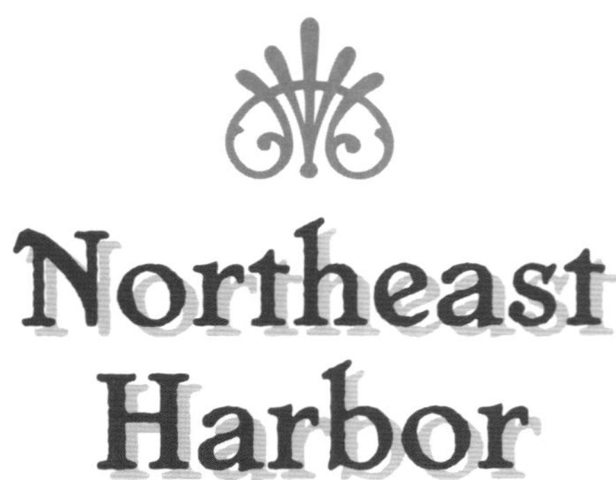

A VILLAGE OF THE TOWN OF
MOUNT DESERT, WHICH
WAS INCORPORATED AS MAINE'S
68TH TOWN ON FEBRUARY 17, 1789

POPULATION IN 1900: 1,600
(TOWN OF MOUNT DESERT)

POPULATION IN 2000: 2,109
(TOWN OF MOUNT DESERT)

Northeast Harbor is the largest of five villages that make up the town of Mount Desert. Like Mount Desert Island, it has depended heavily on its summer colony, but unlike Bar Harbor, it depends only a little on tourists. The summer colony began with the wave of early-day rusticators who were first attracted to Bar Harbor, later spilling over to the "quiet side" of the island. This first wave of tourists enjoyed staying in boardinghouses and living simply, as the natives did. Two decades later, travelers were no longer content with roughing it; the island's great inns were built for the era when the elite would stay for an entire summer.

Although the class distinctions were cultivated and maintained by the upper crust, caretaking provided another means of income to the natives. Many locals developed decades-long relationships of gardening, housekeeping, and maintaining cottages. Historian Lew Dietz described this state of affairs in *Night Train at Wiscasset Station*: "A Maine woman is willing to accept good money working as a cook or a domestic for a summer family so long as it is clearly understood she is not being hired by her betters, but has come in merely to 'help out.' Summer people who don't grasp this semantic subtlety usually find themselves doing their own dirty work."

By 1910 the village had a hundred summer cottages and seven hotels, and by 1915 it was the largest and busiest of the town's villages. The town offices moved onto Main Street two years later. By 1936, Northeast Harbor had the largest yachting fleet east of Marblehead, Massachusetts, and is still one of Maine's largest yachting centers.

The village was spared in the fire of October 1947, and many whose cottages were destroyed elsewhere on the island relocated to Northeast Harbor. Like many desirable coastal communities, housing costs have priced many out of the market. In 1989, only three local families owned shorefront property in the village.

In recent years, the influence of Northeast Harbor native Fred Savage on the local architecture has been recognized. Hardly a village on Mount Desert has gone untouched by his design handiwork, and many of the best-known cottages bear his stamp. He is particularly known for his wide, rambling porches; he felt people came to Maine in the summer to be outdoors, and he designed his cottages specifically to encourage this alfresco setting. While his interiors are functional and spacious, they are not the focal point of the house. Eighty homes, commercial spaces, and other structures in Northeast Harbor alone are of his provenance, including the Asticou Inn. Many of his designs also incorporate his trademark ogee (double-curved) roofs and turrets.

The postcard of Main Street shows the gambrel-roofed A. G. Bain Co., built in 1903, which later became the Hillcrest Market. The words on the striped awning say NEWS DEALERS. The short green building on its left was a fish market, and the dark-colored building next to it was the Des Isles building, which housed the Wood brothers' restaurant. To the right (not shown) was the Pastime Theatre, built in 1913. The buildings on this corner burned in 1965 when a spark at Wallace's Garage started a fire. It also burned the Hillcrest Market and Mrs. Flye's Sandwich Shop. Just across the street was the Gaynor House hotel, which burned in a suspicious fire. It is now the Holmes Store. The village today retains a sort of removed-from-the-rest-of-the-world ambience, untouched by chain motels and tchotchke shops.

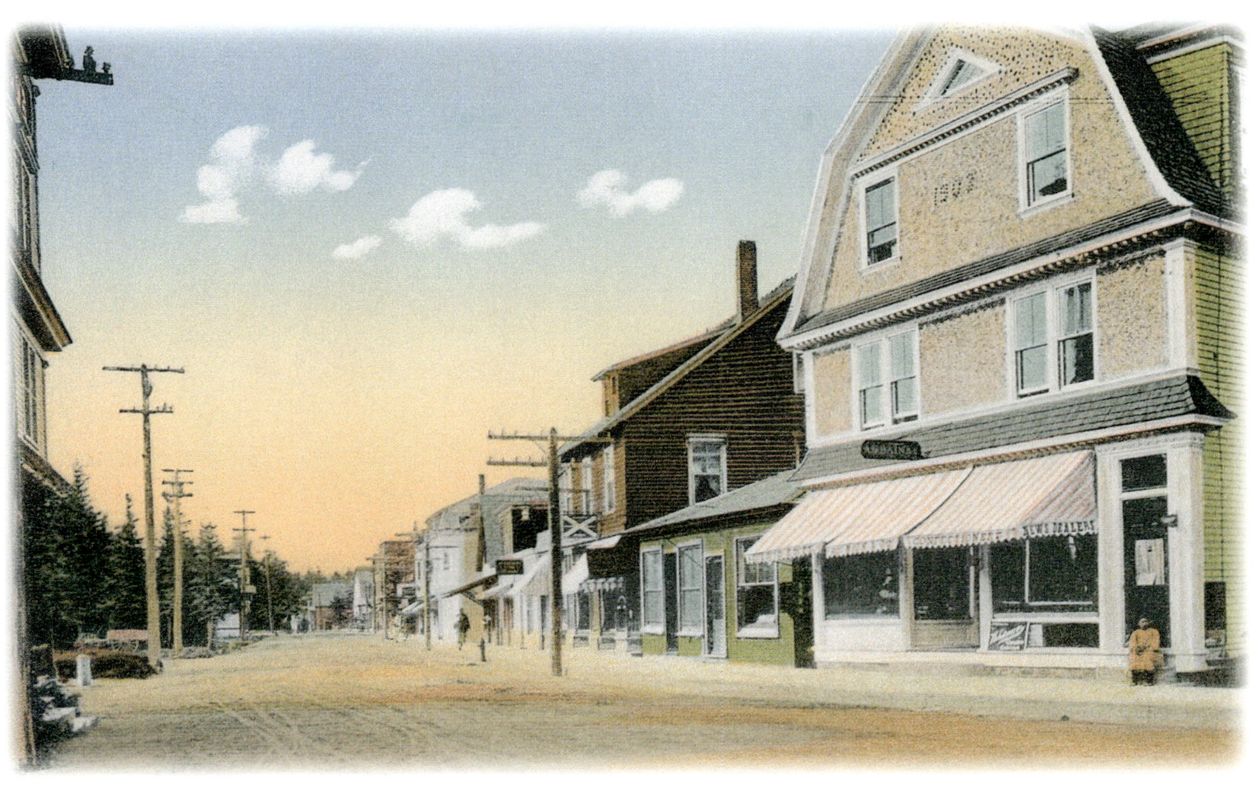

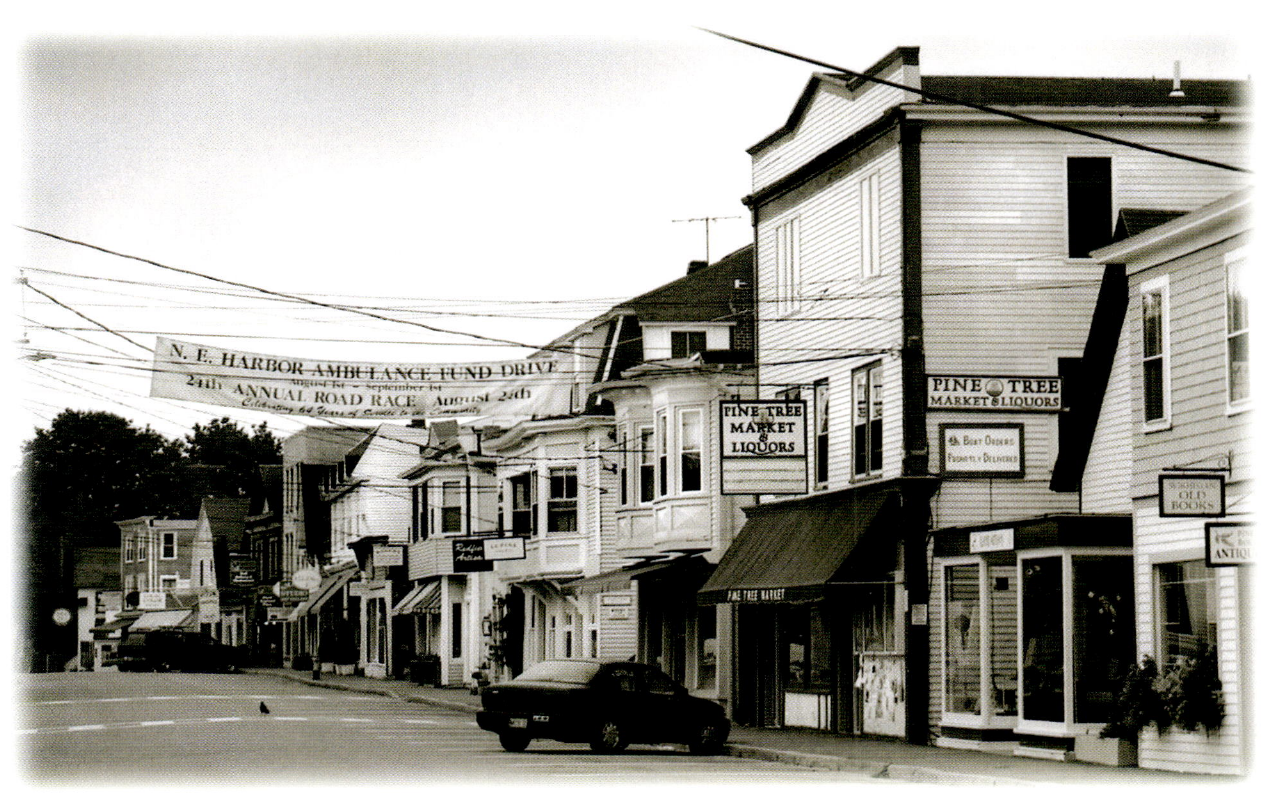
N. E. HARBOR AMBULANCE FUND DRIVE
24th ANNUAL ROAD RACE August 24th
PINE TREE MARKET & LIQUORS
PINE TREE MARKET & LIQUORS
BOAT ORDERS PROMPTLY DELIVERED
OLD BOOKS
PINE TREE MARKET

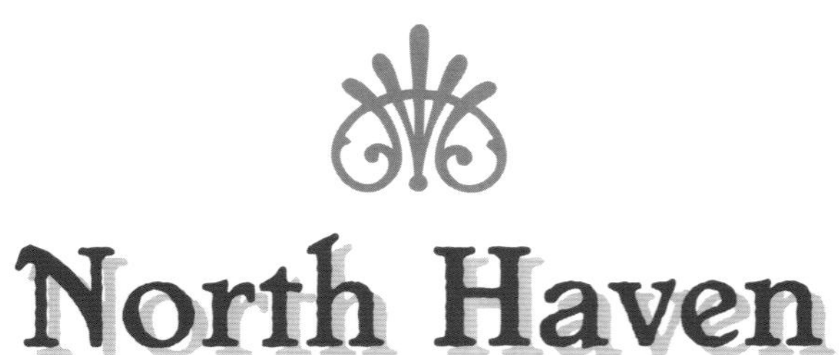

North Haven

INCORPORATED AS MAINE'S
370TH TOWN ON JUNE 30, 1846

POPULATION IN 1900: 551

POPULATION IN 2000: 381

Part of the Fox Islands Plantation along with Vinalhaven Island, North Haven was at first part of Vinalhaven when it was incorporated in 1789. After years of debate, it was set off and incorporated first as Fox Isle, and a year later became the town of North Haven. At various times the Fox Islands belonged to Hancock, Lincoln, Waldo, and Knox counties as they themselves were divided. In her book, *Our Island Town,* Lillie S. Bousfield wrote about one resident who liked to say "he had lived in two states, four counties, and three towns, and had always lived in the same house."

North Haven was also discovered by rusticators in the 1880s, and by 1916 nonresident real-estate valuations exceeded those of residents. But by the 1970s some of them had decided to put down roots and became year-rounders, adding another layer to the island's culture. In summer the population swells to more than four times the year-round figure, and many summer homes have been in the same families for generations. Thus, caretaking has become one of the major occupations for islanders, along with fishing. However, it is not a resort community by any means; there are few facilities for overnight tourists, and day-trippers may find getting to the island on the small ferry from Rockland, the *Capt. Neil Burgess,* to be an exercise in futility.

The postcard shows the Casino Clubhouse Wharf in the center. The Casino was built in 1900 and the North Haven Casino incorporated in 1912, "to encourage yachting, athletic sports, and social meetings . . ." for both North Haven and Vinalhaven. It was a simple one-room building downstairs, with a small sailing-school office and ladies' room upstairs. Teas were the tradition following the yacht races, and continue to this day.

On the wharf was the "salt store" where MacDonald used to provisions boats with supplies—including salt—which he kept in the basement. Some of the wharf buildings later became the Marine Apartments, rented out in the summer months, until they were sold piecemeal after 1911. All of the buildings are now part of the North Haven Casino Yacht Club. The three-story house to the left of the sprawling club is a summer residence, and served as the Kent Store and North Haven's first post office before the turn of the twentieth century.

The building on the hill behind the Casino was Library Hall, which was later torn down and a new library built on the site. In the background is the American Legion Hall. The cluster of buildings to the right included stables, a garage, and warehouses, as well as the ship chandlery, which is now Eric Hopkins's art gallery. The white, four-story building to the right of it had been the C. S. Staples General Store, which later became W. S. Hopkins General Store and wharf. Today it is the North Haven Gift Shop.

The Waterman Company market and variety store, to the far right of the postcard, closed in 1993. A longstanding island landmark, it sold all sorts of general-store merchandise, including penny candy from the glass case now displayed at the North Island Museum. The building was torn down to make way for Waterman's Community Center at the east end of the boatyard.

INTERESTING TIDBIT:

Back in 1977, a special census of the island showed that 398 year-round residents owned 153 dwellings valued at $1.8 million. Seven hundred fifteen seasonal residents owned 199 dwellings valued at $6.5 million.

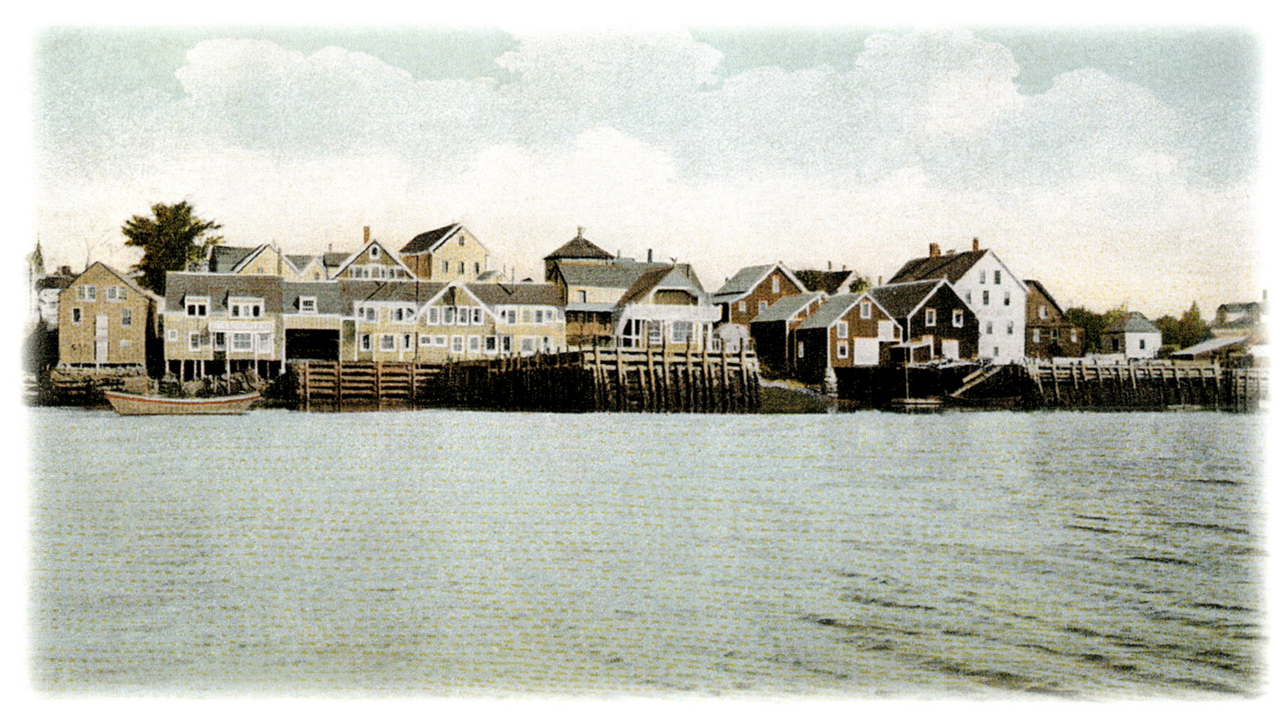

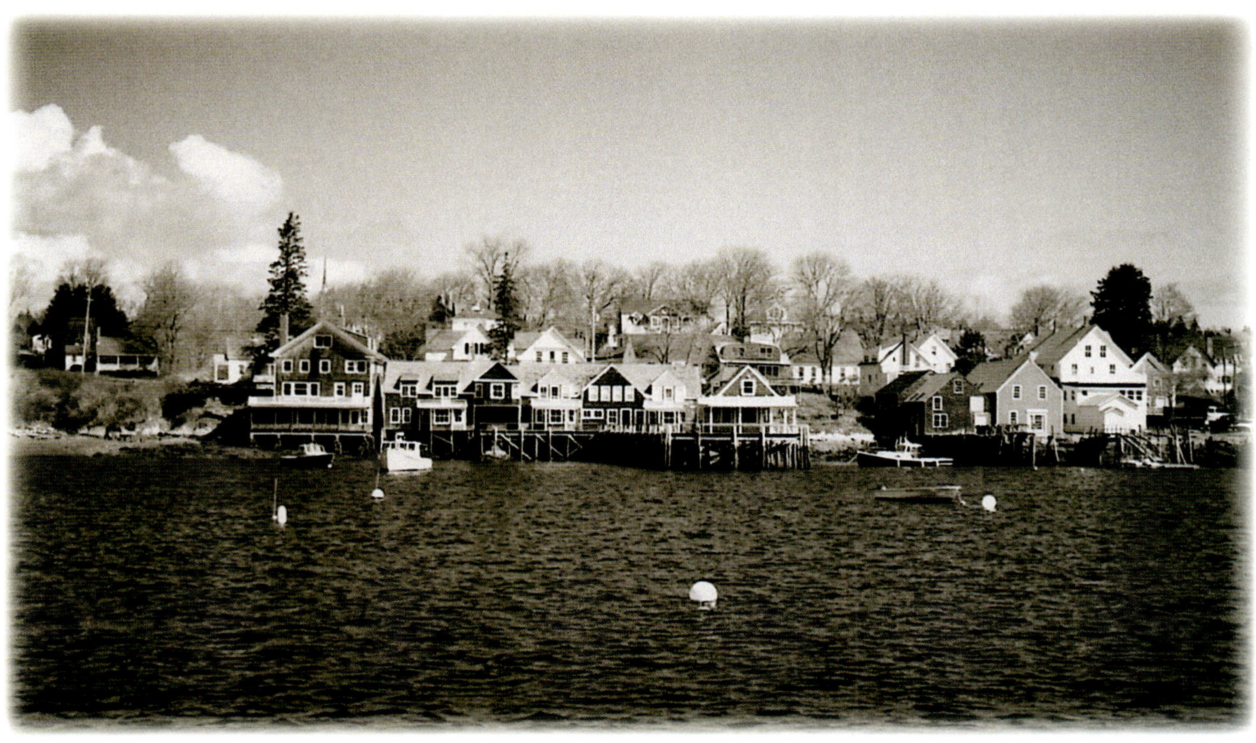

Old Orchard Beach

INCORPORATED AS MAINE'S 447TH TOWN ON FEBRUARY 20, 1883

POPULATION IN 1900: 964

POPULATION IN 2000: 8,856

Old Orchard Beach is Maine's version of Coney Island. Amusement rides, tattoo parlors, wall-to-wall beachcombers, fried onions, and fried bodies—this is Old Orchard in the summer. The pier, with its vendors and lowbrow diversions, is the centerpiece of the seven-mile-long beach. When built more than a hundred years ago, it extended 1,700 feet into Saco Bay, daring the elements with its fragile splendor.

After much planning, Old Orchard Beach began construction on the world's largest steel pier on St. Patrick's Day in 1898. Including the part over the beach itself, the pier was 1,800 feet long, with four pavilions spaced at 460-foot intervals along the promenade. Total seating capacity was 5,000. But Mother Nature has no respect for man-made finery; in December of the pier's first year, a nor'easter destroyed the fourth pavilion.

Grand hotels in typical resort fashion sprang up on the beach. The Hotel Velvet opened across from the pier entrance in 1899, sporting eighty different designs of velvet carpeting. The hotel was later named the Hotel Emerson.

Since 1907 Old Orchard Beach has survived six major fires and many storms, but the grand hotels and casinos did not always fare so well. On a fine August day in 1907, seven hundred people were enjoying themselves on the pier when fire broke out along the waterfront. Flames soon lapped at the oak planking on the walkway, and several men began tear-

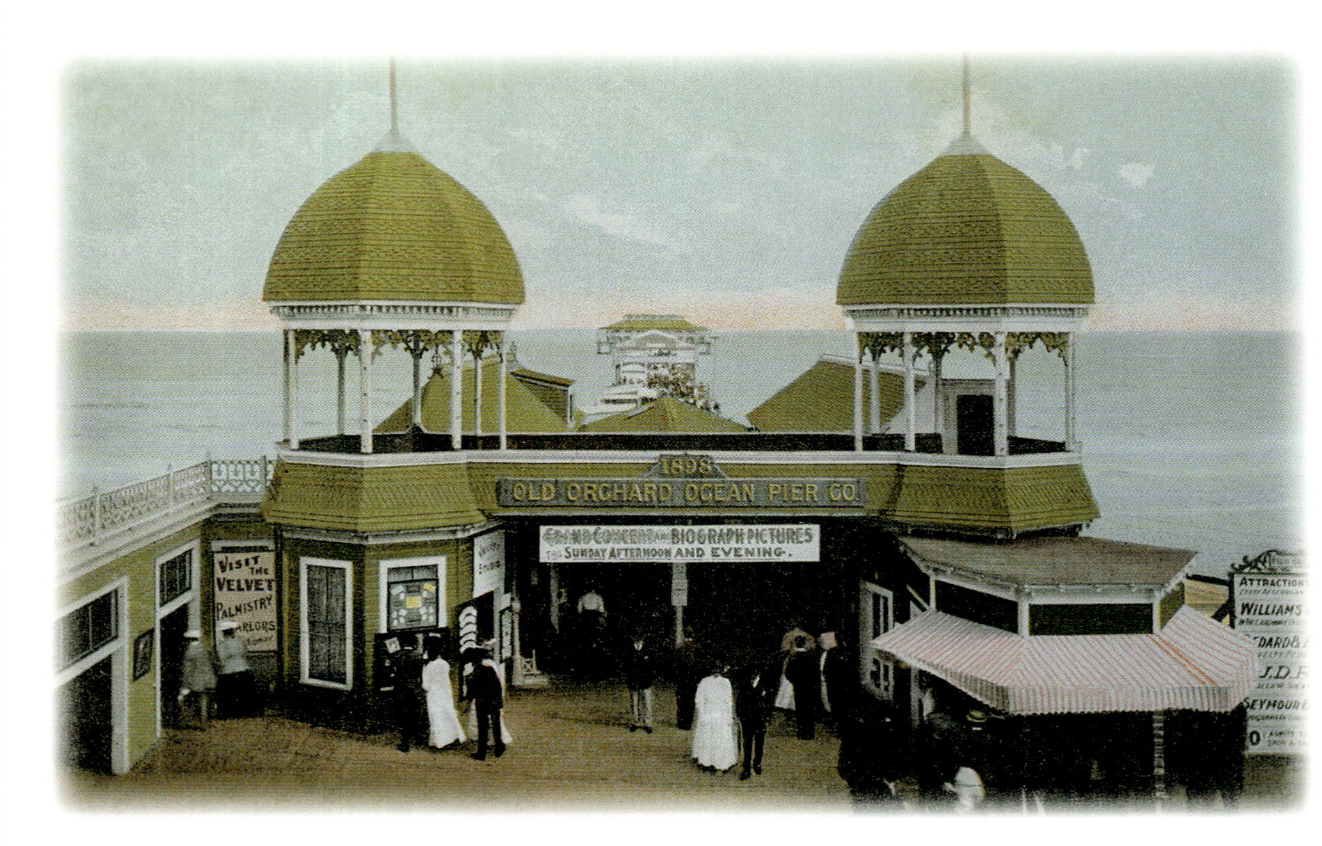

ing off the planking ahead of the fire to prevent the entire pier from burning. When it was over, the pavilion at the entrance and the first hundred feet of boardwalk had been reduced to ashes, and the steel trestle had twisted and buckled from the heat. The Hotel Velvet and sixteen other hotels were consumed in the conflagration, along with sixty cottages and scores of other buildings.

Two years later a March storm blew away the middle section of the pier. Following this event, the pier had a thousand feet lopped off its length and the casino was moved closer to shore. From 1911 to 1912, its deteriorating iron framework was replaced with oak pilings.

In 1913 a new owner introduced the arcades and booth stands, which provided the template for today's carnival-like atmosphere. A 1923 fire didn't make it too far down the pier because firemen tore up the planking at the entrance. But the German-built carousel installed in 1892 perished, as did the pier entrance building. Another carousel was installed in 1924, along with a "curious collection of gaudy amusements" such as Noah's Ark and the Jack Rabbit's Roller Coaster, according to one writer.

From the 1920s to the 1950s, big-name bands played on the pier. Count Basie, Duke Ellington, Cab Calloway, Louis Armstrong, Glenn Miller, Jimmy Dorsey, and others performed, along with local house bands. Dwindling crowds led to the closing of the ballroom in 1956. In the early 1960s it was converted to an 18-hole miniature golf course and aquarium.

In July 1969 another fire destroyed the amusement area and one third of the pier. A penny in the fuse box of the Moonspinner ride, located in the White Way, caused the conflagration. The deteriorating casino was removed the following year, and a snowstorm in February 1972 obliterated the White Way pavilion and 200 feet of boardwalk. A February 1978 blizzard with hurricane-force winds destroyed all but a few twisted shreds of the wooden pier. The present-day pier with its twin entrance towers opened in June 1980 on a wooden foundation that is 396 feet long and 27 feet wide. The postcard view of the entrance was taken from the Hotel Velvet.

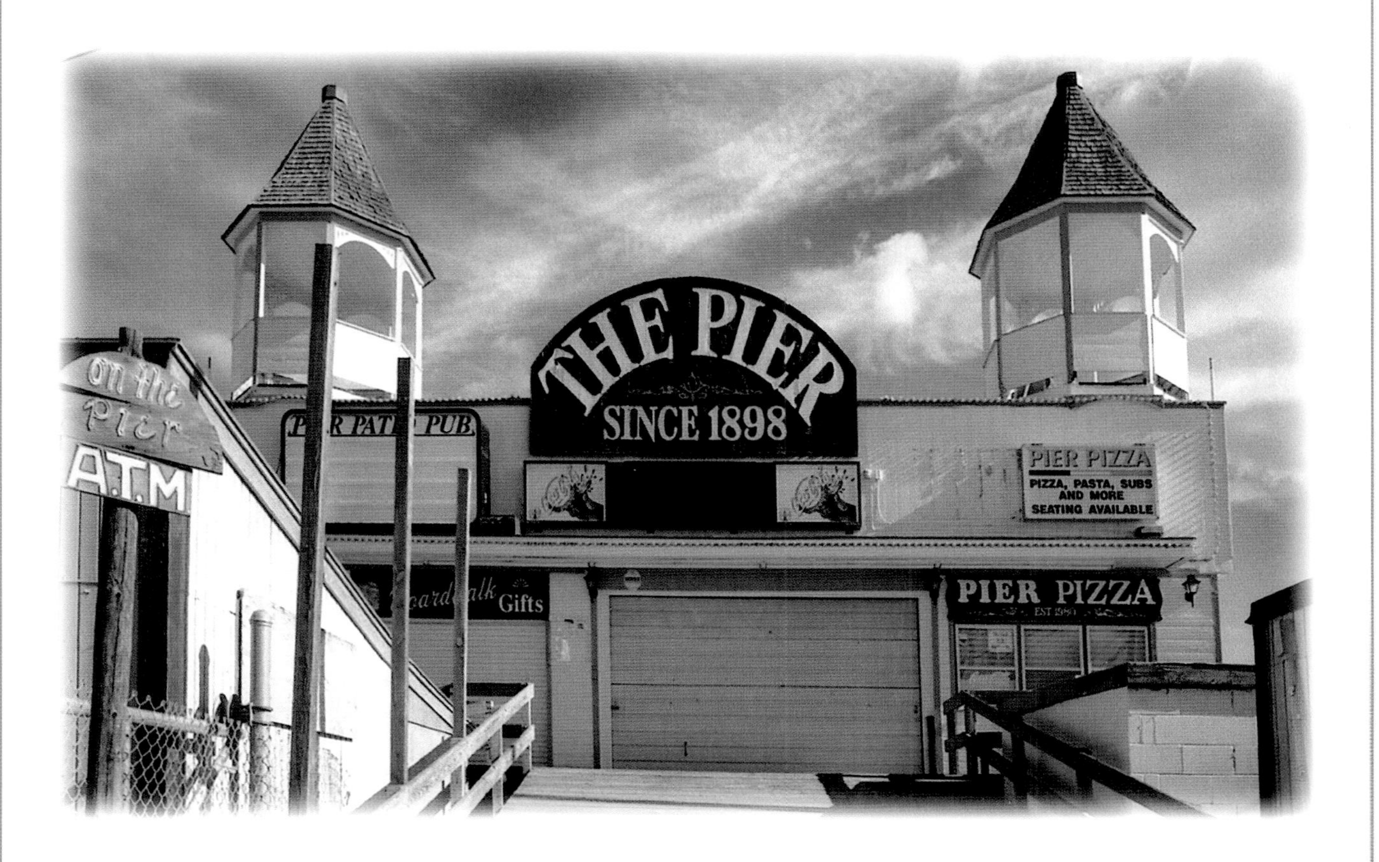

Pemaquid Point Light

The Pemaquid Point Light overlooks one of the most artistic piles of "pulled taffy" bedrock on the Maine Coast—and one of the deadliest. More than one unsuspecting bystander has been swept to sea by a rogue wave crashing high on the rocks. Many ships have also met with peril on the jagged rocks just offshore. Yet countless visitors continue to pay homage to its beauty.

As early day shipping and commerce increased on the Atlantic, so did shipwrecks, mandating the installation of a beam to guide mariners. Built in 1827, the first tower didn't hold together very well, probably because the contractor used salt water to mix his lime mortar. Fresh water was specified for the 38-foot replacement in 1835, which stands 78 feet above water level to this day. The original ten whale oil lamps and reflectors were replaced by a fourth-order Fresnel lens in 1856, which still directs the beam today with a white light flashing every six seconds. It is visible for fourteen miles.

The original stone keeper's house was replaced with a wooden dwelling the following year. The brick fog bell house and tower were constructed in 1897. Like most fog bells at the time, it was hand-cranked; the following year, steam engines were installed, later replaced by a striking machine that could go eight hours between windings. The bell was removed in the 1930s. The tower was destroyed by two storms in 1991 and rebuilt the following year. Even with the lighthouse guardian, ships still ran aground. In 1930 the last keeper of the light, Leroy S. Elwell, received a U.S. Lighthouse Service commendation when he rescued three people from a capsized sailboat under hazardous conditions.

Pemaquid Light was the first in Maine to be automated in 1934. The grounds later became a park leased by the town of Bristol, and the keeper's house was converted into the Fishermen's Museum in 1972. The light is still an active aid to navigation, and in 2000 it was leased by the Coast Guard to the American Lighthouse Foundation, which jointly operates it along with the Friends of Pemaquid Point Lighthouse. Still standing are the 1857 keeper's house, the 1896 oil house, and the fog bell tower, which was rebuilt in 1992.

People standing on solid ground here have been washed out to sea when they misjudged the reach of the waves. Several have been swept to their deaths in the past two decades, and dozens more have suffered broken bones and other injuries. In 1995, the town of Bristol erected a fence to keep the public off the rocks after eleven people had to be fished out of the turbulent waves.

Pemaquid Light appears on the Maine state quarter, released in 2003. The design, which shows the windjammer *Victory Chimes* sailing offshore, was selected over three other finalists by an informal vote of over 100,000 people. It is the first circulating U.S. coin ever to feature a lighthouse. A ceremony with newly elected Governor John Baldacci was held at the lighthouse in June 2003 to honor the release of the quarter, which was minted for only ten weeks.

The state quarter series was initiated in 1999, with the quarters released according to the date each state was admitted to the Union. The Maine quarter is the twenty-third in the series, and the last New England quarter to be minted. Because it was minted in a period of low demand due to the recession, it has the smallest circulation—448,800,000—of any of the quarters minted so far. Virginia, in contrast, has 1,594,616,000.

For the first time ever, volunteers in the summer of 2003 supervised public access to the inner workings of the lighthouse. More than eight thousand visitors from all fifty states and several countries climbed the stairs to the beacon.

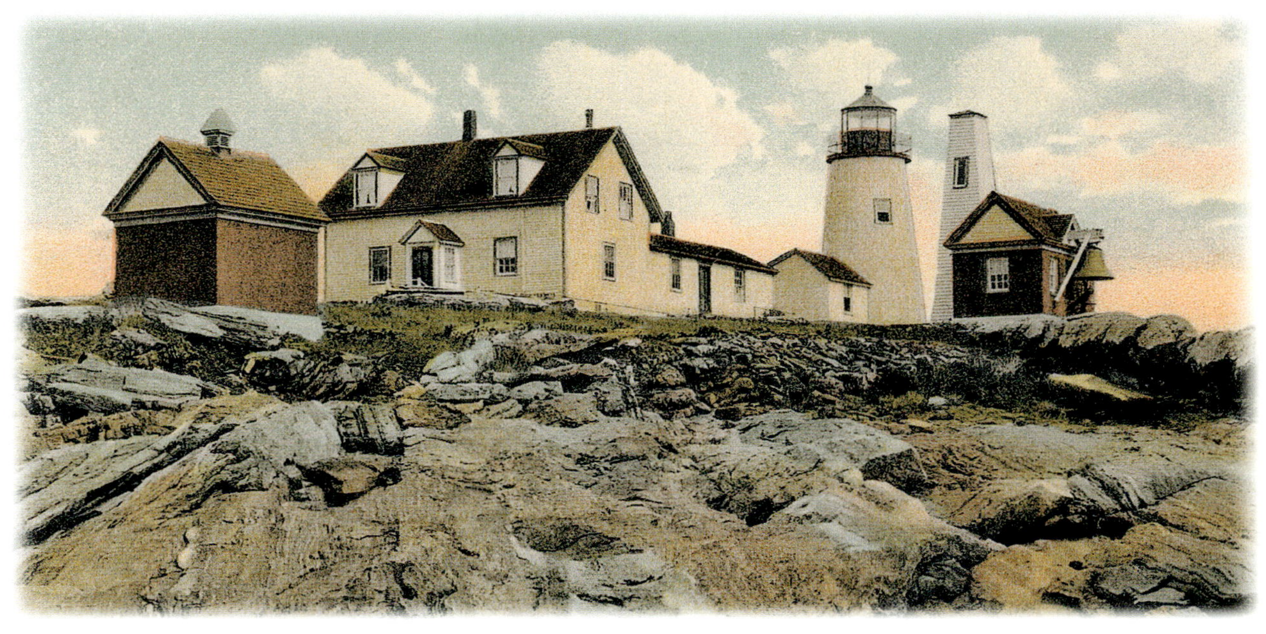

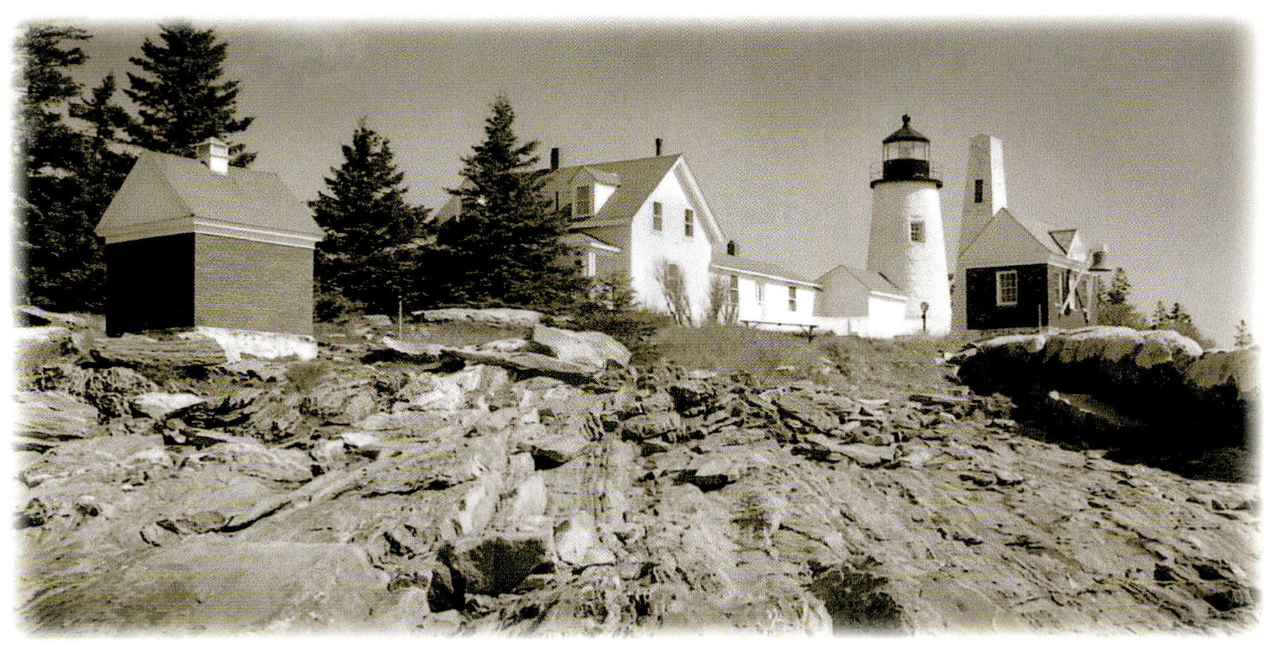

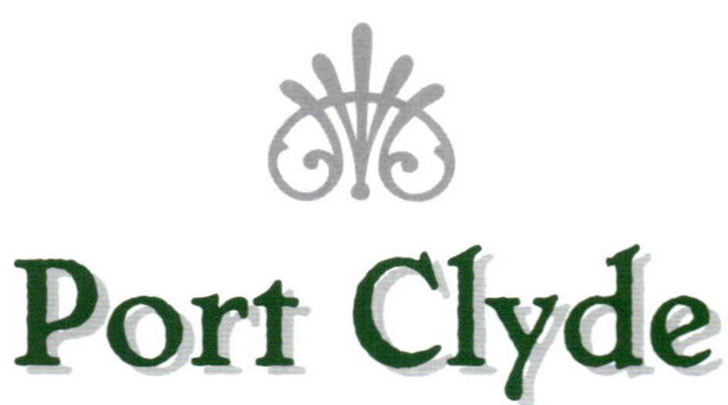

Port Clyde

A VILLAGE IN THE TOWN OF
ST. GEORGE, WHICH
WAS INCORPORATED AS MAINE'S
138TH TOWN ON FEBRUARY 7, 1803

POPULATION OF ST. GEORGE
IN 1900: 2,206

POPULATION OF ST. GEORGE
IN 2000: 2,580

"Nothing really to see or do in Port Clyde. Heaven help the stranded tourist."

Those were the words of author Martin Dibner in 1973. Port Clyde hasn't changed much, thankfully.

Known before 1891 as Herring Gut (*gut* means a narrow waterway), this village at the tip of the St. George peninsula today has a harbor jammed with lobster buoys and a small fleet of fourteen offshore draggers. Hugging its shores are expansive homes owned by families of fortune whose mere presence has caused housing prices to skyrocket. More than half of the property in St. George is owned by nonresidents, and many young lobstermen have to travel from places off-peninsula in order to work their traps in St. George. But enough veteran lobstermen populate the town so that many yards are decorated with stacks of purple, yellow, or green traps snuggling fluorescent buoys when not in their watery quarters in Muscongus Bay.

St. George was a busy place in the nineteenth century; fishing, granite quarrying, and shipbuilding were the mainstays. It was likely the Scottish quarrymen that gave this village its name, after the Clyde Valley of their native country.

When the Burnham and Morrill Packing Company closed in 1900, Port Clyde Packing Company took over its lobster-canning operations. It kept going until September 24, 1970, when a suspicious fire

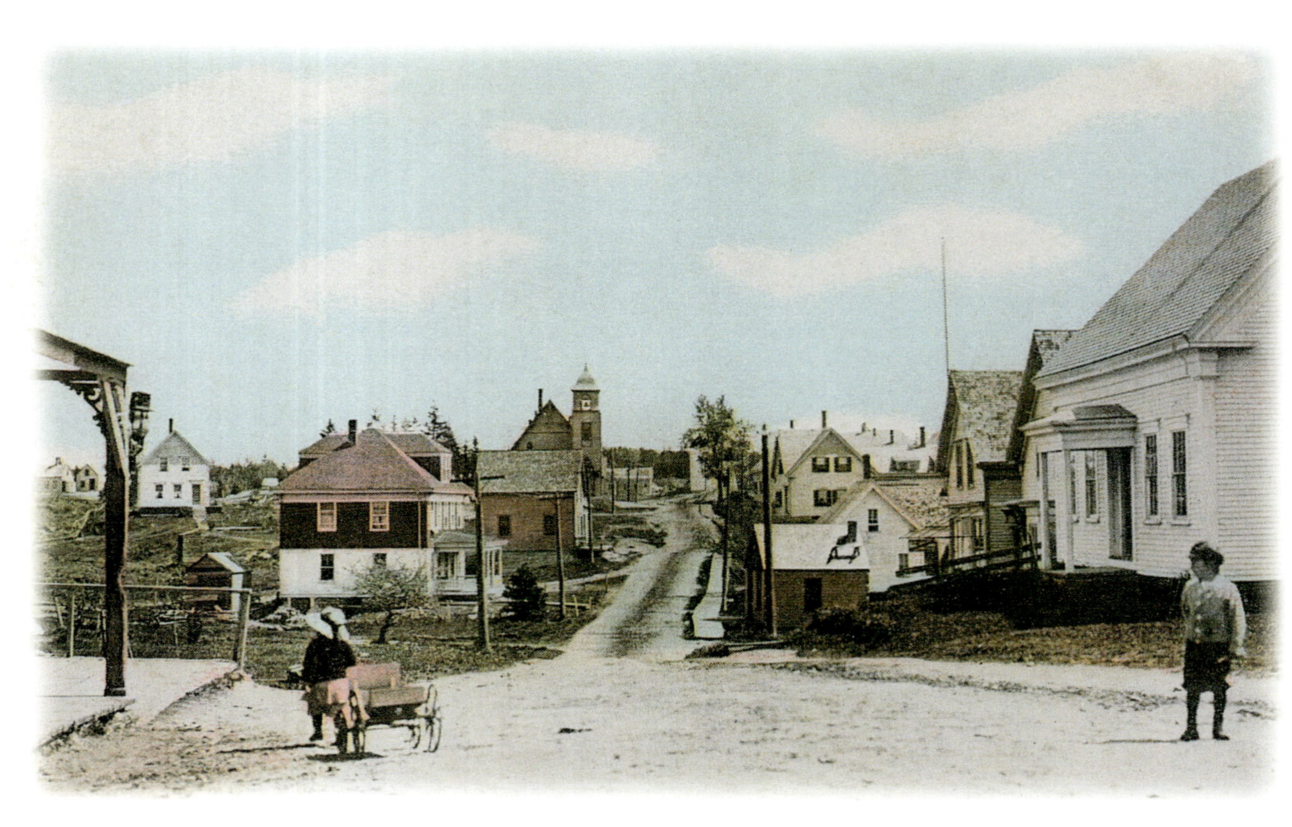

turned it to ashes in just over an hour, putting 200 out of work. Henry Danielowitz, then a 64-year-old shipping manager, was hard at work when the fire started. "We all raced out of the factory carrying whatever valuables we could, including typewriters. By the time we got everybody out, the factory was completely ablaze." His stepson, Carl Schwab, a lobsterman, said the explosion blew sardine cans all the way to Hupper Island a quarter mile away. Even today tin cans can be seen in the waters around the site.

Schwab told of how he used to find herring for the sardine plant. "We'd go out at night and thump on the bottom of the dory with our feet," he said. "It would startle the herring, and they'd stir up the phosphorescence in the water. Mackerel wouldn't startle that way, so that's how we knew where the herring were."

The local scenery has inspired artists from the hobbyist to one of the country's greatest American painters, and Andrew Wyeth sightings (with or without Helga) are common in village eateries. A couple of wire-haired fox terriers are also local celebrities, featured in children's books illustrated by Robert Ensor (one is written by his wife, Eloise). The first, *Nellie the Lighthouse Dog*, featured the rescue of a lost child at Marshall Point Light by the Ensors' dog.

Sarah Orne Jewett summered in nearby Martinsville in the 1890s and wrote her best-known work—*The Country of the Pointed Firs* (1896) and other Dunnet Landing stories—with the village and its people as its inspiration.

Even though there is "nothing to see or do," the area has long provided accommodations for tourists. The Ocean House, perhaps the oldest and most well-known inn, is a stone's throw from the public landing. It was built in 1851, burned in 1888, and then rebuilt. The photograph of Main Street today, looking north, shows the Advent Christian Church (not yet built when the postcard was made). The two-toned house just beyond remained a private home until several years ago, when it became a seasonal art gallery. The 1897 Port Clyde Baptist Church in the background has been a subject for many painters.

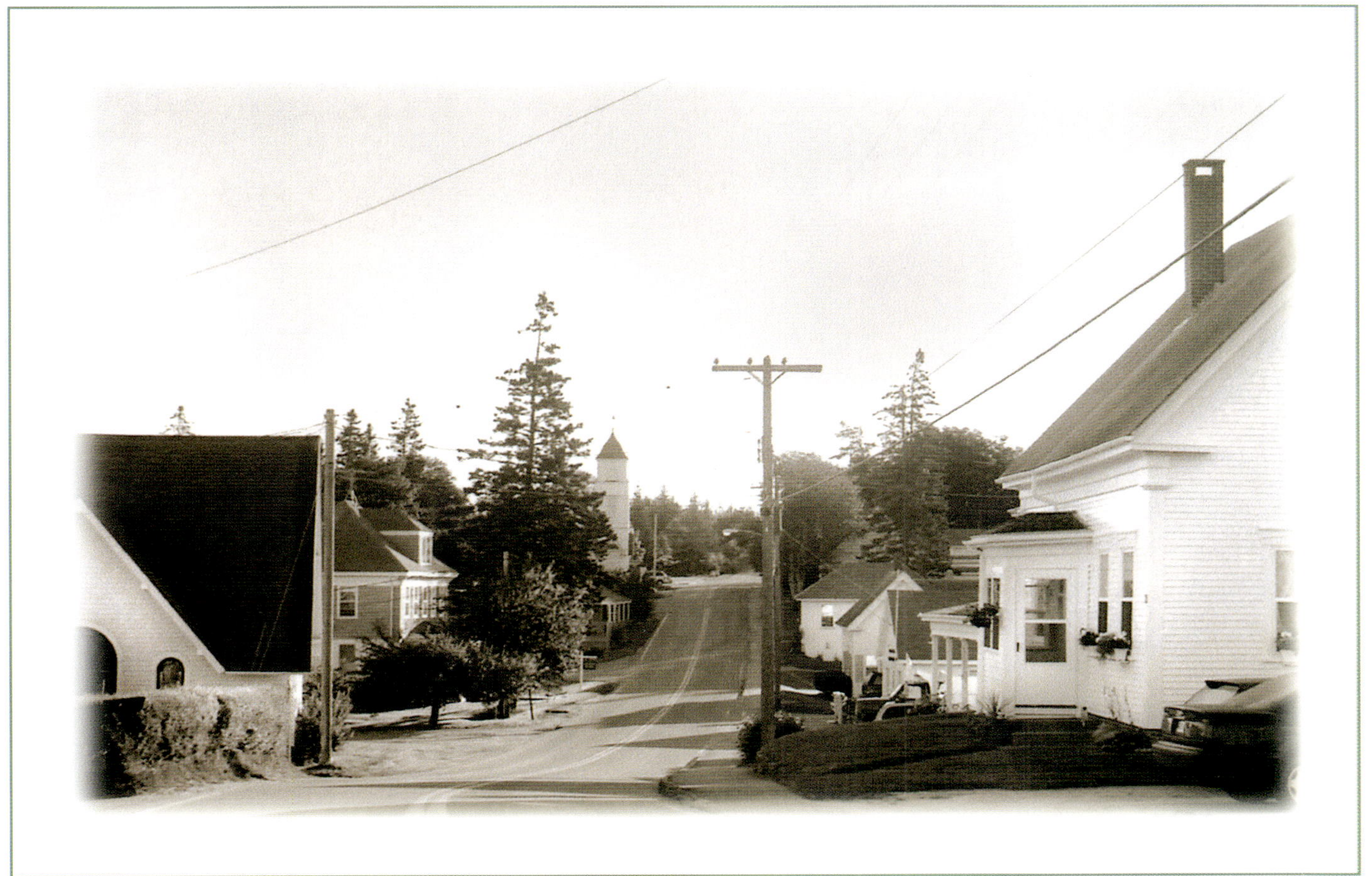

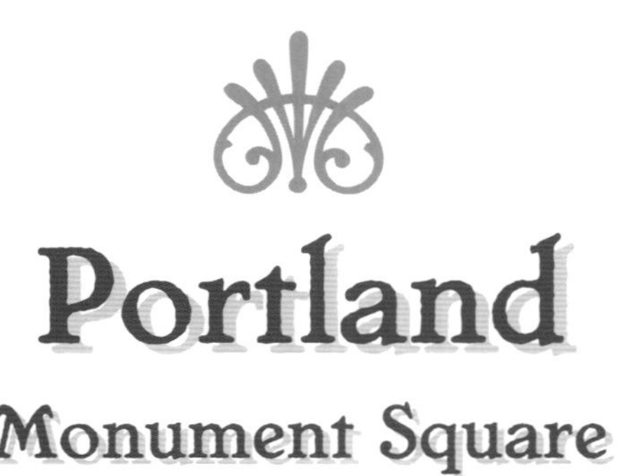

Portland

Monument Square

PORTLAND INCORPORATED
AS MAINE'S 46TH TOWN ON JULY 4, 1786
AND MAINE'S 1ST CITY ON MARCH 26, 1833

POPULATION IN 1900: 50,145

POPULATION IN 2000: 64,249

The town was two thousand souls strong when the Neck portion of Falmouth became Portland in 1786. It was originally Maine's capital, but Augusta was deemed to be more centrally located, and in 1827 it was designated to become the capital. The seat of state government was moved there five years later when the new capitol building was completed in 1832.

At the turn of the twentieth century, Portland billed itself as "The Convention City." It hosted up to a quarter million tourists each year, and the state's principal postcard manufacturers—Hugh C. Leighton and George W. Morris—churned out cards by the millions. A January 1908 fire destroyed the City Hall, and it was rebuilt in 1910 (for the third time). It is now the 3,000-seat Merrill Auditorium, and boasts a stunning pipe organ.

In 1971 the Maine Mall opened in South Portland, further eroding an already dying downtown area. A waterfront renovation soon began and continued through the 1980s, bringing in an international ferry terminal and a new fish pier. Greater Portland Landmarks, Inc. worked in conjunction with the Old Port Exchange to transform derelict buildings into specialty shops, restaurants, galleries, and apartments for young professionals. In 1977 the Cumberland County Civic Center opened with a 9,000-seat capacity. Author Martin Dibner wrote, "The city of Portland seems to inch, cobble by cobble, brick by brick, into the twentieth century."

The postcard shows Monument Square, with all but the monument itself drastically changed in today's photograph. Originally called Haymarket Square when the first town hall was built in 1825, it found a new identity when the Soldiers and Sailors Monument was erected on the old town hall site after it was demolished in 1888. Titled "Our Lady of Victories," it commemorated those who fought in the Civil War. The selection of a design and location took eighteen contentious years to resolve. Maine sculptor Franklin Simmons designed the monument, which features two groups of life-sized military men.

In the center stands Admiral David G. Farragut, hero of the battles of New Orleans and Mobile Bay. The central figure in the group of army soldiers is Brigadier General Francis L. Vinton of Fort Preble, Maine. They were sculpted in Rome, Italy, and shipped from Naples buried in a cargo of loose sulphur. On Memorial Day 1889, an eighteen-inch-square copper box with documents, photographs, medals, and other memorabilia was sealed and placed in the cornerstone. It was dedicated on October 28, 1891. The decision over which names to place on the plaque was also fraught with controversy. Finally it was decided the wording should be: *1861–1865 More than four thousand men were enrolled from Portland in the Army and Navy for the War of the Rebellion. More than three hundred were killed in battle, or died in service. Honor and grateful remembrance to the dead. Equal honor to those who, daring to die, survived.*

In the postcard, the backdrop to the monument is the Edwards and Walker hardware building, which was originally the 1803 Washington Hall hotel. Later it became the Portland House, then the Cumberland House with several expansions, and by 1840, it was the United States Hotel. It escaped the Great Fire of July 4, 1866, and was remodeled in the early 1870s, when a fifth floor was added. The hotel closed in 1900, and two years later the hardware store moved in. The building was sold to Casco Bank in 1965 and replaced in 1970 with a ten-story office building. Its "massive aggressiveness" stands in contrast to the demure monument.

The last electric trolley trundled down Congress Street in 1941. There are seven trolleys in this postcard!

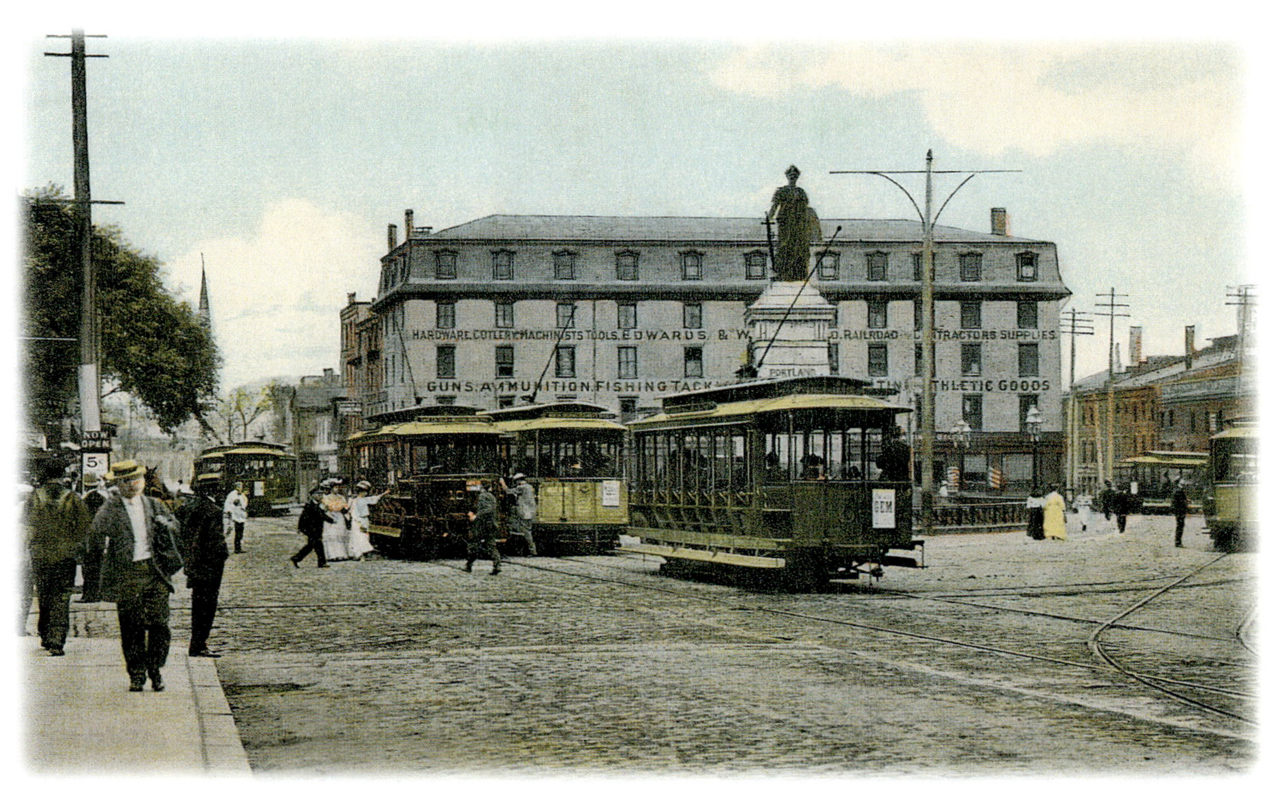
HARDWARE, CUTLERY, MACHINISTS TOOLS.
CONTRACTORS SUPPLIES
GUNS, AMMUNITION, FISHING TACK
ATHLETIC GOODS
PORTLAND
GEM

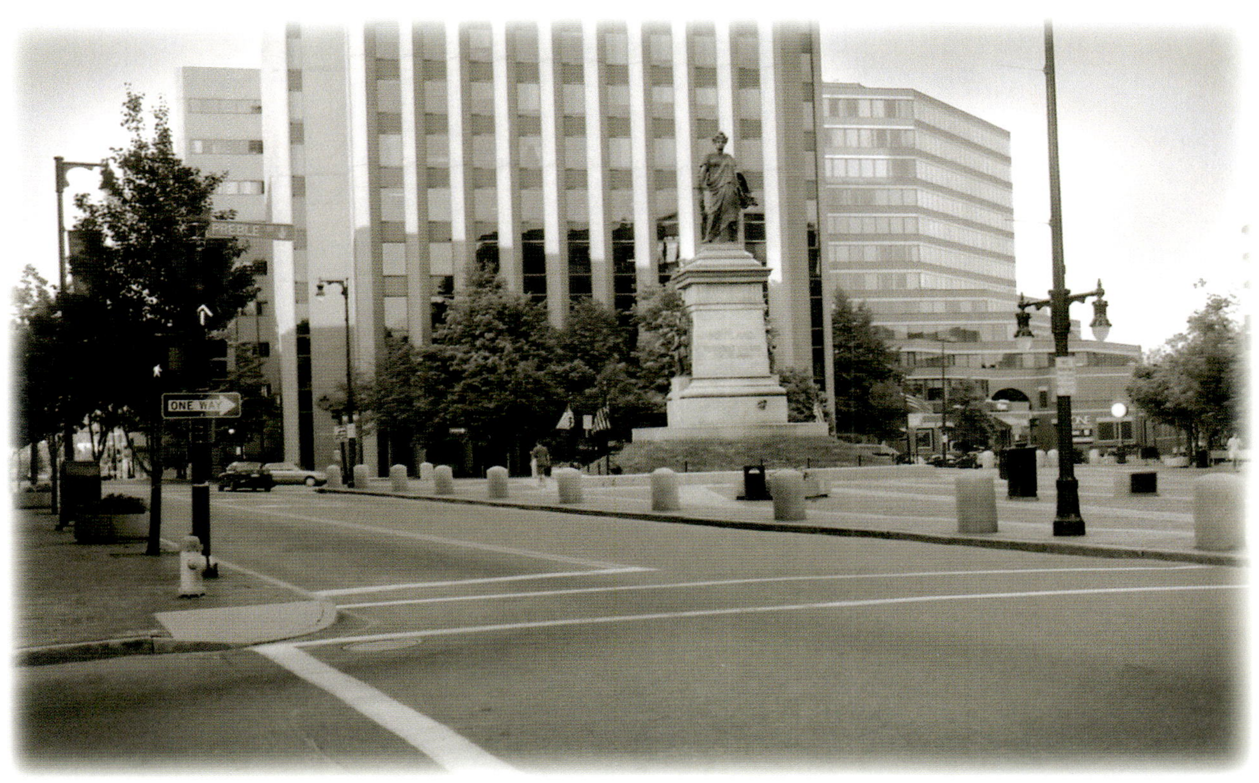
PREBLE
ONE WAY

Union Station

The phrase "urban renewal" has the same *ugh!* factor as, say, strip malls—which is exactly what many historic and artful buildings in Maine became, thanks to urban renewal. Many a Portlander today still mourns the loss of the grand 1888 Union Station. Though meant to memorialize the station with its marvelous clock tower, today's Union Station Plaza strip-mall sign only serves to mock it. Greater Port-land Landmarks, Inc., arose from the public rage over the destruction of this wonderful old building, and since then preservation groups throughout the city and the state have managed to hold on to many of the buildings that would have otherwise been bygones.

Delmar Needham was a conductor on the Maine Central Railroad train that took Franklin D. Roosevelt from Rockland to Portland on August 16, 1941. Roosevelt had signed the Atlantic Charter with British Prime Minister Winston Churchill two days earlier, in a top-secret meeting aboard a battleship off Newfoundland, Canada. The world first heard of the details when Roosevelt arrived in the presidential yacht at Rockland to board the train to Washington. It was presumably Delmar who had the privilege of shouting "All aboard!" on this important day.

Delmar's son John, of Tenants Harbor, said Delmar started with the line as a baggage handler in the late 1920s or early '30s. He loaded mail sacks on the trains, helped them turn around for their next journey, and during the Depression, even cleaned latrines. "That's the way it was," said John. "There was no work for anybody and you did what you could to get by." But things got better. "When my father got his paycheck, I conned him into getting me a soda at Armstrong's Restaurant in the station," he chuckled. "I also got to ride up in the locomotive with the engineer once. I was ten at the time. I was so puffed up by the experience I couldn't get through the door!"

A rarely remembered bit of history about Portland's passenger-train service concerns the African-Americans who served as redcaps—so called because of the red hats they wore as part of their uniform. As many as a dozen redcaps carried bags, cleaned bathrooms, or cooked for passengers at the Union Station. Until 1938, when the various black train workers' unions successfully petitioned for salaries, the redcaps worked solely for tips.

The chateau-style Union Station was renowned for its interior architectural beauty, with elegant exposed wooden beams and decorative ash trim. The fireplace was topped with marble, and the floor was of marble and slate. The granite to build the structure came from North Conway, New Hampshire.

Looking at the postcard, the mail department was at the back end, and the waiting-room entrance was the archway between the two turrets. The Boston and Maine Line boarding area was to the rear, and the Maine Central Line was on the far right. The Rigby Yard Turnaround was four miles away.

Union Station was torn down on August 31, 1961. Half the train shed was moved to Thompson's Point where it is still used for storage today. The clock is currently displayed at ground level in Congress Square in downtown Portland. The building to the left was the Maine Central Railroad office building and is now Margarita's Mexican Restaurant.

In December 2001 Amtrak instituted the first passenger rail service to Maine in three decades with its *Downeaster*, which links Boston with Portland. But no station today is as magnificent as this one was—one of many in Maine lost to urban renewal.

Five trains at Union Station, probably in the 1920's. The airplane was undoubtedly added by the postcard publisher.

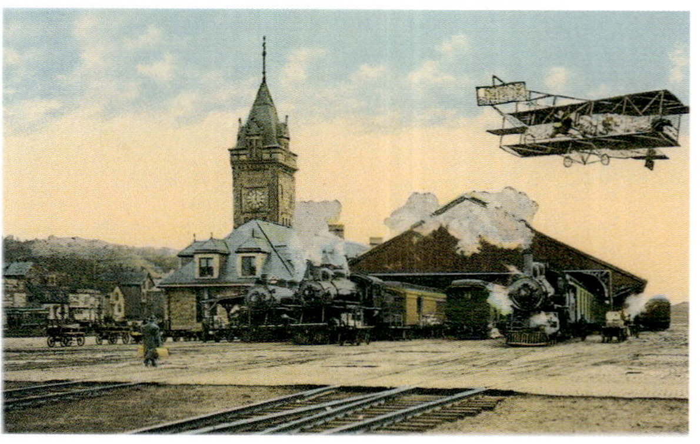

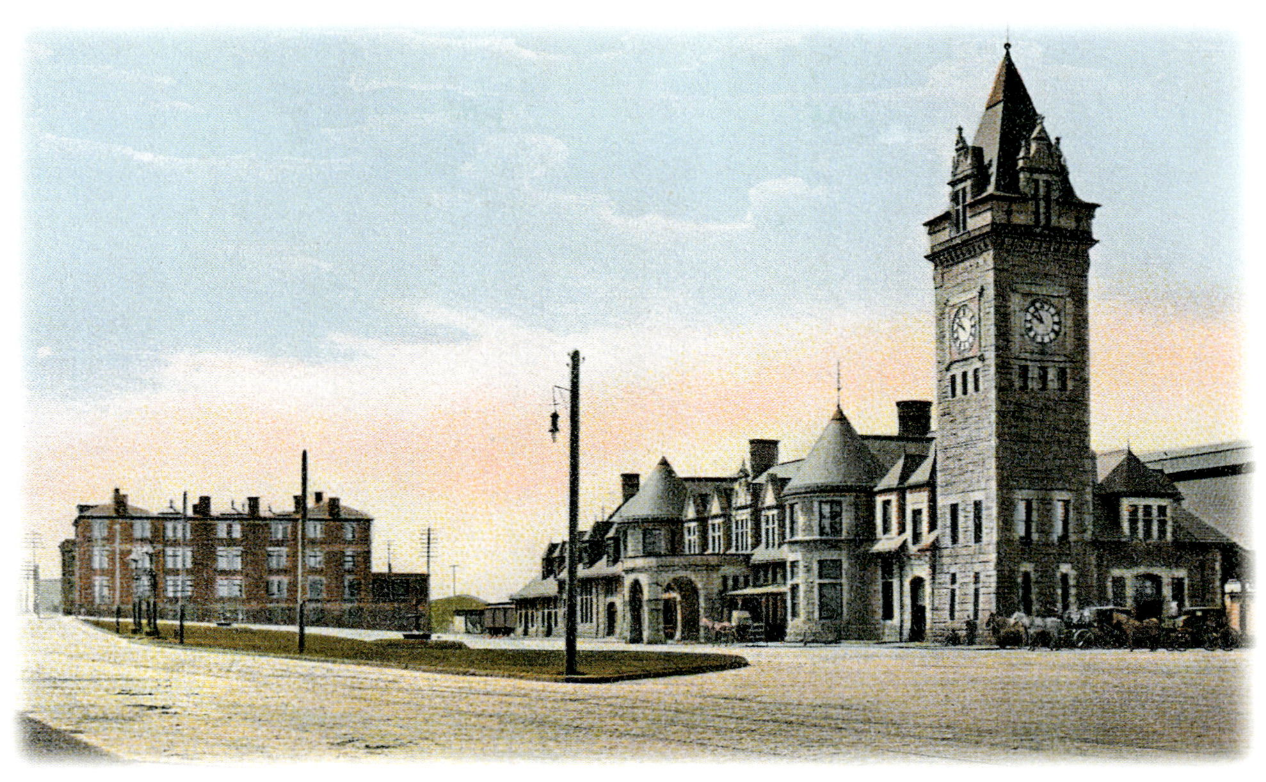

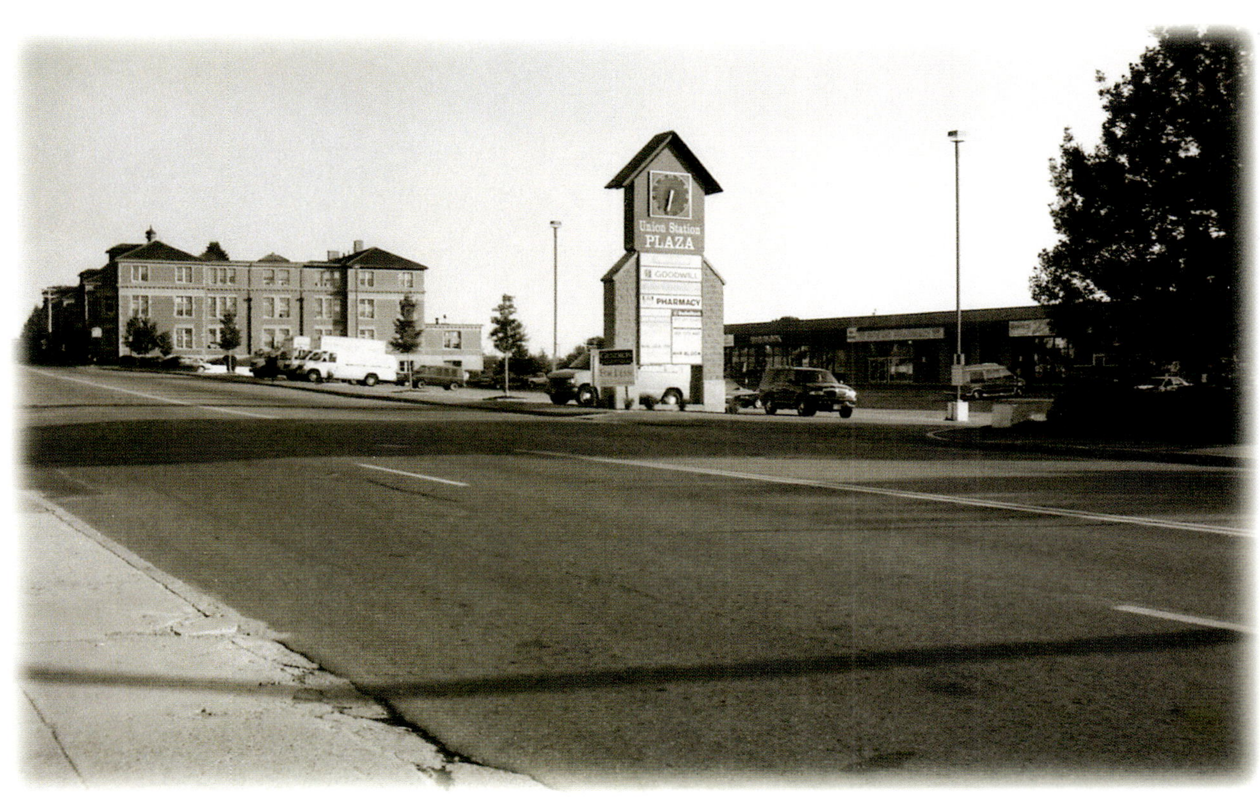
Union Station
PLAZA
GOODWILL
PHARMACY

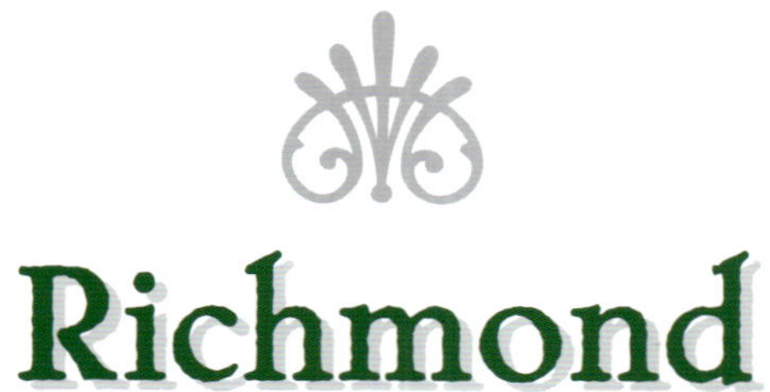

Richmond

INCORPORATED AS MAINE'S
252ND TOWN ON FEBRUARY 10, 1823

POPULATION IN 1900: 2,049

POPULATION IN 2000: 3,298

The Russians came to Richmond during the Cold War, and nobody seemed to mind. Having fled communist rule, they were lured by a Russian army pilot named Baron Vladimir von Poushental who had settled in the area. The Czar's relative, Princess Vera Romanov, also had a summer home in the area, and that might have inspired some to settle here. At any rate, von Poushental bought up many "hardscrabble farms," said town historian Jay Robbins, and advertised Maine living in Russian-language newspapers in the United States. Eventually, the Gardiner-Richmond area had the largest Russian-speaking population in the country, consisting of around five hundred Russians, Ukrainians, and Belorussians. They took up settlement in many of the neglected farmsteads, bringing them back to life and establishing three Orthodox churches. Today the blue onion-domed St. Alexander Nevsky is the only Russian Orthodox Church in Maine.

Richmond was famous for shipbuilding, as were many towns with waterfronts. Many Greek Revival and Victorian homes, now on the National Register, were built by sea captains, merchants, and shipbuilders. The shipbuilding era was at its peak from 1824 to 1885, and the last Richmond-built vessel, the four-masted *Phoebe Crosby*, slid down the ways in 1920. Ice harvesting brought about a second period of prosperity in the early 1900s, and shoe making was important from the Civil War era through the end of the twentieth century. Etonic, manufacturer of golf shoes, was the largest employer for the second half of the twentieth century. When the factory closed in

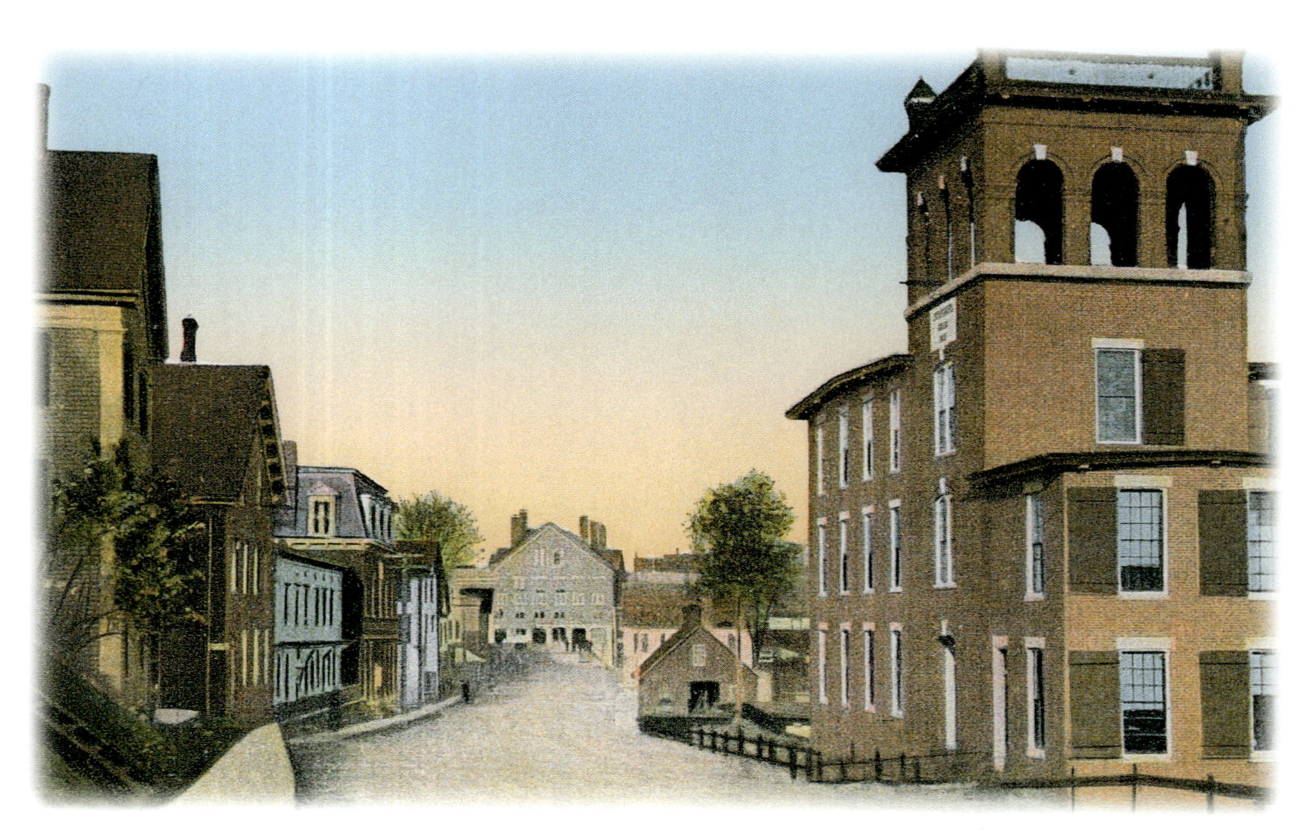

2000, it was converted into the Richmond Business and Manufacturing Center. Among the businesses operating there today are Maine Scientific, which makes components for hearing-aid interface devices, and Maine Composites, which produces carbon fiber products such as ship masts for racing yachts.

In the postcard of Front Street, the 1881 Southard Cotton mill is on the right. It was started by T. J. Southard, whom Robbins describes as a "rags to riches, Horatio Alger- type guy." The first mill burned shortly after it was built, but Southard just put up another. It was eventually bought out by Ames Worsted Mill, and when it closed in the early 1960s it was given to the town, which leases part of it to Richmond Contract Manufacturing, Inc., a company that assembles electronic components.

Beyond the mill was Edward Page's blacksmith shop. Today's public boat landing on the Kennebec River is to the right of the old shop. Facing the street in the center is the Old Post Office Block, also known as the Hathorn Block. It was built by two brothers who each had commercial space to run their shipping businesses. Listed among Maine's Eleven Most Endangered Buildings in 2003, it is currently for lease by its new owner. The post office was once located where the Front Street Market is now. In 1895 a fire started there—although one text claims it actually started in a nearby bank when thieves blew up the safe.

On the left, from the foreground to the background, was a residence, then the mill boardinghouse, the brick tenement for mill workers, the row houses, and the mansard-roofed Southard Bank on the corner of White Street, now occupied by the Richmond Insurance Agency. The Front Street Market is currently on the corner where Front Street intersects with Main Street. In addition to being the post office in its early years, that building has also served as the library, offices for businesses, and a restaurant and provisions store run by African-American Henry Wilkins.

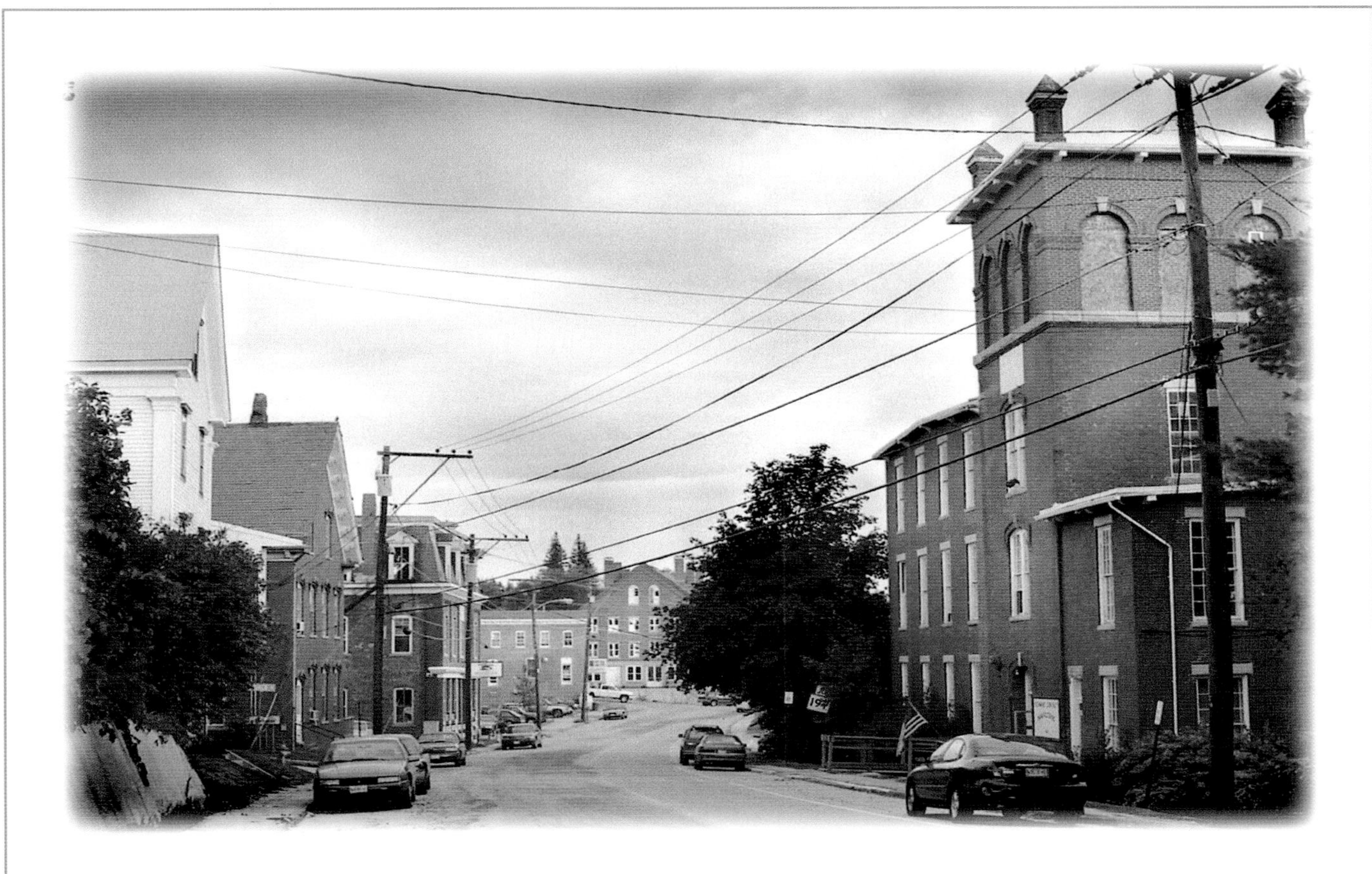

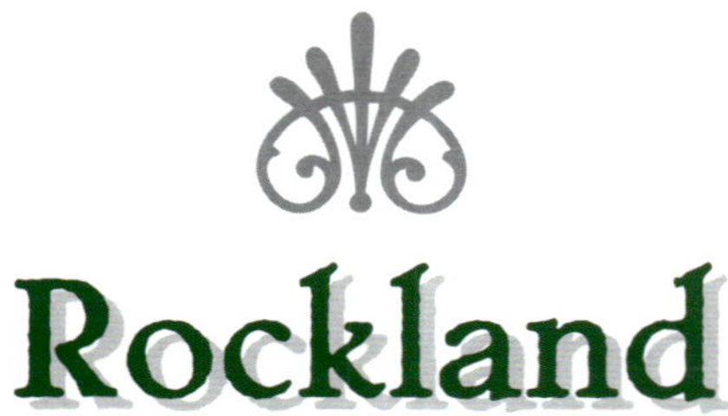

Rockland

INCORPORATED AS MAINE'S
376TH TOWN ON JULY 28, 1848

INCORPORATED AS MAINE'S
9TH CITY ON JUNE 3, 1854

POPULATION IN 1900: 8,150

POPULATION IN 2000: 7,609

Rockland was known as the Shore Village of Thomaston in its early days. In 1848 it was incorporated as East Thomaston, and two years later changed its name to reflect the prodigious limerock industry. Lime was necessary to make plaster, mortar, and cement, among other things, and as long as men were putting up buildings, the lime industry in Rockland and nearby Rockport kept money in the pockets of thousands of men for a hundred and fifty years. "Boston and New York wouldn't have been built until later if it hadn't been for Rockland's lime," said David Hoch, the foreman who put out the fire on the last remaining kiln in 1958. It was the advent of gypsum wallboard, as well as the depletion of the high-quality lime, that signaled the end of the industry that gave the city its name.

It wasn't long ago that the Lime City was known by other, less-flattering names, thanks to the odoriferous Sea-Pro fish processing plant, which closed in 1988. Fish processing and canning were important to the local economy for more than a century. One by one the sardine canneries disappeared. Now Rockland is the Lobster Capital of the World, and there's nothing smelly about that. Rockland has hosted the nationally known Maine Lobster Festival for more than a half century, headlining such notables as Willie Nelson and the Temptations. A hundred thousand people devoured more than 25,000 pounds of the crustacean during the five-day festival in 2004.

Within the last decade, this small mid-coast city has evolved from a gritty industrial town to a gem of a tourist destination, and is now homeport to seven of Maine's windjammers. The expansion of the Farnsworth Art Museum, with the addition of the Wyeth Center several years ago, was the linchpin in the transformation. The center's collection includes paintings by three generations of Wyeths, along with other artists of note.

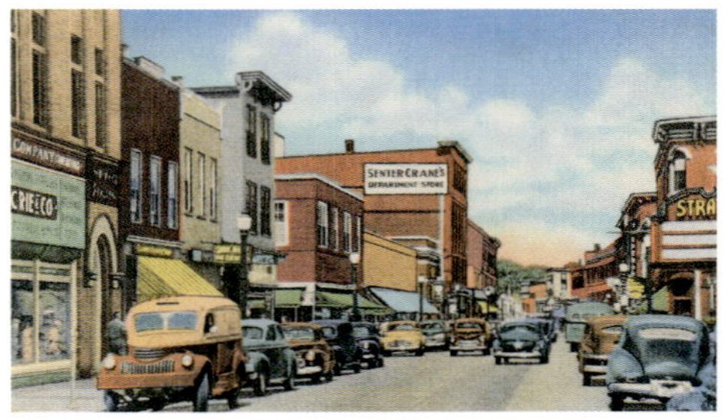

Main Street in the 1940s. The Senter-Crane department store stands in the center. The Strand Theatre (now closed) is on the right.

Several fires changed the face of Main Street over the years. In June 1920, four blocks on the east side went up in smoke, and in 1940 the Masonic Temple burned. Most infamous was the fire of December 12, 1952, which destroyed much of the downtown. The Spear Block with its many businesses, the Hotel Rockland, and the Bayview Hotel were lost.

On the right in the postcard is the Joy Building, with several retail shops such as B. L. Segal Clothing, a luggage store, and a restaurant. Today, G. M. Pollock Jewelry is on that corner, adjacent to an art gallery and an import clothing shop. The round-cornered Thorndike Building at the corner of Tillson Avenue was a hotel from 1855 through the late 1970s. The ground floor housed an optometrist business until the Thorndike Creamery ice cream shop took over in 2003.

On the left side, the household goods store was a Chinese laundry in the 1920s, and housed J. J. Newberry's department store before the Farnsworth expanded to occupy the whole block in the mid-1990s. W. O. Hewett Company on the next corner was replaced by the Security Trust Bank, and is now Harbor Square Gallery. Senter-Crane occupied the Pillsbury Block in 1926; it is now home to the offices of the Island Institute and the Archipelago Gallery.

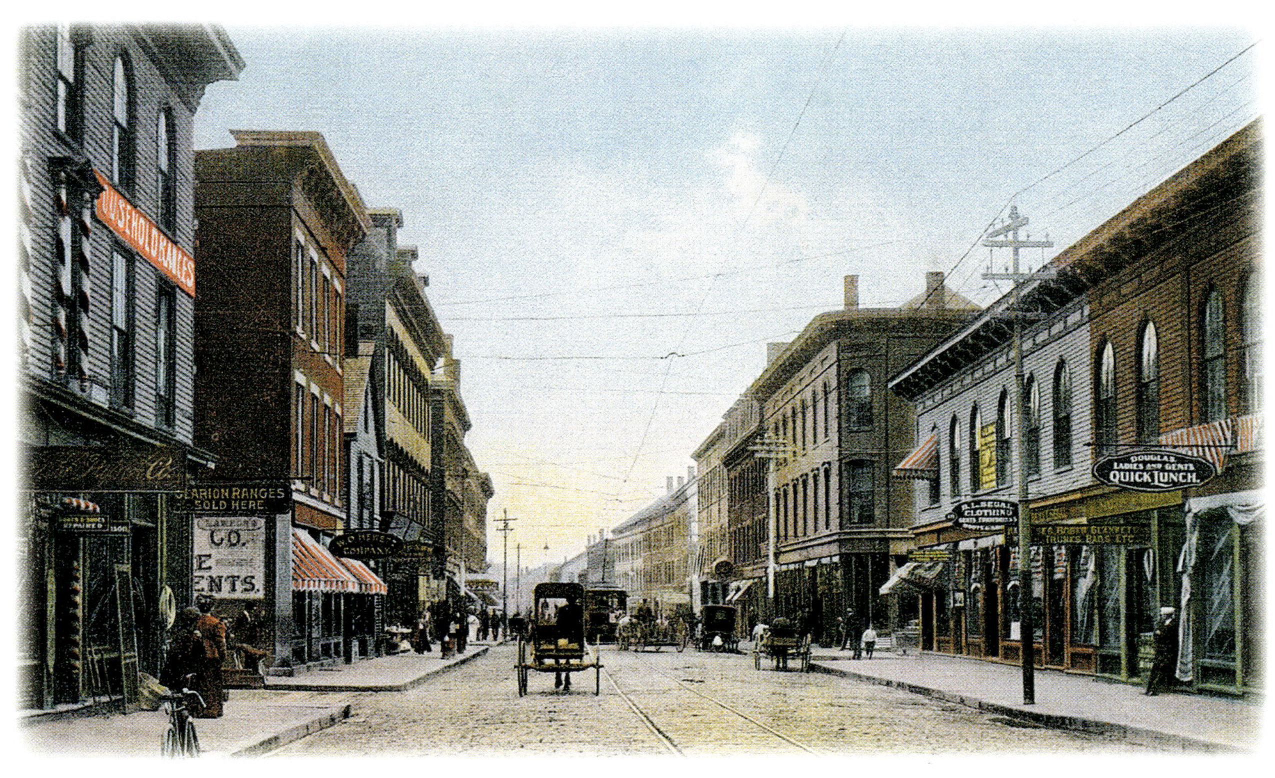
CLARION RANGES
SOLD HERE
DOUGLAS
LADIES AND GENTS
QUICK LUNCH

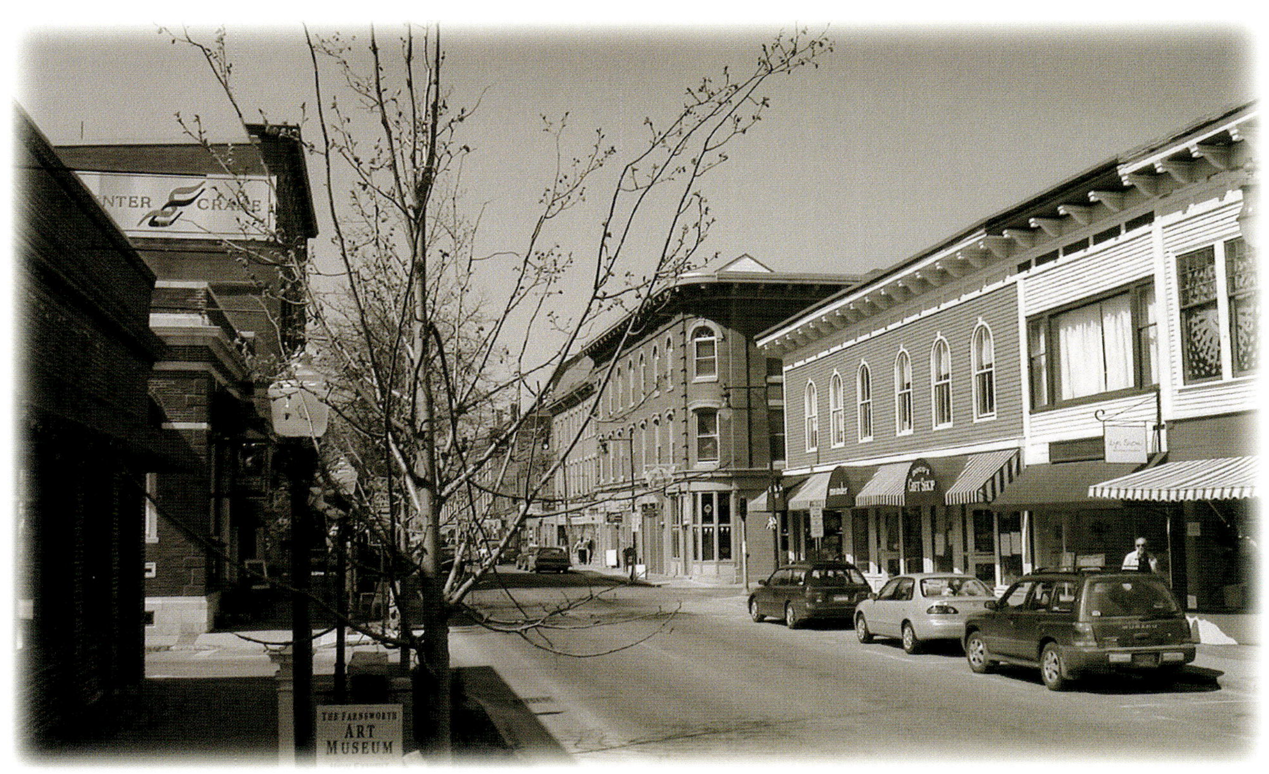
THE FARNSWORTH
ART
MUSEUM

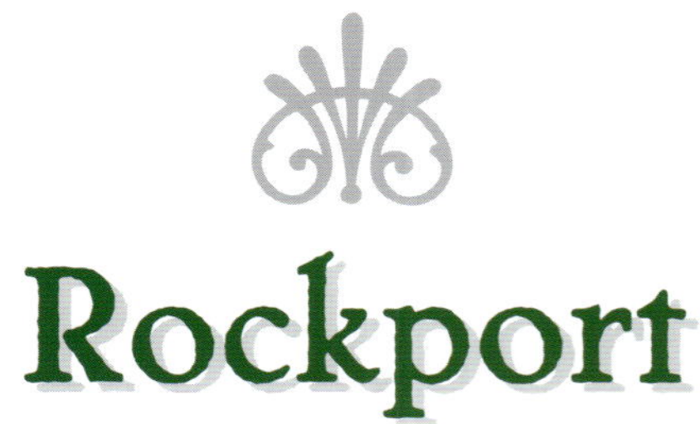

Rockport

INCORPORATED AS MAINE'S
453RD TOWN ON FEBRUARY 25, 1891

POPULATION IN 1900: 2,314

POPULATION IN 2000: 3,209

Along with Rockland, Rockport shared the distinction of having limerock in its topography and its name. Thus it, too, had a number of kilns where limestone was heated to produce quicklime, used in the production of cement. Limestone was burned around the clock, and the lime coaster ships carried it far and wide. Because the chemical reaction of quicklime and water produces a tremendous amount of heat, leaks sometimes caused ships to burn right there in Rockport Harbor. But since a shipload of lime casks that arrived intact at its destination could bring a bigger profit than would most other cargo, ship owners and captains were willing to take the risk.

Rockport also shared kinship with Camden, which once encompassed what are now West Rockport, Rockville, Glen Cove, and Rockport village. It was the Iron Bridge shown in the postcard that ruined relations between the Harbor (Camden) and Goose River (Rockport village). Rockport wanted the bridge over the Goose River to be built; Camden didn't. Rockport prevailed, and on February 25, 1891, the two villages separated over irreconcilable differences. (One legislator said they should have been celebrating their centennial instead of suing for divorce!) The old bridge fell in 1946 when a trailer truck struck an abutment.

Harold Leland was a student at Rockport's school, located at the top of the hill, from kindergarten through high school. He was one of nineteen graduates of Rockport High School's class of 1956. Leland recalls how fellow students would go up the

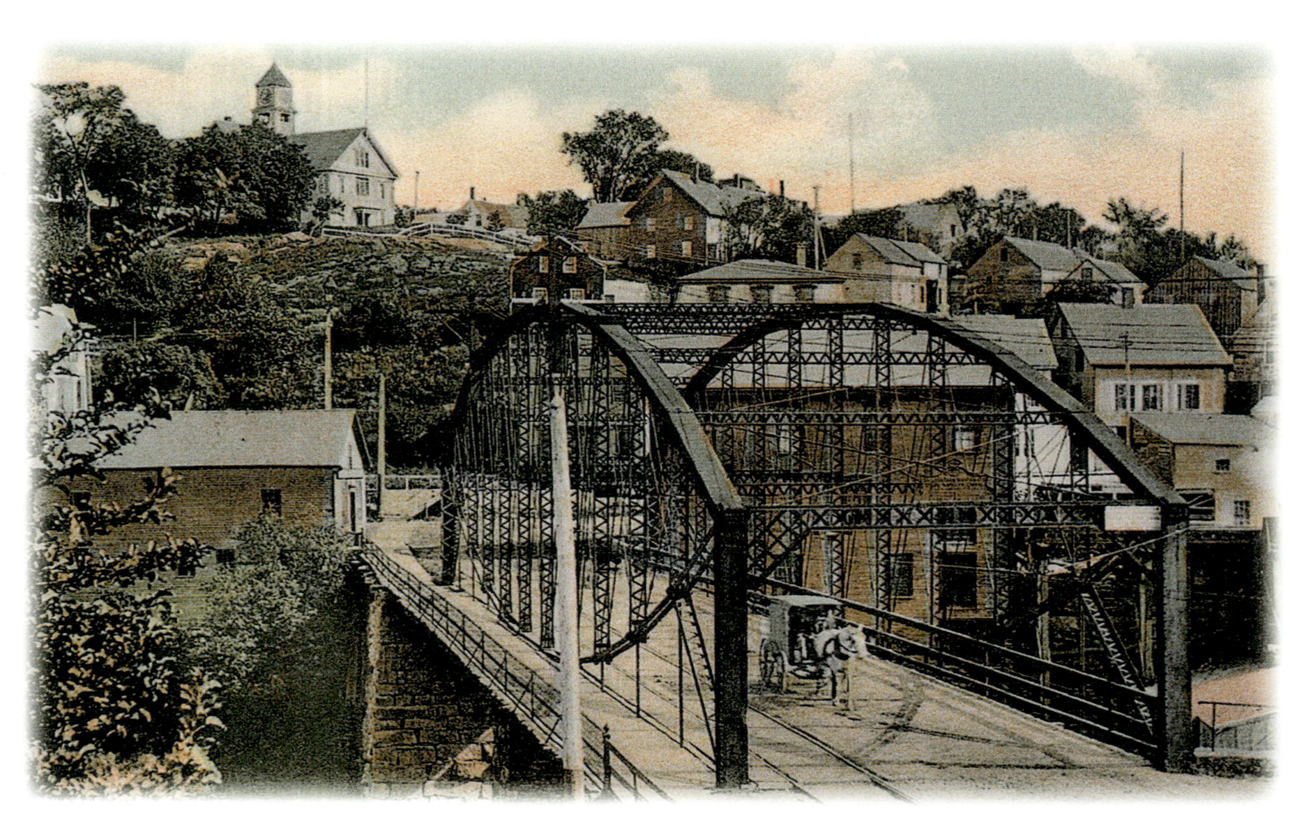

rickety steps to the clock tower along with the janitor to help him wind the clock weights.

The Maine Photographic Workshops in the village has enjoyed a long history of offering nationally renowned summer classes in traditional and digital photography, as well as film and video media. On the same block is the Rockport Opera House, which since its restoration in 1993 has hosted the Bay Chamber Concerts series, started in 1961 by pianist Andrew Wolf and his flutist brother, Thomas.

Andre the famous harbor seal made Rockport his summer home after Harry Goodridge found the abandoned pup in 1961. For nearly a quarter century, Goodridge and Andre entertained thousands at the harbor. The seal was named honorary harbormaster, and became famous for his annual winter migration to Massachusetts, where he was cared for by the New England Aquarium in Boston. He was released each spring, and his progress northward on the 150-mile journey back to Rockport was reported avidly by the national news media. Andre was on hand in 1978 to unveil the statue that stands in his honor at the public landing. He died in 1986, but his adventures have been immortalized in several books and a 1994 movie.

Several miles from the village and the Goose River bridge, in the southernmost corner of Rockport, the famed Samoset Resort stands on a bluff overlooking Penobscot Bay and the Rockland Breakwater Light. It was named for one of the two Native Americans who traveled with (actually, were kidnapped by) explorer George Weymouth. Samoset was a translator for Weymouth and remained a friend of the European settlers, so his name became a symbol of hospitality. The building was originally the Bay Point Hotel, built in 1889. When it was sold to the Ricker family—owners of the Poland Springs House—turrets, porches, and gingerbread trim were added and the name changed to SamOset, with the capital O in the middle. It was sold three more times before the grand old hotel was closed in 1969. It burned on October 12, 1972, and was rebuilt two years later using massive timbers from the old Portland granary.

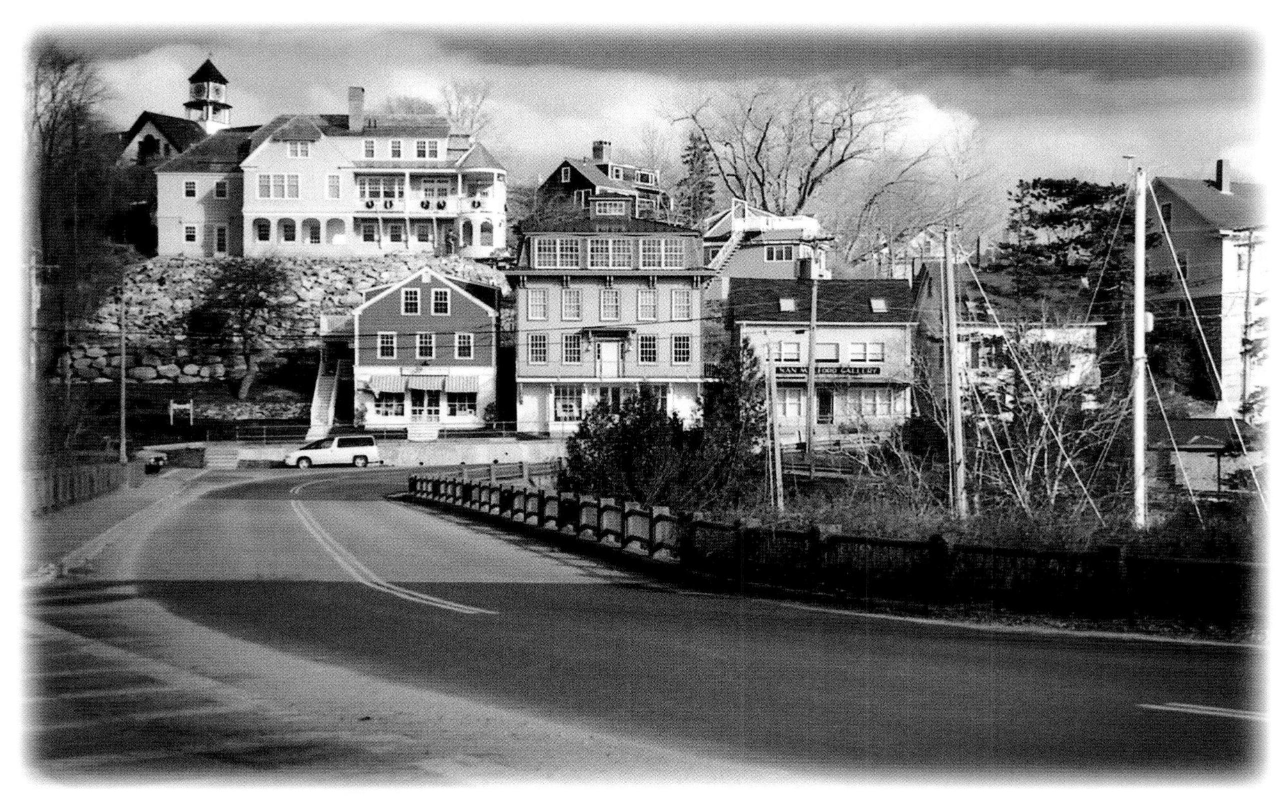

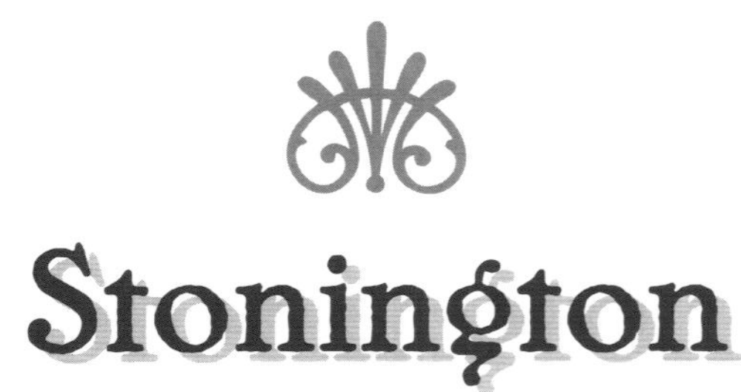

Stonington

INCORPORATED AS MAINE'S 462ND TOWN ON FEBRUARY 18, 1897

POPULATION IN 1900: 1,648

POPULATION IN 2000: 1,152

Located at the tip of Deer Isle in Hancock County, Stonington was originally known as Green's Landing in the Town of Deer Isle, being named for its first settler, Sullivan Green. It was later renamed to reflect its quarrying economy. Several types of pink-toned granite are unique to Deer Isle, and by the turn of the twentieth century, Stonington was quite prosperous because of it. The ethnic diversity matched that of other quarrying towns. Italian stonecutters, Scottish paving cutters, Swedes, and Norwegians came to work in the quarries. Italians in particular were known for their skill at sculpting columns and designs into the stone.

The first quarry opened in 1869, and its output did not start to dwindle until around 1925. Deer Isle granite was used at the Smithsonian Institution, in Washington, D.C., and is featured at several important sites in New York City: the plaza entrance of the Manhattan Bridge, the New York County courthouse, and the Cathedral of St. John the Divine. The Boston Museum of Fine Arts was also built of the pink granite. The last major contract for island granite was in the 1960s, for the John F. Kennedy Memorial inscription stone in Washington, D.C.

During the quarries' boom years, more than fifty retail establishments were built. Many of the buildings were even moved from nearby towns in the early 1900s to meet the demand for commercial space. Today, there is little room for expansion or development, and Stonington's waterfront is a charming array of wooden homes and shops set in a quintessential lobstering harbor. A true working community with more than three hundred lobsterboats, it has less need for tourism than other waterfront towns, and has little in the way of guest accommodations. Nonetheless, the day-trippers and summer residents find their way downtown, and even townspeople dependent upon summer trade sometimes resent the congestion they bring.

As has happened in many fishing towns, the fishermen of Stonington have been squeezed out of property on the very waterfront they depend on for their livelihood. Most of the village homes, sold at high prices, are vacant much of the year, and fishermen must live inland on lots large enough to store their traps in winter. On its Web site dedicated to yachting, the Maine Coast Guide says "The frontier-town attitude is often cultivated on the water, too. Without a doubt and not by accident, Stonington's lobsterboats are the loudest on the coast, and the men at their helms seem to take perverse pleasure in buzzing nearby yachts at predawn hours or cutting across their bows."

To celebrate its lobstering heritage, the town hosts its annual Lobster Boat Race, where souped-up "stallions of the sea" churn the waters as they vie for points and prizes. This is one of several such races held in various harbors on the Maine coast.

New fisheries come and go on the Maine coast, and Stonington has seen its share of changes. It happened in the 1920s and '30s, after scientists warned that the town's lobster cannery was depleting the stocks. Maine's catch fell from 20 million pounds in 1910 to 8 million in 1930, and hundreds of lobstermen were forced out of the fishery, but catches rebounded after World War II. Stonington's harbor once sheltered a fishing fleet that ventured all the way to the Grand Banks off the coast of Newfoundland, the ground fishery is all but dead today thanks to declining catches and federal regulations. When fads and supplies converged, the fishermen here have also harvested sea cucumbers and urchins for the Asian palate. Urchins are harvested by divers, who hand-pick them, and urchining was so lucrative for a short time in the 1990s that men came all the way from the Pacific coast to get in on the action. But now the only sizable fishery left is that of *Homarus americanus*, the American lobster.

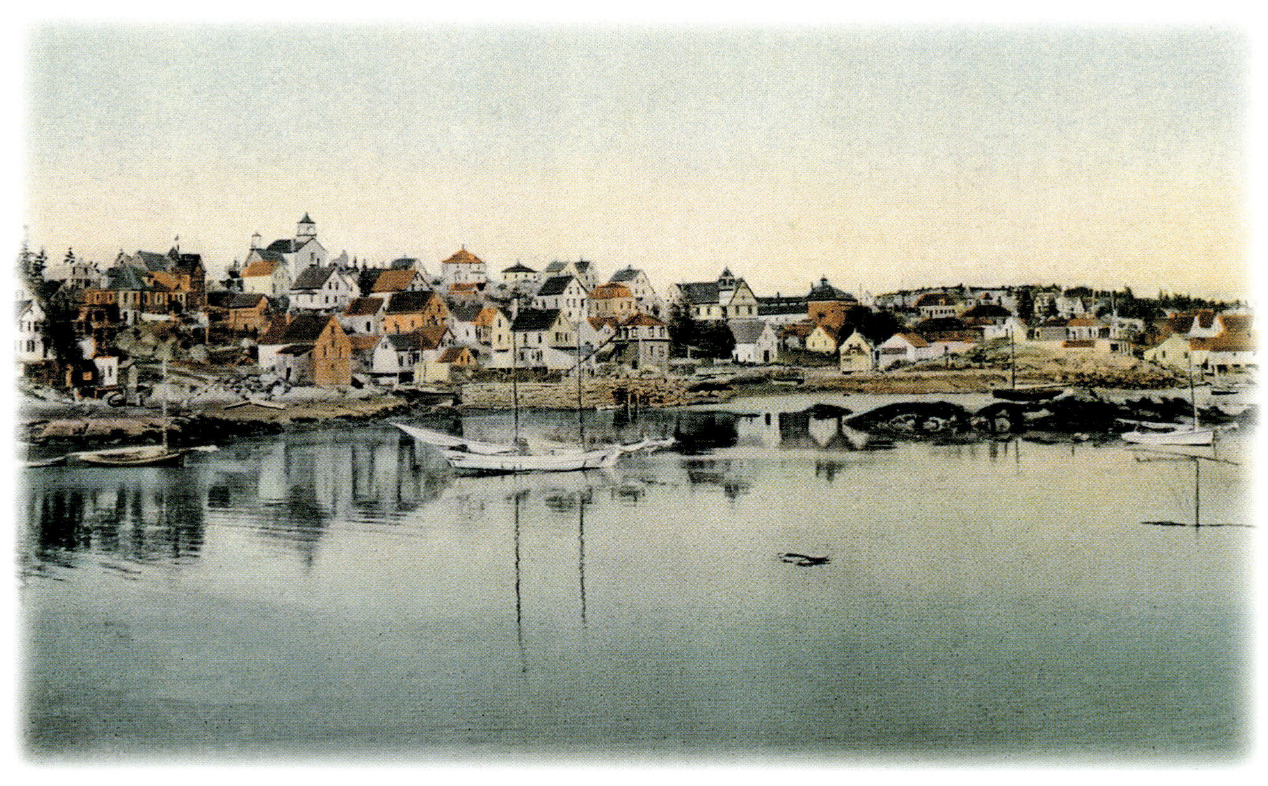

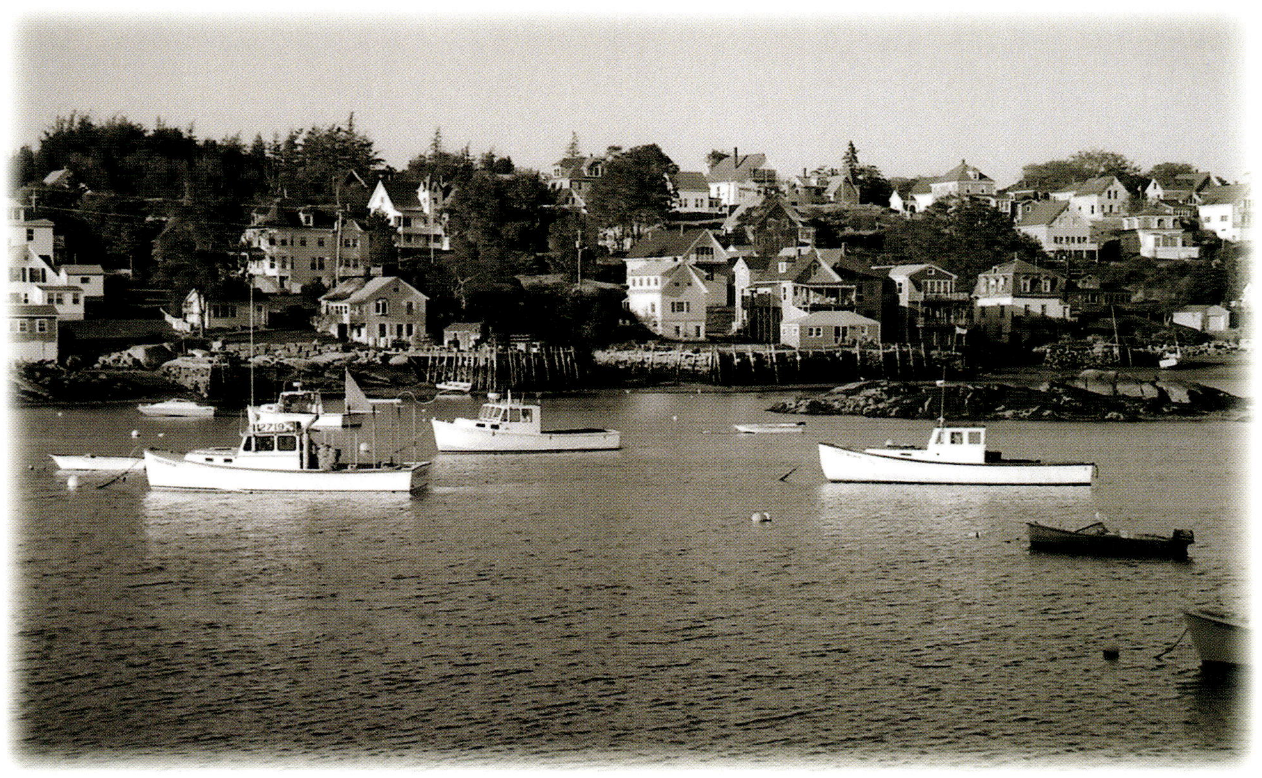

Tenants Harbor

A VILLAGE OF THE TOWN OF ST. GEORGE

POPULATION OF ST. GEORGE IN 1900: 2,206

POPULATION OF ST. GEORGE IN 2000: 2,580

The town of St. George was set off from Cushing in 1803 because it lay on the other side of the St. George River, and attending town meetings in winter was difficult. The town was composed of eleven villages with indistinct boundaries, and mail came twice a day by stage to the seven post offices. The St. George post office in Wiley's Corner closed in 1993, and today there are only three left: Port Clyde, Tenants Harbor, and Spruce Head.

Captain George Weymouth sailed the *Archangel* up the Georges River in 1605, and named the peninsula "St. George's Island" after the patron saint of England. The origin of the village's name is uncertain, but maps from the 1700s on spell it Tarrent's, Tarance, Terrence, Talant's, Tennant's, Tenas, and finally, Tenants (although a recent mailing from a selectman showed its spelling as Tenant's).

Granite helped define the peninsula's economy in its early days. Quarrying began in the 1830s, and boomed after the Civil War, when paving and building stone were needed by the growing nation's cities. St. George granite was particularly suitable because it naturally runs in thin sheets of varying thickness. In Long Cove, tiny quarrymen's cottages still line the road to the granite quarry. English stonecutters already living there gave the village its nickname of Englishtown, and Maine's first Finnish settlement of any consequence arrived here in the 1880s to cut

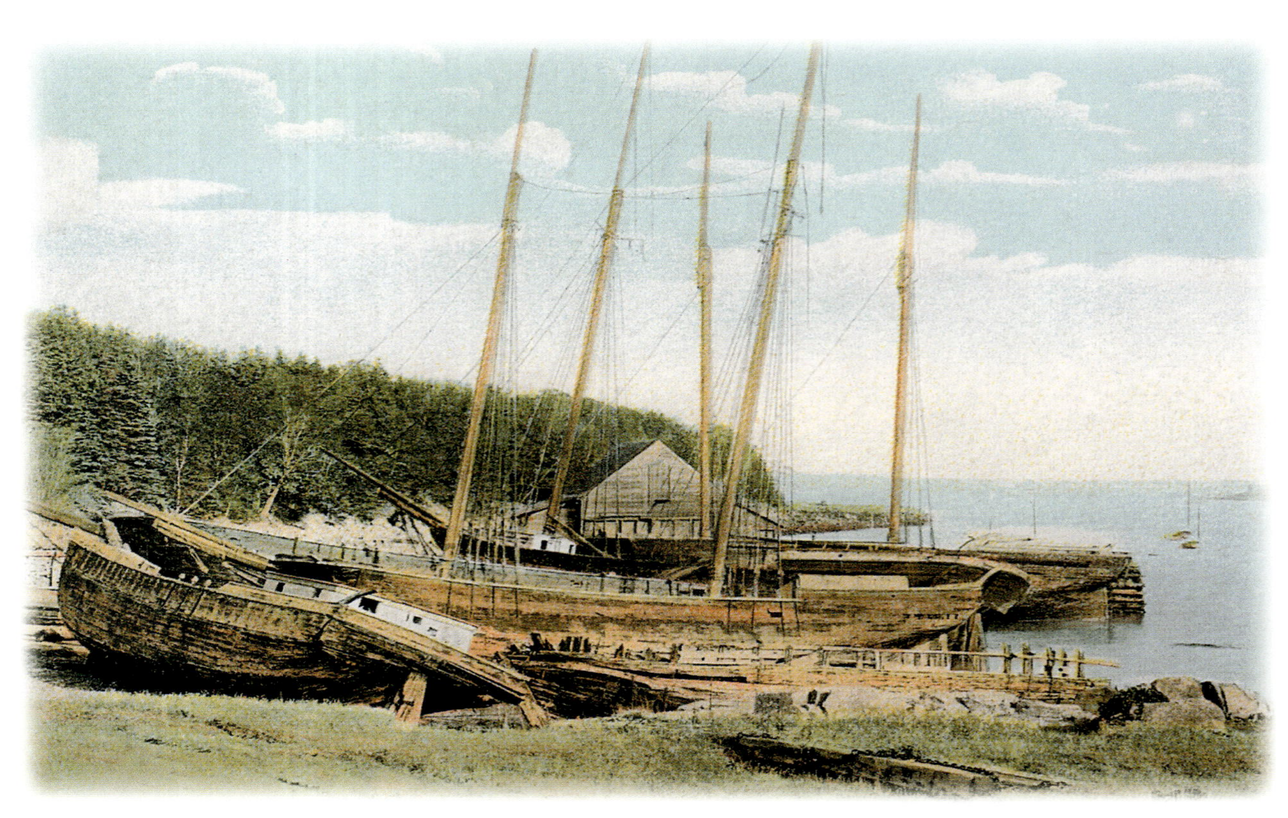

paving blocks, along with the Swedes, Scots, Irish, Italians, and Welsh. "By 1920 virtually every mailbox along the River Road had a Finnish name scrawled upon it," wrote Lew Dietz.

Many a fine sailing ship was built in St. George, and in the mid-1800s there were 90 master mariners and 225 seamen on record with St. George residences. Wooden boats are still made at the Tenants Harbor Boatyard. George Emery said he envisioned a business "rebuilding old thoroughbred yachts—the old beauty queens," and today he handles several types of vessels, both wooden and fiberglass.

Tenants Harbor is very much a lobstering community today, but its fishermen also reap another important harvest from the sea—mussels. Adjacent to the Long Cove quarry is the Great Eastern Mussel Farms, Inc. which moved there in 1982 from Edgecomb. It has the only bottom-culture dragger in North America, and is also making a foray into rope-grown mussels, harvesting about 100,000 pounds of the bivalves each week.

The postcard shows the schooner graveyard off Sea Street; the boatyard in the background is where Isaiah Gilchrest and others built wooden ships. Historian Albert Smalley wrote that unscrupulous shipowners would often hire someone to bore holes in a vessel to promote its "accidental" sinking. "The graveyard of vessels at Tenants Harbor was a most eloquent testimony to the integrity of the St. George shipowners," he wrote. "It proves beyond any doubt that they chose to wear a vessel out and lay her up in preference to letting the insurance companies pay for her loss, by employing an augur mate." The scuttled ships were burned in the 1920s, but as the modern photo shows, the splayed skeletons are still visible at low tide.

Notable Native:

A man best known by his voice lives in a butter-yellow house at Wiley's Corner. The "humble Farmer" (humbly lowercase), Robert Skoglund, airs a weekly program on Maine Public Radio featuring his self-deprecating humor, dry Maine witticisms, and "old-fashioned music."

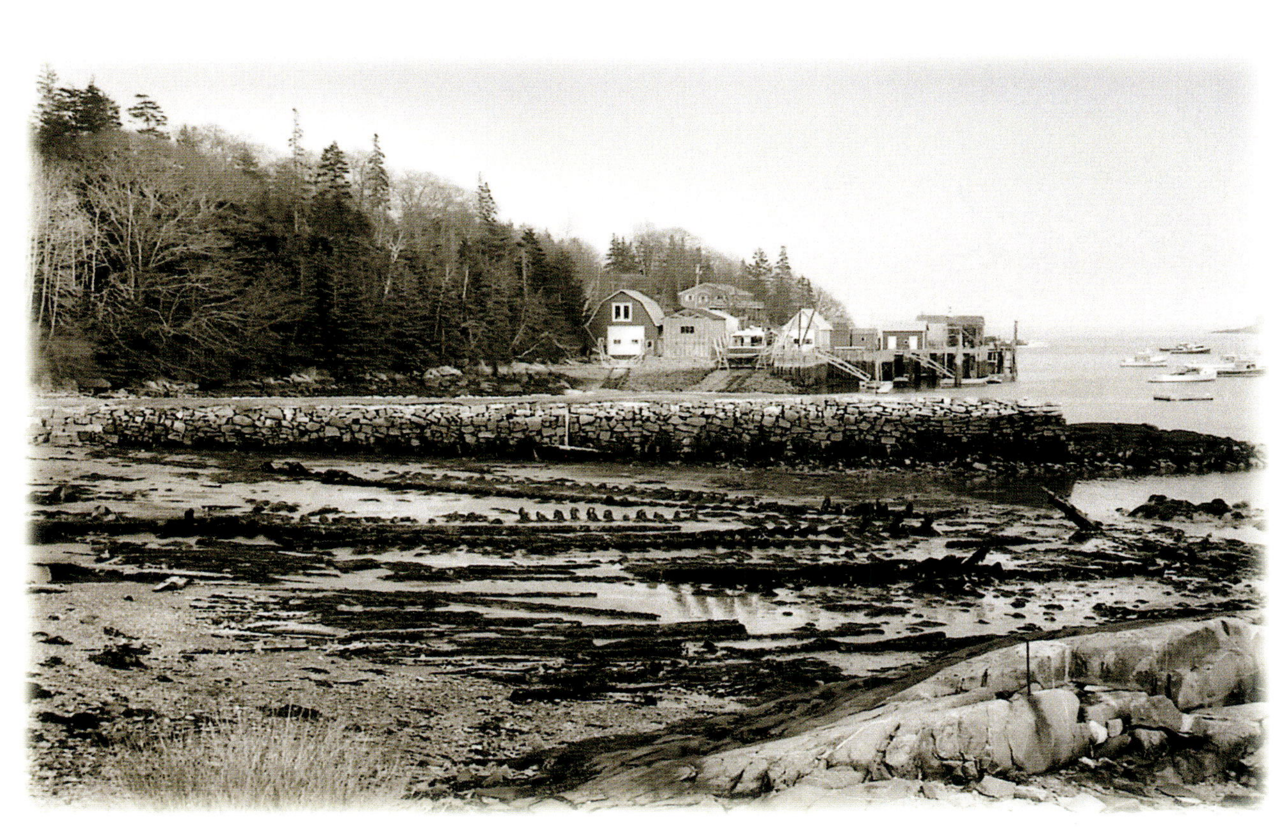

Thomaston

INCORPORATED AS MAINE'S 37TH TOWN ON MARCH 20, 1777

POPULATION IN 1900: 2,688

POPULATION IN 2000: 3,748

More nineteenth-century sailing ships were built in Thomaston than in any other place in America—nearly seven hundred in all. Before the Civil War, Thomaston ships were so active in the cotton trade that a street in Liverpool, England, was named for the town, according to writer W. H. Bunting. (It's still there, though it's a pretty short street.)

At Lyman-Morse Boat Building, Inc., the tradition continues, albeit with different materials. The company recently expanded after buying the nearby Steele & Marshall Company, which will allow it to build metal-hulled boats in addition to those with fiberglass. Its century-old firm built Alden Malabar schooners and Friendship sloops before switching to custom sailing and motor yachts. Dunn and Elliott was another early-day boat builder that made three- and four-masted schooners.

The Maine State Prison in Thomaston was built four years after Maine achieved statehood in 1820. In 2002 a new prison was completed in Warren, and after the prisoners were transferred to the new facility, the landmark Thomaston site was opened to the public for a once-in-a-lifetime tour. Eleven thousand people came from all over the state to see where the prisoners had lived. The cells were so small that the walls were the width of a man's outstretched arms. The quarry hole was filled in with demolition debris, and in a few short months, an institution that was two centuries old had vanished, replaced by the new Supermax Prison in nearby Warren.

Like its neighbor, Rockland, Thomaston also engaged in quarrying and burning limerock, with many kilns located on the waterfront. A cement plant, which used the lime, was built in 1928. After the landmark Maine Indian Land Claims Settlement in 1980, the Passamaquoddy Tribe bought and operated the plant from 1983 to 1988, selling it for a $56 million profit. The tribe also developed a scrubber to reprocess waste and control sulphur dioxide emissions at the plant. Today, the Dragon Products Company is owned by a Spain-based company and employs 230 people at its Thomaston location—New England's only cement manufacturing plant. Blasting of the limerock still goes on from time to time, and huge tailings piles are quite prominent along U.S. Route 1 and the Old County Road.

Located near the plant, sitting majestically on the hill at the head of the St. George peninsula, is a mansion called Montpelier—General Henry Knox Museum. Originally built in 1795 for the retired commander of artillery in the American Revolution, it was demolished in 1871 when the railroad bought the decaying building. In the early 1900s, the Knox chapter of the Daughters of the American Revolution formed an association to build a replica of the original home about a half mile from its first location. Many of the furnishings, which had wound up with Knox descendants or been sold at auction, gradually made their way back to the mansion. In 1995 it was refurbished to prevent it from once again falling to the wrecking ball, and the Friends of Montpelier now own and manage it. Volunteer tour guides in full period costume lead visitors through the museum, pointing out the gorgeous architecture and furnishings and describing the life of the man who was one of George Washington's most trusted friends and fellow soldiers.

Both Main and Knox Streets are on the National Historic Register. Approximately 85 percent of the seven hundred homes in Thomaston are more than a century old.

The postcard view of the waterfront from "Brooklyn Heights" shows the bridge on the left. The four-masted ship is likely a coal carrier making a delivery, and probably was not a Thomaston-built ship, according to a local historian.

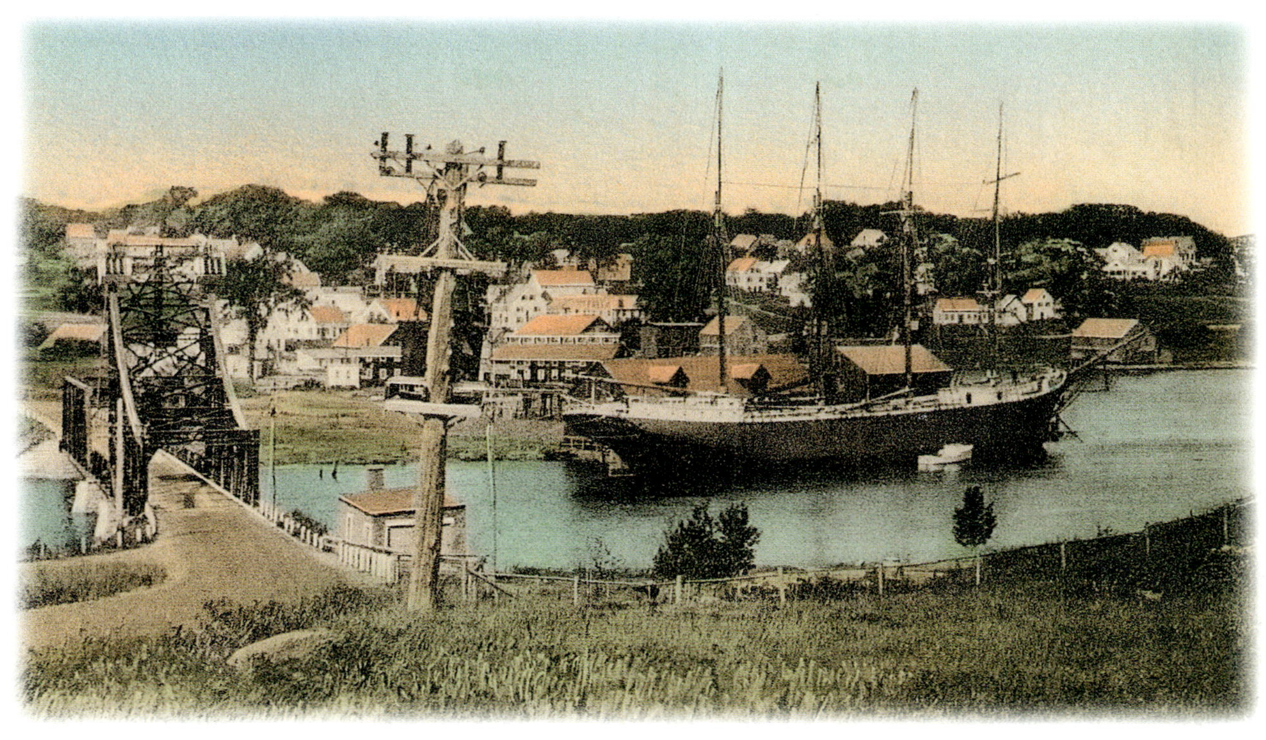

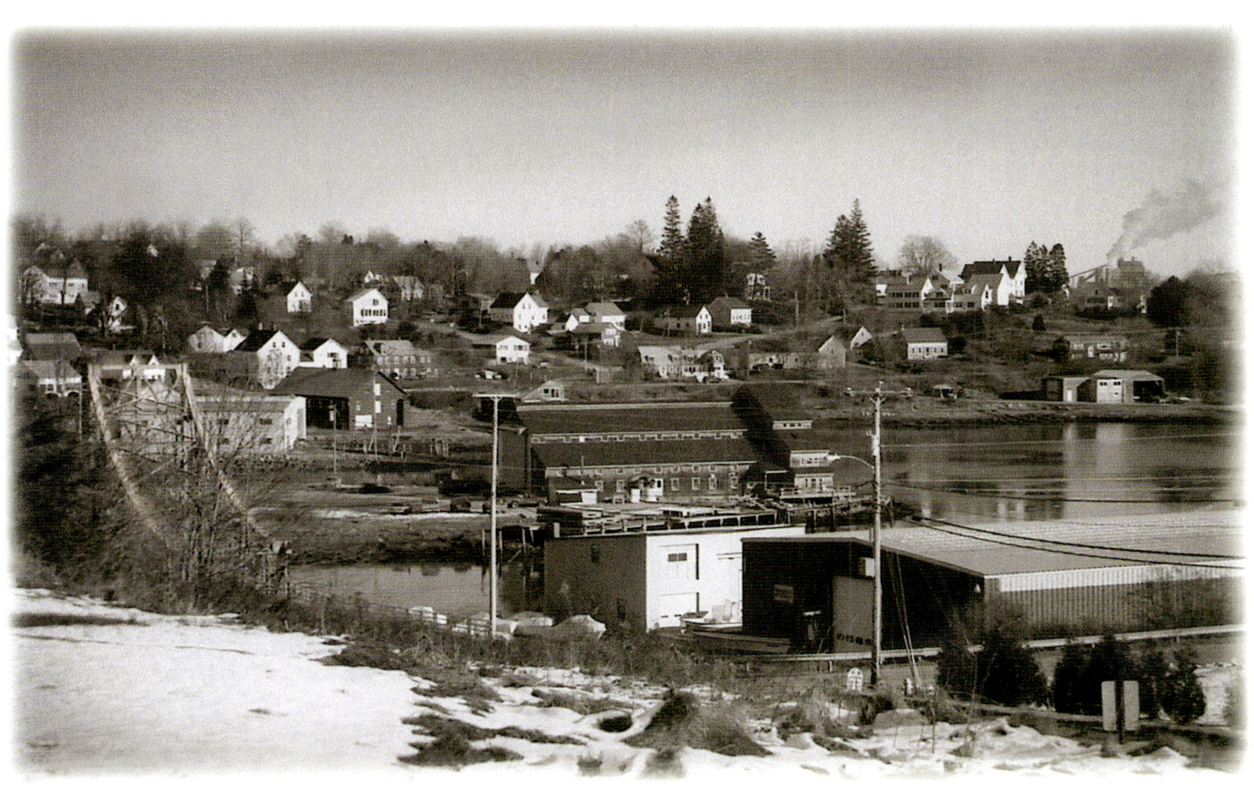

Vinalhaven

INCORPORATED AS MAINE'S 71ST TOWN ON JUNE 25, 1789

POPULATION IN 1900: 2,358

POPULATION IN 2000: 1,235

Vinalhaven was one of the Fox Islands, along with North Haven, and was named for John Vinal, the Boston attorney who represented the islanders in their incorporation petition. In addition to the usual fishing, farming, logging, and boat-building occupations, the enterprise of net making was at one time important on the island. It was mostly a job for the women, who not only made nets for fishing, but also to protect horses from flies. As many as 1,800 nets and "ear tips" were sent out each week to a Boston company for shipment throughout the country. The horse-net factory closed in 1926, but women continued to knit from their own homes, producing fishing nets, lobster bait bags, trap heads, pool table pockets, and other pieces for many years to come.

Granite quarrying on the island began in 1826, and by the mid-1800s was a formidable mainstay of the economy. The Bodwell Granite Company dominated the industry from 1871 through the ensuing four decades, at times employing more than fifteen hundred men. Extremely ornate designs were often carved into granite faces, lintels, and other decorative pieces by skilled Scottish stonecutters before being shipped. Eight polished columns for the nave of the Cathedral of St. John the Divine in New York City were made in two sections. The longest segment (at 36 feet) weighed 90 tons. They were installed in 1904 and the cathedral was built around them. The largest granite quarry closed in 1919, though the paving-block industry continued until 1939. Granite was briefly quarried in the early 1970s, but for the most part the old quarries have become de facto swimming

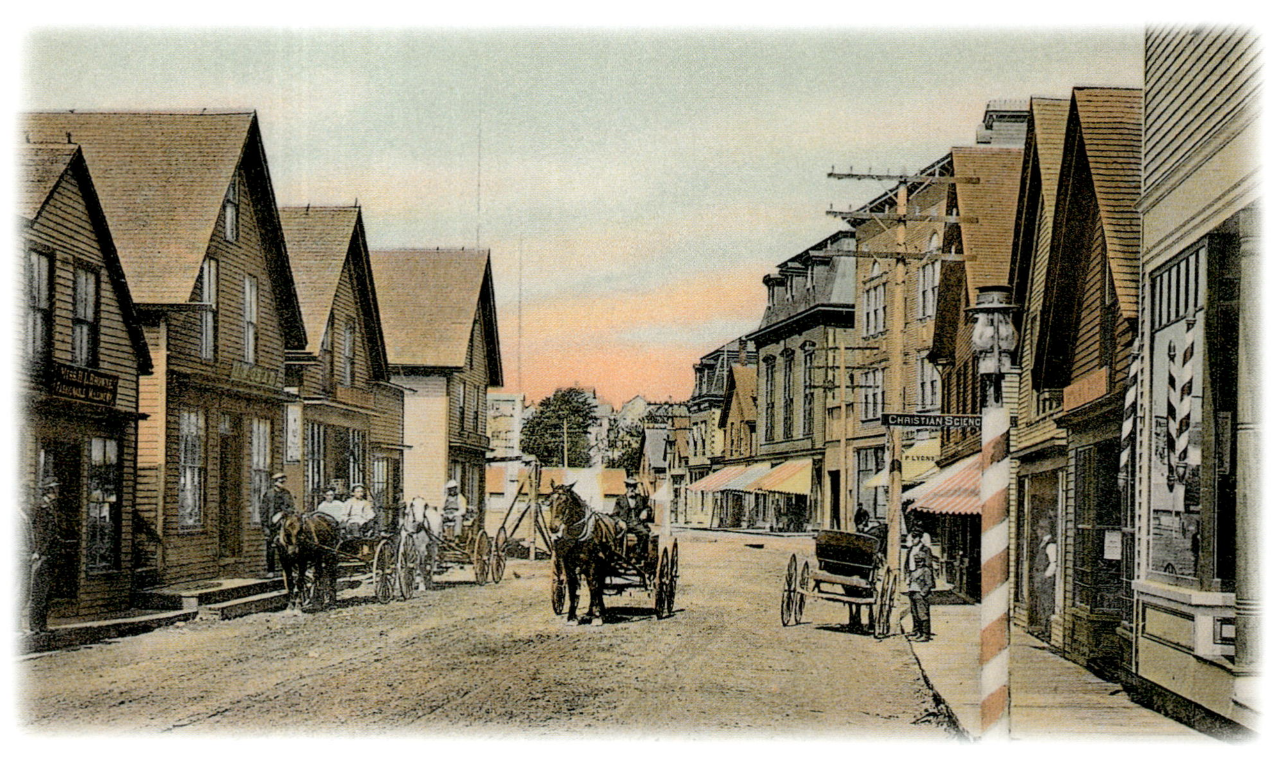

holes, two of which are maintained by the town for that very purpose.

In 1903 the Vinalhaven Fish Company was the principal fish-curing plant in Maine and one of the country's largest, handling between seven and eight million pounds of fish. That year approximately twelve million pounds of groundfish were landed in Penobscot Bay ports by around four hundred fishermen. The company also produced cod liver oil, glue, and fertilizer as by-products. Today, the ground fishery is all but dead, but lobster fishing is a family affair, and has given many a teenager (both male and female) an income better than that of a schoolteacher. Vinalhaven is one of Maine's largest lobstering communities, with more than two hundred fishermen.

In the postcard view of Main Street, the mansard-roofed structure (right center) is the Masonic Building, constructed in 1879. The Bodwell Granite Company's store occupied the first two floors. The store, which sold groceries, clothing, hardware, and "all the necessary material for the construction of a house from cellar to garret," closed in 1919, along with the quarry. Other stores, including an A & P, moved in, and Johnson's pool hall occupied the building in the 1940s. The building succumbed to fire in 1967.

The distinctive edifice just up the street from this building was Memorial Hall, which was razed in 1973. Next door (with the top steeple barely visible) was the Star of Hope Lodge of the Independent Order of Oddfellows, now the home and studio of artist Robert Indiana. After World War II the men's fraternal order never resumed the meetings that were suspended during the war, and though the upper stories were vacant, a drugstore and newsstand occupied the ground floor. Near the yellow awning was O. P. Lyons Jewelers, and just up the street was the Christian Science Reading Room.

The building on the far left sports a sign that says MISS H.L. BROWNE—FASHIONABLE MILLINERY. Next door was the shop of J. W. Gray, followed by Charles B. Smith Provisioners, now the Haven Restaurant. The building beyond was the original Engine House, still the home of the 1888 steam fire engine.

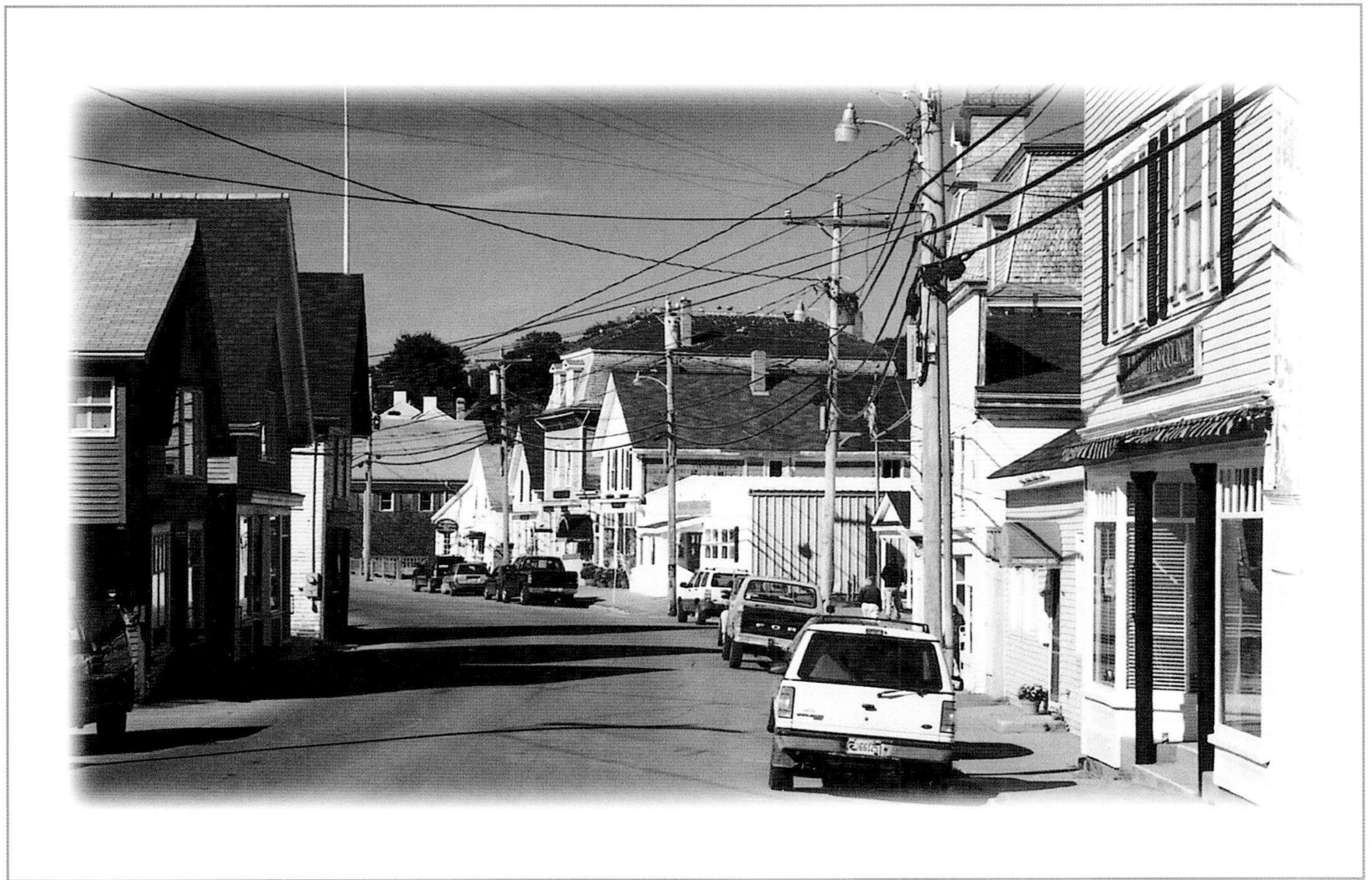

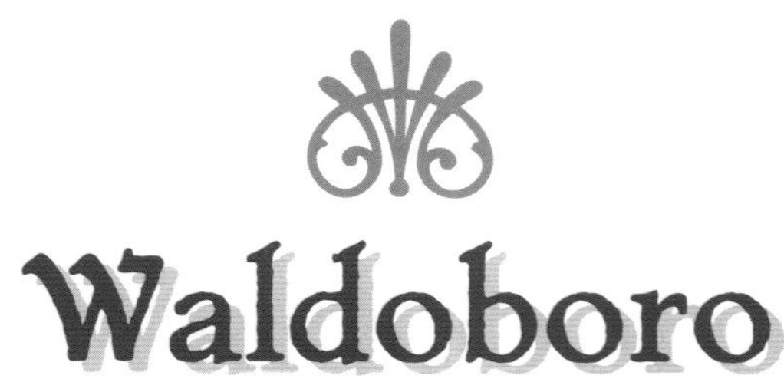

Waldoboro

INCORPORATED AS MAINE'S
27TH TOWN ON JUNE 29, 1773

POPULATION IN 1900: 3,145

POPULATION IN 2000: 4,916

In the early part of the eighteenth century, Samuel Waldo went to Germany to find settlers for the new British colony of Massachusetts. He must have been a great salesman, for his promises of a well-supplied village and a parcel of land for each family filled a ship with German Protestants. In 1739 these immigrants sailed up the Medomak River and were met with unbridled wilderness. (It is from this encounter that the expression "Where's Waldo?" originated—well, maybe not!) But the going was tough, and although the first colony in "Waldoborough" sputtered out, more Germans came, thanks to the salesmanship of the German-born Waldo.

Although it is situated five or so miles upriver from Muscongus Bay, Waldoboro was a major shipbuilding center in the 1800s. More than four hundred ships were built on the banks of the Medomak, which widens nicely just south of the business center. The country's first five-masted schooner, the *Governor Ames*, was built here in 1888.

Clothing manufacture was also a part of the economy. The Waldoboro Pants Factory was built in 1893, and in 1909, Isaac Gardner Reed opened a shirt factory that employed fifty people in the making of blue chambray work shirts. It closed in 1920, the year the Paragon Button Corporation opened in the old shoe factory building. In the 1930s, it was the area's major industry, employing eighty people who made pearl buttons out of shells imported from Australia, Manila, and the Fiji Islands. It closed in 1993, and today the building is being remodeled for various uses.

Food seems to be another of Waldoboro's calling cards. Morse's Sauerkraut started in 1918 when Virgil Morse used a secret mixture of sugar and salt to cure his cabbage, and in the 1950s the business produced twenty-five to forty tons of kraut a year. Today's kraut is still made the same way by the company's new owners.

Moody's Diner has long been a Waldoboro institution, and even though it doesn't stay open all night anymore, it comes pretty darn close. It was immortalized in humorist Tim Sample's "Saturday Night at Moody's Diner" first published in 1985 (revised 1996). And across the street from Moody's is Borealis Breads, specializing in artisan-type breads.

Friendship Street is the commercial section, and in the postcard the store with the wall sign was later a five-and-dime; Fernald's Five-and-Ten has occupied this spot since 1998. John Black, code-enforcement officer for the town, remembers the other buildings from the 1940s: Wincapaw Jewelers, an A & P grocery, Weston's Hardware, Jameson's Plumbing, Clark's Drugstore, and a First National Store on the corner. The tallest building was the Oddfellows Block, until the organization built a new one just down the street in 1904. The drugstore is now Waltz's and also occupies the corner spot.

On the right side the major building is the Sproul Block, built in 1854 after a fire destroyed the first block erected by George Sproul in 1835. In the late 1940s it housed apartments upstairs and retail stores on the ground floor, including the Roseway Restaurant. Despite local opposition, the brick edifice with arched windows and a steel balcony was demolished in 1981 in favor of a no-frills block of subsidized apartments. One resident said the new building "had the charm of a block of Velveeta cheese."

The tall chimney in the distance was the Engine Hall on Glidden Street, where the fire hose was hung to drain after use. There was also a lockup in the basement for ne'er-do-wells, and the town offices were on the third floor. The building was later an auto body shop before it burned in the 1950s. The building in front of the chimney, on the corner of Friendship and Main Streets, housed a series of retail shops, including Teague's butcher shop, Benner's shoe store, and Ethel's dress shop. It burned in the 1980s. The current building was built by attorney Sam Cohen, who operates his law offices there.

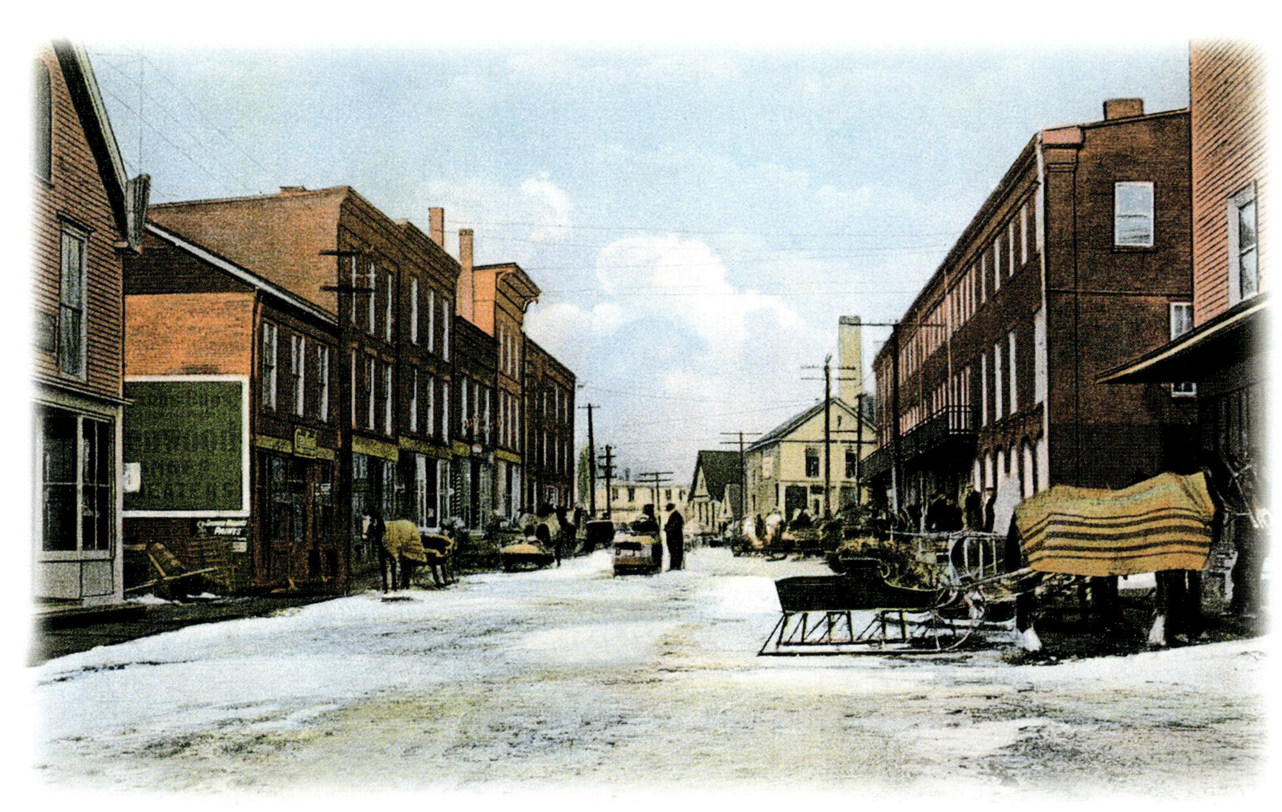

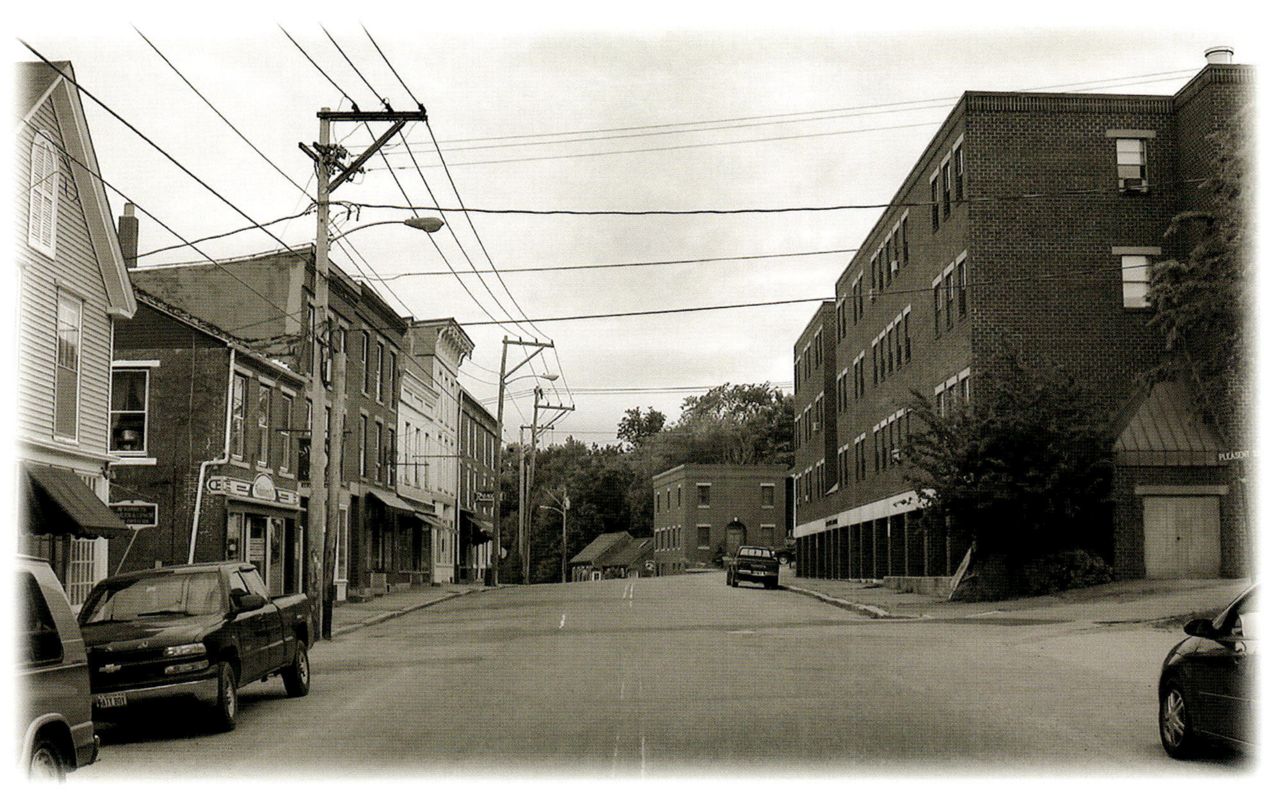

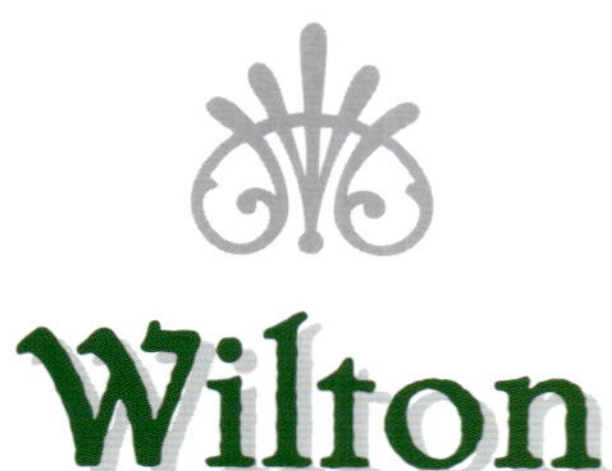

Wilton

INCORPORATED AS MAINE'S
148TH TOWN ON JUNE 22, 1803

POPULATION IN 1900: 1,647

POPULATION IN 2000: 4,123

Wilton was Bass Shoe, and the Bass family was Wilton. In 1876 George H. Bass opened a factory and began a five-generations-long relationship with the community that made his shoes famous. Writer Frank Sleeper said the Bass family practiced "enlightened capitalism" because it contributed in so many ways to the town's well-being. Charles Lindbergh wore Bass aviation boots when he made his first transatlantic flight. James Dean's rebel image came, in part, from rolled-up jeans, a white T-shirt, and Bass footwear. Students wore the Weejun "penny loafers" in the 1960s. All were made in Maine.

But in the 1970s the company was sold to Chesebrough Ponds, Inc., and then sold again in 1987 to Phillips–Van Heusen. When the Bass shoe factory closed for good in 1998, it was just another company taking its work to Puerto Rico and the Dominican Republic, where labor costs are cheaper. Wilton lost 350 jobs, and part of the building became the Boiler Room Restaurant. The final blow came when the company decided to shut down the rest of its Maine operations in 2004, including the Wilton distribution center that had employed 125 workers. From now on, Bass shoes will be made by Brown Shoe Co. of St. Louis.

The Bass factory is prominent in the postcard, behind the monument. It was built on the site of Everett Hiscock's lumber mill. George Bass started out making his fourteen-inch leg boots with hand-pegged soles in a wood-frame building on Main Street. He also peddled them throughout the countryside, and the boots were seen on log drives from the St. John River

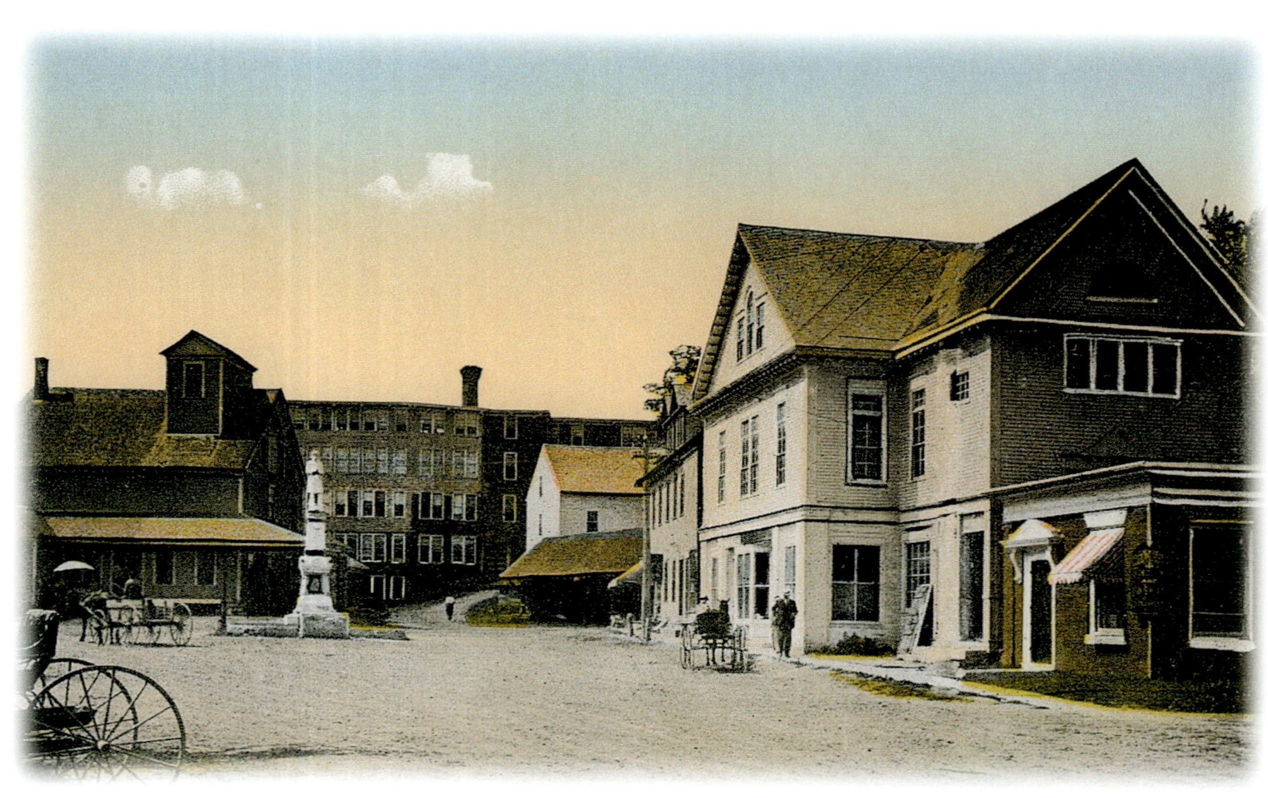

to the Pacific Ocean. His small factory also made farmer's plow shoes and footwear for outdoor guides. The first Bass moccasin appeared in 1906. At its peak, the G. H. Bass Company employed twelve hundred people.

Fernald's grist mill, which was taken down in the 1930s, is to the left of the monument in the postcard. To the right was the R. B. Fuller House, later the Wilson Lake Inn. The horse shed is in the center of the view and the W. E. Sawyer & Company grocery store is on the corner.

The Soldier's Monument, built to honor those who served in the Civil War, was installed by the Grand Army of the Republic in 1911 where the hay scales and horse trough had been. A time capsule in the base is to be opened in 2103, the town's tricentennial.

Originally Tyng's Township, Wilton was named by Abraham Butterfield who came from Wilton, New Hampshire. He agreed to pay for the town's incorporation expenses if it would carry that name. In 1893 a fire wiped out part of Main Street, and in 1960 the old town hall and the Hotel Wilton burned. The Wilton Woolen Company, built at the site of the old canning factory in 1901, also provided jobs for the community, remaining in operation through 1958. In 1960 the Forster Manufacturing Company bought the factory and employed more than four hundred people to make croquet sets and assemble snap clothespins, among other things.

A 165-foot-long ice skating rink was located off lower Main Street, where the Academy of Winter Carnivals was based. The Wilton Academy hockey team won a state championship in 1932. The rink was discontinued in the early 1960s.

In August the town celebrates the wild bounty of the fields with a Blueberry Festival. Fiddleheads—an unusual edible long prized by New Englanders—are canned by W. S. Wells & Sons. The newly emerging fronds of the ostrich fern, coiled like a fiddle's head, grow along rivers and streams. A backwoods staple for generations, fiddleheads are now featured on the menus of many fine restaurants, and the company ships canned fiddleheads all over the country.

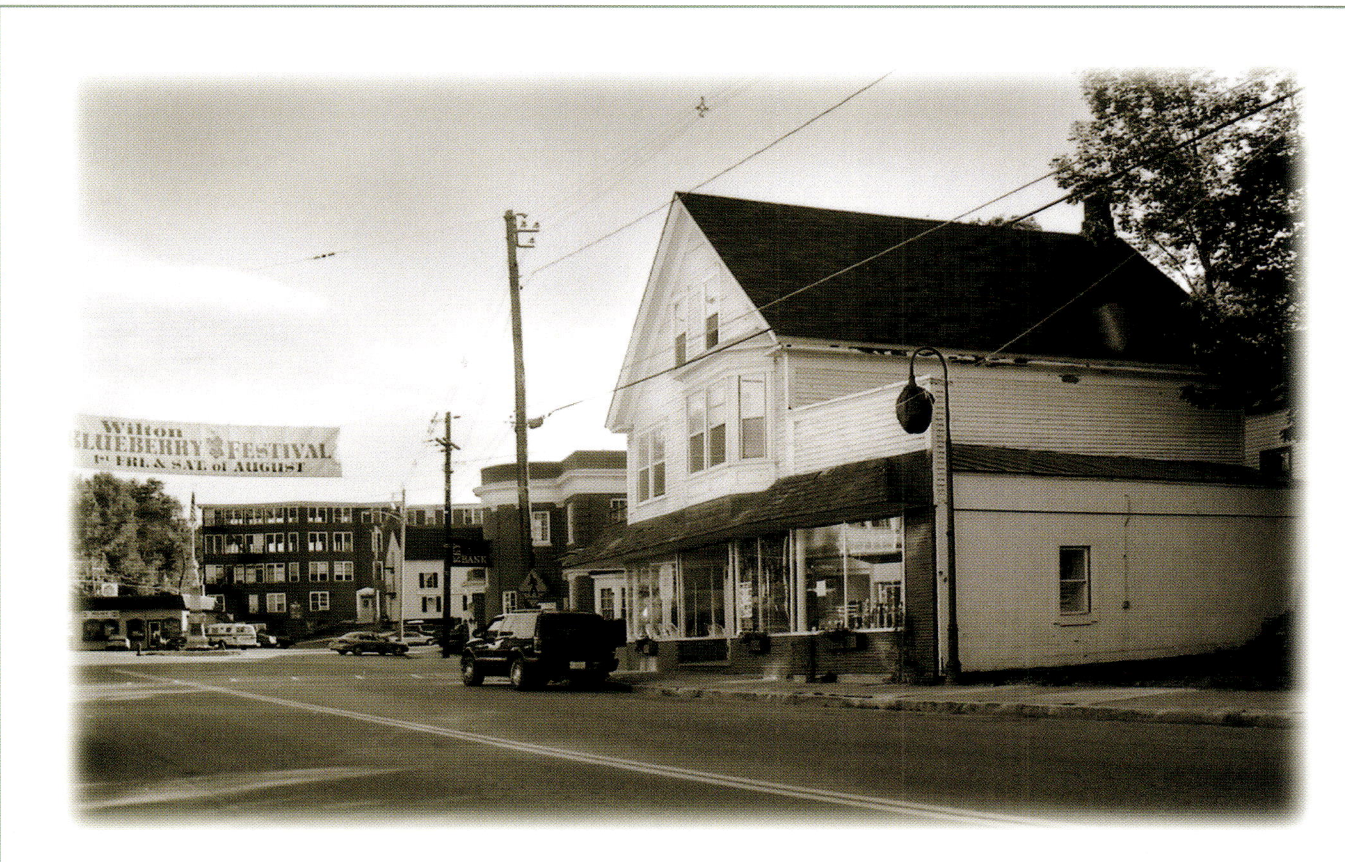

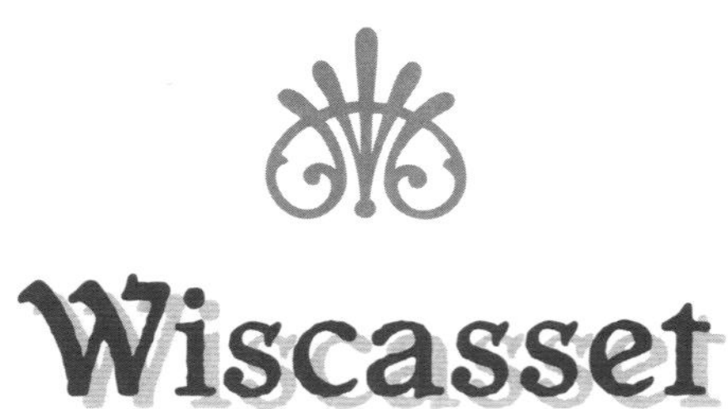

Wiscasset

INCORPORATED AS MAINE'S
16TH TOWN ON FEBRUARY 13, 1760

POPULATION IN 1900: 1,273

POPULATION IN 2000: 3,603

Wiscasset was once in the running to be the seat of Maine government, but it was bypassed by one vote in favor of Augusta. Speaking of bypass, the town that bills itself as "The Prettiest Village in Maine" is debating the nature of a highway bypass that will alleviate the dreaded summer-traffic bottleneck. Such a detour of U.S. Route 1 has been debated for decades, and there is little consensus even today as to which route would be best, or even if one should be built at all.

Named Pownalborough after Thomas Pownal, colonial governor of Massachusetts, the town was renamed in 1802 for what the Native peoples called the confluence of the Sheepscot, Marsh, and Back Rivers—*Wiscasset*. (Or maybe the name had another meaning—that's the way it is with Indian names.) It has one of the deepest harbors in Maine even though it is fourteen miles from the sea; up to one hundred sailing ships at a time could berth in Wiscasset's waters.

A 1953 *Ford Times* article called the town "a northern Williamsburg" with "wine-glass elms, architectural elegance, and true 'down East' flavor." In 1973, twenty-two buildings spread over several blocks, including Main Street, were placed on the National Register of Historic Places. Today, many—including old sea captains' homes—are antiques shops, galleries, and specialty stores.

The postcard looks toward the bridge over the Sheepscot River, now named the Donald Davey Memorial Bridge in honor of a police officer who died in the line of duty in 1984. The postcard calls it "the longest bridge in Maine." One of the bypass options would eliminate this bridge in order to divert U.S. Route 1 away from Main Street.

For decades Wiscasset was notable for the wrecks of two four-masted schooners—the *Hesper* and the *Luther Little*—which greeted travelers as they crossed the bridge. They were already past their prime when they were purchased in 1932 by a man who wanted to bring coal from Boston to Wiscasset and return south with lumber. The plan never materialized, and the schooners were dragged onto the mudflats near the shore. There they remained, serving as landmarks and inspiring artists and souvenir hunters for seven decades. The 204-foot-long *Luther Little*, built in 1917, was closest to shore; the *Hesper* was built in 1918. Many fires over the years, as well as storms and natural decay, finally rendered them into mere piles of rotted wood, and in 1998 they were dredged out of the river. The remnants were offered to the public, and one entrepreneur even made commemorative ballpoint pens out of the wood.

Another Wiscasset landmark, though less cherished, is the Maine Yankee nuclear power plant. It was put into operation on Montsweag Bay in 1972 as the largest nuclear facility in New England, and was Maine's largest electricity generator until it was decommissioned due to safety concerns in 1997. Another power plant, the oil-burning Mason Station—formerly run by Central Maine Power—was sold in January 2004. Maine Yankee was at one time Wiscasset's largest employer, and has been purchased by a company specializing in environmental cleanup and redevelopment of former industrial sites.

Wiscasset has also been known as the Worm Capital of the World, in honor of the sandworms and bloodworms—much prized by recreational fishermen—that are dug from the mudflats of the Sheepscot estuary at low tide.

In the postcard, the red brick building on the right side of Main Street is the Rundlett Block, built in 1871 and occupied today by a restaurant on the ground floor. The Wawenock Block is the second brick building from the left, today occupied by an art gallery and a florist. The wooden buildings just before the bridge are no longer standing, replaced by the tiny but renowned Red's Eats.

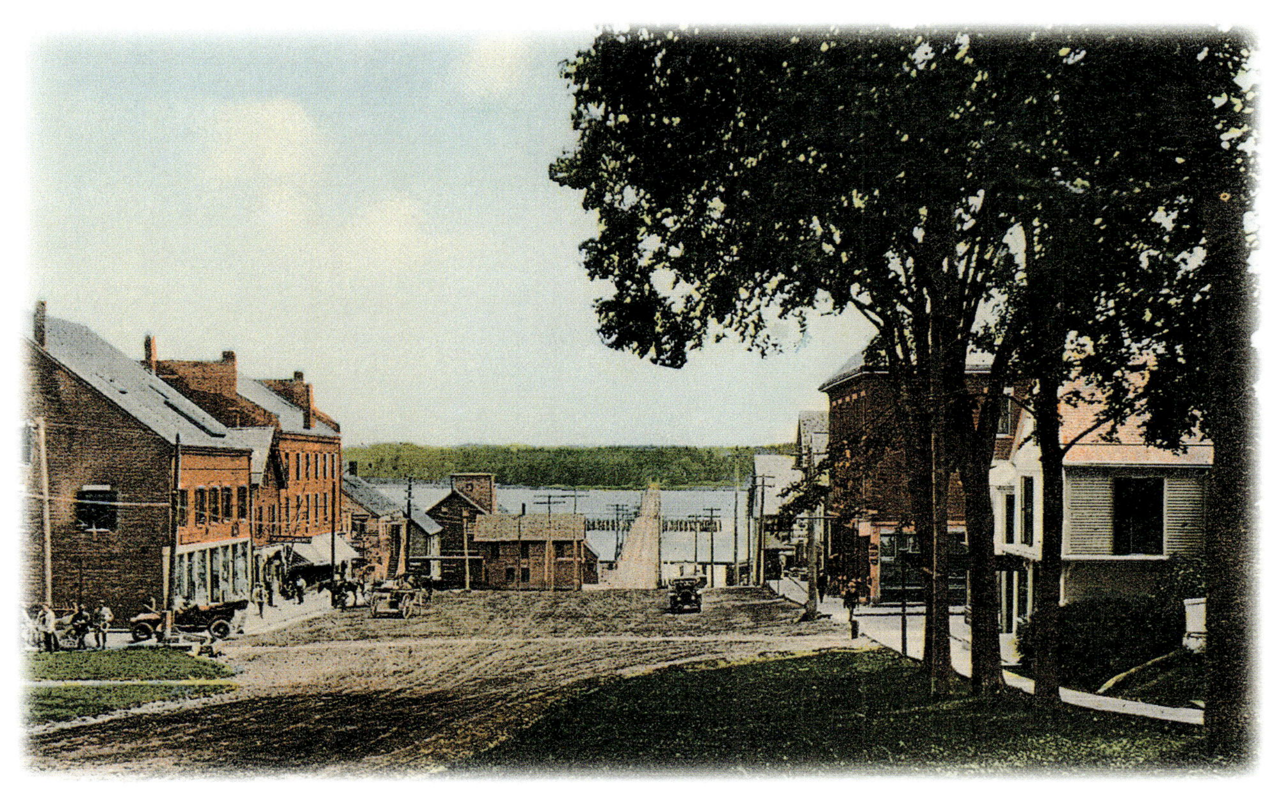

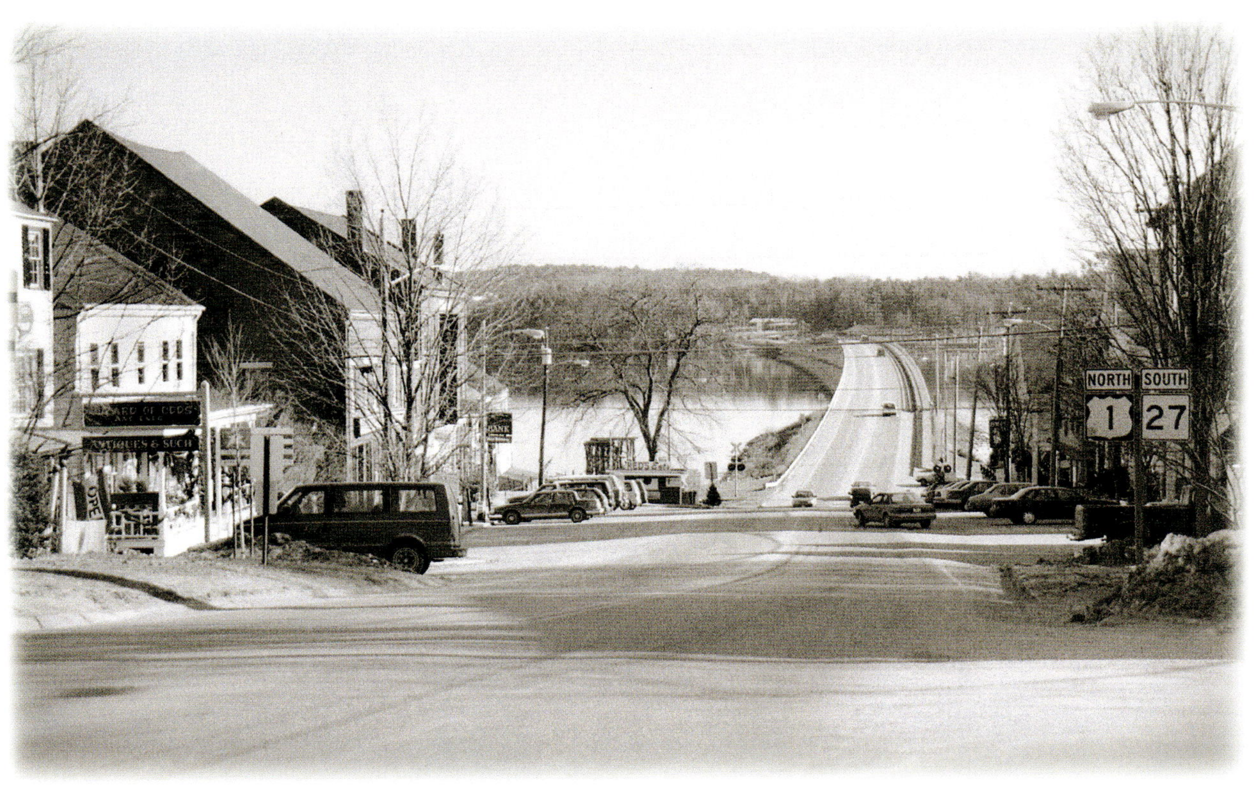
NORTH
SOUTH
1
27

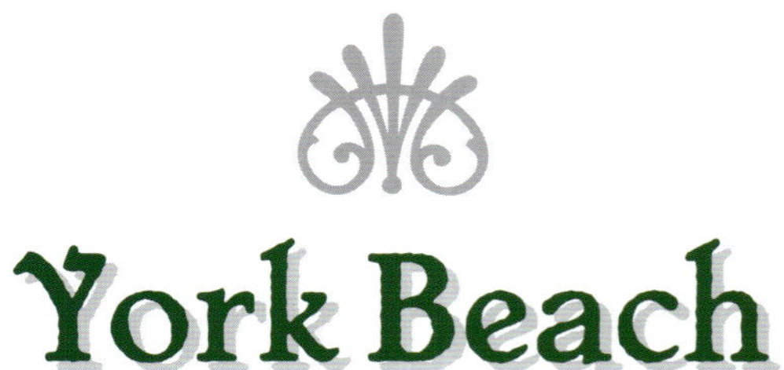

York Beach

YORK WAS INCORPORATED AS MAINE'S 2ND TOWN ON NOVEMBER 22, 1652

POPULATION IN 1900: 2,668

POPULATION IN 2000:3,321

York is Maine's second-oldest town, celebrating its 350th anniversary of incorporation in 2002. It was named in 1652 to honor a victory in the English Civil War, when Cromwell defeated the king's forces in the town of York, England.

There are three separate entities in the town that carry the name: York Village, York Beach, and York Harbor. The tourism boom that started after the Civil War made York Beach the vacation hot spot for ordinary folk, many of whom came from New Hampshire blue-collar towns. Blessed by wide sand beaches, the area burgeoned with summer homes, hotels, amusements, and summer businesses that catered to vacationers.

Most of the year-round residents lived in York Village, while the wealthy tourists were attracted to York Harbor's shore and rocky cliffs. Conflicts often arose between the competing desires of the two groups: the wish of the upper class to preserve their York Harbor enclave, and the similar longings of working-class people to enjoy the ocean, too. And because the farmers and regular folk outnumbered the shore residents, they often voted against improvements for the Harbor or the Beach.

In 1901 the Beach and Harbor areas formed separate village corporations that allowed them to remain a legal part of the town of York but gave them the ability to govern themselves and to keep 65 percent of the tax revenue they'd otherwise have to pay to the town. In 1909 the coastal residents even attempted to establish themselves as a separate town called Gorgeana, and it went—unsuccessfully—to a statewide vote.

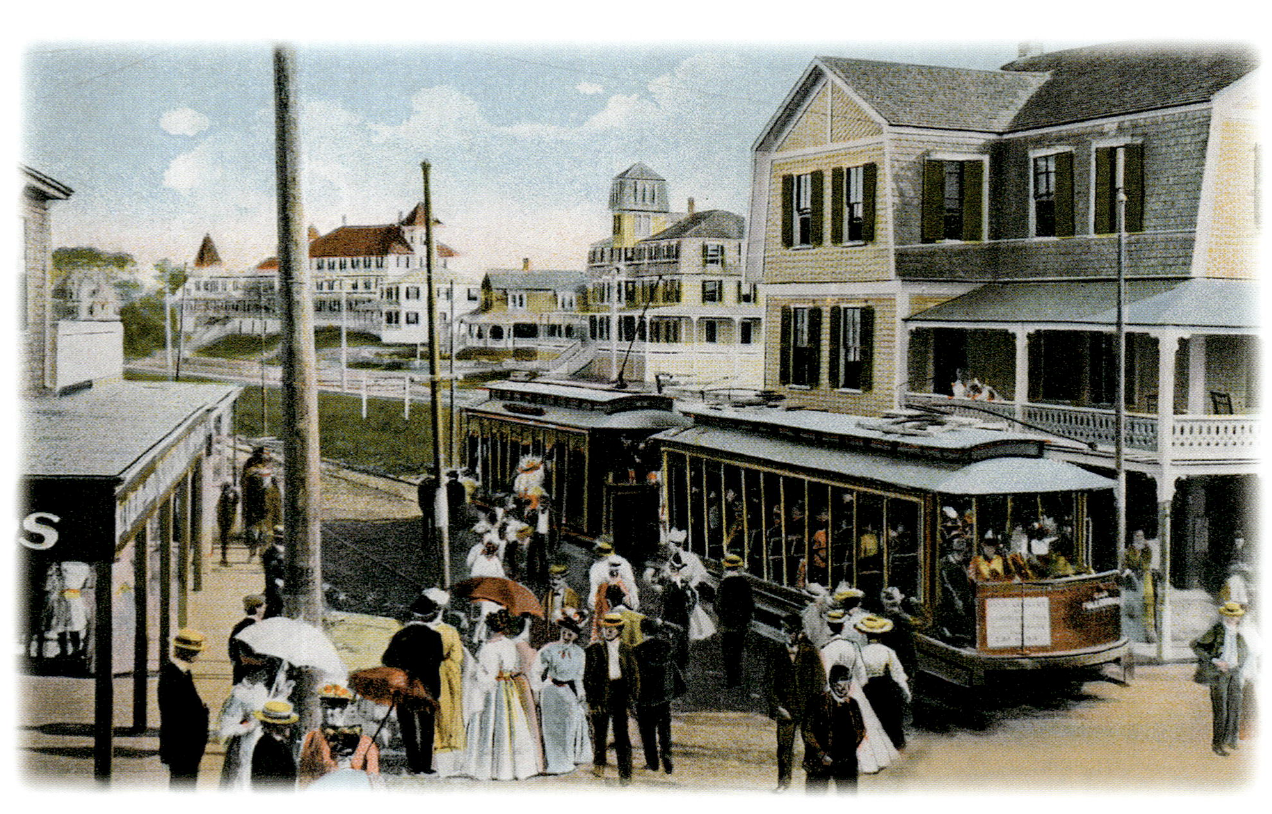

The residential suburb of Cape Neddick is the location of the Cape Neddick (Nubble) Lighthouse, and the early settlement there pre-dated that of York Village. In the 1970s the village corporations disbanded, leaving York a unified township today—although the communities still have individual post offices.

Trolley service to "the Yorks" began in 1898 and ended in 1923. The Portsmouth, Kittery and York Railway merged with the Portsmouth, Dover and York line (dubbed the Pull, Drag and Yank) in 1906 to become the Atlantic Shore Railway. The last of the old rails were removed from York Village in the mid-1960s.

The postcard of the Square at York Beach looks west toward Short Sands Beach. The Goldenrod bakery and ice cream parlor, established in 1896, is on the corner, with the trolleys parked in front. The Goldenrod has been in the same location for more than a century and is famous for its saltwater-taffy kisses. In the old days the candy was hand-pulled from a hook on the wall, in full sight of visitors peering in the window. Today passersby can watch the taffy being cooked in big copper kettles and poured onto cooling tables. Once it cools to the right temperature, the sheets are transferred to the pulling machines, which fluff it up a bit, pull it, roll it, and feed it to the cutting machine, which churns out 180 kisses a minute. That's nine million saltwater taffy kisses a year.

To the left of the Goldenrod is the 124-room Hotel Rockaway, which burned in 1958 and was later replaced by the Sands Hotel. In the background is the Ocean House Inn, which burned on May 20, 1986, while it was being renovated into condominiums. The inn had been built in the 1870s as a roller rink with birch floors, and it expanded in the late 1880s to become the first of the grand hotels on York Beach. The Ocean House Condominiums now occupy the spot. On the left side of the street in today's photograph are the Whispering Sands Gift Shop and the Surfside Restaurant.

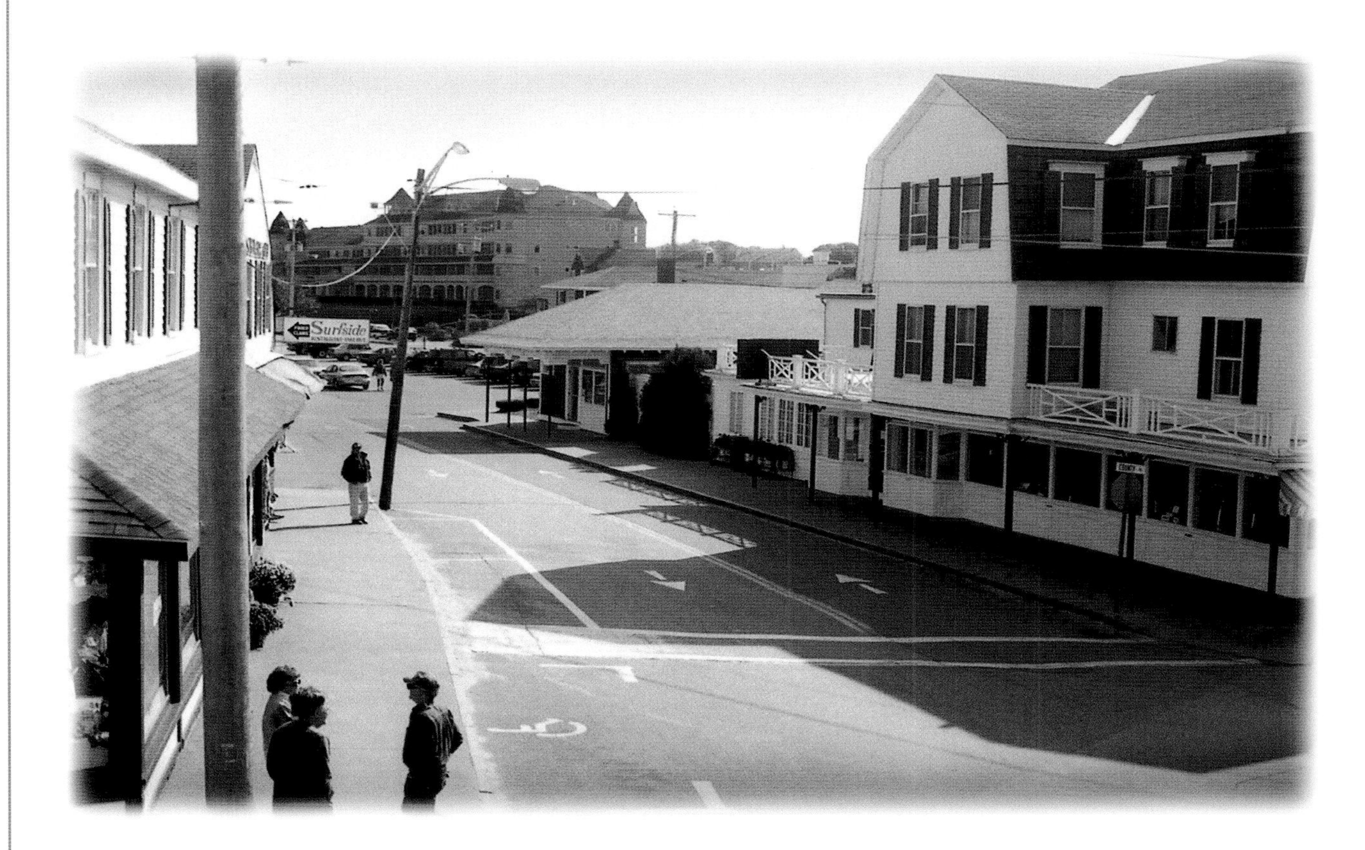

Acknowledgments

Many thanks go to everyone who helped in even the smallest way. You may not find your name in here, but your good deed will not go unrewarded in the Karmic Cosmos. I apologize in advance for omitting anyone who should have been mentioned.

I owe particular thanks to those who bailed me out during the holidays, since an auto accident in November stole valuable time from this project and forced a blitzkrieg of desperate pleas at a time when people were extra busy or even out of town.

EARLE G. SHETTLEWORTH JR., Maine Historic Preservation Commission

JUNE THOMPSON, City of Auburn

BANGOR MUSEUM AND CENTER FOR HISTORY

DEBORAH DYER, Bar Harbor Historical Society

ROBIN A. S. HAYNES (Bath)

PERLESTON PERT, Bath Historical Society

DR. TIM HUGHES (Belfast)

CHARLES L. BUTLER, Biddeford Historical Society

RICHARD BOULET, Blue Hill Public Library

BARBARA RUMSEY (Boothbay Harbor)

JUDY BLAKE and SUE BLACK, Bridgton Historical Society

BRAND LIVINGSTONE

BARBARA DYER (Camden)

CLAIRE RANDOLPH (Caribou)

JUDY CORROW

KAREN MOTYCKA (Castine)

MATT FILLER (Damariscotta)

CAROL FEURTADO, Dexter Historical Society

CINDY WHITE and BARBARA MOORE, Dover-Foxcroft town office

MARY ANNIS (Dover-Foxcroft)

MARK E. HONEY (Ellsworth)

DICK FLICK, Farmington Historical Society

NATE TUTTLE (Gardiner)

DR. EVERETT L. PARKER, Moosehead Historical Society

SUMNER WEBBER (Hallowell)

KAY BELL (Houlton)

BARBARA BARWISE, Kennebunkport Historical Society

GERRY PETTY, Ypsilanti (Michigan) Historical Society

FRANK ANICETTI (Lisbon Falls)

BILL BARR (Lisbon Falls)

BRUCE D. WILSON, West Quoddy Head Light Keepers Association

NORMAN DEAN, Madison town office

LEO and BETTY DEMCHAK (Madison)

RUSS DAY (Mechanic Falls)

DANA LEE (Mechanic Falls)

RICHARD FARRELL (Monhegan)

ANNA CARR, Northeast Harbor Library

HELEN M. POPP, North Haven Historical Society

BEVERLY CROFOOT, Bayside Historical Preservation Society

DAN BLANEY (Old Orchard Beach)

RICHARD MELVILLE, Friends of Pemaquid Light

MICHAEL LORD, Androscoggin Historical Society

ROBERT ENSOR (Port Clyde)

ROBERT SKOGLUND (Tenants Harbor)

BRIAN HARDEN, Rockland Historical Society

JAY ROBBINS, Richmond Historical Society

RICHARD AVERY (Stonington)

LINDA NELSON (Stonington)

EVE ANDERSON, Thomaston Historical Society

JOHN BLACK and MARJORIE FREEMAN (Waldoboro)

RANDY GROSS and STEVE CARTWRIGHT, Waldoborough Historical Society

VINALHAVEN HISTORICAL SOCIETY

TOM JOHNSON, Old York Historical Society

MARK GREEN, York town office

Postcard Notes

Unless otherwise indicated, all postcards shown were printed in Germany. The G. W. Morris and Hugh C. Leighton companies were in Portland, Maine. If there is a postmark date, it is noted. Local publishers probably contracted with another company whose item number appears on the card. The Albertype Company, of Brooklyn, New York, produced cards on a photographic paper stock that could be hand-colored.

ACADIA NATIONAL PARK

Sieur de Monts: hand-colored; Albertype Co., Brooklyn; published by the Acadia Corporation, Bar Harbor

Bubble Pond: hand-colored; Albertype Co., published by the Acadia Corporation, Bar Harbor

AUBURN

Goff Block, Court Street: Divided-back; published by H. L. Tarr & Co., Auburn A-27474

AUGUSTA

Water Street: Divided-back; 1909; The Robbins Bros. Co., Boston

Waterfront: Divided-back; Metropolitan News Co; Boston

BANGOR

Main Street: Undivided-back; G. W. Morris; 1906 postmark

Market Place: Divided-back; Publisher James F. Snow, Brunswick; C. T. Photochrom

BAR HARBOR

Main Street: Divided-back; Raphael Tuck & Sons series 2584; 1908

Harbor: Leighton #4159

BATH

Centre Street: no publisher listed, no. 812; 1909

BAYSIDE

Undivided-back; Leighton #4505

BELFAST

Main Street: Divided-back; Leighton #4498

BIDDEFORD

Main Street: White border, C. T. American Art A-102910

BLUE HILL

Hand-colored, signed S. G. Hinckley; Albertype Co., Brooklyn

BOOTHBAY HARBOR

Waterfront: Leighton #7294

Commercial Street: Divided-back, published by W. M. Prilay, Pittsfield, Maine

BRIDGTON

Pondicherry Square and Main Street: Divided-back; The Leighton & Valentine Co., New York City, #29449; printed in U.S.

BRUNSWICK

Maine Street: Divided-back; no publisher listed

CALAIS

North Street: Divided-back; no publisher listed

CAMDEN

Main Street: Divided-back; 1910; Leighton #2725

Harbor: Curt Teich & Co., Chicago, from a folder, postmark 1924

CARIBOU

Sweden Street: White border; C. T. American Art #113466

CASTINE

Dice Head Light: Undivided-back; Morris #88156

DAMARISCOTTA

Main Street: Divided-back; 1912; Leighton & Valentine Co., New York City, printed in U.S.

DEXTER

Main Street showing Gerry Block: Divided-back; Leighton #27192

DOVER-FOXCROFT

Union Square: Undivided-back; 1907; publisher Berry Paper Co. #3834

EASTPORT

Water Street: Divided-back; no publisher listed

ELLSWORTH

Main Street: Divided-back; Leighton #5934

FAIRFIELD

Main Street: Undivided-back; Metropolitan News Co., Boston #5579

FARMINGTON

Broadway looking west: Divided-back; published for Hardy & Tarbox

FREEPORT

Post Office Square and Clark's Hotel: Divided-back; published by F. E. Merrill, Freeport #404958

GARDINER

Water Street: Undivided-back; S. Langsdorf & Co.; published by C. H. Beane, Gardiner #S-1077

GREENVILLE JUNCTION

Divided-back; Leighton #25094

HALLOWELL

Water Street: Divided-back; Morris; 1907 #117276

HOULTON

Looking up Court Street: Undivided-back; Morris

KENNEBUNKPORT

Post Office Square looking West: Divided-back; published by Geo. Bonser & Son

KITTERY

Old Block House, Fort McClary: Undivided-back; G. W. Morris # 84674

LEWISTON

Lisbon Street looking down from Main Street: Leighton; 1911; #1092

Lisbon Street with McGillicuddy Building: Curteich folder D9411, 1950

LISBON FALLS

Main Street: Divided-back; Leighton #3636

LUBEC—WEST QUODDY LIGHT

Undivided-back; no publisher, #584

MADISON

Main Street looking east: Undivided-back; Morris; #87291

MECHANIC FALLS

Undivided-back; Morris #88149

MONHEGAN

Harbor: Divided-back; Leighton #2840

NORTH HAVEN

Divided-back; Leighton #6011, 1907

NORTHEAST HARBOR

Main Street: Published by A. G. Bain Co., Northeast Harbor #12595

OLD ORCHARD BEACH

The Pier from Hotel Velvet: Divided-back; Leighton, 1907; #4861

PEMAQUID POINT LIGHT

Undivided-back; Morris

PORTLAND

Monument Square: Divided-back; Leighton & Valentine Co., New York City, printed in U. S.; 1914; #27546

Union Station: Undivided-back; published by Chisholm Brothers, Portland # 296

PORT CLYDE

Main Street looking north: 1911; published by W. M. Prilay, Pittsfield

RICHMOND

Front Street looking north: Divided-back; Mason Brothers & Co., Boston #591

ROCKLAND

Main Street looking north: Divided-back; Robbins Bros. Co., Boston #55482

ROCKPORT

Iron Bridge: Undivided-back; Morris #85383

STONINGTON

Deer Isle from the water: Divided-back; Leighton #4927

TENANTS HARBOR

Old Condemned Vessels: Undivided-back; Leighton #3661

THOMASTON

Harbor scene: Hand-colored, published by E. D. West Co., S. Yarmouth, Cape Cod, Massachusetts

VINALHAVEN

Main Street West: Undivided-back; Morris #84644

WALDOBORO

Friendship Street: Divided-back; Leighton #25353

WILTON

Village Square and Soldiers' Monument: Divided-back; J. V. Hartman & Co., Boston

WISCASSET

Main Street—showing the longest bridge in Maine: Divided-back, no publisher listed, 1914

YORK BEACH

The Square: Divided-back; Leighton #5283, 1911